THE SENTIENT ARCHIVE

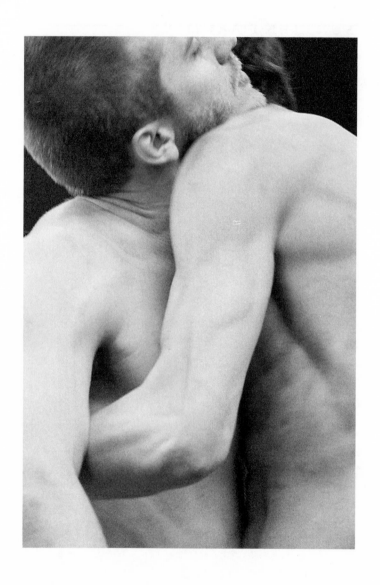

The Sentient Archive

BODIES, PERFORMANCE, AND MEMORY

Edited by BILL BISSELL and LINDA CARUSO HAVILAND

WESLEYAN UNIVERSITY PRESS Middletown, Connecticut

Wesleyan University Press
Middletown CT 06459
www.wesleyan.edu/wespress
© 2018 The Pew Center for Arts & Heritage
All rights reserved
Manufactured in the United States of America
Typeset in Quadraat by Tseng Information Systems, Inc.

Library of Congress Cataloging-in-Publication Data
Names: Bissell, Bill, editor. | Haviland, Linda Caruso, editor.
Title: The sentient archive: bodies, performance, and memory / edited by
Bill Bissell and Linda Caruso Haviland.
Description: Middletown, Connecticut: Wesleyan University Press, [2018] |
Includes bibliographical references and index. | Identifiers: LCCN 2017026923
(print) | LCCN 2017050853 (ebook) | ISBN 9780819577764 (ebook) |
ISBN 9780819577740 (cloth : alk. paper) | ISBN 9780819577757 (pbk. : alk. paper)
Subjects: LCSH: Dance—Philosophy. | Human body (Philosophy)
Classification: LCC GV1588 (ebook) | LCC GV1588 .S46 2018 (print) |
DDC 792.8—dc23
LC record available at https://lccn.loc.gov/2017026923

5 4 3 2 1

CONTENTS

Foreword / ix
  Paula Marincola

Acknowledgments / xi

Introduction: A Body Comparable / xiii
  Bill Bissell and Linda Caruso Haviland

Considering the Body as Archive / 1
  Linda Caruso Haviland

I. BODIED KNOWING
  Introduction by Linda Caruso Haviland / 19

Everyone Has Something to Tell / 23
  Alain Platel

Stalking Embodied Knowledge—Then What? / 28
  Tomie Hahn

The Sensing and Knowing Body: Choreographing Action and Feeling / 46
  Juhani Pallasmaa

Use Me / 55
  Meg Stuart

A Body-Mind Centering® Approach to Movement through Embodiment / 58
  Bonnie Bainbridge Cohen

Pleasure / 61
  Ralph Lemon

Slow / 62
  Ralph Lemon

II. MEMORY, HISTORY, AND RETRIEVAL
  Introduction by Linda Caruso Haviland / 63

Memory Has Its Way with Me / 67
  Barbara Dilley

The Body Makes You Remember / 69
  Ivo van Hove

Touching History / 73
  Ann Cooper Albright

My Discovery of Dance / 82
  Allegra Kent

We Dance What We Remember: Memory in Perceiving and
  Performing Contemporary Dance / 87
  Catherine J. Stevens

The Stories in Our Bodies / 110
  Emily Johnson

III. THE BODY IN THE ARCHIVE
  Introduction by Linda Caruso Haviland / 115

& We Should Live and Be Well: Five Artist Statements, 1995–2007 / 117
  David Gordon

The Embodied Performance of Museum Visiting: Sacred Temples
  or Theaters of Memory? / 126
  Laurajane Smith

Sideways Glances: Painting and Dancing / 143
  Sarah Crowner

Leap Before You Look: Honoring the Libretto in *Giselle* and *Apollo* / 146
  Nancy Goldner

Body as Signifier / 183
  Patricia Hoffbauer

IV. PERFORMING THE ARCHIVE
  Introduction by Linda Caruso Haviland / 191

Untitled / 193
  Bebe Miller

My Body, the Archive / 198
  Deborah Hay

Choreographing Somatic Memories and Spatial Residues / 200
  Jayachandran Palazhy

Tremulous Histories / 209
  Jenn Joy

Exit/Exist—Embodiment / 223
  Gregory Maqoma

V. AFTERLIVES AND TRANSFORMATIONS
  Introduction by Linda Caruso Haviland / 227

Pavilion of Secrets / 229
  Marcia B. Siegel

Archiving Indeterminate Systems of Ecosystems and
  Improvisational Dance Strategies / 263
  Jennifer Monson

Them: Recombinant Aesthetics of Restaging Experimental Performance / 268
  Thomas F. DeFrantz

New Bodies, New Architecture / 293
  Mariana Ibañez and Simon Kim

Choreographic Angelology / 297
  André Lepecki

Contributors / 321

Index / 327

Color illustrations follow page 206.

FOREWORD

The Pew Center for Arts & Heritage is a multidisciplinary grant maker, funded by The Pew Charitable Trusts, dedicated to fostering a vibrant cultural community in greater Philadelphia. As a funder, the Center invests annually in ambitious, imaginative projects in the Performance and Exhibitions & Public Interpretation programs, in individual artists' fellowships, and in catalytic organizational development. Our efforts foster and showcase the great cultural richness and vitality of our region, enhancing public life and reaching many different audiences.

The Center also actively engages in an ongoing exchange of ideas concerning artistic and interpretive practice and functions as a hub for discourse and knowledge sharing about crucial issues in current creative practice. In that capacity, we create opportunities for inquiry, debate, and analysis, from lectures and workshops to newly commissioned writings. Beginning in 2006, with an anthology of texts on curatorial practice, *What Makes a Great Exhibition?*, followed by *Letting Go? Sharing Historical Authority in a User-Generated World* (2011) and *Pigeons on the Grass Alas: Contemporary Curators Talk About the Field* (2013), we have regularly produced print publications on topics that grow directly out of and respond to our experience as cultural grant makers.

In addition, our danceworkbook series of publications, in the form of DVDs and Web-based productions, has established a body of reference materials for choreographic creation and development. They provide a view into the process and backstory of making dance or, as in the case of *A Steady Pulse: Restaging Lucinda Childs, 1963–1978* (2015), present a rich and interactive archive documenting an important stage in an artist's trajectory. All our publishing efforts aim to generate insights and further discussion for artists, curators, presenters, producers, critics, and scholars alike and to make a contribution to the fields we serve that amplifies the impact of our grant dollars.

The Sentient Archive grew in part out of the audience response to lectures by Dr. Susan Leigh Foster, hybrids of performance and theory that were produced in 2011 by the Center with the cooperation of the Philadelphia Live Arts Festival. These were subsequently collected in the danceworkbook publication *Susan Foster! Susan Foster! Three Performed Lectures* (2013). Question-and-answer sessions following Foster's presentations revealed certain divisions among practitioners, theorists, and critics, most notably in some practitioners' rejection of theory's "intrusion" into the privileged territory of the body. The coeditors of this anthology, Bill Bissell, director of Performance here at the Center, and Linda Caruso Haviland, founding director of the dance program at Bryn Mawr College, envisioned an approach to bridging the gap by commissioning a diverse set of writings by artists, theorists, and scholars. As this idea evolved, practitioners and researchers in other disciplines were invited to be part of the collection. As a way to foreground the analytical and the experiential in equal measure, the coeditors began by positing the sentient, living body as an archive of knowledge and experience, the nucleus of every approach to performance. Dance is at the core of this investigation, but the anthology aims to reach beyond dance, even performance, by drawing on contributors who work with the body in other fields. The result is a shared space for multiple voices to spark insight and fruitful discussion across disciplinary and professional boundaries.

What you hold in your hands, then, is a rich compendium of texts—from analytical to anecdotal, from memoir to research—that we hope will find a welcome reception among its many potential audiences. Bill and Linda, as coeditors, have demonstrated both vision and extraordinary commitment in bringing this publication to fruition, and I want to acknowledge and applaud their tremendous work here, along with the writers and other contributors to The Sentient Archive.

Most important, none of the Center's work would be possible without the extraordinarily generous support and rigorous strategic leadership of our funder, The Pew Charitable Trusts. Their belief in the value and impact of the Center's activities forwards and sustains our endeavors. It is indeed our privilege to work on Pew's behalf in the cultural arena.

—Paula Marincola
Executive Director
The Pew Center for Arts & Heritage

ACKNOWLEDGMENTS

The Sentient Archive: Bodies, Performance, and Memory could not have been realized without the significant support of numerous people. First and foremost, we must thank The Pew Center for Arts & Heritage, Philadelphia, through which this book came to fruition. It was a happy coincidence that early conversations about the anthology with coeditor Linda Caruso Haviland occurred just as Paula Marincola, the Center's executive director, and Doug Bohr, former director of the Philadelphia Program, The Pew Charitable Trusts, offered me the opportunity to develop a publication project as part of my work as director of the Center's Performance program. Paula, in particular, has always believed in *The Sentient Archive* and stayed the course with me over its circuitous path to completion. And most important, all of our work at the Center is made possible by the generosity of our funder, The Pew Charitable Trusts, and we can never adequately express our appreciation to them for their generous support of our efforts.

Coeditor Linda Caruso Haviland also acknowledges the administration of Bryn Mawr College for allowing her the time to finish this project, and credits colleagues at Bryn Mawr for their continual encouragement, as well as her students at Bryn Mawr and Haverford College, who over the years have kept her "thinking and on her toes." She honors the influence of Jean Williams and Selma Jeanne Cohen, of dance artists Merce Cunningham and William Forsythe and, importantly, of Hellmut Gottschild. In particular, Linda also calls out Edrie Ferdun, Ann Cooper Albright, André Lepecki (for his initial enthusiasm for the project), and Susan Leigh Foster (for her continuing inspiration).

Linda and I must both thank Peter Nesbett (former specialist at the Center, now executive director of Washington Project for the Arts) for his rigorous feedback, his perceptive editing of Linda's lead essay, and his expertise in guiding publisher interest in the manuscript. Lucy Warrington and Erin Read of the Center's Performance program assisted in coordinating correspondence and managing important details of the project.

Josie Smith, a specialist in the Performance program at the Center, has provided important continuity and has been steadfast and diligent in readying the manuscript's visual and textual materials for publication. Max Margulies assisted Josie and me on research, including the invaluable work of collating the images amassed for *The Sentient Archive*—or as it was called then, *Body as Archive*—

and deserves special mention. In addition to Max and Josie, of course, we thank all of the photographers and artists who have permitted us to use images of their work. In particular, I wish to acknowledge the late Violette Verdy and her assistant, Robin Allen, who combed the ballerina's extensive archives for images for Nancy Goldner's essay; Erin Hestvik, manager of the New York City Ballet Archive; and Ellen Sorrin, director of the George Balanchine Trust, for their consideration and help in obtaining additional images for Goldner's essay.

One of the first people I spoke with at the start of this process was dance writer Suzanne Carbonneau, who helped catalyze my determination to proceed. I also want to remember Kilian Kröll, who compiled the appendixes for both the Marcia B. Siegel and Goldner essays, in addition to documenting moving-image references.

No longer with us to thank personally is the late Gregory T. Rowe, former director of Culture Initiatives and deputy director of the Philadelphia Program at The Pew Charitable Trusts, a dear friend to all of us who work at the Center. He believed in all our capacities as program directors. I think he would be proud of this book, and I hope it serves as testimony to how he, along with then Culture Program senior director Marian Godfrey, felt the Center might contribute to the vitality of ideas in contemporary culture.

On a personal note, Linda thanks her husband Jeffrey for his patience with the process. I wish to thank my partner Raymond J. Ricketts for his as well.

While any faults in this book are Linda's and mine alone, we save the virtues of the manuscript for our final acknowledgment: the gratitude we direct to the work of all our contributors—they *are* the feeling body.

—Bill Bissell

INTRODUCTION
A Body Comparable

> [O]ur body is comparable to a work of art. It is a nexus of lived meanings.
> — Maurice Merleau-Ponty, *Phenomenology of Perception*

We began this project with dance. This is because the questions we are asking have been most consequential to dancers, choreographers, pedagogues, critics, and scholars, who for centuries have sought to include the body—particularly as we know it in the embodied experience of performance—within the larger orbit of cultural discourse. But this project also brings makers and thinkers from other disciplines into the conversation, in an effort to acknowledge that what is at stake is much more complex than can be addressed through any single perspective.

We take as a given that artistic practices constitute important research into how a body "knows," practices that parallel the methods of traditional forms of scholarship, including critical analysis, the tracking of behavioral patterns, scientific measurement, and data assessment. This book places artists side by side with scholars from both within and outside the landscape of performance; all are connected by an interest in the body as the source of consciousness. Equal to appreciating how artistic practice is scholarship, we also value how scholars find their way into embodied knowledge through the ideas and data that inform their writings. Each writer in this collection is a witness to his or her own archive: entering the realm of the body, understanding his or her material intuitively or critically, speaking from the bodies that occupy his or her work. One form of pedagogy is not privileged over another.

As coeditors we first discussed the germ of this book as part of our response to comments from audiences attending a series of three performed lectures by Dr. Susan Leigh Foster, sponsored by The Pew Center for Arts & Heritage at FringeArts in Philadelphia between March and September 2011. The value of theory, as well as the problems in translating ideas from critical thinkers and how those ideas connect artists with scholars, emerged in the conversations after each of Foster's lectures. Both of us imagined how different forms of inquiry might be collected together. We asked each other if gathering writings on the body from various perspectives could help us proceed beyond simplistic binaries, such as "thinking and doing." Our starting point was a belief that the domain of the body is the site of consciousness, regardless of particular disciplinary approaches.

Inquiry and debate about the nature of dance and its status in Western culture have their roots in the philosophical writings of classical antiquity and in Renaissance-era dance manuals and treatises. In the eighteenth century choreographers emerged as apologists for the field, adding their voices to the nascent philosophical subdiscipline of aesthetics.[1] By the nineteenth century, however, the emergence of the critic as enthusiast ushered in popular depictions of ballets and ballerinas, which doubled as voyeuristic odes to the beauty and availability of female bodies. Bodied and ephemeral, dance came to be seen as an art that could never generate or communicate important ideas, further ensuring that the dancer as body, sex, and object was meant to be seen and not heard.

The situation changed in the first half of the twentieth century, with the advent of modern dance in Europe and North America. This new form of dance not only elicited responses from philosophers; it gave birth to a different kind of critic and prompted a spate of artist-driven writing and research that bridged the false dichotomy of body and mind.[2] Though too often discounted, the writing of three early women pioneers—Loïe Fuller, Isadora Duncan, and Ruth St. Denis—gave evidence of their passionate yet astute engagement with their art. Their voracious and wide-ranging reading included the philosophy of Friedrich Nietzsche, movement theories of François Delsarte, Walt Whitman's poetry, Victorian ethnographies, and travel literature of a decidedly orientalist bent. In addition, they engaged in research in museums, artists' studios, salons, and theaters on three continents.[3] These three dance makers then put muscle to mind, experimenting in the studio and, in Fuller's case, the laboratory, to develop new movement forms or stage technologies that could hold their radical aesthetics.[4] In time, fame afforded them proximity to great writers and practitioners in the arts and sciences and further guaranteed their familiarity with the aesthetic and scientific theories that fed the zeitgeist in which they were creating and performing work.

Subsequent generations of dance artists, along with scholars investigating the theoretical or semantic and semiotic capacities of the dancing body, further affirmed that the analytical or empirical, on the one hand, and the immersive or experiential, on the other, do not undermine one another.[5] Instead, they together deepen our understanding of dance without ever exhausting its meaning. This book, then, should be understood as an expansion of dance studies, joining together artists, practitioners of cognitive psychology, philosophy, cultural archaeology, and anthropology, along with somaesthetic perspectives on the performing body.[6] Our multidisciplinary approach is meant to counter the reality that connections between dance and other disciplines are still too often ignored. In the United States the body as a subject has been tinged by moral suspicion and an assumed lack of cognitive capacities. Western culture has been reluctant to admit what might be called "an unruly body"—a body that refuses to be constrained by the demands of objective analysis or to remain passive in the course of investigation—into its midst. Although the realm of dance has benefited from a tremendous surge of theoretical and scholarly activity in the past three decades, there remain sharp divides in style, methods, and reception of inquiry or research. This is unfortunate, because those who are investigating the body across various discourses and practices could generate fruitful dialogue together. We offer this book as our contribution to furthering such dialogue.

As you begin to read, it is important to remember that "archive" throughout most of Western history has alluded to material objects: important documents and records intended for long-term retention, as well as the sites constructed in which to hold them. The body's mortality has disqualified it from consideration as an archive, in either sense of the word. Today, our notion of the archive is changing, and scholars, curators, and artists understand the body as a cognitive system that draws on its own experiences and memories. Among the questions being asked are, "What would it mean to say the body is an archive?," or more specifically, "What sort of investigations or practices might facilitate the archiving of bodied acts or events, as well as their potential for retrieval and reenactment?" and "What is being stored, retrieved, or transmitted, and what or who shapes the body in storing or recovering its knowledge?"

To be sure, this collection is not exhaustive, nor does it fully put into perspective investigations about body knowledge taking place globally. Nevertheless we offer here initial responses to the question, "What if a book were informed by contributions from theorists, historians, dance writers, practitioners, researchers, and artists from several disciplines, all gathered around the human body as the active intersection of knowing, memory, and performance?"

The contributors' perspectives, topics, ideas, and key phrases relate in substantial ways to other essays in this collection, even those from different fields of inquiry. Our path starts with bodied knowledge, moves through memory and retrieval, considers the body in the archive, observes how the archive might be performed, and then imagines the capacity for the body's transformations and afterlives as (and within) the archive. This is only one possible way to assemble the writings, one that we hope will prove fruitful to stimulating generous discussion on the topic and encourage us all to consider, more fully, the archives we embody daily.

— Bill Bissell and Linda Caruso Haviland

NOTES

The epigraph is from Maurice Merleau-Ponty, *Phenomenology of Perception*, trans. Colin Smith (London: Routledge & Kegan Paul, 1962).

1. This tradition continues beyond eighteenth-century choreographers and theorists (such as John Weaver and Jean-Georges Noverre) in the work of August Bournonville, Michel Fokine, Doris Humphrey, Merce Cunningham, Deborah Hay, Simone Forti, Ralph Lemon, and William Forsythe, among many others.

2. The work of oratory pedagogue François Delsarte and music educator Émile Jaques-Dalcroze was influential for artist-driven research and writing; both had a profound effect on early modern dance pioneers such as Mary Wigman, Isadora Duncan, and Ted Shawn. More directly influential was dancer and theorist Rudolf Laban, whose theoretical works began appearing with regularity in 1926. The new critics of dance, all men, included Paul Valery, *Dance and the Soul* (London: J. Lehman, 1920/1944; trans. 1951); André Levinson, "The Idea of the Dance: From Aristotle to Mallarmé," in *André Levinson on Dance: Writings from Paris in the Twenties*, ed. Joan Acocella and Lynn Garafola (Hanover, NH: Wesleyan University Press, 1991), 47–54; and John Martin, *The Modern Dance* (New York: Barnes, 1933) and "The Dance," *Dance Scrapbook*, *New York Times*, May 20, 1945. For more on the transformation of criticism from avocation to profession, see Elizabeth Prettejohn, "Aesthetic Value and the Professionalization of Victorian Art Criticism 1837–78," *Journal of Victorian Culture* 2, no. 1 (1997): 71–94; and Anna Brzyski, *Partisan Canons* (Durham, NC: Duke University Press, 2007). For more on the professionalization of art history and arts criticism, see Roger Fry, "The Artist as Critic," *Burlington Magazine for Connoisseurs* 64, no. 371 (February 1934): 78–80; and the work of mid-twentieth-century art critic Clement Greenberg.

3. For an overarching study of the period that includes these three female dance artists, see Elizabeth Kendall, *Where She Danced* (New York: Knopf, 1979). For Fuller, see *Fifteen Years of a Dancer's Life with Some Account of Her Distinguished Friends* (London: Herbert Jenkins Limited, 1913); for Duncan, see *The Art of the Dance*, ed. Sheldon Cheney (New York: Theatre Arts, 1928) and *Isadora Duncan, My Life* (1927; New York: W. W. Norton, 1995); and for St. Denis, see *Ruth St. Denis: An Unfinished Life* (New York: Harper and Bros., 1939).

4. Many of the ardent male artists/intellectual fans/supporters who raved about the work of these female dance pioneers also presumed that they were not able to talk about what they do. As well-meaning as they might have been, writers like Anatole France and Konstantin Stanislavsky frequently categorized dancers/artists/choreographers as geniuses working purely from instinct. France, who admired Loïe Fuller's intelligence, celebrated the artist as working entirely out of the unconscious — an observation echoed by the choreographer herself in her autobiography. Duncan quotes Stanislavsky at length, including his comment that "Duncan does not know how to speak of her art logically and systematically. Her ideas come to her by accident, as the result of the most unexpected everyday facts." These assertions discounted the female dancer's ability to speak or write about her work, much less analyze or theorize about it. See *Isadora Duncan, My Life*, 123; and Fuller, *Fifteen Years of a Dancer's Life*, ch. VI. Although Fuller (in agreement with France) refers to her stagecraft

work as "intuition ... instinct, and nothing else" (p. 66), chapter VI clearly indicates her familiarity with the scientific, technical, and aesthetic functions of electrical lighting; while she discloses no technical knowledge in her thinking, throughout the book there are numerous mentions of her extensive work with her electricians to create a specific "apparatus" for each of her dances.

5. One of the first modern philosophers to engage in an analytical approach to the experiential aspect of dance in a significant way was Susanne K. Langer; see *Philosophy in a New Key: A Study in the Symbolism of Reason, Rite, and Art* (Cambridge, MA: Harvard University Press, 1942); *Feeling and Form: A Theory of Art* (New York: Scribner, 1953); and *Problems of Art: Ten Philosophical Lectures* (New York: Scribner, 1957). Shortly after Langer's books were published, scholarship began to emerge from philosophical considerations within fields of movement practice, including, among others, Maxine Sheets Johnstone's *Phenomenology of Dance* (1966) and Eleanor Metheny's *Movement and Meaning* (1968).

6. Somaesthetics is becoming an accepted concept beyond philosophy in areas as diverse as art history, literary criticism, and human-computer interaction design. This concept is attributed to philosopher Richard Shusterman. See "Somaesthetics: A Disciplinary Proposal," *The Journal of Aesthetics and Art Criticism* (Summer 1999): 299–313, for a brief introduction.

LINDA CARUSO HAVILAND

CONSIDERING THE BODY AS ARCHIVE

The many kinds of dance actions, events, and experiences, and the varying levels of expertise at which all of these can be practiced, both require and make evident not only the conscious intellection historically associated with constructs of mind but also the knowledge that resides deep within and throughout the body. The body can generate, assimilate, and process knowledge and is an archive able to store such knowledge.

Bodiedness must thus be understood as a legitimate cognitive state and the knowledge one finds in the body considered as important as any gleaned from what might be thought of as more rational approaches or disciplines. In dance, muscles are informed by the corporeal remnants of the performer's personal and cultural pasts, and the creative process entails the ability to experiment, value, and make choices at unconscious as well as conscious levels. Recent research has confirmed that a dancer's knowledge and memories are part of a dynamic cognitive system that operates on the levels of nerve, muscle, and the physiology of the brain, as well as of thought and language. On all these levels prior experience is retrievable, but never as static facts; every action is called up through bodies that are dynamic and ever-changing.[1]

A consensus is building that "knowing body" is neither an oxymoron nor a romanticized metaphor, but a legitimate topic of study. Research on the subject now engages with a range of scholarly and artistic pursuits, including considerations of the body as a site of consciousness and cognition and its involvement in the recovery and reenactment of memory. At the same time, the body and the archive are being reexamined as entities that are completely entangled with politics and power, capable of both profoundly shaping and being shaped by historical and cultural forces. As is evident in this anthology and elsewhere, scholars and practitioners in dance and other performance forms have brought their own perspectives to these conversations.[2]

Imagining the body as an archive necessitates rethinking the meaning of both "body" and "archive." It requires a radical openness to the possibility that knowledge can be both legible and embodied, that it is not only accessed through texts, but also generated and understood through physical states and actions. Moreover, if the body is to be understood as a fundamental cognitive agent, then other modes or disciplines of human inquiry must acknowledge

1

that their own methodologies are infused with knowledge derived from human corporeality. This repositioning irrevocably changes both body and archive, because it presumes a *sentient* archive: a sensate structure infused with cognitive potential, inseparable from its archived contents.

To move toward a notion of the body as a repository of knowledge also entails turning a critical eye on older models of the archive and on its history. This demands a questioning of the underlying assumptions behind the theory of such structures and practices and making visible that which has been overlooked or excluded. Investigations that have compelled this rethinking have numerous roots, including, in the 1920s and 1930s, the writings of German philosopher and critic Walter Benjamin. Benjamin challenged long-standing Western commitments to fixed, linear narratives in historical and art-historical texts, replacing these with a radical model of history in which the present can reengage with the past, compelling constant reconstruals of past, present, and future. He further argued for multiple interpretations of all "texts," and his focus on the potency of the image acknowledged the possibility of various modes of intelligibility in addition to language. In effect, Benjamin made consideration of the body as archive a viable construct.[3]

However, looming on the horizon a few decades after his death in 1940 were, depending on one's perspective, either the twin pillars or the Scylla and Charybdis of new thinking in the West about the archive: the work of French thinkers Michel Foucault and Jacques Derrida.[4] Many attribute the "archival turn" to their controversial but influential writings in the 1980s and 1990s.[5] Their lines of inquiry not only signify the ubiquity of the archive in theory and in culture in the last three decades, but also turn on or upturn the notion of "archive," investigating its influential nature and functions within the realms of human knowledge and power. Foucault's and Derrida's works theorize how the body is part and parcel of the archive.

MICHEL FOUCAULT'S IMPRINTED BODY

In many of his writings, Foucault noted that bodies are shaped by the regulatory power of the archive and its discourses. Stripped of agency or the capacity to function as discourses in themselves, they are "totally imprinted by history and the process of history's destruction of the body."[6] Nevertheless, the body's inscribable nature suggests a capacity to receive and store knowledge that, in turn, can be read. Even at this level the body becomes a site of legibility, and like the skin of Epimenides or tattooed flesh in various cultures, may hold magic or power in its deeper folds.[7] Foucault himself allowed that even "the very gesture of the painter" could be sites of embodied knowledge.[8]

Foucault provided a way of rethinking history through new approaches to archival research. In rejecting standard historiographical models, he "sketched out" a history of the ways "that humans develop knowledge about themselves," appropriating two different but complementary research practices that he designated "archaeological" and "genealogical."[9] Archaeological research looked past authoritative interpretations to the documents themselves to reveal the fragmented nature of human knowledge and its capacity to be grouped and regrouped into multiple but distinct "discourses." The archive as imagined by Foucault was not just a physical structure but a "density of discursive practices": a system, or the "law of what can be said."[10] If archaeology helped to make the workings of these internally cohesive systems visible, it was genealogy as a methodological practice that countered any singular or authoritative narrative. Genealogy uncovered irregular, accidental, and unexpected paths of descent, revealing the contingent nature of discourses along with the operations of power that emerged from or within them.[11]

Foucault's new model of the archive enabled linguistic events within a discourse "to undergo regular modification"; that is, to be arranged differently according to other generative and organizational dynamics.[12] The search for an original in such an archive is futile, since multiple entries into the archive could reveal "several pasts, several forms of connection, several hierarchies of importance, several networks of determination, several teleologies, for one and the same" work, artist, performance, or genre, and even point to those excluded from the established archive.[13] In this reading, continual excavation of the archive yields multiple emerging, disintegrating, overlapping, transformative, or contesting discourses.

Although Foucault has been criticized for abstracting the human body in his writings primarily to theorize his ideas, bodies continue to insist on emerging in all of their full physicality. For example, his genealogical investigation of knowledge and power revealed that "descent" (in the sense of lineage) is completely "attached" to the body, even to its "nervous system [and] digestive apparatus," and that every internal and behavioral system and sign is maintained and manifested as a sort of "stigmata of past experiences."[14] Each body stores its own particular history of living and is also as a body ordered and disciplined by a history of the cultural pressures within which it matures, part of a phylogenic (or developmental) archive of the regulations of conduct and communication commanded in any particular epoch. Foucault's theories on the body and its discourses have also been generative for contemporary thinkers in the area of performance. Countering, amending, or extending his ideas, writers and practitioners have identified performance as discourse capable of coexisting with other established or already legitimized discourses. This writ-upon body also writes; it activates, engages, or disrupts as a discourse in its own right, a force in itself that participates in constructing and conferring meaning on the world.

JACQUES DERRIDA: REENTERING THE ARCHIVE

Many archivists argue that Derrida's notions of archive are lamentably parallel to Foucault's: too abstract, and oblivious to the realities and practices of archives and archival science.[15] Derrida provided an etymology of "archive," beginning with the Greek *arkhe*, which holds at once a double, and doubly powerful, meaning, as the point or moment of origin—"where things commence"—and also as the principle of commanding or ordering—"there where authority, social order are exercised." *Arkheion*, the second word of his etymological search, also had two meanings: the physical dwelling places of rulers or archons and the official documents stored therein, as well as the power of those archons to select, organize, and interpret the documents as law.[16] Derrida made it apparent that this conflation of archive and power had escaped notice for centuries. Nevertheless, "archive" retained the signification of both site and its contents and acted as the verb that constructs both. From the beginning, "archive" also raised questions about its function and its relation to history and thus to past, present, and future—all terms that themselves are contested and render any definitions both regional and partial.[17]

There were archivists who applauded Derrida's disruption of notions of objectivity traditionally attributed to archive and archivist alike; they found his ideas instrumental in rethinking the nature of both.[18] Derrida, whose methodology exposed hidden contradictions in texts and the camouflaged instabilities of meaning, notoriously observed that, "Nothing is less reliable, nothing is less clear today than the word 'archive.'" Further, he posited that emerging technologies would further undermine any inherited or fixed concept of the archive.[19]

Like Foucault, Derrida looked through the concretized meanings attached to the contents of the archive to the documents themselves as texts in potentially endless relations with other texts. He also recognized both hidden and overt forces in the archive. "There is no political power without control of the archive, if not of memory," he warned, for to create and maintain an archive, to select, categorize, and interpret its contents in service of a unified narrative, is also and always an act of violence in its concomitant acts of exclusion and erasure.[20] Though Derrida paralleled Foucault's aversion to standard historiographical practices (and how archives were used within them), much of his investigation was intimately connected to notions of how a person remembers.

The archive for Derrida arose at the place where memory fails or is expected to fail, and therefore provided a substrate onto which the act of remembering could be consigned and further be retrieved, reproduced, or reiterated in some way. In dialogue with Freud's notions of the death-drive, Derrida argued that we build archives because we suffer from a *Mal d'archive*—"archive fever"—that can escalate to a "compulsive, repetitive, and nostalgic desire . . . to return to the most archaic place of absolute commencement," to origin or oblivion—an impossible task for historian and analyst alike.[21] Archive fever drives us to return to the origin or to hold back death and forgetfulness by recording, repeating, and recalling through texts, objects, monuments, or data files—the very acts that at the same time eliminate our need to remember and efface the experience of remembering. Derrida, however, suggested multiple interpretations of *mal d'archive*, which frame archiving and retrieving the archive as both a debilitating *and* necessary venture.[22]

Derrida's investigations into archive fever, particularly his meditations on psychoanalysis and circumcision, led him to puzzle over the boundary separating the body's interior from its exterior: "Where does the outside commence?" This reinforced the possibility that the body can exist as archive, one that is able to receive information from outside itself.[23] In addition, he argued that "archivable meaning is also and in advance codetermined by the structure that archives."[24] This suggests that the body not only stores knowledge and meaning, but is capable of producing and shaping them as well. The body serves as a prosthesis for memory, able to "assure the possibility of memorization, or repetition, of reproduction, or of re-impression."[25]

Derrida's notion of archive reflected the forces that determine the archive's structure and contents, but Derrida also considered the practical and conceptual problems that undermine any such power, resulting, as already noted, in a seemingly endless proliferation of archives. Its contents and meaning, for example, can only be understood in retrospect, "in the times to come," making the archive a promise or responsibility, open toward the unknown.[26] The act of the researcher entering the archive, and of retrieving to reenact, "inscribes" or adds this act of entry into the very archive she is investigating, irrevocably changing it. "By incorporating the knowledge which is deployed in reference to it, the archive augments itself," endlessly but unpredictably.[27]

5

THE ARCHIVAL IMPULSE

The writings of Foucault and Derrida on the archive, as well as those of their contemporaries, were highly influential and compatible with work being carried out across multiple disciplines, which included experiments in the visual and performing arts.[28] Still, it is fair to ask: Why this return to the archive? Was it symptomatic of a conservative desire to maintain the status quo? Did it feed what Andreas Huyssen called the "modern disease" of nostalgia—a way to recycle or perpetually market material, including ideas, that already existed? Or was it evidence of the further death of artistic imagination?[29] Art critic and historian Hal Foster worried that the archival impulse might be a concept haunted by the failure of cultural memory.[30] But he saw in what he termed "archival art" the potential for continuing the transformations of art, art maker, and audience. Archival art could retrieve obscure or "failed art," revisit landmark artworks or events, or in other ways reexamine or intervene in the past. By this means, artists working in the archive might set loose alternative meanings or countermemories, disturb present perspectives and practices, or instigate social and political commentary and action.[31] As an effect of the theories produced during the "archival turn" (by Benjamin, Derrida, and Foucault), however, the researcher's entry into the archive requires a critical self-examination of stance, motive, and context.

Of course enormous alterations in the way that humans process, store, and communicate information—often in lieu of noticing and remembering—have also forced paradigmatic shifts within the field.[32] Growing concern with the archive has intersected with what has been described as a cultural obsession with the memory industry.[33] Technologies of photography and film have encouraged the creation of archives as ubiquitous as the family album and as chillingly specific as the thousands of individual headshots documenting the Cambodian genocide of the mid-1970s.[34] With roots that reach back into the nineteenth century, interests in archive and memory have merged and accelerated over the last forty years and exploded in the last twenty, equally supported and exacerbated by new computing and virtual technologies. Less referenced in the social, cultural, and philosophical commentary on this "memory boom" were those crucial voices addressing body and archive within the neurosciences, even as advances in brain-imaging technologies produced new models of how memory functioned.[35] In these studies, remembering is an act that fuses together elements of both past and present experiences in a "highly fluctuating excitation pattern formed by continuously changing connections of cells . . . and circuits

6

... in permanent flux."[36] The entire cerebral cortex is constantly altered by experience, so the trajectories of excitation can never return exactly to the same location. Therefore, remembering is "recategorical" because, despite the illusion of exact recall, a past action cannot be replicated exactly. In these models, the brain counters the notion of archive as static storage. It instead resembles Benjamin's, Foucault's, or Derrida's notions of the archive, in which the temporal continuum is regularly disrupted and the archive shifts with the flux in organizational forces.

KNOWING MORE THAN DANCERS SAY

Dance has explored connections among memory, cognition, and body in work produced since at least the 1930s, including that of Mabel Elsworth Todd and her protégé Lulu Sweigard. They employed imagined movement or "ideokinesis" in therapeutic or pedagogic settings; rather than focusing on using voluntary muscular efforts to direct the body into corrective positions, Todd and Sweigard cultivated the "subtle effects of the mind on movement" in order to develop a body-based practice that utilized imagery and visualization. They theorized that focusing on "the idea of the movement" would activate neural pathways to reconfigure muscular-skeletal alignments, resulting in efficient and full use of human movement potential.[37]

This exploration of connections has increased in the last few decades, with the inclusion of a cognitive psychology component in the field of dance medicine and the move within dance studies to embrace interdisciplinary perspectives, including those of the sciences. Scholars and practitioners, augmenting their own studies with findings from research on learning, remembering, performing, and perceiving dance, have produced new conceptual structures or language that have enhanced their understanding of dance and dancing. Yet despite all this, contemporary Western culture remains reluctant to fully consider dance. Dance is still viewed as a product of trained reflexes, spontaneous emotions, or cultivated innate skills and consequently disengaged from the sort of intellection that earns status in this culture. On the popular stage, this attitude is reinforced by televisual dance competitions, which in the early decades of the twenty-first century joined a host of other phenomena that foregrounded the body, including instruction in fitness, yoga, and conditioning; body-revealing high fashion; and a glut of medical, forensic, zombie, and vampire dramas. These dance competitions focus on supersized and over-the-top dancing—how big, how many, how virtuosic—replete with overwrought emotions and attitude, and sexy as well. This emphasis on an aesthetics of the physical extreme too often simply updates the age-old split between mind and body and the categorization of dance as sheer physical entertainment.[38]

BODY AND DANCE

Restricted to the categorization of dance as merely amusing and trivial or even sinful, the study of dance was not generally considered a serious area of research. Nevertheless, evidence of the significance of dance to human society appeared as early as Mesolithic rock carvings and paintings indicating that people have been dancing for at least twelve millennia. They have continued to do so throughout the accretion of Western culture, despite often severe proscriptions. For every warning of damnation, angels danced in the painted clouds of cathedral domes. For every designation as savage or primitive, kings performed in splendid spectacles, secured by their divine power and royal treasuries.

But eschewing the perceived effeminacy of the monarchial court as well as the vulgar physicality of the working class, the nineteenth-century man found the male dancing body its least appropriate representation. The female dancing body—all nature, ephemerality, and sex—was the forbidden yet desired fruit that took center stage in the romantic period, even as she was dismissed from the respectability of polite society. The debasement of the male dancing body and the conflation of female dancer with body and sex did little to confer intellectual status on the dancing body within the larger worlds of culture and academe.[39] However, within the narrower canon of dance research the story, of course, is quite different. Essays appeared during the brief period in the eighteenth century when the emerging field of aesthetics coincided with the consideration of dance as a serious art; these took their place on library shelves adjacent to assorted volumes by ancient and Renaissance philosophers and dancing masters. The late nineteenth and early twentieth centuries produced writing by choreographers and critics as apologists for dance as well as by enlightened anthropologists, who began to generalize their findings on the functions of dance beyond "primitive" societies. But in the 1960s thinking and writing about the body underwent a seismic shift. Multiple critiques of those binaries that had undergirded Western philosophy for most of its history, such as the mind/body split, produced theories that undermined those models and reevaluated the status of the body in human history and society. In turn, this cleared the way for a rapid expansion of scholarship and research into dance and the dancing bodies of artists and everyday movers alike.[40]

DANCING IN THE ARCHIVE

All performing artists learn through moving within the limits of their abilities, through their particular interactions with the world or broader collective and cultural cues, and within the specific contexts and demands of art practices. Audiences, similarly, draw on their own archives of movement to help make sense of what they see in performance.[41] But the meaning or intent that is created and communicated by those who make or perform the work, which is received and remade by audiences, may not rise completely to the level of articulation in language. We all know more than we can say.

That is why the radical rethinking of the archive by Foucault, Derrida, and others—as mutable, transformative, open to the future, inviting reentry, able to explode into and disrupt the present—has had such an enormous impact on dance scholarship. In Western dance tradition, for example, there has long been an assumption that whole dances should be repeatable, meaning that doing so requires mining the archives of others' bodies, limited or idiosyncratic notational schemes, or disembodied visual media to reconstitute an original in bodies that are inherently incapable of duplicating the dances exactly. More recently, persons, events, and works identified in the archive, although anchored in a remembered past, have been understood to generate fluid historical narratives with multiple implications and shifting significances in the present. In other words, each entry into the archive can also uncover a new meaning that "the originating instantiation of the work kept in reserve," rendering reconstruction and reenactment processes of identifying "in a past work still non-exhausted creative fields."[42]

Body-centered approaches to research and the archive have also influenced various kinds of fieldwork in the social sciences. Some scholars, such as Sally Ann Ness, decided to break with standards of academic writing by refusing to "clean up" their field notes. In addition to writing up their findings in discipline-specific formats or tabulating quantitative data, they may also include or substitute their responses to field observations in raw, unmediated, and unrefined states, even for publication. In this way their full archive retains a more vivid and robust record of their work—one that embodies its condition rather than its clinical interpretation. Field notes have also been interpreted within the framework of performances or transformed into performance, for example the work of archaeologist Michael Shanks in performative archaeology or archaeologies of presence and the work of artists in this anthology, such as Jennifer Monson and Emily Johnson.[43]

No gesture is made, no matter how inventive or improvised, that does not draw in some way on a past bodily movement. This constant reenactment within dance generates both problems and possibilities, some of which are shared across the arts and others of which are specific to dance itself. Although serious writing about these and other questions about dance can be found earlier, it is really only in the last three decades that dance researchers and practitioners have focused on revisioning the dancing body as archive and in the archive.[44] As a consequence, dance research has become a richer proposition. These new efforts, utilizing bodied as well as textual or iconological approaches, presume that there is value in entering and reentering an archive to reconstruct near or distant performances of any scale. In contrast, some theorists and practitioners argue that actions or events can only be identified as "performance" by the presence of live bodies in the here and now, that the instantaneity of performance should not be violated or commoditized by attempts to record, document, or reconstruct its original moments.[45] Still, as one dance theorist wrote, "This historian's body wants to consort with dead bodies, wants to know from them," even as she recognized that this methodology always implicates the researcher's bodied history and is granted no authority beyond its power to thicken and animate the historical descriptions of dance.[46]

The impulse to archive and to reenter and retrieve, and in some cases the need or even moral imperative to do so, is fraught with practical, philosophical, and political problems, yet it remains compelling. It is further complicated by continuing redefinitions and reconfigurations of history, archive, and bodied cognition. Nevertheless, these new models unleash multiple opportunities to explore and understand the dynamic frictions among reimagined pasts, constructed presents, and unknown futures. Given the universal and inescapable materiality of humanness, the bodied nature of thought, and the powerful appeal of both history and memory, the notion of the body as and in the archive has import for us in all aspects of our lives.

NOTES

1. Jens Brockmeier, "After the Archive: Remapping Memory," *Culture & Psychology* 16, no. 1 (2010): 5–35, 19–25, esp. 24. See also Emily S. Cross, Antonia F. Hamilton, and Scott T. Grafton, "Building a Motor Simulation de Novo: Observation of Dance by Dancers," *Neuroimage* 31, no. 3 (2006): 1257–67; Ruth S. Day's research page, "Memory for Movement" (http://people.duke.edu/~ruthday/m4m .html); essays in two collections: *The Neurocognition of Dance: Mind, Movement and Motor Skills*, ed. Bettina Bläsing, Martin Puttke, and Thomas Schack (New York: Psychology Press, 2010), and Dee Reynolds, Corinne Jola, and Frank E. Pollick, eds., *Dance Research: The Journal of the Society for Dance Research Electronic* 29, no. 2 (2011); and Catherine J. Stevens, "We Dance What We Remember," in this volume.

2. Regarding the use of "memory" and "history" in this essay, memory begins as a person's neurobiological response to an experience of natural or social surroundings, followed by the various processes that enable retrieval or recall. Memory is lived and personal, subject to forgetfulness or re-remembering differently; it may be externally embodied or recorded, exist without or outside of permission or authorization, but be subject to erasure or marginalization.

History begins as memory. In attempting to distinguish itself from memory, history has sought to base itself in sources articulated in texts or comparably stable forms documenting events alleged to have actually occurred, which provide objective, verifiable, and "true" accounts or records of those events, even though they began as memories. History is the investigation of those accounts or records and the materialization in some form of what, nevertheless, can only be a reimagined or reconstructed past.

3. Benjamin proposed that original works of visual art emitted an "aura," an ineffable but powerful presence radiated by the work that was conferred on its material presence by a history that traded on the work's longevity, singularity, authenticity, and elite ownership. While a reproduction of a painting or a sculpture by mechanical or technological means diminished its aura—not necessarily a negative, as far as Benjamin was concerned—this did not hold true for performance. The materiality of the live body in performance generated an "auratic" presence as well but one that was both conscious and capable of creating meaning. Despite their ephemerality, bodies and performances are capable of temporalizing experience: intensifying a sense of the present, physicalizing a sense of moving in time, and evoking a developmental archive or genealogy of the history of signifying human motion. The auratic body, or the bodied archive, similar to books, photographs, and other ephemera stored in repositories, is susceptible to nostalgia or corruption. But this material, including that residing in the body, is also open to continual reentry and reengagement. It may transform itself or act as a transformative force, reinventing, reinterpreting, or even rupturing the present and the past in unimagined ways for all who encounter them. See Benjamin, thesis IX, "Theses on the Philosophy of History," in *Illuminations: Essays and Reflections*, ed. Peter Demetz (Berlin: Schocken, 1969), 257–58; "Convolute N [On the Theory of Knowledge, Theory of Progress]," N3, 1, in *The Arcades Project*, trans. Howard Eiland and Kevin McLaughlin based on the German edition, ed. Rolf Tiedemann (Cambridge, MA: Harvard University Press, 1999), 463; theses V, VI, and A in "Theses" and "Central Park," in *Walter Benjamin: Selected Writings*, vol. 4, *1938–1940*, ed. Howard Eiland and Michael W. Jennings, trans. Edmund Jephcott and Howard Eiland (Cambridge, MA: Harvard University Press, 2003), 183. See also Jenn Joy, "Tremulous Histories," in this volume.

4. Scylla and Charybdis were mythological creatures; their names refer metaphorically to adjacent natural hazards, between which it is nearly impossible to navigate without risking danger or death.

5. One of the earlier uses of this term can be found in Ann Laura Stoler, "Colonial Archives and the Arts of Governance," *Archival Science* 2 (2002): 87–109. Stoler also lists several works that mark the "archival turn" in the decade preceding Derrida, but credits his work with elevating archive to "a new theoretical status" by "providing an explicit and evocative vocabulary for its legitimation in critical theory" (p. 92).

6. Michel Foucault, "Nietzsche, Genealogy, History," in *The Foucault Reader*, ed. Paul Rabinow (New York: Pantheon Books, 1984), 76–100, 83.

7. Among the stories about Epimenides, a sixth-century BC Cretan prophet and poet, was that his skin, tattooed with secret writings and verses, was preserved in the courts of Sparta (thanks to

Radcliffe Edmonds for pointing me toward this figure). For a contemporary perspective on body/ skin as archive, see also sociologist Deborah Davidson's *The Tattoo Project*, a cross-disciplinary project to digitally archive "memorial" tattoos, at thetattooproject.info.

8. Foucault, *The Archaeology of Knowledge and the Discourse on Language*, trans. A. M. Sheridan Smith (New York: Pantheon Books, 1972), 194. See also painter Sarah Crowner's contribution in this book, "Sideways Glances."

9. Foucault, "Technologies of the Self," in *Technologies of the Self: A Seminar with Michel Foucault*, ed. Luther Martin, Huck Gutman, and Patrick Hutton (Amherst: University of Massachusetts Press, 1988), 17.

10. Foucault, *Archaeology of Knowledge*, 128–29.

11. Foucault, "Nietzsche," 76–100.

12. Foucault, *Archaeology of Knowledge*, 130.

13. Ibid., 5.

14. Foucault, "Nietzsche," 82–83.

15. See Carolyn Steedman, "Something She Called a Fever: Michelet, Derrida, and Dust," *American Historical Review* 106, no. 4 (October 2001): 1159–80. While supporting Derrida's construction of the archive as a nonneutral site of political and cultural power, Steedman attempts to retether Derrida's account to the material realities of the archive and the physical nature of working within it. A more typical criticism is reflected in William J. Maher's 1997 presidential address to the Society of American Archivists, in which Maher argued that "the nonprofessional appropriation of the term 'archives' appears to be part of an attempt by the scholar or database builder to lend panache or cachet and an air of respectability to what otherwise might be little more than a personal hobby or collecting fetish." "Archives, Archivists, and Society," *American Archivist* 61 (Fall 1998): 254.

16. Jacques Derrida, "Archive Fever: A Freudian Impression," trans. Eric Prenowitz, *Diacritics* 25, no. 2 (Summer 1995): 9.

17. See International Council on Archives, ica.org/125/about-records-archives-and-the-profes_ sion/discover-archives-and-our-profession.html; or The Society for American Archivists, www2 .archivists.org/glossary. For more on the history of archives see Jacques le Goff, *History and Memory* (New York: Columbia University Press, 1996); and Terry Cook, "What Is Past Is Prologue: A History of Archival Ideas Since 1898, and the Future Paradigm Shift," *Archivaria* 43 (Spring 1997): 17–63.

The most famous eighteenth-century example of a textual archive is *Encyclopédie, ou Dictionnaire raisonné des sciences, des arts et des métiers* (Encyclopaedia, or classified dictionary of sciences, arts, and trades), comprising twenty-eight volumes of text and plates (others were added later), published over a decade and edited chiefly by Jean d'Alembert and Denis Diderot; see Frank A. Kafker, "Some Observations on Five Interpretations of the 'Encyclopédie,'" *Diderot Studies* 23 (1988): 85–100.

Manual for the Arrangement and Description of Archives (1898) was written by Dutch archivists Samuel Muller, Johan Feith, and Robert Fruin. Although manuals had been published as early as the sixteenth-century, this volume is considered the first systematic presentation of the modern archival paradigm. See also Terry Cook, "The Concept of the Archival Fonds: Theory, Description, and Provenance in the Post-Custodial Era," *Archivaria* 35 (Winter 1992–1993): 24–37; and Marlene Manoff, "Theories of the Archive from Across the Disciplines," *Portal: Libraries and the Academy* 4, no. 1 (2004): 9–25.

18. Derrida worked out these ideas in his controversial and influential lecture and book of the same title: *Archive Fever: A Freudian Impression*, trans. Eric Prenowitz (Chicago: University of Chicago

Press, 1996), and "Archive Fever: A Freudian Impression," 9–63. The question of whether the physical body can serve as archive was answered, in part, by Derrida's discussion of both Freud's psychic apparatus—an internal and immaterial structure that Freud never completely dislodged from physiological body—and by the heritage of circumcision. In part, Derrida read Freud's psychoanalysis as an attempt to unravel the conundrum of human behavior by constructing a model of our psychic apparatus that seems constantly to "repress the archive while archiving the repression" in an "internal substrate" that results in "symptoms, signs, figures, metaphors, and metonymies," some of which are archived more visibly in "bodily dispositions, tics, or restructurings." This process, he argued, clearly indicates "an archival documentation, i.e., psychic or bodied, where the 'ordinary historian' identifies none" ("Archive Fever," 43). Circumcision as act, and its mark, a figural circumscription, is visibly connected to body as a sign of a covenant, similar to the role of tattoos or body incisions in various cultures. Circumcision is configured as a "writing, the trace, inscription, on an exterior substrate . . . and which, though never leaving you, nonetheless has come about, and is no less exterior . . . right on your body proper" ("Archive Fever," 22; see also 12, 19).

19. Derrida, "Archive Fever," 57.

20. Ibid., 11.

21. Ibid., 5.

22. See ibid., 19, 57, in which Derrida defined *mal d'archive* variously as evil, illness, trouble, passion, needing, or in need of—read either as a dependency or a simple fact of necessity. See also multiple sources in Anastasia Proshutinskaya's bibliography in "Archive Fever: Performance Art," *Research Papers* 146 (2011): 6; Derrida, "An Interview with Professor Jacques Derrida," by Michal Ben-Naftali, Jerusalem, January 8, 1998, trans. Dr. Moshe Ron (http://www.yadvashem.org/odot_pdf /Microsoft%20Word%20-%203851.pdf); and Steedman, "Something She Called a Fever," 1162.

23. Derrida, "Archive Fever," 12.

24. Ibid., 18.

25. Ibid., 14. *Prosthetic memory* refers to how processes that mediate memory, from handwriting or recording to computer RAM to technologies yet to be developed, contradict the personal, lived, ambiguous nature of memory—though not the function of power exercised in selection and archiving.

26. Ibid., 27.

27. Ibid., 45.

28. For example, cultural critic Andreas Huyssen and historian Pierre Nora both located the possibility of resistance to cultural amnesia in categories of places, objects, or events other than the archive, but in which materiality and a sense of temporality still adhered. Huyssen posited that one possible antidote for the modern "mnemonic fever caused by the virus of amnesia that at times threatens to consume memory itself" might be the museum and its contents, which, saturated with symbolic potency, could function as anchors of material and temporal fact, creating still pools of present time in the incessant flow of virtual information and rush to the future. Nora identified the potential for resistance in what he designated as *lieux* (realms or sites) of memory that included not only monuments but cultural rituals and performances as well. Replacing lived memory with remains of a past that have been invested repeatedly over time with symbolic cultural importance, these *lieux* nevertheless possessed the capacity to metamorphose in an "endless recycling of their meaning and an unpredictable proliferation of their ramifications." While both were aware of the dangers of nostalgia, the supplanting of live memory, and potential of co-optation by power struc-

tures, they also recognized the potency and potential of physical materiality, invested with symbolic and cultural import however multiple its meanings, to "resist the progressive dematerialization of the world," as well as the cultural or political dynamics of informational overload that generated amnesia. These theories made space for bodies and performance to be considered sites of memory; indeed, Nora makes the claim directly, noting as well that bodied performance is both conscious and capable of creating meaning. Despite their ephemerality, bodies and performance are capable of temporalizing experience: intensifying a sense of the present, physicalizing a sense of moving in time, and evoking a developmental archive or genealogy of the history of signifying human motion. Andreas Huyssen, "Introduction: Time and Cultural Memory at Our Fin de Siècle" and "Escape from Amnesia: The Museum as Mass Medium," in Twilight Memories: Marking Time in a Culture of Amnesia (New York: Routledge, 1995), 1–7 and 13–35; see also Huyssen, "Present Pasts: Media, Politics, Amnesia," Public Culture 12, no. 1 (2000): 27n13; Pierre Nora, "Between Memory and History: Les Lieux de Mémoire," trans. Marc Roudebush, in "Memory and Counter-Memory," special issue, Representations 26 (Spring 1989): esp. 7, 12, 13, 19, 24. Over the course of seventeen years Nora, a French historian, directed the compilation of the multivolume Les Lieux de mémoire (translated as realms or sites of memory, as suggested above), a study of the national history and cultural memory of the French nation.

29. Huyssen, "Nostalgia for Ruins," Grey Room 23 (2006): 7; Huyssen cites Svetlana Boym, The Future of Nostalgia (New York: Basic Books, 2001): "[It] reveals that longing and critical thinking are not opposed to one another, as affective memories do not absolve one from compassion, judgment or critical reflection."

30. See Foster's influential "An Archival Impulse," October 110 (Autumn 2004): 3–22. In this essay Foster documents the creative use of archival materials at the turn of the twenty-first century. He notes how artists are repurposing archival materials in their entirety, sampling from one or multiple archives, or reworking materials into new forms of archives. Curators joined art makers in investigating the power of art that draws on the archive, as evidenced in numerous exhibitions of repurposed "documents." This was soon followed by a broadening of efforts on the part of curators and artists to restage or re-present entire historical exhibitions or reenact seminal performance artworks. Examples are When Attitudes Become Form: Bern 1969/Venice 2013, curated by Germano Celant with Thomas Demand and Rem Koolhaas, presented by Fondazione Prada, Venice; and a restaging of Live in Your Head, curator Harald Szeemann's 1969 exhibition originally mounted in the modernist spaces of the Bern Kunsthalle and restaged in the Ca' Corner della Regina, Venice. See also "How the Art World Caught Archive Fever," Artspace, January 22, 2014; and Reesa Greenberg, "'Remembering Exhibitions': From Point to Line to Web," Tate Papers, no. 12 (2009). See also Marina Abramović, Seven Even Easy Pieces, Guggenheim Museum, New York City (2005), in which she reperformed works by performance artists that were premiered in the 1960s and 1970s in Düsseldorf, New York, and Paris.

31. See, for example, Never The Same: Conversations about Art Transforming Politics & Community in Chicago & Beyond, an archival project concerned with socially and politically engaged art in Chicago since the 1960s that invites people to activate the material of the archive in informal events called "unfurlings" (never-the-same.org); and Nataša Petrešin-Bachelez's two-part "Innovative Forms of Archives," e-flux, Journal 13 (February 2010) and Journal 16 (May 2010).

Another creative redeployment of archival materials addresses the marginalization or deliberate erasure of people or their past, leaving gaps in the historical record. These texts, which include film, sociopolitical essays, and creative nonfiction, frequently mesh traditional archival research into records and files, interviews, oral histories, and memoir; they are described by André Brink as "stories—in which not history, but imaginings of history are invented." "Stories of History: Re-imagining the Past in Post-Apartheid Narrative," in *Negotiating the Past: The Making of Memory in South Africa*, ed. Sarah Nuttall and Carli Coetzee (Cape Town, S. Africa: Oxford University Press, 1998), 42. See also Erica Johnson's analysis of what she calls the "neo-archive" in "Building the Neo-Archive: Dionne Brand's *A Map to the Door of No Return*," *Meridians* 12, no. 1 (2014): 149–71. Dance, too, partakes in this archival art making; see André Lepecki, "The Body as Archive: Will to Re-Enact and the After-lives of Dances," *Dance Research Journal* 42, no. 2 (Winter 2010): 28–48, and Patricia Hoffbauer, "Body as Signifier," in this volume.

32. Donna Haraway's classic essay "A Cyborg Manifesto Science, Technology, and Socialist-Feminism in the Late Twentieth Century," in *Simians, Cyborgs and Women: The Reinvention of Nature* (New York: Routledge, 1991), 149–81, is a good place to begin to consider the intersections of nondualis-tic construals of the body, technology, archive, and sociopolitical dynamics. For the impact of new technologies on archive, memory, and the making of dances, see Jennifer Monson, "Live Dancing Archive," and Mariana Ibañez and Simon Kim, "New Bodies, New Architecture," in this volume.

33. For the origin of the term "memory boom," see Jens Brockmeier, "After the Archive: Re-mapping Memory," *Culture & Psychology* 16, no. 1 (2010): 5–35, esp. 5 and 28n4, in which Brockmeier also includes a summary of "four fields" of memory study and a useful bibliography. For more on the "memory industry," see Gavriel D. Rosenfeld, "A Looming Crash or a Soft Landing? Forecasting the Future of the Memory 'Industry,'" *Journal of Modern History* 81 (March 2009): 122–58, esp. 123n2; Andreas Huyssen, "Introduction," in *Twilight Memories*, 1:7, and 5; and Nora, "Between Memory and History," 7, 12, 13. See also Huyssen, "Present Pasts," 27n13.

Other theorists have also rejected more traditional loci and practices of the archive while re-taining some of the functional definition and relocating the archive to other material possibilities. See Diana Taylor's oft-cited *The Archive and the Repertoire: Performing Cultural Memory in the Americas* (Dur-ham, NC: Duke University Press, 2003); see also Huyssen, "Escape from Amnesia," 13–35; Joan M. Schwartz and Terry Cook, "Archives, Records, and Power: The Making of Modern Memory," *Archival Science* 2, nos. 1–2 (March 2002): 1–19 and "Archives, Records, and Power: From (Postmodern) Theory to (Archival) Practice," *Archival Science* 2, nos. 3–4 (September 2002): 171–85; and Paul J. Voss and Marta L. Werner, "Towards a Poetics of the Archive: Introduction," *Studies in the Literary Imagina-tion* 32, no. 1 (Spring 1999): i–vii.

34. See Boreth Ly, "Devastated Vision(s): The Khmer Rouge Scopic Regime in Cambodia," *Art Journal* 62, no. 1 (Spring 2003): 66–81. For a more general examination of the political or cultural uses of photography, see Allan Sekula, "The Body and the Archive," *October* 39 (Winter 1986): 3–64.

35. See Freya Vass-Rhee, "Integrating Dance and Cognitive Science: Toward Emancipatory Re-search," in *Proceedings of the 38th Congress on Research in Dance* (Tempe, AZ, 2006). See also Catherine J. Stevens, "We Dance What We Remember," in this volume; and Corinne Jola, Frank E. Pollick, and Dee Reynolds, "Dance and Neuroscience—New Partnerships," *Dance Research: The Journal of the Society for Dance Electronic* 29 (2011): 259–69.

36. Brockmeier, "After the Archive," 24.

37. Mabel Elsworth Todd, *The Thinking Body* (Princeton, NJ: Dance Horizons, Inc., 1973); Lulu Sweigard, *Human Movement Potential: Its Ideokinetic Facilitation* (New York: Harper & Row, 1974); and "To Strengthen Muscles After Bone Break, Just … Imagine," *Philadelphia Inquirer*, January 18, 2015, G2.

38. While problematic for many dance artists and educators, the popularity of hyperbolic danc-ing compels consideration of cultural trends, including those that shape concert dance genres.

Virtuosity, variously defined, has been highly valued in many eras and cultures. It may signal competency, leadership, or social status, or establish and maintain important identity factors, such as gender. While its role and impact continue to be debated within Western concert dance, virtuosity is a visible component of dance worldwide; see Elizabeth Kendall, "Artistry's Delicate Balance," *Dance Magazine* (May 2014); and Anya Peterson Royce, *Anthropology of the Performing Arts: Artistry, Virtuosity, and Interpretation in a Cross-cultural Perspective* (Lanham, MD: AltaMira Press, 2004). For virtuosity's connection to masculinity in Western dance, see Ramsay Burt, *The Male Dancer: Bodies, Spectacle, Sexualities* (New York: Routledge, 2007). Hybrid, folk, and vernacular forms frequently value virtuosity. Thomas F. DeFrantz, in "The Black Beat Made Visible: Hip Hop Dance and Body Power," in *Of the Presence of the Body: Essays on Dance and Performance Theory*, ed. André Lepecki (Middletown, CT: Wesleyan University Press, 2004), 64–81, considers the function of virtuosity in hip-hop dance. Sally Sommer's documentary *Check Your Body at the Door* examines virtuosity as identity in the underground house dance scene in 1990s New York City (dir. Charles Atlas, Michael Schwartz, and Sally Sommer, 2011). Franca Tamasari is one of many anthropologists who evaluate the role of dance virtuosity in culture; see "The Meaning of the Steps Is in Between: Dancing and the Curse of Compliments," in "The Politics of Dance," ed. R. Henry, F. Magowan, and D. Murray, special issue, *The Australian Journal of Anthropology* 11, no. 3 (2000): 36–48. See also Sherril Dodds, *Dancing on the Canon: Embodiments of Value in Popular Dance* (New York: Palgrave Macmillan, 2011).

39. For more on ballet and body, gender, and ephemerality, see Susan Leigh Foster, *Choreography & Narrative: Ballet's Staging of Story and Desire* (Bloomington: Indiana University Press, 1996); and *Rethinking the Sylph: New Perspectives on the Romantic Ballet*, ed. Lynn Garafola (Hanover, NH: Wesleyan University Press, 1997).

40. We can refer to Foucault as an exemplar of these changes: from his earlier works, such as *Madness and Civilization* (1967; originally from *History of Madness*, 1961), to his later writings, the body was a focus of his research. See John Protevi, "Body," in *The Cambridge Foucault Lexicon*, ed. Leonard Lawlor and John Nale (Cambridge, MA: Cambridge University Press, 2014), 51–56.

41. See Susan Leigh Foster, *Choreographing Empathy: Kinesthesia in Performance* (New York: Routledge, 2010); Bettina Bläsing, Beatriz Calvo-Merinob, Emily S. Cross, Corinne Jolaf, Juliane Honischg, and Catherine J. Stevens, "Neurocognitive Control in Dance Perception and Performance," *Acta Psychologica* 139, no. 2 (February 2012): 300–8; and see bibliography at The Watching Dance Project (www.watchingdance.org).

42. André Lepecki, "The Body as Archive," 31; Mark Franko, "Repeatability, Reconstruction, and Beyond," *Theatre Journal* 41, no. 1 (March 1989): 56–74, http://www.jstor.org/stable/3207924. Also, scholars and practitioners in the field of performance studies have contributed greatly to research into the knowing body and body as archive, including Diana Taylor, Richard Schechner, Joseph Roach, and many others.

43. See Sally Ann Ness, "Dancing in the Field; Notes from Memory," in *Corporealities: Dancing Knowledge, Culture, and Power*, ed. Susan Leigh Foster (London: Routledge, 1996), 129–54; and Paul Wolffram, "'He's Not a White Man, He's a Small Bird Like You and Me': Learning to Dance and Becoming Human in Southern New Ireland," *Yearbook for Traditional Music* 38 (2006): 112. See also Michael Shanks's writings on the archaeology of performance at www.mshanks.com, as well as *Theatre/Archaeology* (London: Routledge, 2001), written in conjunction with theater director Mike Pearson.

44. Mark Franko, André Lepecki, Thomas F. DeFrantz, Ann Cooper Albright, and Ramsay Burt

explore these themes, some of them in performance as well; several have contributed to this volume. Choreographers have been mining the archive as well, including Meredith Monk, Bebe Miller, Patricia Hoffbauer, and Jennifer Monson; reflections on several of these works can be found in this volume.

45. One of the better-known proponents of this view is Peggy Phelan: "Performance cannot be saved, recorded, documented . . . once it does so, it becomes something other than performance"; and "Performance implicates the real through the presence of living bodies. In performance art spectatorship, there is an element of consumption: there are no leftovers, the gazing spectator must try to take everything in. Without a copy, live performance plunges into visibility—in a maniacally charged present—and disappears into memory, into the realm of invisibility and the unconscious where it eludes regulation and control. . . . It saves nothing; it only spends." *Unmarked: the Politics of Performance* (New York: Routledge, 2004), 146, 148.

46. Susan Leigh Foster, "Choreographing History," 6–7, and other essays in *Choreographing History (Unnatural Acts: Theorizing the Performative)* (Bloomington: Indiana University Press, 1995).

I. Bodied Knowing

Bodied knowing is a state of being long familiar to dancers and other performers. Historically, dancers and others who wrote about dance and movement frequently grappled with articulating the experience of bodied knowledge in learning and teaching as well as in the expressive or communicative capacity of performance. If philosophy has lost primacy of place to science in recent centuries, it still lent credibility to a suspect art; writers who took a particular interest in bodied knowing provided language and conceptual frameworks that enabled movement artists to more convincingly legitimize their experience to those who were skeptical of the cognitive dimensions of dance.[1] The idea of body as archive must start here, at the moment that bodied experience interacts with the world and ideas, creates history, holds memories, and moves in the present and into the future.

Alternative notions of cognition as more fully embodied and situated in the world were reflected in the work of early theorists such as William James and John Dewey, Jean Piaget, and Maurice Merleau-Ponty, as well as dance physiologists and educators such as Mabel Elsworth Todd and Margaret H'Doubler.[2] If you search the Internet today for "body" and "knowing," you will get hundreds of hits for essays, monographs, books, lectures, symposia, institutes, and university departments featuring "embodied cognition." This robust field of study challenges the more traditional approach to cognition, which—developing from the emerging sciences of experimental and empirical psychology as well as neurobiology in the nineteenth and early twentieth centuries, and strongly influenced by parallel research in computer science and artificial intelligence in the 1950s—focused almost exclusively on brain function.[3]

Science-based critiques of traditional cognitive theory increased in numbers, and by the 1970s empirical research in the developing and interrelated fields of situated, embedded, enactive, and embodied cognition confirmed that the body as a whole is integral to cognition and the acquisition and processing of knowledge, and that this knowledge is influenced by the body's sociocultural context.[4] These scientific advances coincided with a renewed interest in phenomenology, gender studies, poststructuralism, postmodernism, and postcolonialism, and any contemporary discussion of the body as an archive must take all these developments into account. Despite variations in theoretical approaches, there

19

is growing acknowledgment of the "bodily nature of cognitive agency."[5] In a culture that primarily lends value to phenomena that can be verified objectively and scientifically, this attention to embodiment as a new paradigm is welcome.

In this section of the book, Alain Platel locates the performer's body as a site that knows more than it can say, asking dancers to dig deeply into the archive of their own or others' bodily movements to create new and shared movement that in turn augments their own repertoires of movement action and memory. Tomie Hahn turns her eye on the performances of individuals' embodied archives and on both the structures that transmit this knowledge into the world and the reciprocal shaping of these structures of transmission by the outside world. Juhani Pallasmaa writes that architecture, like dance, moves outward from the body in acts of expression, constituting a sphere of externalized order and memory. Meg Stuart contributes a warm-up plan that asks performers to not only be physically vulnerable but also to draw on their own archives of memory to become more cognitively aware, responsive, and imaginative. The research and practice of Bonnie Bainbridge Cohen focus on the systematic deepening of awareness about all that the body remembers and archives, starting in the womb and tracing through the development of human movement patterns. Ralph Lemon's two brief pieces of writing invite us to consider and experience his processes of living, dancing, and making, beginning with pleasure as biology or memory and moving to the tension between the insistent memory of the trained body and the creative act.

—Linda Caruso Haviland

NOTES

1. A short list of dance writers who have emerged as important voices in the last thirty years or who have begun to add to the discourse in just the past decade would include Susan Leigh Foster, Sally Banes, Brenda Dixon Gottschild, Mark Franko, Susan Manning, Ramsey Burt, Kariamu Welsh, Marta Savigliano, Kapila Vatsyayan, Ann Cooper Albright, Thomas F. DeFrantz, André Lepecki, Susanne Franco, and Yutian Wong, among many others. Anthologies to consult that give some indication of the scope of research include those edited by Alexandra Carter and Janet O'Shea, Sondra Horton Fraleigh and Penelope Hanstein, Susan Leigh Foster, Andrée Grau, Gay Morris, and Jane Desmond.

2. William James, The Principles of Psychology, vol. 1, particularly chs. VIII and IX, "The Relations of Minds to Other Things" and "The Stream of Thought" (1890); William James, "I. The Function of Cognition," in The Meaning of Truth (lecture delivered to the Aristotelian Society, December 1, 1884, first published in Mind 10 [1885]); Maurice Merleau-Ponty, Phenomenology of Perception, trans. Colin Smith (London: Routledge & Keegan Paul, 1962); "The Primacy of Perception and Is Philosophical Consequences" (address delivered to Société Française de philosophie, November 23, 1946); The Primacy of Perception: And Other Essays on Phenomenological Psychology, the Philosophy of Art, History, and

Politics, trans. James Edie (Evanston, IL: Northwestern University Press, 1964), 12–42; John Dewey, "The Reflex Arc Concept in Psychology," *Psychological Review* 3 (1896): 357–70, and throughout various works, including *Experience and Nature* (1925), *Art as Experience* (1934), and *Experience and Education* (1938); and Jean Piaget, *The Language and Thought of the Child* (1926), *Origins of Intelligence in the Child* (1936), and *The Origins of Intelligence in Children*, trans. M. T. Cook (1952).

3. The notion of embodied cognition has early roots in the nascent anatomical investigations of the seventeenth and eighteenth centuries and was further explored in the emerging sciences of experimental and empirical psychology as well as neurobiology in the nineteenth and early twentieth centuries. Disciplines such as biology, neuroscience, anthropology, philosophy, mathematics, computer science, artificial intelligence, psychology, and linguistics eventually also fed both discipline-specific and interdisciplinary streams of research. Some key figures emerging in the late 1960s and moving forward into present-day research include linguist George Lakoff and collaborators philosopher Mark Johnson, mathematician and linguist Mark Turner, and cognitive psychologist Rafael E. Núñez. A small sampling of others whose work has been directly or indirectly influential could include biologist and neurophenomenologist Francisco Varela, cognitive psychologist Eleanor Rosch, philosopher Evan Thompson, developmental psychologist Esther Thelen, roboticist Rodney Brooks, and neuroscientists Giacomo Rizzolatti and Christian Keysers. Alternate lists could easily be produced of important researchers within these expanding and overlapping fields of inquiry. Useful overviews include Margaret Wilson's "Six Views of Embodied Cognition," *Psychonomic Bulletin & Review* 9, no. 4 (2002): 625–36; and Andrew Wilson and Sabrina Golonka's "Embodied Cognition Is Not What You Think It Is" in *Frontiers in Psychology* (February 2013). For additional historical context see Robert A. Wilson's and Lucia Foglia, "Embodied Cognition," in *The Stanford Encyclopedia of Philosophy* (2017), https://plato.stanford.edu/archives/spr2017/entries/embodied-cognition/. Dance has been of particular interest to cognitive science in the last several years to those working from a perspective within dance, such as Freya Vass-Rhee, and to those working from the frameworks of science research, such as Catherine J. Stevens, a contributor to this volume.

4. Wilson and Foglia, "Embodied Cognition."

5. Ibid.

EVERYONE HAS SOMETHING TO TELL

When I graduated from university (Ghent, Belgium) in the early 1980s with a master's degree in psychology and educational sciences, my ambitions were clear: I would become a good remedial educationalist in one of the cerebral palsy centers where I had worked as an intern. Now, thirty years later, I realize that I have spent most of my active life as a dance theater director in a company called les ballets C de la B. What started out as a small group of friends and amateurs making short dance theater performances has evolved into a professional dance theater company performing on stages all over the world.

Personally, I like to speak of the history of les ballets C de la B as a joke that got a little out of hand. Still, it has become clear to me that my education as a remedial educationalist has had a great influence throughout my career as a dance theater director. As a remedial educationalist, I was already particularly interested in the functioning of the "wounded body." Physical disabilities and the way in which people try to compensate for them were extremely fascinating to me. Their beauty was unique, I thought, and I remember how people around me could be shocked when I pointed that out. It is my belief that people with a disability have some kind of advantage over the so-called normal people, as if the disability has made them aware that there is no time to waste to make something special out of life. Finally, it is my long-held conviction that there is no such thing as "normality." Working as a director has really taught me that.

As I already mentioned, the company started more or less by accident. We were a group of friends hanging out together, ready to change the world, drinking cheap wine and smoking cigarettes. And we also liked to go and see young and experimental theater. That's how we discovered Pina Bausch's work. Her work was very different from all other modern dance theater performances (which on looking back were rather neoclassical). The dancers that Pina put on stage did not look like dancers. What's more, she introduced a special way of creating: she asked questions of her dancers and used their answers to create the performance. She gave her dancers back their name, and after having watched some of her performances, we really felt as if we knew the dancers personally: Mechtild . . . Dominique . . . Jan . . . Nazareth . . . Malou.

Pina worked with virtuousic, trained classical dancers, yet they looked like

Rehearsal for *pitie!* (2008) by Alain Platel, in Ghent, June 2008. Mathieu Desseigne Ravel (on left) and Romeu Runa (on right). (See plate 1 for color image.) Photograph by Chris Van der Burght.

ordinary people who just happened to be in her dance performance. "I'm *not* interested in how people *move but* what *moves* them." That had become her motto.

And that is why we became so inspired by her work. It made us believe that everyone can have something to tell on stage and that every movement can lead to a little dance.

At first, les ballets C de la B was a nice hobby. The original group consisted of a cheese maker, a medical doctor, a criminologist, a student in communication sciences, and me. None of us had any dancing or acting experience whatsoever, and we had no professional ambitions. None of us was good at speech, so our performances had little text. None of us had any dancing skills, but we liked to move, so we created a sort of dance theater, called physical theater. We could only create performance material based on the personal history and physical capabilities of the participants, and that was rather limited at first. Only much later, when professional dancers took an interest in our work, did the physical potential we could work with increase.

The first turning point in the career of les ballets C de la B proved to be *Bonjour Madame* in 1993. It was a performance about "manhood." I recruited ten boys/ men ranging from eleven to thirty-three years of age. Some were professional dancers with classical or contemporary dance training; others were amateurs (meaning dance lovers with no professional training).

When the rehearsals started, I was very well prepared, as usual. But every single day the most amazing and interesting things happened in that studio, things that required no organizing or "directing." It did not take long for me to understand that my preparation was of no use at all. These men simply wanted to find out how they could share their talents and skills.

I created exercises to boost that process. For instance, I would ask the dancers to turn personal experiences into dance phrases. The ballet dancer would create a typical classical dance phrase and the hip-hopper would make a hip-hop phrase. When I would ask the hip-hopper to learn the ballet phrase and add his personal experience to it, something really interesting would happen with the classical phrase. The continuous passing on of these reworked phrases that were reinterpreted over and over again resulted in a kind of dance beyond classification. I called it the "bastard dance," and we made it our trademark.

It was even more fascinating to see how the professional dancers tried to create dance phrases that could be performed by children without making too many concessions on the level of difficulty. And vice versa, I would also ask the children to create phrases that the professionals had to learn.

This way, a unique repertoire of movements was created, based on the personal history of each participant and adapted and reinterpreted by his colleagues. During rehearsals, it was mainly my job to suggest themes to inspire the participants, themes that would go beyond the purely personal level to address a wider audience.

It was obvious that the dance/physical language created by the participants was inspired by their own physical abilities, their training and experience in movement, their roots, and their personal history.

The social body determined the form and content of the work. And ever since *Bonjour Madame*, when I started working with an international and multicultural cast, people have been looking for a political message in our work. We were not aware of that at first, but gradually it became one of the themes we worked around during rehearsals: the social body as a political statement.

The second turning point came along while creating *vsprs* in 2006. For this particular performance, I was inspired by short films made by Arthur Van Gehuchten, a psychiatrist who filmed his patients at the beginning of the last century. These old films show people making fierce involuntary movements, as if the body wants to express what words cannot say. Anyway, I did not see sick

Still shots from *Films médicaux* (1904) by Arthur Van Gehuchten. As Alain Platel observes, "the body wants to express what words cannot say." (See plate 2 for color images.)

people in these films. I prefer to call them people who are hypersensitive toward life. And that was something that the dancers recognized immediately when I showed them these films: as if examining this physical language enabled the dancers to dig deeper into themselves and their peers, as if they were able to tap into layers of (collective) sub- and unconsciousness.

Now that I know that the term "choreographer" is derived from the medical term "chorea" (which is a collective term for disorders of the nervous system that manifest themselves by involuntary movements), I can reconcile myself with the idea of being called a choreographer. We have come full circle, so it seems, and my training as a remedial educationalist has proven to be a good preparation for what I am doing today.

In one way or the other, dance will always be a language that is trying to physically express the "big emotions." Of course there are thousands of dialects, and they differ according to time and place. But all these dialects are one big family, I like to think.

STALKING EMBODIED KNOWLEDGE — THEN WHAT?

PART 1: STALKING EMBODIED KNOWLEDGE

In slow motion
a woman on the bleachers meticulously applied lipstick.
I could only see lips in her tiny mirror.
Cherry red.
"Check ... it ... OUT!" a teenage boy hollered from the chain-link fence
as the demolition derby cars paraded into the arena.
Tires kicked up dust
joining the plumes of engine exhaust.
Chaotic, unnatural energy.
These engines, carefully crafted from old parts in the heat of summer,
would be re-sculpted in seconds by impact.
High gloss.
Let's get ready to rummmmm-ble![1]

For many years I have been stalking the ephemeral: how we come to embody cultural knowledge. The very process of comprehending embodiment appears to dissipate the closer I get. The embodiment of knowledge presents a paradox, a perpetual loop that teases me. Although the body stands as a very real, physical entity in the world, the flow of knowledge into and from the body is not always discernible, or clear. That the body changes once it learns and embodies information continues the paradoxical loop. At first glance the notion of the body as archive appears to address the body as a stable corporeal object, yet the reality of how archives are created and reside *within* the body winks to the ephemeral paradox of change and growth that characterizes that very body. In different cultures and in different time periods, the relationships between the body and mind have been philosophically and scientifically diverse. The study of mind, cognition, and embodied cognition have shifted the examination of the mind-body relationship to a point where the dichotomy fades and we can consider embodied consciousness.[2] Can embodiment be a process of archiving knowledge?

When we observe human activities, such as movement, that outwardly display the embodiment of knowledge or knowledge transfer, we are provided with abundant opportunities for understanding knowledge acquisition over time.

Because repetition of movement reinforces the retention of embodied knowledge, there are numerous opportunities for us to observe an ephemeral, time-based process that literally presents the moment of knowledge transfer.

One of the aims of this essay is to heighten our awareness of how movement is learned, or embodied, through observation. As a result of that expanded awareness we can ask: *Then what?* What can we create from observations of an experience? I see the body as a site of emergent knowledge—as a wonderfully dangerous zone, encouraging or maybe discouraging experimentation through creative practices. I offer the demolition derby vignette that opened this essay as an example of experimentation. While it does not provide a strict Geertzian "thick description" of the derby, which has its place in other kinds of texts, I believe it reflects a particular sensibility and perspective of my experience.[3]

Practicing Moves

As an ethnographer and as a performer, I am trained to observe, but in different ways and for different purposes. In playing these dual roles, I feel strongly that theory and practice inform each other. The crossroad where theory and practice meet locates a surreal yet rich context for understanding embodied cultural knowledge. The juxtaposition of creative art making, practice, and research within this crossroad provides insights not normally revealed through the practice of just one of these disciplines. Some people assume that research and creative practices related to the body can be isolated from each other or even consciously separated, while others find them inseparable. In this essay I focus on observation and experimentation not only as two methods that link theory and practice, but also as methods to identify the structures that help us to develop creative expression and research (or prevent us from doing so). It is fortunate that movement is an outward display of energy and exists as an observable display of embodied knowledge.

Because observing embodiment engages me as both a dancer/mover and scholar, I find it useful to (re)connect the research and creative aspects of my everyday life and to draw attention to the perspectives of both movers and observers. As a mover, I ask: What value is there in knowing structures of embodiment and transmission (the cycle of teaching and learning)?[4] As an ethnographer, I ask: What does observation reveal? From the perspectives of both mover and observer, I ask: What is interesting about movement? Why move? How does moving or observing movement assist in our cultivation of embodied cultural knowledge, memory, or creative expression?

First, let's agree on one thing: the body is a medium of expression. How we express ourselves through the body reveals a great deal about our personal, cultural, and social backgrounds. When the body outwardly displays knowledge—while speaking, moving, touching—we have opportunities to observe the elements of an individual's embodied "archives." The various modes of communication emphasized during such outward displays are important to note: spoken or written word, touch, movement, or gaze, to list a few. The sensory experience of movement expression is rich, but in this essay I focus on enactive knowledge (knowledge gained through action) and display.[5] How does movement reveal embodied knowledge?[6]

The wide range of movement expressivity is staggering, from a casual gesture to a pas de chat in ballet or an *osuberi* in Japanese dance. When I stepped back and included modes of movement expression beyond "dance" in my frame of awareness and research, a flurry of insights emerged about the expressivity, meaning, creativity, and transmission of the moving body. For this reason, I have expanded the breadth of my research scope from dance to include expressive movement.[7] Subsequently, more questions arose: What embodied cultural knowledge and sensibilities are conveyed through movement? How does movement support, or negate, what is verbally articulated? People "say" a lot with their bodies, but people often rely *so* heavily on the words used by others that frequently what the body conveys through movement goes unnoticed. Sometimes facial expressions and movements support or enhance what is being said orally, but at other times movements and facial expressions belie and contradict these words.

A Brief Story

Recently, while discussing sound and movement practices with a group of artists and scholars, an established professor of music sincerely declared, "I don't dance at all." Yet as he said this he energetically whirled his arms around in outward circles like broad brushstrokes. Such expressivity seemed to arise naturally when coupled with speech, although these animated gestures contradicted his words. He continued speaking, marveling about the dramatic movement expressivity and communication between performers in classical chamber music ensembles. Fascinated by how he displayed the very ideas he was communicating through his movements and sounds, I drew little outward circles in the margins of my paper to note his "dance" for my pocket archive of embodied stories. Then what? My archived sketch later inspired a brush painting, and the story now also resides on these pages.

Foundation Building

The *Oxford English Dictionary* (OED) defines "embody" in multiple ways. Curiously, the definitions mirror the theoretical threads I problematize in this essay. Although several definitions are obsolete or refer to other disciplines, I include all of the entries, for contextualization, below. Note especially the first, third, and fourth entries, which I have highlighted in boldface type:

1. **To put into a body; to invest or clothe (a spirit) with a body;**
2. To impart a material, corporeal, or sensual character to. *rare.* Also *intr.* for *refl.*;
3a. **To give a concrete form to (what is abstract or ideal); to express (principles, thoughts, intentions) in an institution, work of art, action, definite form of words, etc. b. Of institutions, works of art, actions, forms of words, etc.: To be an embodiment or expression of (an idea, principle, etc.);**
4. **To cause to become part of a body; to unite into one body; to incorporate (a thing) in a mass of material, (particular elements) in a system or complex unity;**
†5. *Chem.* and *Physiol.* a. *trans.* To form into one body. b. *intr.* for *refl.* To coalesce, draw together, solidify. *Obs.*
6a. *trans.* To form into a body or company for military or other purposes; to organize. **b.** *intr.* for *refl.* To form or join a body or company for military or other purposes.[8]

These emphasized entries directly address the core themes in this essay. The first entry presents us with the two necessary characteristics of "embody" as a transitive verb—that "embody" is an action verb and that it *needs* a direct object (or person), a what or a whom that, in a sense, sits still to receive the action. But the intertwined relationship between action and object highlights the paradox of the ephemeral; transitive also connotes something or *someone in transition.* Entry 3a draws our attention to the process or act of giving form to something abstract. Entry 4 brings me to one of the more salient topics of this essay: incorporating things or elements into a system (or complex unity). Structure. Taken together, they reveal another paradox of the ephemeral. The body-as-structure for abstract knowledge *is also structured by* outside practices. This in itself is not a new idea; many scholars have noted how culture or society organizes bodies.[9] I point out these three definitions of "embody" because they identify the slippery nature of embodiment, the human body both changing within and changing culture, as well as the mirroring and the reciprocal structuring between bodies and context or knowledge.

Sensational Hunting

While stalking the ways that we learn through the body, I logically began my hunt with the body. The senses quickly emerged as the vehicles for the transmission of embodied cultural knowledge. My subsequent research on pedagogy derives from a long-term study of embodied practices and transmission—more specifically, how the senses act as the conduit for the body and self to comprehend the world.[10] The senses exist as our physical interfaces to the world, both what is experienced inside our bodies and what is "out there" in the environment. The body learns not only about itself but also about the world around it through the senses and, in pedagogical settings, how to attend to sensory information. This raises some questions: What sensory modes does a teaching practice emphasize for transmitting knowledge? What can be noted about a pedagogical system by observing how the particulars of sensory information are imparted?

The study of the structures of knowledge transmission reveals how teaching methods instill cultural concepts of the body and embodiment, while also identifying which elements a culture deems to be vital to transmit. Teaching methods include personal interactions, direct or tacit methods employed by larger institutions or organizations or media, such as notation, Skype, audio, or video transmissions. Noting the particular cultural context of the instruction—how practitioners behave, their metacognitive awareness of the process, pedagogical practices—can offer a wide range of insights into the nature of embodied cultural knowledge, embodied cognition, and creative expression.[11]

Creativity emerges at least twice in the research process when observing transmission: creativity within the practice we are observing and then in what we (creatively) produce after our observations. I see transmission and creativity intertwine in fascinating ways, particularly when observing structures of transmission that might inherently encourage, or discourage, experimentation and innovation. A subculture, genre, or discipline, driven to maintain a traditional performance practice, for example, generally maintains structures of transmission that limit the degree of experimentation allowed within the practice in order to foster continuity. Other subcultures, genres, or disciplines may specifically encourage innovation and experimentation as part of their performance practice. How might the structures of transmitting embodied cultural knowledge influence notions of creativity, both in the cases we observe, and in how we (creatively) display what we observe?

Noticing Transmission: Knowledge Building(s)

Many educational settings build structures that organize our experiences of the world, art, and information. I want to use just such a setting to draw attention to the continuum of information flow in order to problematize small-to-large organizations of knowledge or corporeal structures. On one side of the continuum we encounter the subtle details of ephemeral sensory information transmitted through bodies: between performers or teacher and student. On the other end of the spectrum are the large-scale structural patterns of moving bodies, such as the design of pathways on a college campus or highways for vehicle travel.

Standing central to the entire transmission affair is the body, with the senses transmitting the flow of information. Culture and upbringing color our worlds. As human beings, our selective sensory awareness at any given time, influenced by cognitive filtering and enculturation, shapes how we attend to the stream of information around us. Cultural hierarchies of the senses, as well as personal/individual filters, affect the transmission of particular sensory information.[12] These filters problematize notions of sensory "translation," or how we make sense of our experience.

Academia shapes our environment and the structures of knowledge flow. Regarding the design of campuses, architect Gregory Kessler keenly observed, "The built environment communicates ideas, values, and beliefs that reflect the material culture of our civilization. In this way, our spaces and places can be understood as a language of communication in the same way that our written and verbal language allows us to communicate with each other."[13] I want to expand Kessler's statement to include the time-based, ephemeral arts, by positing that the built environment also communicates the *nonmaterial* culture of our civilization. The organization of university campuses shapes the flow of our movements, juxtapositions of buildings create associations, and populating these living spaces shapes knowledge and the valuing of this knowledge.

It is vital to understand how our academic cultures have compartmentalized the sensory order of our studies of expressivity and the acquisition of knowledge in general. The campus maps out, or reconfigures, our bodies and research: people who study music, "ear people," are "housed" in one building; the visual arts or "eye people" generally work in a different building; and dancers or others who move their entire bodies inhabit yet another building on the outskirts of campus. In addition, in some universities people who create art make their work in locations on the margins of the campus and distant from the "head" people, those working within traditional academic parameters of intellectual research or theory. This is curious and further obfuscates the organization of knowledge flow. Campus designs often mirror a conventional notion of the philosophical mind-body split, even in the face of contemporary theories of embodied cognition, in which the brain is not the sole keeper of knowledge. The entire body holds knowledge.

But you get my point: when the sensory modes are compartmentalized in the academic arena, we lose the perspective of the humanity—the diverse social and cultural qualities of being human—of the whole expressive, sensory being. In everyday life, the senses are not discrete. There is a great deal of sensory overlap; perhaps the greatest examples appear in the connections between smell and taste or sound and touch. So why do we compartmentalize them in academia or even in many artistic practices? Understandably, there are practical and formal reasons, as well as spatial concerns. Yet I feel it is our responsibility as artists and scholars to identify the structures that shape our lives. Collaborating across disciplinary or practice boundaries is one way to reconnect divisions, yet only collaborations that integrate the senses/arts/research in deep ways will counter and reconstruct such structural forces.

I contend that it's essential to pull back the structural frames—and, in taking notice, to seek out, write about, and be creative with the knowledge we embody. There's creative movement, sound, visual, and other sensory expressivity in our everyday lives. I beg that we take notice. Observing context and structure is key.

PART 2: THEN WHAT?

To the Reader: A Self-guided Tour

Let's not overlook the transmission of ideas via text as part of our embodiment of knowledge! Fostering creativity in how we write about movement expression will hopefully challenge our sensibilities about transmission. This part of the essay is written in segments that may be read in any order. Please choose your own path. Readers will find stories, theoretical texts, and "activating moves"— exercises that I hope will challenge readers to consider movement and observation in unique ways. Simply flipping pages forward and back prompts body-mind activity and decision making. Be rebellious: jump ahead, then flip back, or start in the middle and spiral out. How might these choices initiate subtle movements of the fingers and hand? Also, consider how the sequence of sections shifts your embodiment of knowledge, comprehension, and creativity. If you are reading this text with a group, why not compare your varied paths through the text and the similarities and differences in how each of you responds to those juxtapositions? Since I mentioned that the embodiment of enactive knowledge generally requires repetition, I have included repeating motifs in this text. I hope you find them.

Archiving Liveness

Being alive is moving. Energy. Vibration. Feeling.
Archives appear to gesture to history. Time.
The presence of bodies, or being in the body, locates
liveness and energy.
Embodied knowledge gestures to a present time.
A situatedness. Embeddedness.
Caught in a fascinating ephemeral flow of an immediate present
soon-becoming-past, the body reaches and extends forward.
Lurches. Gravitates. A continuous becoming.

Body as a Site

The body is a field site. Let me explain. While conducting ethnographic fieldwork on Japanese dance, I realized that each dancer I encountered provided distinct, individual experiences of movement. I immediately noticed the differences and similarities in individuals' experiences. Dancers studying with the same teacher embodied similar experiences, yet each dancer also conveyed discernible nuances through her movements and the ways in which she articulated her experiences. In order to deeply understand the subtleties of their embodied experiences, I realized it was necessary to observe and speak to as many dancers as possible. While dancers studying in the same studio traversed similar spaces, their internal landscapes—their subtle physical experiences—revealed that each dancer represented a *particular* field site.[14] I wondered: how and what can we learn from the rich and varied experiences of dancers? The body is an ephemeral field site. Movement leaves no trace, making research on enactive knowledge challenging and humbling. Noting the diversity of our particular experiences while also acknowledging similarities reveals our perpetually changing state of becoming, of embodying knowledge through experience.

Activating Moves

Consider the variety of ways you might express what you learn through observation: write a poem, draw, draft a scholarly paper, dance/move, or sculpt. Consider experimenting with and engaging in a creative practice that is outside your norm, if only as a means of understanding the experience from a different point of view and to ponder how you might be different as a result of your heightened awareness.[15]

Enactive Meanderings

Current research on the brain, awareness, and identity reveals significant links to movement. Neuroscientist Rodolfo Llinás, for instance, writes that the brain evolved because organisms needed to move for survival. Step one: intention.

> Mind or mindness state, is that class of all functional brain states in which the sensorimotor images, including self-awareness, are generated.... When using the term sensorimotor image, I mean something more than visual imagery. I refer to the conjunction or binding of all relevant sensory input to produce a discreet functional state that ultimately may result in action.[16]

A few pages later he adds, "From the earliest dawning of biological evolution it was this governing, this leading, this pulling by predictive drive, *intention*, that brought sensorimotor images—indeed, the mind itself—to us in the first place."[17] He goes on to emphasize the implications of his findings: "*that which we call thinking is the evolutionary internalization of movement.*"[18] The perspective of movement and intention as it relates to what Llinás calls mindness lures me into this discourse. I can imagine observing dancers as moving thought. Embodied consciousness.

Story: Archiving and Noting Awareness

In the last ten years I have been incorporating a freeform notation of movement in my field notes as an attempt to record what I observe people "saying" with their bodies during fieldwork: tacit knowledge. My idiomatic jottings are not meant to be a systematic notation, but instead a process of broadening my awareness of movement. In this section I am not addressing the long-standing theoretical tangle in music and dance scholarship—to notate or not to notate— or *how* and *why* one would notate something. Instead, I offer a story about an on-the-fly method of notation that helps expand my awareness of expressive movement. I want to see if my knowledge gleaned from dance, through both the expressive body and research, can inform an awareness of the relationships of movement to other sensory information, such as sound, touch, and visual aspects of experience.

While doing fieldwork at the Tachibana dance studio in Tokyo I learned a

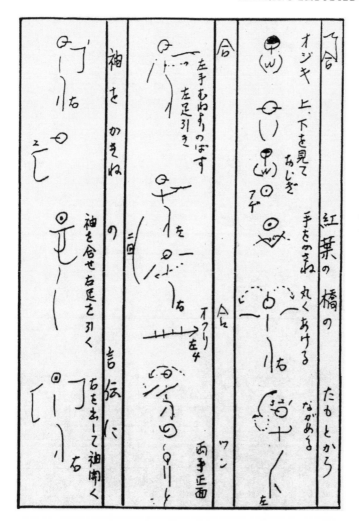

Tachibana school notation for the opening of the dance *Momiji no hashi*, from Tomie Hahn, *Sensational Knowledge: Embodying Culture through Japanese Dance* (Wesleyan University Press, 2007).

simple style of notating Japanese dance that would forever change how I conceptualized and analyzed movement. As an example of the simple, stick-figure style of notation, see the illustration above, the notation for the opening of the dance *Momiji no hashi*. The next illustration offers a breakdown of the dance's first few steps. In these examples we can see how this basic notation captures enough information for a traditional dancer to recall the dance from memory. It is a memory aid to support embodied cultural knowledge and is not intended to be the primary means of transmitting the dance. I found the notation quite intuitive, and it influenced the way I currently conduct interviews, choreograph, and notate movement. I find myself notating everyday expressive body lan-

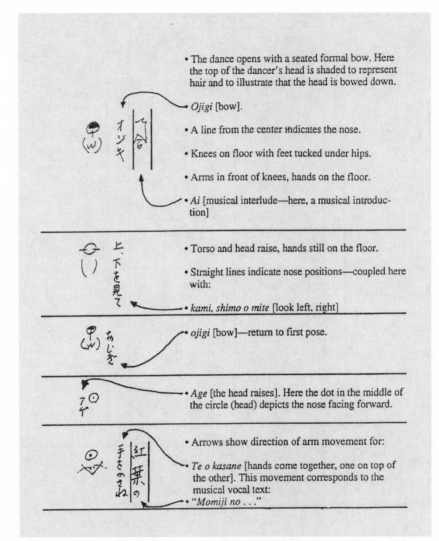

Explanation of opening sequence from preceding figure, from Tomie Hahn, *Sensational Knowledge: Embodying Culture through Japanese Dance* (Wesleyan University Press, 2007).

guage, gaze, and facial expression—from the actions of monster-truck builders, dancers, and musicians. I hope you will try it too.

Notice how just the bare essentials of movements and poses are inscribed. The notation stands merely as a reminder of embodied memory. As a memory aid, it remains an archive for the future. A circle with a line intersecting it offers a simple representation of the head and the direction of the nose. The shaded part of the circle represents hair. Similarly, the hand with a thumb pointing down (see middle column, top stick figure) records where the palm faces. Dotted lines with arrows indicate movement direction. This notation helps dancers of Japanese dance to recall movements and sequences, orient the body in space and time (with the music), and most important, maintain a living cultural tradition.

Activating Moves

How can we analyze and understand the embodied intelligence from movement derived from the articulate body? Beyond dance movements, how would we notate expressive gestures made while someone is talking? Position yourself where you can observe others in an everyday setting, perhaps a library, street corner, or café. Without attracting attention to the process, nonchalantly draw a few gestures using only one or two strokes. *These jottings are only considered memory aids.* I encourage you to review these notes later and flesh them out for your particular purpose. What did you notice about the gestures? Were they socially motivated? Pragmatic? Did you see the same gesture repeated by one person and/or by others? If so, were there visible similarities, differences, and nuances in the repetitions? Looking at your notes later, what was significant about your memory of the experience?

Enactive Meanderings

In the 1960s psychologist Jerome Bruner, known for his profound contributions to the philosophy of education and cognition, noted the importance of observing structures of learning. He proposed three ways people organize knowledge and interact in the world: enactive (action), iconic (image), and symbolic modes of representation (language).[19] I am particularly drawn to enaction—knowledge that comes through action—as one mode of being in and representing the world. Bruner's inclusion of enactive knowledge as a way a person can be in the world bears significant relevance to the study of embodied transmission and the body as archive. But the challenge remains: How can we broaden our awareness of movement, observe its relationship to other sensory modes of expression, and find ways of conveying our observations through writing or other creative avenues?

Activating Moves

Take a moment to consider a specific activity, a movement that you often repeat. The movement can be anything: turning a doorknob, skipping across the dance floor, or brushing your teeth. Next time you perform this activity, pay attention to details. Note precisely when the movement begins. Are you able to mark the starting point? Repeat the movement. See any changes? Has your consideration of the movement transformed or altered the activity? Discerning details, including beginnings and endings, helps us to bring conscious mind into the body. Perhaps the process initiates a different sort of archiving as embodiment, or embodied cognition. Now, how would you informally notate this activity? The process of notating provides another layer of knowledge building, in which translating lived movements and enactive knowledge into two-dimensional symbols reinforces one's embodied knowledge.

Ra-a-a-aa!!! Moving Monsters

When I interviewed Scott Pontbriand, driver of the monster trucks *Grave Digger* and *Undertaker*, I audiotaped our conversation.[20] Luckily I had a notebook in hand to jot down a few of his gestures using my freeform notation system, borrowed from Japanese dance. I asked him to describe what it's like to fly in such an extreme vehicle:

> Well, you know you work on the truck for, hey, forty hours making sure everything's ready to go, the bolts and everything. When you get in the truck, as soon as you're in there ... you just kinda, I don't know, I kinda zone out into my own little world and I'm at one with the truck. You know, there's not a part on the truck that I'm not aware of at any given moment when I'm in it. I mean, you become one with it, you know? When you're flying up in the air, you know, *Ra-a-a-aa!!!* [he makes a motion with his arms outstretched skyward] You get up in the air and it's like, you know there's times when you're up there and it's like, "Okay, I know I just jumped, but when am I going to land? [laughs] [A]m I going to land?"[21]

When Scott exclaimed "*Ra-a-a-aa!!!*" he darted both arms diagonally upward, palms down, fingers reaching forward. While Scott's roar was caught on my audiotape, the combination of the power of his loud speech with his startlingly swift arm movements made clear his extreme experience of flying a ten-thousand-pound vehicle in the air. Passion. Presence. Raw, moving energy. Without looking at my notebook, my pencil etched one single line—a diagonal from lower left to upper right—then hooked down about at a forty-five-degree angle, signifying a hand palm down. Before I drove away, I wrote "Ra-a" next to this scratchy line, lest I would find the scrawl meaningless later. Later, at home, I transcribed the interviews from the day and aligned Scott's "*Ra-a-a-aa!!!*" with his physical expression of the moment.

Monster truck
*Maximum
Destruction,*
driven by
Tom Meents,
in flight,
Lebanon Valley
Speedway,
West
Lebanon, New
York, 2005.
Photograph by
Tomie Hahn.

Why note and recall Scott's movements? Why is it important? Since I have never experienced flying a monster truck, I found that Scott's gestures that day, most notably his effusive arm thrust, imparted a particular quality of the monster-truck-in-flight experience that helped me to imagine experiencing it. In this moment, Scott conveyed the force of a ten-thousand-pound truck launching into the air, coupling his movements with his loud, gravelly voice yelling "Ra-a-aa!" His animated state conveyed the charge of energy during flight.

Interviewing Scott and other monster-truck drivers had an impact on my awareness about movement. Drivers choreograph how trucks perform: races, wheelies, jumps, and even how they crash. Of course tense moments arise when the unexpected occurs, but that adds to the thrill.

Multisensory Orientations

Staring at your hand, as yourself, how does it know how to pick up a pencil and write? Or type on a keyboard? How does your hand know how to dance? Contemplating this for a moment while looking at your hand might reveal a host of memories—perhaps a schoolteacher demonstrating cursive writing while hovering over your desk or your first try at a dance class. Perhaps this was long ago, or just yesterday. Information learned through more than one sense tends to orient our bodies in space and time. Multisensory learning also reinforces memory of the activity and the associations we have with it. Imagine the following scenario. You hear a friend say, "Wow, look at those brown birds flocking!," and out of the corner of your eye you see her lips form each word; the sound and vision aid your comprehension of her sentence. Then she taps you on the elbow to direct your attention to the flock; she opens the window and suddenly you hear birds squawking as they fly by. You have received a lot of sensory information to reinforce her words. This lush array of information—sound, touch, movement, sight—helps us to understand how movement relates to other sensory modes. The multisensory experience also reinforces your memory of this experience. Learning through multisensory modes of transmission reinforces our understanding, supports knowledge building, and imprints the experience in our memories in deeper ways.[22]

Motor Coordinations
Monster-truck rally spectacles, as movement or as entertainment, emerge, in part, from a long-term development of a truck's body design and identity. Each decision made when building a truck—which bolts, zoomie headers, or suspension to use, for example—affects the overall performance. Monster-truck builder-driver Robbie "Flying" Dawson recalled:

> The first Undertaker that I drove was a rear-engine truck. And the man that built that liked rear-engine trucks because it would do a lot more radical freestyles. And those things will do wheelies like nobody's business, I mean you go straight up. We had to build a big bumper just out past the tailgate just because it landed straight up and down all the time. But that was the perfect combination for freestyle. And that was what he was more concerned about, and [he] thought that that was what people paid more attention too. But it made it a little less successful in the drag racing end, in the straight-line drags, simply because it was such a handful going straight, you know, trying to go as fast as you can [to crash] cars and having your nose ten feet up in the air. . . . Oh it was incredible. It was just, just a wild ride.[23]

Of course, which driver races the truck at the rally makes a difference as well. Monster truck fans favor certain trucks and particular drivers of each truck. Fans' appreciation for particular performers and how they engineer moves is a major aspect of the rally scene.

Activating Moves
Notice actions in your habit memory vocabulary for the next hour. For example, do you gesture when you speak? Flick or twirl your hair periodically? Consider how these movements are idiomatic—part of your personal, embodied archive

Monster truck *Stone Cold 3:16*, driven by Calvin Carrington, jumping, Riverside Park Speedway, Agawam, Massachusetts, July 1999. Photograph by Tomie Hahn.

of actions—and ponder if there are social or cultural associations. How did you learn this movement?

Then what?

It's time to experiment.

NOTES

1. Demolition Derby, Columbia County, New York, September 2, 2004.

2. The concept of a mind-body split or "problem" is long-standing in Western philosophy, with its roots in ancient Greek philosophy, but is most commonly exemplified in Cartesian dualism. See René Descartes, *Meditations on First Philosophy* [1641], trans. Michael Moriarity (Oxford: Oxford University Press, 2008). Regarding different theoretical perspectives in cognitive science and embodied cognition see Lawrence Shapiro, *Embodied Cognition* (New York: Routledge, 2010). "By *embodied* we mean reflection in which body and mind have been brought together. What this formulation intends to convey is that reflection is not just *on* experience, but reflection is a form of experience itself—and that reflective form of experience can be performed with mindfulness/awareness. When reflection is done in that way, it can cut the chain of habitual thought patterns and preconceptions such that it can be an open-ended reflection, open to possibilities other than those contained in one's current representations of the life space. We call this form of reflection *mindful, open-ended reflection*." Francisco Varela, Evan Thompson, and Eleanor Rosch, *The Embodied Mind: Cognitive Science and Human Experience* (Cambridge: MIT Press, 1993), 27.

3. The phrase "Geertzian thick description" refers to Clifford Geertz's assertion that the interpretive practice of observation and analysis demands a more detailed and complex description of observable human behavior, including the sociocultural factors and public codes that influence its function and meaning within a cultural context. See Clifford Geertz, "Thick Description: Toward an Interpretive Theory of Culture" in *The Interpretation of Cultures: Selected Essays* (New York: Basic Books, 1979), 3–30.

4. In this essay I use the word "transmission" to include the entire teaching and learning cycle, and because it references the history of research on cultural transmission within anthropology.

5. See the work of psychologist Jerome Bruner, *The Process of Education* (Cambridge, MA: Harvard University Press, 1963) and *Toward a Theory of Instruction* (Cambridge, MA: Belknap, Harvard University Press, 1966).

6. David McNeill wrote, "In 1992 the emphasis was on how gestures reveal thought; now it is how gestures fuel thought and speech. The new step is to emphasize the 'dynamic dimension' of language—how linguistic forms and gestures participate in a real-time dialectic during discourse, and thus propel and shape speech and thought as they occur moment to moment. As in the earlier book [*Hand and Mind*], gestures, language and thought are seen as different sides of a single mental/brain/action process. They are integrated on actional, cognitive, and ultimately biological levels. The difference is that now I present gestures as active participants in speaking and thinking. They are conceived of as ingredients in an imagery-language dialectic that fuels speech and thought." *Gesture and Thought* (Chicago: University of Chicago Press, 2005), 3. See also David McNeill, *Hand and Mind: What Gestures Reveal About Thought* (Chicago: University of Chicago Press, 1992); and Susan Goldin-Meadow, *Hearing Gesture: How Our Hands Help Us Think* (Cambridge, MA: Harvard University Press, 2003).

7. For research that focuses on movement that is not considered to be dance within its cultural context, yet provides extensive information about the meaningful nature of movement, see Matthew Rahaim, *Musicking Bodies: Gesture and Voice in Hindustani Music* (Middletown, CT: Wesleyan University Press, 2012).

8. *Oxford English Dictionary* online, 1989. Accessed June 25, 2013. http://www.oed.com/.

9. See Marcel Mauss, "Les Techniques du corps," *Journal de la Psychologie* 32, nos. 3–4 (1936): 271–93; Mary Douglas, *Natural Symbols: Explorations in Cosmology* (Harmondsworth, UK: Pelican Books, 1970); Michel Foucault, *The Archaeology of Knowledge & Discourse on Language* (New York: Pantheon, 1972); and Michel Foucault, *The Order of Things: An Archaeology of the Human Sciences* (New York: Routledge, 1970).

10. Tomie Hahn, *Sensational Knowledge: Embodying Culture through Japanese Dance* (Middletown, CT: Wesleyan University Press, 2007).

11. Pablo Briñol, Richard Petty, and Benjamin Wagner, "Embodied Validation: Our Bodies Can Change and Also Validate Our Thoughts," and Lawrence Sanna and Kristjen Jundberg, "The Experience of Thinking: Metacognitive Ease, Fluency, and Context," in *Social Metacognition*, ed. Pablo Briñol and Kenneth DeMarree (New York: Psychology Press/Taylor & Francis Group, 2011), 219–39, 179–98.

12. Constance Classen, *Worlds of Sense: Exploring the Senses in History and Across Cultures* (London: Routledge, 1993); David Howes, ed., *The Varieties of Sensory Experience* (Toronto: University of Toronto Press. 1991); David Howes, ed., *Empire of the Senses: The Sensual Cultural Reader* (Oxford: Berg, 2005); and Sarah Pink, *Doing Sensory Ethnography* (London: Sage Publications, 2009).

13. Gregory Kessler, "Designing with a Visual Language: Elements and Ordering Systems," in *The

Built Environment: A Collaborative Inquiry Into Design and Planning, ed. Wendy McClure and Tom Bartuska (Hoboken: John Wiley & Sons, 2011), 75.

14. Hahn, *Sensational Knowledge,* x.

15. See Arnd Schneider and Christopher Wright, eds., *Between Art and Anthropology: Contemporary Ethnographic Practice* (New York: Berg Publishers, 2010), for examples of collaborations between anthropologists and artists; it includes discussions of ethical and collaboration concerns.

16. Rodolfo Llinás, *I of the Vortex: From Neurons to Self* (Cambridge: MIT Press, 2001), 1.

17. Ibid., 3.

18. Ibid., 35 (emphasis in original).

19. Bruner, *Process of Education* and *Toward a Theory of Instruction.*

20. Tomie Hahn, "'It's the RUSH': Sites of the Sensually Extreme," *Drama Review: Journal of Performance Studies* 150, no. 2 (2006): 87–96.

21. Interview with Scott Pontbriand, Sturbridge, Massachusetts, September 10, 1999.

22. E.g., Ladan Shams and Aaron Seitz, "Benefits of Multisensory Learning," *Trends in Cognitive Science* 12, no 11. (2008): 411–17.

23. Interview with Robbie "Flying" Dawson, Sturbridge, Massachusetts, September 10, 1999.

THE SENSING AND KNOWING BODY
Choreographing Action and Feeling

> All architecture functions as a potential stimulus for movement, real
> or imagined. A building is an incitement to action, a stage for movement
> and interaction. It is one partner in a dialogue with the body.
> —Kent C. Bloomer and Charles W. Moore

We continue to hold a dualistic attitude toward our bodies. On the one hand, physical characteristics and appearances have a growing significance in human interactions, but on the other, the role of embodiment in our sensory and mental functions and cognitive capacities continues to be underestimated. The corporeal and the mental are still seen as separate realms. One consequence of the detachment of the body and the mind is that the self is commonly understood to be separate from the world. Works of art and architecture are likewise regarded as autonomous objects outside of ourselves and our embodied relationships with our settings. Yet as philosopher Maurice Merleau-Ponty argues, we exist in "the flesh of the world," so the body or the mind cannot be detached from the world.[1] The world and the self constitute a single continuum, like the magical Mobius strip with its two sides but only one surface. This curious intertwining is described by Merleau-Ponty thus: "The world is wholly inside, and I am wholly outside myself."[2]

This philosopher, whose thinking provides a firm ground for the understanding of the human existential condition and artistic phenomena, also points out that both the making and experiencing of art are fundamentally embodied processes: "The painter takes his body with him. . . . Indeed, we cannot imagine how a mind could paint."[3] The same is certainly true of the art forms of dance and architecture, as they arise directly from our embodied existence and aspire to a poetic articulation and expression of this existential and embodied condition. As Heinrich Wölfflin, the Swiss art historian, stated at the end of the nineteenth century: "We always project a corporeal state conforming to our own, we interpret the whole outside world according to the expressive system with which we have become familiar from our own bodies."[4] Adrian Stokes, the British artist and writer, expanded the significance of the body in artistic expression to all art forms: "All art is of the body."[5]

Regrettably, these crucial views of the significance of human embodiment have been neglected in most of modern scientific, artistic, and pedagogical theorizing. Another underestimation in modern thought concerns the role of metaphors in thinking and communication. Yet Aristotle assured us of the power of the metaphor: "The greatest thing by far is to be master of metaphor, the one thing that cannot be learned from others; and it is also a sign of genius."[6] Significantly, our metaphors in thought, language, and art are frequently related to the body and embodied experiences. Philosopher Mark Johnson and linguist George Lakoff have shown that all our thinking is fundamentally metaphorical, and the metaphors we most commonly use derive from our own bodies.[7] In addition, both philosophical analyses and neurological research have recently established that even sensory perception and memory cannot exist without their fundamental grounding in human embodiment and imagination. This view is expressed in philosopher Edward S. Casey's assertion: "[B]ody memory is ... the natural center of any sensitive account of remembering. . . . There is no memory without body memory."[8]

We tend to think that architecture is merely a form of aestheticized constructional rationality. However, our buildings are also existentially grounded and richly metaphorical. One of the central metaphors is the unconsciously mirrored imagery of buildings as organic bodies, on the one hand, and the body as an architectural construction, on the other. In Michelangelo's view, understanding the human body is mandatory for understanding architecture in general: "There is an essential relationship between architecture and the proportions of the human body, and he who has not made himself master of the human form and especially anatomy, will understand nothing of architecture."[9] The unique emotive expression of Michelangelo's architecture becomes understandable after one realizes that his structures are actually metaphorical muscular and skeletal ones, halted in their movement; unconsciously through our embodied simulation we experience these melancholic buildings as if they were bodies in mourning. Even the smallest of profiles expresses a restrained movement and tension as if it were a tendon or muscle, and the entire building seems to be holding its breath. Renaissance architecture in general was based on proportionality, which aimed at unifying the macrocosm and the microcosm, the realms of God and mortals, through the use of proportional systems resonating with the measures and proportions of the human body, which was understood to reflect cosmic principles. The two systems were the Pythagorean principle of harmonic proportions, also applied in Western music, and the golden section, referred to first by Luca Paccioli, the Renaissance mathematician and friend to Michelangelo.

47

The body metaphor in architecture is not limited to facades and appearances, as it is extended all the way to the metabolic functions of both our bodies and buildings. Even Le Corbusier, "the Purist," points out this correspondence: "A plan arranges organs in order, thus creating an organism or organisms. The organs possess distinctive qualities, specific difference. What are they? Lungs, heart, stomach? The same question arises in architecture."[10] This preconscious reciprocity between the body and architecture is also presented in the writings of Sigmund Freud and Carl G. Jung, as well as in numerous artistic images of fused bodies and buildings, such as *Femme maison*, the many drawings and sculptural works of Louise Bourgeois that combine images of the female body with those of architectural constructions. Rudolf Steiner concretized the view of the essential dialectics between the human body and architecture: "All the laws present in the architectural utilization of matter are also to be found in the human body. When we project the specific organization of the human body into the space outside it, then we have architecture."[11]

Our lived experiences of self and existence are surely embodied sensations, and my body knows and remembers who I am and how I am located in the world. We tend to place our consciousness in the brain, but there is a strengthening line of thinking in philosophy and neuroscience that suggests that consciousness is part of our complex and dynamic relationships with the world rather than concealed within our skulls. In the view of philosopher Alva Noë, consciousness takes place not in the brain but within the "joint operation of brain, body, and the world," and it is thus an achievement of "the whole animal in its environmental context."[12] The body is a knowing body, and learning any skill implies the gradual transference of the task from a conscious and deliberately learned activity into an unconscious performance of the body. This applies similarly to the task of the painter, musician, architect, craftsman, juggler, athlete, and dancer; it takes about ten thousand hours of intense practice to master any bodily skill. The poet Rainer Maria Rilke assures us of the significance of unconsciously embodied memories in creative work: "For it is not yet the memories themselves (that are useful). Not till they have turned to blood within us, to glance and gesture, nameless and no longer to be distinguished from ourselves—not till then can it happen that in a most rare hour the first word of a verse arises in their midst and goes forth from them."[13]

Altogether, in our quasi-rational culture, the prevailing understanding of ourselves as biological, cultural, and historical beings continues to be grossly simplified. To start with, the realm of our senses extends far beyond the five Aristotelian senses. Steinerian philosophy names twelve human senses,[14] and it has been recently suggested that we deploy more than thirty categories of sensory interaction in our relationships with environments.[15] Contradicting their medical definition, even our endocrine glands seem to serve our connectedness with the world, instead of being sealed in the interior of the body.[16] Thus it is no wonder that the pragmatist philosopher Richard Rorty makes a surprising argument about the miracle of the human body: "If we had understood the body, no one would have thought that we have a mind."[17]

Creative intuition also arises from the body and unconscious memory, or more precisely, from our integrated sense of existence rather than a detached intellect. Even the concept of intelligence is currently being redefined in relation to our full embodied existence. In *Intelligence Reframed*, Harvard psychologist Howard Gardner posits an alternative to the single-category mode that is measured by IQ tests and suggests that we have as many as ten categories of intelligence, many of them arising from our embodied and sensuous being. Gardner's categories are linguistic, logical-mathematical, musical, bodily-kinesthetic, spatial, interpersonal, intrapersonal, naturalistic, spiritual, and existential intelligences.[18] In my writings I have suggested three further categories of intelligence beyond Gardner's list: emotional, ethical, and aesthetic.[19]

Moreover, my recent studies in the significance of ambiences, feelings, and moods in environmental and architectural experiences suggest that we should acknowledge the existence of another category: an atmospheric sense.[20] We underestimate particularly the role of emotions in our cognitive acts. Yet Mark Johnson argues firmly: "There is no cognition without emotion, even though we are often unaware of the emotional aspects of our thinking."[21] Emotional intelligence could, in fact, be the most instant, synthetic, holistic, integrated, and reliable among our systems of reacting to complex environmental and social situations, because it is related to the deep, primordial layers of the mind and less corruptible by convention. Through emotions, we judge complex situations, such as ambience, mood, and atmosphere, of a space or place. Mood may well be the most synthetic of architectural features, although it has rarely been consciously analyzed or theorized. Indeed, as artists and architects, we need to sharpen at least twelve categories of sensing and the same number of modes of intelligence in order to succeed in our work.

Since the late eighteenth century, architecture has become increasingly instrumentalized for purposes of utility, economy, and the assertion of hegemonic power. However, the task of buildings is not only to provide physical shelter, functional efficiency, and physiological comfort. They also serve to structure our view of the world and enable us to dwell in the world through providing cultural, metaphorical, and symbolic meanings, as well as a domicile for our memories, dreams, and fears. In addition to shaping space, architecture structures and articulates time. As philosopher Karsten Harries points out, "Architecture is not only about domesticating space, it is also a deep defense against the terror of time. The language of beauty is essentially the language of timeless reality."[22] Like cinema, architecture has the capacity to slow down, accelerate, and halt experiential time. The buildings of our time tend to express a fast and nervous time, whereas great buildings of history are museums of benevolently slow time and silence. All the arts, in fact, transform endless natural duration into experiential time, scaled to the rhythms of human biological processes and consciousness. Through our buildings we empower and expand ourselves and project order into our relationships and interactions with the world. The art of architecture creates specific horizons and frames for perception and understanding. Cities, buildings, and works of art constitute a sphere of externalized order and memory, knowledge and emotion, an extended body and mind. Indeed, we extend and externalize our biological faculties through countless physical, cultural, and mental extensions, from clothing, buildings, and cities to cultural and mental constructions and belief systems.[23]

Architecture is also a form of spatial choreography, an architectural dance, as it were, a subtle means of stimulating and guiding action, movement, human interaction, and emotion. The empathetic choreography of architecture guides us through the practicalities, activities, and mental experiences of spaces in particular ways, similarly to the way that musical scores give rise to and guide music making, although mostly unconsciously. Spatial choreography and experiences are usually implicitly mediated by architectural drawings and models, but there have been interesting attempts to create specific symbolic procedures for the purpose of describing the complex behavioral and experiential dimensions of environmental design, such as the "pattern language" of Christopher Alexander[24] and the "scores" by Lawrence Halprin.[25] Yet a sensitive designer is able to imaginatively mediate between spatial configurations, even imagined ones, and the consequent human behavior and feeling. This transference from a physically nonexistent, imagined situation to an imaginatively felt emotive experience is likely to be the most precious quality of human imagination. That is the ground of empathy: the capacity to sense what other people feel and even to sense the emotional impact of imaginatively projected forms and spaces.[26]

Architectural spaces and structures are invitations to and facilitators of actions, from the acts of entering and exiting to the multifarious functions and acts of life. Instead of providing mere visual objects external to us, architecture implies verb-form actions; a window is not architecture, whereas looking through the window into a garden or at distant mountains turns the situation into an authentic architectural experience. The essential role of the window is to mediate distance and connectedness between spatial categories. Similarly, passing through a door from one spatial realm to another is a true architectural event, while seeing the door frame, however beautiful it may be, is not. In fact, deep architectural experiences arise from distinct primary images instead of being mere formal fabrications.[27] In the constitutive case of a house or home (architecture arises from two notions, dwelling and celebration or ritual), there are about a dozen of such images or experiences. Wang Shu, the Chinese Pritzker Prize Laureate in 2012, confesses that all buildings are houses for him in terms of their emotive imagery: "To me, any type of architecture, no matter its function, is a house. I only design houses, not architecture. Houses are plain. They always maintain some sort of interesting relationship with true existence and life."[28]

I suggest that the primary images of dwelling are the following: floor, roof, wall, door, window, fireplace or hearth, stairway, bed, table, chair, and washing place or bath. I suggest further that this is the ontological order of their appearance in the mental history of building. I wish to emphasize that these images obtain their emotive power from the actions that they give rise to or facilitate. They are not primarily formal architectural objects or aesthetic entities; the form of an architectural object attains its suggestive emotive power from the underlying image of action, not from mere formal abstraction. That is why formal aestheticization or reduction, devoid of deep mental intentions and meanings, produces lifeless art and architecture.

The floor is the constitutive first "element" of architecture, and it invites us to stand up, move, or perhaps dance, or to set up a table or chair and establish one's domicile. The roof invites us underneath its protective intimacy and shelters us against weather, and it promises us a feeling of protected dwelling and a sense of home. The roof, more than any other ingredient of the house, suggests protection, and it is regrettable that modern architecture has often completely eliminated the image of the roof and turned it into a mere technical flat surface. Consequently, the rich images and feelings that the roof can mediate have disappeared. The fireplace promises us intimate warmth, togetherness, and safe moments of dreaming. All the primary images of architecture can be analyzed similarly in terms of their ontology and hidden imagery. No doubt buildings are scripts and scores for life, work, and other activities, as well as human interactions. Empathetic design does not force our behavioral choices into fixed and rigid frames, as it predicts and anticipates our intentions and acts and supports them gently. Architecture always anticipates distinct action and emotion; a sensitive building foresees our needs, preferences, and desires. It is always an invitation to act and a promise of an appropriate response.

Art and architecture are not primarily about aesthetics, as is usually believed, but about how to be a human being in this world. Artistic and poetic imagery is always grounded in our lived existential experience. Great works of art and architecture enable us to realize our own humanity, sensitize our experiences, and expand our realm of existential and emotive knowledge. Through art and architecture, we can experience our own being-in-the-world, refined and reinforced by the embodied perceptions and images of some of the world's greatest creators. We can see through the eyes of Piero, touch through the hands and skin of Michelangelo, hear through the ears of Mozart, and feel through the heart of Rilke.

"Architecture glorifies and eternalizes something" Ludwig Wittgenstein states. "[W]hen there is nothing to glorify, there is no architecture."[29] The philosopher's assertion invites us to ask ourselves: Are we losing the qualities of life worthy of architectural glorification in our surreally consumerist and quasirational way of life? My answer to this question is a firm "yes." Meaningful architecture concretizes ideals and mental dimensions of life, and as the current materialist and one-dimensional lifestyle tends to eliminate the second level of reality, the reality of ideals, myths, and dreams, it also eliminates the mental ground for true architecture. Profound architecture can arise only from the reanimation and resensualization of life; a rediscovery of its physically embodied and symbolic dimensions. As the psychologist E. F. Edinger states, "Modern man's most urgent need is to discover the reality and value of the inner subjective world, to discover the symbolic life. . . . The symbolic life in some form is a prerequisite for psychic health."[30]

NOTES

The epigraph is from Kent C. Bloomer and Charles W. Moore, *Body, Memory, and Architecture* (New Haven, CT: Yale University Press, 1977), 59.

1. Merleau-Ponty describes the notion "the flesh of the world" in "The Intertwining—The Chiasm," in *The Visible and the Invisible*, ed. Claude Lefort (Evanston, IL: Northwestern University Press, 1992), 130–55.

2. Maurice Merleau-Ponty, *Phenomenology of Perception*, trans. Colin Smith (London: Routledge & Kegan Paul, 1962), 407.

3. Maurice Merleau-Ponty, *The Primacy of Perception* (Evanston, IL: Northwestern University Press, 1964), 162.

4. Heinrich Wölfflin, *Renaissance and Baroque* (New York: Cornell University Press, 1966), 77–78.

5. Adrian Stokes, *Image in Form: Selected Writings of Adrian Stokes*, ed. Richard Wollheim (New York: Harper & Row, 1972), 122.

6. Aristotle, *Poetics* 59a8–10, as quoted in Arthus C. Danto, *Beyond the Brillo Box: The Visual Arts in Post-historical Perspective* (New York: Farrar, Straus and Giroux, 1992), 73.

7. Mark Johnson and George Lakoff, *Metaphors We Live By* (Chicago: University of Chicago Press, 1980).

8. Edward S. Casey, *Remembering: A Phenomenological Study* (Bloomington: Indiana University Press, 2000), 148, 172.

9. Michelangelo Buonarroti, quoted in Matteo Marangoni, *The Art of Seeing Art* (Shelley Castle, 1951), 248.

10. Le Corbusier, *My Work* (London: Architectural Press, 1960), page unknown.

11. Rudolf Steiner, *Architecture: An Introductory Reader*, ed. Andrew Beard (Forest Row, UK: Sophia Books, 2003), 36.

12. Alva Noë, *Out of Our Heads: Why You Are Not Your Brain, and Other Lessons from the Biology of Consciousness* (New York: Hill and Wang, 2009), 10.

13. Rainer Maria Rilke, *The Notebooks of Malte Laurids Brigge*, trans. M. D. Herter Norton (New York: Norton, 1992), 26–27.

14. Albert Soesman, *Our Twelve Senses: Wellsprings of the Soul* (Stroud, UK: Hawthorn Press, 1998). The twelve senses in Steinerian thought are touch, life sense, self-movement sense, balance, smell, taste, vision, temperature sense, hearing, language sense, conceptual sense, and ego sense.

15. *The Sixth Sense Reader*, ed. David Howes (Oxford: Berg Publishers, 2011).

16. Edward T. Hall, *The Hidden Dimension* (New York: Doubleday, 1966), 33. Hall refers to the 1960s research findings of A. S. Parkes and H. M. Bruce, who coined the term "exocrinology" (as contrasted with endocrinology) to express the expanded view of the chemical regulators to include the products of odoriferous glands scattered throughout the bodies of mammals.

17. Richard Rorty, *Philosophy and the Mirror of Nature* (Princeton, NJ: Princeton University Press, 1979), 239.

18. Howard Gardner, *Intelligence Reframed: Multiple Intelligences for the 21st Century* (New York: Basic Books, 1999).

19. Juhani Pallasmaa, "Architecture and the Human Nature: Searching for a Sustainable Metaphor" (lecture presented at the 2011 National Architecture Conference, Melbourne, Australia, April 14–16, 2011), 7.

20. Juhani Pallasmaa, "On Atmosphere: Peripheral Perception and Existential Experience," in *Juhani Pallasmaa, Encounters 2: Architectural Essays*, ed. Peter MacKeith (Helsinki: Rakennustieto Publishing, 2012), 237–51.

21. Mark Johnson, *The Meaning of the Body: Aesthetics of Human Understanding* (Chicago: University of Chicago Press, 2007), 9.

22. Karsten Harries, "Building and the Terror of Time," in *Perspecta, the Yale University Architectural Journal* 19 (1982): 59–69.

23. The idea of an extended phenotype as a biological concept is developed in Richard Dawkins, *The Extended Phenotype: The Long Reach of the Gene* (New York: Oxford University Press, 1999).

24. Christopher Alexander, Sara Ishikawa, and Murray Silverstein, *A Pattern Language: Towns, Buildings, Construction* (New York: Oxford University Press, 1977).

25. Lawrence Halprin, *RSVP Cycles: Creative Processes in the Human Environment* (New York: George Braziller, 1970).

26. For a discussion of the empathic imagination, see Juhani Pallasmaa, "Empathic Imagination: Formal and Experiential Projection," *Architectural Design* 84, no. 5 (2014): 80–85.

27. For the idea of primary architectural images, see Juhani Pallasmaa, "The Lived Metaphor," in *Primary Architectural Images: Seminar Document 2001/2002* (St. Louis, MO: School of Architecture, Washington University, 2002), 2–10.

28. Wang Shu, Chinese Pritzker Laureate 2012. "A House as Sleep," in Shu, *Imagining the House* (Zurich: Lars Müller Publishers, 2012/2013).

29. Ludwig Wittgenstein, *Culture and Value*, ed. Georg Henrik von Wright, in collaboration with Heikki Nyman. (Oxford: Blackwell, 1998), 74e.

30. E. F. Edinger, *Ego & Archetype: Individuation and the Religious Function of the Psyche* (Baltimore, MD: Penguin Books, 1974), 109, 117.

USE ME

How does a choreographer like Meg Stuart create work? How does she speak about her poetics and method? An internal perspective on Stuart's work is a red thread throughout the book *Are we here yet?*, which embraces the views and voices of several Damaged Goods collaborators by way of interviews, essays, documents, performance texts, photographs, and so forth. *Are we here yet?* is a container brimming with memories, projections, reflections, and images close to Stuart's choreographic practice, a heterogeneity of materials that have a certain gravity of their own and continue to resonate and stir up new questions for future work.

A true accumulation of discourse embedded in the work is to be found in the tasks and fictions that make up the many exercises spoken out loud by Meg Stuart in workshops. These exercises have gained structure and clarity over the years and, due to the pedagogical context, appear unburdened by the vagueness that characterizes a creative process. They highlight the nar-

Philipp Gehmacher and Meg Stuart in *the fault lines* (2010) by Meg Stuart. Video by Vladimir Miller. Museum Moderner Kunst, Vienna, February 3, 2011. (See plate 3 for color image.) Photograph © Eva Würdinger.

ratives and principles underpinning the work and reveal aspects of its construction. Carefully transcribed and organized into a manual, the exercises of Meg Stuart and Damaged Goods are at the heart of *Are we here yet* and an apt place to start discovering Stuart's language of making. You could take her words as a partner into a dance studio and work with the following exercise, letting the tasks slowly overwhelm your body: *Use me.*

—Jeroen Peeters

A duet exercise. Your partner lies down passively, as in bodywork. Notice the image of the other's body and digest it. Lie next to the person and double the image. Take some distance; stand across the room and just look at that flat, resting body. Try different actions to find different relationships, stories, images. Put your head on their shoulder, imagining they are your lover. Tell a story in their ear. Work with memories of touch, like scratching, kissing or tickling. See them as an abstract shape. Sculpt them into a position you would like to see them in. See them as a package and wrap them. Be their twin. Be a live body next to a dead one. Lie on top of them. Let them hold your weight. Measure the length and width of their body parts, their weight and density. Imagine that the person has given up on living and try to resuscitate them, give them reasons why life is worthwhile. Put them in a sitting position. Take a picture together. Abandon them by leaving the room for a while. Return to them. Hold them tight. Teach them how to move, working with your maternal instincts. See them as a hostage. See them as a heavy weight that you're responsible for. Drag them across the room. Slow dance with them. Ultimately, the passive partner gets to standing. Switch roles.

Both partners' identities shift as they stay in the fixed occupations of passive or active. Following is a list of roles that you can try (or will arise naturally).

Active	Passive
Lover	Lover
Intruder	Hostage
Voyeur	Object
Vampire	A familiar place
Protector	A fantasy
Mother	Ghost
Seducer	Angel
Healer	Enemy
Show-off	Corpse

Sibling	Landscape
Guardian	Victim
Sculptor	Puppet
Collector	House pet
Playmate	Photograph
Adviser	Sleeper
Rescuer	Burden
Joker	Baby
Bully	Camera
Twin	Twin
Mirror	Mirror

Usually when a person performs body work on a partner to prepare them for dancing, the performative state of the people involved is never thought about. What do they look like as they do these actions? How can the actions be read? I have always been interested in the theatrical situation between a passive and an active body. In most relationships there is not an equal reciprocal dialogue. One person almost always has a certain amount of power over the other. The nature of relationships is usually unpredictable; the ground is shifting, prone to drama and change.

The exercise "Use me" is one that I come back to over and over again. It works well as a warm-up. We usually do it for about forty-five minutes in each role. By bringing the exercise into different scenarios the dancers consider the circumstances around their actions and become aware of their inherent states. They not only manipulate the other's body, but create memories and suggestions around it. This makes them improvise, create different scenarios, ride through emotions and be aware of the image they are producing. They are not only warming up a body, but also their own imaginations and sensitivity. Private intimate exchanges, like one person whispering into the ear of the other, can have as much value and power as big dramatic moves, like jumping on someone's back. It has a quiet urgency which I find very moving to witness. And "Use me" insists that the passive person be patient as they find ways to assist their partner complete the image they are envisioning.

AUTHOR'S NOTE

Slightly revised excerpts from Meg Stuart/Damaged Goods, *Are we here yet?*, edited by Jeroen Peeters (Dijon: Les presses du réel, 2010).

A BODY-MIND CENTERING® APPROACH TO MOVEMENT THROUGH EMBODIMENT

The seeds of my explorations lie in both dance and therapy. As a lifelong dancer, from the womb to now, in my seventies, I have sought how to fully know and express the vibrant spirit that enlivens this body in which I live.

Spinal paralysis at the age of four; at ten years, a broken right arm that remained significantly restricted; and in my mid-fifties a total collapse due to post-polio syndrome that left me first housebound and then unable to move freely in the world for nearly a decade, all led me to search for the roots and essence of healing.

My extensive study of anatomy beginning in 1958 has also become a foundational map upon which to focus this process of self-knowing.

When I was teaching a group of dancers in the 1960s and 1970s, we focused on bringing detailed awareness to our bones, joints, and muscles. Through our bones and joints we found basic structure and alignment. Through our muscles we found effortless strength and flexibility. However, I realized that there was much more to the experience, expression, and aesthetics of dance than we manifested through finely differentiating our bones and muscles.

In 1976 I began to develop and share the initiation of our movement through breathing, moving, and vocalizing from our organs and endocrine glands. This offered an amazing array of dynamics and integration of movement and emotion.

Feeling the power of this expanded awareness, I applied this emerging cellular consciousness and engagement from the tissues themselves to the nerves and ligaments. The nerves brought in our senses and perception and the role of the nervous system in recording the pathways of cellular experiences. The ligaments manifested as direct clarity of articulation and directed both the bones and muscles.

Until this point all of the systems I had researched had specific locations in the body on which we could consciously focus our attention. Our fluids, on the other hand, presented an additional challenge. Except for synovial fluid located in our joints, where was the place of entrance into the vastness and encompassing vista of our other fluids circulating throughout the body?

It took about two years of meditative searching before, in 1981, I was able to differentiate my blood from my lymph. This opened my consciousness into the other fluids: cerebrospinal fluid (CSF) of the nervous system; interstitial fluid, our inner sea; and cellular fluid contained in each cell. Eventually the continuous gliding of fascia and the sensuousness of fat emerged as semiviscous fluids. Two other fluids also joined the repertoire: periorgan fluid (serous fluid) around the organs and transitional fluid, the fluid flowing through the outer (plasma) membrane of cells. Each fluid contributes a unique quality of flow, rhythm, and feeling.

My exploration of body systems and tissues led me to the place where embodiment is the direct, fully known consciousness of the experienced moment initiated from the cells themselves. Here, the cells experience first and the brain is the last to know.

Since the early 1970s I have also been exploring the developmental process of how we came to be as we are. This aspect began with what I call the basic neurocellular patterns (BNP), movement patterns we have in common with animals.

The BNP begin with the underlying vibration of all forms. The next patterns are found in prevertebrate animals (those without a spine), including single-cell organisms ("Cellular Breathing"), sponges ("Sponging"), jellies ("Pulsation"), starfish ("Navel Radiation"), sea squirts ("Mouthing"), and lancelets ("Prespinal"). The vertebrate movements we have in common include the spinal movements of fish, the homologous movements (symmetrical right/left) of amphibians, the homolateral movements (asymmetrical right/left) of reptiles, and the contralateral movements (diagonal limbs) of mammals.

Underlying the BNP are the primitive reflexes, righting reactions, and equilibrium responses (RRR), simple to complex automatic responses to internal and external stimuli. The stimuli can be the position and movement of the body and in body parts in relation to gravity, space, and timing. The responses can be changes in tone in the torso and/or limbs involving flexion, extension, lateral flexion, and rotation.

Ontogenetic movement from fetal life through the first year after birth to standing and walking carries us through the sequential phases of development. This can be viewed in four three-month phases. The first phase, from birth to three months, is concerned with transitioning from life in the ocean of the womb to life outside of the womb. This includes survival functions, coordination of nursing, movement in a gravitational space around a central midline, bonding to family and environment, and feeling comfortable in oneself.

The second phase, from four to six months, is concerned with gradual increases in strength and coordination to flex, extend, lateral flex, and rotate the spine and limbs while in a horizontal relationship to the earth (lying on the belly, back, and side). Rolling in this phase is the first pattern of locomotion.

The third phase, seven to nine months, is concerned with developing loco-motion skills on the belly and hands and knees along the earth and coming to standing. Crawling on the belly and then creeping on the hands and knees are the second and third patterns of locomotion through space. Coming to sitting is the first vertical pattern.

The fourth phase, from ten to twelve months, is concerned with further ver-ticality through standing and bipedal locomotion, beginning speech, more mature manipulation of objects, and further explorations of the environment as other than self.

My most recent research, since the late 1990s, is exploring our embryological development as it manifests in the moment. We were each present in the form-ing of our bodies. As tissues and structures develop, some remain with us, some are transformed into other structures, and some fade into the background, no longer existing or recognizable as the original structure. As with all develop-ment, though the original processes are no longer with us, they have left us with deep-rooted patterns and templates that affect our movement, mind, and spirit. In exploring embryological development, we discover the primal roots of our structure, perception, respondability, and presence. Re-membering this pro-cess opens us to the state of being that integrates form and flow into a unified whole. In this study we enter into the clear realization that the past, present, and future exist as one time in the Now.

Our experiences imprint in all of our tissues. As we bring awareness to our bodies, our cells awaken to themselves and reveal to us the memories of these experiences. This allows them to emerge from the shadow of our unconscious into fresh insights and the possibility for transforming us into deeper compas-sion, wisdom, and ease.

Through the years I have studied with wonderful teachers who have inspired my continued searching and research. Together, those who have been pursuing this study with me over the past forty years and I have created a path for embodi-ment of body, movement, and consciousness called Body-Mind Centering®.

AUTHOR'S NOTE

Material in this essay was taken from "An Introduction to Body-Mind Centering®" by Bonnie Bainbridge Cohen, 2012 (http://www.bodymindcentering.com/introduction-body-mind-centering), and from Body-Mind Centering® Training Manuals, 1989–2012.

PLEASURE

Thinking about pleasure (um) as a mental state, (um) (and) is it something that I (um) am thinking about or is it more sensorial, and the body, or my body, (um) has some organic, natural need to feel pleasure? Or is feeling pleasure some reaction to (um) some pause, or (um) ointment, medicine for something that's not pleasurable? Thinking about it as a reaction, or as just biologically human. And then if you (one) take(s) the sound or the actual word pleasure (sonically) and how we have or how I have coded (embodied) it in my life, then what is that biological activity, that energy, that (um) the body is actually creating? Its need, and probably more the fact, its function.

(And) you know, you know historically, like, for, I think, all of human existence there has been a relationship to (um) pleasure, (and) often times you know under the (um) inducement of plant-drugs, and (um) and (um) how (cough) that could be its (pleasure's) relationship to (um) celebration, (um) organization of our agriculture. (Food. A means to our existence.)

SLOW

I've been thinking about (um) theoretical ideas about slow, or small (um). These ideas aren't so much about being minimal (um) but more to do with challenging the idea of virtuosity, and you know, skill, great technique, you know within a creative practice (um). Yes, I confess to feeling uncomfortable (um) when I'm working with materials that I am producing, or creating or even thinking (provisionally) about that has some element of technical prowess (um), that it feels like an interesting kind of protest to that, which is about my own history and (um um) education, acquisition of knowledge, this information, training, becoming of an artist, and then trying to disavow that. And you know the cycle of that may be a little silly but it feels important, that I could be virtuosic if I wanted to and choose not to. And then the challenge of not doing that creates these situations that can be about nothing. But if it's nothing, what is there to share? And if you're sharing nothing, that kind of quiet, or slow, is that not just as dogmatic, aesthetically?

And then there is an element about being older where I, I, my body and mind just doesn't want to think about too much.

II. Memory, History, and Retrieval

Memory, history, and archive, while maintaining distinct if unstable definitions, have long engaged in a dance of changing relationships and power. For at least two millennia, humans have striven to understand the human capacity to bring the absent past into the present through memory. Contemporary neurobiological and cognitive research have provided important information about the physiological processes of perception, encoding, storage, and retrieval that constitute human memory and have in fact revealed the constructive and plastic nature of memory.[1] Nevertheless, its relationship to history, archive, and even personhood and subjectivity remains an area of speculation across the cultural landscape and multiple disciplines.

When the need or desire to record and retain outstrips human capacity for memory, then history is born, and writing, documents, memorializing artifacts, and recordings take over. Stored in archives, libraries, on solid state drives, or using systems as yet nonexistent, these memory prostheses, in purporting to guarantee objectively recorded fact and permanence, put history in tension with the personal, lived, ambiguous nature of memory. Plato's dialogue, *Phaedrus* (360 BC), warned of the danger of turning to writing as a prosthetic that would replace living memory and knowledge.[2] Two millennia later, Pierre Nora expressed his concern that "with the appearance of the trace, of mediation, of distance, we are not in the realm of true memory but of history."[3]

The archive—as both those written records and the structures that house them—can either salvage and supplement memory or destroy the need for it. Thus, from their beginning these memory prostheses have prompted public discourse about the nature and function of bodied memory, about the role of memory in constructing histories and the historiographical models that govern their documentation, about the relationship of archive to the historical narrative, about the ever-increasing technological erosion of human memory functions, and even about the value or necessity of memory. Of course this brief chronology oversimplifies the complex relationships among memory, history, and archive, but it does confirm the continuing interest in researching or utilizing memory as part of a methodology to investigate the past and understand how it contributes to knowledge building in the present.

The body, like any archive, stores its history, but it does so as memory—in the complex circuitry of the brain and neuromuscular systems and the sophisticated movement possibilities generated at the junctions of biology and culture.

"Looking back" is a common phrase that validates the visual as fact or metaphor in the effort to recover the past, and clearly, texts, images, and artifacts are important data in recovering dance. But these may document both evidentiary and experiential accounts that, taken together, can create portals for a more bodied approach to research. A range of scholars and practitioners have incorporated strategies into their work for both themselves or others to feel, move, and dance back into the near or distant past; reinvestigating and reimagining both the recorded fact and remembered experience. In doing so they have discovered that various forays into bodied research may not only release new evidence but also refocus or reshape modes of transmitting their findings. This research may produce new kinds of historical insight, prompt new perspectives in empirical and experimental inquiry, affirm the revelatory power of memory as commensurate with that of history, and stimulate the creation of new modes of intellection as well as new choreographies.

In this part of the book, Barbara Dilley's poetic ruminations on memory and dance remind us of the slipperiness of memory over time, the elision as well as the chasm between dancing now and the dancing before this moment. Ivo van Hove recalls how, in working with actors in his company, Toneelgroep Amsterdam, the actor's body leads not just to meaning making within each play, but to a larger understanding of the capacity of the body to call out states of being that lie buried in consciousness. Ann Cooper Albright interrogates her writing methodology in her books on Isadora Duncan and Loïe Fuller, in which her historical investigation into textual evidence, images, and memoir is permeated by her own physical research into the effort, sensation, and impact of reembodying their dance works. Allegra Kent takes us back to her childhood encounters with dance and forward again as the ballerina reminisces about what lives in memory from working with George Balanchine as he created for—and on— her body one of their signature works together. Catherine J. Stevens, drawing on her own interest in and experience with dance as a cognitive psychologist, discusses her investigations into the nature and function of long-term memory in the perception of dance and dance performance from the perspectives of both dancers and observers. Emily Johnson draws on her lineage as an Alaskan Native American Yup'ik to create performance works often catalyzed by dreamscapes and memory.

—Linda Caruso Haviland

NOTES

1. John Sutton, "Memory," in *The Stanford Encyclopedia of Philosophy*, ed. Edward N. Zalta (2012), http://plato.stanford.edu/archives/win2012/entries/memory/.

2. Plato, *Phaedrus*, trans. Benjamin Jowett. (Blacksburg: Virginia Tech, 2001), 38.

3. Pierre Nora, "Between Memory and History: Les Lieux de Mémoire," in "Memory and Counter-Memory," special issue, *Representations* 26 (Spring 1989): 8.

MEMORY HAS ITS WAY WITH ME

BEGINNING

Writing about dancing is like writing on water. Stick breaks surface tension, enters pond, swirls. The beginning is gone by the time the ending arrives. The gesture is there, for sure—then, in the blink of an eye, gone.

Now I am writing about dancing, making a book, an archive: archive is object, is outer, outside; memory is subject, is inner, inside. Archive triggers memory. And then there is forgetting.

(*What are those fresh words that fly around the classroom above folks lying on the floor seeking kinesthetic delights?*) This writing is about teaching thinking dancing. I translate from words alive in space to words captured on a page. (*Will they sing to you?*)

And the young ones want stories. They say *Tell us how it came to be that you do what you do in the way that you do it.* I peer into my archive, make frontal lobes quiet, listen for instructions.

I remember.

Stay in the **middle** *of the event.*
Listen for messages.

PHOTOGRAPHS

Photographs/ephemera are organized into folders: from performances of the Princeton Ballet Society to Merce Cunningham's epic dances 1963–1968; from the New York downtown art ecosystem, 1968–1975, to arriving at the Naropa Institute in Boulder, Colorado, where I study my mind, my mind. All through these years, small/large black/white photographs, these captured moments in time, continue to land in my hands.

But what of the experience of dancingdancingdancing?
What of yours watchingbreathingseeing?

I look into a photograph, this archive of dancing with Merce, Los Angeles, 1963, my first tour with the company. We are dancing *Suite.* I don't remember the gesture caught in the photo, downstage left. I am up in the air, both feet off the ground, arms in a pose, head turning to the left. I do remember the space that Marvin Silver sees and photographs. The center of this archive I am peering into is empty. I remember this.

I know there is a body memory of the arabesque; that elegant ballet gesture. (Will I ever forget how to do an arabesque?) With a gust of desire, memory flows along finely honed body-mind pathways. One day, however, I am standing on the path, older and slow, peering into the glooming. Looking at a photograph from fifty years ago, I don't remember the dancingdancingdancing. All I have is this very moment, standing here.

EVOLUTION OF KNOWING

Long ago I let go of practiced moves, choreographed and rehearsed. Learn the dance. Adjust the gestures. Repeat. Repeat. On the other hand, I love taking class, a place and time to follow instructions and to explore. Here I feel an evolution of knowing, of inner and outer levels of awareness folding back and forth.

And then there is improvisation, the body-mind practice of Now. There is a simple score:

Beginning   Middle   End.

We spill into dancingdancingdancing;
memories merge with kinesthetic delights.

NOT TWO AND NOT ONE

Is body memory different from mind memory? Suzuki Roshi, Zen meditation teacher, says "body and mind are not two and not one." Is this where Now dancing resides? Between being not two and being not one?

> "This Very Moment is Always the Occasion."
> —Chogyam Trungpa Rinpoche

Decades later, kinesthetic delights emerge from this very moment, right here, right now. After all, it is always the occasion, right? Where does memory fit in? Does it get in the way? Is memory a bright scarf I wrap around my shoulders? If I stay in the middle of the event and listen for messages, sometimes memory appears and, yes, sometimes it trips me up. I want to feel the way I did before, before this very moment.

END

IVO VAN HOVE

THE BODY MAKES YOU REMEMBER

Thinking of highlights in my theater work, it strikes me that I spontaneously think of moments in which the almost purely physical performance of an actor moved me, brought me to tears. In 2009 I made *Cries and Whispers*, based on Ingmar Bergman's filmscript. It played in New York at BAM in 2010, but we also played in Amsterdam, Paris, and Brussels, and everywhere this production provoked the same reaction. At the end of the short, ninety-minute-long evening, most of the audiences were crying, holding onto each other, deeply moved by what they had seen. This might seem strange since the text of Bergman is only some twenty pages long and the dialogues are rather bare. The whole production was based on the physical and psychological performance of the actors.

One scene stands out for me. It is the scene when Agnes dies. The story of *Cries and Whispers* is simple: Agnes, an artist, has decided to stay with Anna, a servant, in the house where her parents once lived and raised their daughters. Agnes is dying, and her two sisters come to spend the last months, weeks, hours with her. For me the importance of bringing this filmscript to the stage was that Ingmar Bergman with very few words made me think of life in a big way. We all know that when somebody dies who is very dear or near to us, life becomes meaningless. Death confronts us in the most extreme way with the sense of our temporarily life on the earth. Ingmar Bergman didn't write a traditional filmscript for *Cries and Whispers*, but he wrote a long letter to his actors, a kind of short novel containing his thoughts about the story and the characters. Reading that letter, I discovered something strange. Bergman described the death of Agnes twice. Analyzing the text, it became clear to me that he wanted to decide later which death he would choose to put in the movie. I made the brutal choice to direct them both. The first death represents the way we want death to be. Everybody would like to die surrounded by people who care and whom one cares for. I had, as in the movie, the sisters and Anna surrounding the bed of Agnes, like a warm bath. A moment of togetherness and tenderness. But it is the second death that took even me, who had directed the scene, by surprise.

When we first rehearsed the scene Chris Nietveld, who played Agnes, asked me if I had an idea about this second death. I explained to her that this second death was death as I fear it would be: a death struggle, a horrible painful fight against dying, a visceral desire to keep on living. She wasn't satisfied and asked

Chris Nietveld in *Cries and Whispers*, directed by Ivo van Hove. De Singel, Antwerp, March 16, 2009. (See plate 4 for color image.) Photograph © Jan Versweyveld.

me if I had an image for the scene. I said that Agnes could create her last paint-ing, as if it were her testament. I talked about the way performance artists in the 1970s made paintings with their own bodies, so called action paintings. Chris quietly listened and said, "Okay, I understand." I checked with sound to see if they were ready to go. I had all the props ready for Chris to use, and I said, "Chris, we're ready whenever you are." And then one of the most striking mo-ments in the more than thirty years I had directed theater happened to me. The music started, and as a possessed madwoman Chris cleaned the space, put a large white canvas on the floor, poured blue paint on the canvas, and dived into it, making with all the energy that was left in her deathly sick body this wild painting, this expression of a lust for life, this ultimate fight against the inevi-table. It went on for only a few minutes, but to me it seemed hours, and I started to cry. It was a moment of pure cruel beauty.

There is also a second moment I recall, coincidentally also a production based on a filmscript by Ingmar Bergman. In *Persona*, which opened in 2012, we witness a star actress who suddenly stops acting in the middle of a performance of *Electra*. She ends up in a hospital for treatment. This text also has few words but is emotionally and physically very intense and challenging. Marieke Heebink played the actress, who doesn't speak a word, except for one at the end when she says "nothing." How could I show this inexplicable behavior and mysteri-

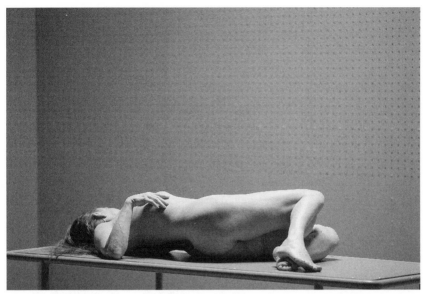

Persona, directed by Ivo van Hove. Pictured is Marieke Heebink. Théâtre de Liège, Liège, Belgium, November 30, 2012. (See plate 5 for color image.) Photograph © Jan Versweyveld.

Berlinde De Bruyckere, *We Are All Flesh*, 2009. Wax, polyester, and steel on wooden plinth, 105 x 165 x 196 cm (41³⁄₈ x 65 x 77¹⁄₈ in.). Private Collection © Berlinde De Bruyckere. This image is of De Bruyckere's sculptural work with the human figure, a portrayal of a "naked body in agony," which Ivo van Hove discusses in his essay. Courtesy the artist and Hauser & Wirth. (See plate 6 for color image.) Photograph by Mike Bruce.

ous mental state of this character. I showed Marieke a sculpture by Berlinde De Bruyckere, a renowned Flemish artist: a naked body in agony lying on a kind of large pillow or mattress. Marieke undressed and totally transformed into this sculpture; she became a sculpture, a body in terrible pain, unable to make even the slightest movement.

Never have I seen mental pain so mercilessly represented. It gave me an instant physical reaction: goose bumps. I mention explicitly the two actresses who played these quintessential scenes. Of course being the director, I came up with the inspirational images and ideas, but these two fabulous actresses performed the scenes ruthlessly and shamelessly, not trying to please for one second, greedy to deliver these irrational moments of intense pain in a way I had never before witnessed on a stage. It was only by their performances that I was totally overwhelmed by my own creation. The body is the ultimate expression of all that is going on in a human being, emotionally and psychologically. You are your body. That's why theater, opera, and dance can be life-changing experiences. The body is like an elephant; it remembers very well and in detail. And because it remembers well, the body makes us remember.

TOUCHING HISTORY

This essay begins with a question: How is one touched by history? The verb is chosen with care. I am not asking how one is affected by history. Nor am I asking what one learns from history. Instead, I want to think about how one is *touched* by history. Touch; touching; to be touched—these words evoke a relationship in which self and other are joined in an exchange that opens up the boundaries of critical discourse to the subtle energies of live performance. To be touched by history directs the research process into a perceptual experience, the measure of which cannot easily be quantified in terms of facts or dates. As Toni Morrison discusses in her moving essay "The Site of Memory," it requires an act of imagination to locate the various "truths" that have been overlooked by mainstream histories. Discussing how she re-creates the interior lives of African American slaves in her fiction, she writes: "[T]he crucial distinction for me is not the difference between fact and fiction, but the distinction between fact and truth. Because facts can exist without human intelligence, but truth cannot."[1] These "truths" touch one with a kinesthetic charge that registers differently from other kinds of historical documentation. They are grounded in a somatic awareness, what Morrison describes as "what the nerves and the skin remember as well as how it appeared."[2]

Our skin is the medium of touch, the first site of any tactile exchange with the world. As we know, skin is one of our largest and most sensitive organs. It covers the entire human body, and it is impossible to exist in the world without one's skin. Ironically, many people go through their lives with little awareness of their skin as a perceptual faculty. This is because our current postindustrial culture reifies the visual almost to the exclusion of our other senses, including those of touch, hearing, and kinesthesia. Many people use sight almost exclusively to navigate the world—offline as well as online. Usually we become aware of our skin only in extreme situations such as fear (the skin crawling up the back of my neck), awe (it gave me goose bumps), or pleasure (the tingling sensation of a lover's caress).

We can conceive of our skin as either a boundary or a conduit, and this shift in perception leads to a radically different understanding of the relationship between self and other, inside and outside. If my skin is seen as a barrier to disease, infection, or any kind of contamination, I might well approach life with a certain cold war mentality, shoring up any breaches in my defense system and using my skin as a wall or a container meant to keep me safe from dangerous influences. If, on the other hand, I experience my skin as the porous interface between my self and the world, then I will be more apt to engage my skin as a permeable, sensitive layer that facilitates that exchange, allowing me to touch and be touched by my environment. This attention takes practice, and clearly there are risks involved. Reaching out to touch something or someone insists on its own reciprocity, for it is impossible to touch in a way that does not also implicate one's own body. This is true in the case of fire and other people, as well as history.

These ruminations are occasioned by a retrospective harvesting, a kind of glance backward to the motivating curiosities and methodological principles of my last two books, at the moment of launching a new project. I am intrigued by how the somatic awareness cultivated in many contemporary movement forms can also help us engage our kinesthetic perceptions in the act of writing dance history. As both a scholar and a mover, I try to find ways to use my physical intelligence to help understand what is at stake while researching a particular historical moment, choreographer, or movement form. I think of this engagement as creating an embodied archive that parallels the written or visual archive, helping me to locate more than mere facts. Of course, as Susan Leigh Foster notes in her introduction to *Choreographing History*: "This affiliation, based on a kind of kinesthetic empathy between living and dead but imagined bodies, enjoys no primal status outside the world of writing. It possesses no organic authority; it offers no ultimate validation for sentiment. But it is redolent with physical vitality and embraces a concern for beings that live and have lived. Once the historian's body recognizes value and meaning in kinesthesia, it cannot disanimate the physical action of past bodies it has begun to sense."[3] That sensing is both mysterious and insightful. Surrounding myself with images and words, I try not only to analyze the textual and visual representations, but also to imagine the kind of dancing that inspired such visions. That is to say that I allow myself to be touched by what remains only partially visible.

> *Let's begin with traces. Traces of the past. Traces of a dance. Traces of light . . . and color and fabric. Traces of a body, animating all these sources of movement. Traces of a life, spent spinning across nations, across centuries, across identities. How do we trace the past? Reconfigure what is lost? Are traces always even visible?*

Long ago, I chanced upon an exhibition of early twentieth-century dance photographs at the Rodin Museum in Paris. I bought the small catalog, and from time to time I would page through the striking black-and-white images searching for dancing inspiration. I always paused at a certain one of Loïe Fuller. There she is, radiant in the sunlight of Rodin's garden, chest open, arms spread like great wings, running full force toward the camera. It is an image of a strong, mature woman, one who exudes a joyful, earthy energy. A copy of this photograph, taken in 1900 by Eugène Druet, still hangs above my desk, inspiring me daily.

I had been thinking about writing a book on Fuller for some time, but it took me awhile to come to terms with how I wanted to respond to the less visible traces of her work. *Traces of Light: Absence and Presence in the Work of Loïe Fuller* began with a question: Why do so many critics and historians dismiss the bodily experience of her dancing in their discussions of Fuller's theatrical work? I felt that many scholars covered over the kinesthetic and material experience of Fuller's body in favor of the image, rather than reading that image as an extension of her dancing. Then, too, there were all those apologies and side notes about how Loïe Fuller didn't have a dancer's body, or any dance training really, as if the movement images were solely dependent on the lighting, as if it were all technologically rendered. (One typical example: "The influence of Loïe Fuller upon the theater will always be felt, particularly in the lighting of the scene and in the disposition of draperies. *But she was never a great dancer. She was an apparition.*"[4]) There was an odd urgency in my response; my whole body revolted with the kinesthetic knowledge that something else was going on.

> In all writing, a body is traced, is the tracing and the trace — is the letter, yet never the letter, a literality or rather a lettericity that is no longer legible. A body is what cannot be read in a writing. (Or one has to understand reading as something other than decipherment.) Rather, as touching, as being touched. Writing, reading: matters of tact.[5]

Despite its linguistic unwieldiness, the preceding quotation from Jean-Luc Nancy's "Corpus" signals what is for me a profound difference in my approach to history. Moving from traces to tracing incorporates the tactile and thereby refuses the traditional separation of object from subject. Reaching across time and space to touch Fuller's dancing means that I allow myself, in turn, to be touched, for it is impossible to touch anything in a way that does not also implicate one's own body. Touching, then, becomes the space of our interaction, a mutual engagement. As I touch Fuller through my historical research, both textual and physical, I am touched in return, allowing me to write history from inside the vibrations of its ongoing motion. Working on this book helped me solidify an intellectual approach to the past that not only recognized the corporeal effects of the historian's vantage point, but also mobilized my body within the process of thinking and writing.

> Perhaps we should lose the noun, which renders us nostalgic, maybe even melancholic at the extreme. Replace our ambition to find out what happened with a curiosity about how it came to be that it was happening. Replace traces with tracing — the past with the passion. Tracing the contours of fabric which spiral upward and outward, we spill over beyond any one historical or aesthetic discourse. This act of tracing can help us become aware not only of what's visible, but also what is, has been, will always be, less clearly visible. Beyond the image into the motion.

This metaphysical conundrum (How is one touched by history?) has, in my case, a very physical complement, a form of contemporary dance called *contact improvisation*. In contact, the actual point of contact (defined, most usually, in terms of physical touching, although it can be rhythmic, visual, or kinesthetic) creates an improvisational space in which assumptions about what the dance will be like (future tense) are eschewed in favor of a curiosity about what is happening now (present tense). The meeting point of contact improvisation creates an interconnectedness of weight, momentum, and energy that channels a common physical destiny.

The partnering in contact is not simply an addition of one movement to another, but rather a realization that both movements will change in the midst of the improvisational duet. In addition to learning how to meet others in a dance, contact dancers train in extreme spatial disorientation. Releasing the uprightness of the body and learning how to be comfortable upside down, rolling and spiraling in and out of the floor, falling without fear — these are all aspects of a training that redirects visual orientation into a kinesthetic grounding.

I think of the physical aspects of my research on Loïe Fuller in terms of a contact duet. My body is influenced by her dancing as I imagine how she must have used her spine, her head, her chest. Spinning with my arms raised high and my head thrown back, I begin to understand the historical descriptions of Fuller laid up in bed with excruciating pain and ice packs on her upper back, begin to make sense of that as I literally incorporate some aspects of the physical tolls her nightly performances must have incurred. I realize that Fuller may have slipped a disc in her cervical spine. Even on an intellectual or metaphysical level, I think of our interaction as a contact duet, a somatic meeting set up by the traces of history. I believe that envisioning this relation in terms of an improvisational duet usefully redefines the traditional separation of a historical subject (treated as the "object" of study) and the omniscient writer of history. When, for instance, I review the enormous variety of images of "La Loïe"—the posters, photographs, paintings, prints, and program covers—I try not only to analyze the visual representation of her work, but also to imagine the kind of dancing that inspired such visions. That is to say that I allow myself to be touched (these "matters of tact") by what remains only partially visible.

My next book, *Modern Gestures: Abraham Walkowitz Draws Isadora Duncan Dancing*, was inspired by the incredible archive of watercolors by Abraham Walkowitz. Traced and colored throughout his life, these free-form images of Isadora Duncan spoke to me with such gestural force that I had to stand up in order to witness their large format with my whole body. (Needless to say, this caused considerable alarm among the librarians in the special collections at Lincoln Center.) When I later decided to write about these images of Duncan, I was surprised by a friend's observation that I had been thinking about Duncan for a long time. I had never envisioned writing a book on Duncan before. Nevertheless, it was true that I had written about Duncan early on in my career, in an essay focused on autobiography and dance. In addition, one of the first pieces that I ever published was an essay called "Writing the Moving Body," which also featured some Walkowitz drawings as examples of work that captured the immediacy of Duncan's dancing gestures.

Looking back, I realized that Duncan had surfaced repeatedly throughout my dancing career, although if someone had asked me if I thought of myself as a Duncan scholar, I would have said no. It's funny what we fail to recognize sometimes. Whereas I engaged my tactile sensibility while I was working on Loïe Fuller, it was the breath-like rhythms and musical phrasing, not to mention the importance of repetition—of entering the same movement again and again—that propelled my dancing and writing exchanges with Isadora Duncan.

> This one is one having been doing dancing. This one is one doing dancing. This one is one. This one is one doing that thing. This one is one doing dancing. This one is one having been meaning to be doing dancing. This one is one meaning to be doing dancing.[6]

Gesturing toward Isadora Duncan's monumental performance presence, Gertrude Stein builds her prose portrait of the famous dancer, "Orta or One Dancing," on a series of "ones." Cascading along with an evolving sequence of present participles, the "ones" ring out within a repetitious succession that loops forward and back in much the same way as the wavelike patterns of Duncan's dancing. Although Stein begins with the simple yet enigmatic "Even if one was one she might be like some other one," soon this "one" is threading her way through a labyrinth of increasingly complex states of being: "This one is the one thinking in believing in dancing having meaning."[7] These gerunds—being, doing, dancing, all the way to existing—describe Duncan's intriguing combination of historical influence and modern artistry by literally inscribing her movement into language.

Similarly, Abraham Walkowitz drew and painted images of Isadora Duncan in multiple series of movement phrases that also cycle back on themselves to evoke a "one" dancing. Like Stein, Walkowitz is not only interested in capturing a single precise moment, but also in approaching his subject again and again through an enactment—on paper—of her physical gestures. Dance is an elusive art. It requires the rehearsal of movements to train the body for a performance that disappears the moment the curtains close. To really embed the movements in the muscles and the bones requires constant repetition of specific actions. The French word for rehearsal is, tellingly, répétition. Through repetition, Stein and Walkowitz retrace Duncan's dancing presence, crafting unique representations of the famous dancer through new approaches to their respective media. Radically shifting the priorities of language and drawing to include an improvisational and performative element, Stein and Walkowitz create a composite portrait of Duncan, an artist who was always in the process of becoming "one."

> This one is the one being dancing. This one is the one thinking in believing in dancing having meaning. This one is one believing in thinking. This one is one thinking in dancing having meaning. This one is one believing in dancing having meaning. This one is one dancing. This one is one being that one. This one is one being in being one being dancing. This one is one being in being one who is dancing. This one is one being one. This one is one being in being one.[8]

Within a page or two of Stein's ninety-nine-stanza portrait of Duncan, most readers have to make a conscious choice about how to continue. Either one begins to skim over the repetitious phrases, looking only for the pattern of variation such as how "being" evolves into "doing" and "thinking" shifts into "believing," or one takes a deep breath, calls forth a somatic sensibility that expands beyond the symbolic meaning of words, and begins patiently to read the words aloud. With the reader's voice carrying the textual repetition of "one" into live sound, Stein's language begins to resonate, like a musical canon, in the surrounding space. At this moment, Duncan's gestures, expressed by Stein's writing, carry a profound power as they reverberate both inside and outside of the reader's body. I believe that these are the moments that Walkowitz tried to capture in his images of the dancer. The declarative power of her outstretched arms, the expansive quality of her mature body filling the frame, and the reverberations of past motion swirling in the backgrounds — these were the elements of Duncan's dancing that Walkowitz was both drawn to and drew out, over and over again.

When I teach Duncan in my twentieth-century dance history class, I take the students outdoors to a memorial archway. Standing between the columns, we draw on what we have learned of the cultural milieu of early modern dance and, inspired by the monumental architecture and open sky, we try to embody something of Duncan's expressive movement. When we return to the classroom, I give them copies of Gertrude Stein's prose portrait and Abraham Walkowitz's sketches of Isadora Duncan and ask the students to synthesize their physical experience with those primary sources. Over the years, I have become increasingly aware that these young dancers often have very little sense of space. They do not "see" it; they do not "feel" it; and they certainly cannot "sculpt" the space in any meaningful way. Kinesthetically, they remain inside their own physical reach space, dancing only with their reflection in the mirror. Any three-dimensional expansiveness that affects the space beyond their bodies seems outside the scope of their experience. I believe that by looking at and listening to Walkowitz's drawings, they can begin to envision a dialogue between motion and space. Through practice, they can attend to the vibrations of movement beyond the confines of their skin. Opening their bodies to her dramatic gestures, they learn to expand beyond the limits of their training to imagine other possibilities.

In his collection of essays *A Sense of Sight*, John Berger writes of the experience of his father's death. At the moment of his passing, Berger felt himself compelled to draw his image. Gradually, as time went on, this drawing became increasingly meaningful, not as a marker of his father's disappearance, but rather as a process of his becoming, what Berger refers to as "the simultaneity of a multitude of moments": "The drawing, instead of marking the site of a departure, began to mark the site of an arrival. . . . The drawing was no longer deserted but inhabited. For each form, between the pencil marks and the white paper they marked, there was now a door through which moments of a life could enter."[9] For me, this movement from the past to the present describes exactly the trajectory of Walkowitz's drawings of Duncan dancing. When I first looked at them, they marked a historical loss and another time. Now that they have become familiar to me, they hold a vibrant life in the present. They sing to me, inspiring me to look at and listen to the world with a little more awareness—and a little more joy.

Simone Forti was born in Florence, Italy, twenty-five years before I was born on an air force base in Illinois, yet circumstances and a lifelong commitment to improvisation have brought us together occasionally over the years. Forti is of the same generation as Yvonne Rainer and Steve Paxton, and although she did not participate directly in The Grand Union, her early dance constructions, such as *Huddle* (1961), inspired many of the investigations of postmodern dance in America. Forti is also known for her movement studies of animals in the zoo, as well as for her devotion to exploring the forms and structures that appear in nature: plants, rocks, and the weather. Her teaching seeks to develop an awareness of individual bodily sensations within the changing landscape of a movement environment. This internal attention often gives her dancing an absorbing deliberateness. Usually when I watch Forti, I feel as if I am right next to her, listening to the physical forces that guide her dancing.

Over the last two decades Forti has shifted the focus of her improvisatory research to a writing and dancing practice she calls "logomotion." In her performances she blends talking and moving to investigate the embodied resonance of topics as diverse as the latest news, the environment, or her own experiences gardening or traveling. In an essay called "Animate Dancing," Forti describes this practice:

> I started speaking while moving, with words and movement springing spontaneously from a common source. This practice has been a way for me to know what's on my mind. What's on my mind before I think it through, while it is still a wild feeling in my bones. My subject matter tends toward landscape, ruminations on the news, my family, garden, vegetables, weeds, roots, the way in spring a worm will dash for cover as I pull out the winter rye. The thoughts and images seem to flash through my motor centers and my verbal centers simultaneously, mixing and animating both speech and physical embodiment. Spatial, structural, emotional. I call this moving the telling or Logomotion. I see it as a performance form, and as a practice.[10]

That piece was published in *Taken by Surprise*, a book I coedited with David Gere. I want to relate the genesis of this essay because I believe it illustrates an approach that I would describe as embodied archiving. In the early 1990s I traveled to Mad Brook Farm, the rural Vermont community where Steve Paxton, Lisa Nelson, and Simone Forti lived at the time. While I was visiting, Forti and I talked and wrote and moved together, and I encouraged her to collect some of her journal writings into a longer article. She later sent me a series of uncon-nected bits and pieces of reflections about her practice improvising. Receiving these, I went into my dance studio and laid out all of the writings on the floor. I spent a long afternoon arranging and rearranging the individual paragraphs into an order that seemed to flow and make narrative sense. I was very aware of my movement at the time and how I was improvising my way through her writ-ing. It was a wonderfully fun and physical way to edit someone's work, and that sense memory has remained in my backbone for twenty years.

Based on that and other "moving the telling" experiences, I have recently de-cided to write a book on Simone Forti. As I contemplate how this new writing project might engage my dancing, I am drawn to the idea of connective tissue. Connective tissue is a collection of multifunctional fibers that envelop, connect, and support our physical structure. As a system that is responsive to both our physical and psychic states of being, connective tissue is tremendously adapt-able and resilient. I also find connective tissue to be a suggestive image for the ways that Forti and I inhabit similar dancing environments (the related circles of contact and contemporary improvisation) and share curiosities about the inter-sections of writing and dancing. Within the cycle of a year that is filled with teaching and other responsibilities, I am hopeful that I can keep this inspira-tion alive in the core of my physical imagination, opening my connective tissue to the myriad ways that I can continue to be touched by her history—and mine.

NOTES

1. Toni Morrison, "The Site of Memory," in *Marginalization and Contemporary Cultures*, ed. Russell Ferguson et al. (New York: The New Museum of Contemporary Art, 1990), 303.

2. Ibid., 305.

3. Susan Leigh Foster, "Choreographing History," in *Choreographing History*, ed. Susan Leigh Fos-ter (Bloomington: Indiana University Press, 1995), 7.

4. J. E. Crawford Flitch, *Modern Dancing and Dancers* (London: Grant Richards, 1913), 88; empha-sis added.

5. Jean-Luc Nancy, "Corpus," in *Thinking Bodies*, ed. Juliet Flower MacConnell and Laura Zakarin (Stanford, CA: Stanford University Press, 1994), 24.

6. Gertrude Stein, "Orta or One Dancing," in *A Stein Reader*, ed. and introd. Ulla E. Dydo (Evans-ton, IL: Northwestern University Press, 1993), 122–23. All quotations that accompany examples in this section are from "Orta or One Dancing," 121–36.

7. Ibid., 123.

8. Ibid., 123–24.

9. John Berger, *Permanent Red* (London: Methuen, 1960), 23.

10. Simone Forti, "Animate Dancing," in *Taken by Surprise*, ed. Ann Cooper Albright and David Gere (Middletown, CT: Wesleyan University Press, 2003), 57.

MY DISCOVERY OF DANCE

In 1946, when I was nine years old, my mother placed me in a progressive boarding school located in Ojai Valley, California. Her reasons were inexplicable; I suppose she thought it would be a great experience for me, but she was wrong. Loneliness set in on the first night; I didn't cry, though. Who would care or listen? During that first year, I felt I was losing my childhood before completely experiencing it. Nostalgia was creeping into my young soul. To offset this despair, I decided to become famous at something and receive a lot of attention.[1] But what would that something be? I didn't know. One activity was a consolation. In the dark atmosphere of nearly night, the children played a game called Ditch and Run, really Hide and Seek. I liked being chased, and I loved outdistancing my pursuers. A big triumph for a small person. I was in control of my athletic self.

During my second year at school, I became despondent. But then, at midterm, folk dancing was introduced as a once-a-week evening activity. I loved it passionately and decided that dance would become my destination and maybe my grown-up profession. And then my childhood would last forever. Dancing would make my life elastic—with it my life would expand; love could be captured. I couldn't jump into my mother's arms, but dance would embrace me.

The school had a spacious living room, a Victrola, and a collection of three records, which I played endlessly, dancing in my own style. My ideas and inspiration came from the music, its rhythm, and what I felt to be its message. The dream of dancing caught fire within me, and I decided to become a ballerina. The odd thing was that I had never seen a ballet or even a picture of a ballerina, but I understood it was a grown-up profession.

I had no idea that there was structure and technique in classical ballet, so I just danced on. A little plant flourished forward, fed by wind, water, desire, and the three records.

I sent my mother many letters about my decision to dance. The moon was in Ojai, but the stars were in my head. I wanted to become one. That summer I changed my name from Iris to Allegra. I had discovered my new persona. That fall I began to study ballet in Los Angeles, at age eleven—nowadays considered late. Although I was a beginner, the only dance school that interested my mother was that of Mme. Bronislava Nijinska, who had no beginners' class.[2] However, there was an intermediate level taught by her daughter, Irina, so I joined it. After finishing my first class, I seriously considered giving up, but my moxie ruled the moment. The opening exercises were pliés; the knees bend: the whole world pliés. The final steps were grand jetés—huge leaps that I could do with flying passion. But the whole middle of the class was beyond my reach. Deeply bewildered, I asked my mother to take me to the library so I could at least learn the names of the steps. I checked out many books and saw what ballerinas looked like; some were on their toes, a point of interest to me. I also included a biography of Anna Pavlova.

Looking back, I see that my mother's choice about my course of study was odd, but she wanted me to start with Nijinska, the sister of Vaslav Nijinsky. That was a glorious but impractical idea. Still, Nijinsky was a legend, and the power of his name was magnetic. Ballet was in their family's bloodline. With Nijinska, dance unfolded forward as her memories unfolded backward. Perhaps her ideas would be born anew in her receptive students.

After less than three weeks, my coordination and natural ability came together, and my body easily achieved something wonderful: a tour jeté—a towering leap. It was a simple step but great fun to do and consisted of a twist in the air during which a high leg in front becomes a high leg in back. My body clicked like a silent castanet; I was inspired. I will never forget that moment—it was mine forever.[3] I had found something that motivated my mind, muscles, and passion. Yet I still had not seen a ballet on stage. My ideas of what a performance would be like were still shadowy. But to watch Nijinska teach a class was a wonder. At the moment, that was enough.

My first evening at the ballet arrived five months after I started to study. My expectations weren't met, and I was very disappointed. But then, on the second program, *Night Shadow* (now called *La Sonnambula*) was presented.[4] That was my first experience of seeing a Balanchine ballet. Now I knew there were wonders in this art form. Curiously, I only read the ballet's name and its cast. The word "choreography" was not in my vocabulary—not yet. But that ballet leapt into my psyche. I knew I had chosen the right profession after all.

Eventually I started to study with Carmelita Maracci, who spoke English, was a brilliant teacher, and also told her students fascinating stories about dancers and performances she had seen by Carmen Amaya, Anna Pavlova, and Martha Graham.[5]

After I had spent three years of intense study in Los Angeles, Mother decided to move to New York City. Carmelita Maracci suggested we go to the School of American Ballet, where her friend Muriel Stuart taught.[6] There I took classes with many great Russian teachers, including my beloved Felia Doubrovska, who in 1928 danced the original Siren in Balanchine's *Prodigal Son*.[7] She was a superb teacher and enchanting to watch. She emphasized elegant footwork, beautiful port de bras, and feminine grace. After one year at the school, when I was fifteen, Balanchine asked me to join the New York City Ballet (NYCB).

There I learned about performing, and I could stand in the wings and observe closely the technique, musical phrasing, and wit of many great ballerinas, including Maria Tallchief, Tanaquil LeClercq, and Nora Kaye.[8] There I heard music that I had never heard before, by Igor Stravinsky, Maurice Ravel, Georges Bizet, and Paul Hindemith, among others. I also saw the amazing array of Balanchine's ballets in the company's repertoire that grew larger with each new season.

In the fall of 1954 Mr. B was creating *Ivesiana*, a new work for the company. The music was to be a selection of short symphonic pieces by Charles Ives, a composer not widely known at that time.[9] Rehearsals took place at the School of American Ballet, then located at 59th Street and Madison. Every day after work the dancers checked the call board to see what their schedules were for the following day. After my last rehearsal, I also did this. My eyes caught the words "The Unanswered Question," and next to it were the names of five men and one "Kent." I was thrilled but stayed composed. I might have a principal part in this section, but I couldn't be sure, and I didn't want to be disappointed. No one had given me any advance notice of something so momentous—not the ballet mistress, not Mr. B—so I would just have to wait.

The following day, when I entered the classroom, everyone was present: the four corps men and Todd Bolender, who was a principal dancer.[10] Mr. B asked all of us to gather together in one corner of the room where the barres intersected and instructed me to take off my shoes and climb up on the barre. The four men were arranged in a square configuration, and I was to stand on the shoulders of the two front men, who would grasp my ankles and calves to ensure my stability. When the music started Mr. B instructed us to proceed forward slowly on the diagonal, with Todd in front of us walking backward. Mr. B nodded to the pianist, who started to play a transcription of the orchestral score. When we heard a theme of five solemn notes, Mr. B asked me to slowly sit: he had the two men make a chair for me with their hands, and from there, I curled backward and was threaded through their legs.

All this time, Todd was walking backward, his arms outstretched—he had encountered a mysterious vision that he longed to understand. At a certain point in the dance, when the music became twisted with erratic notes, Todd performed wild contortions, but to no avail. He could never enter my world.

At another moment, after I was held high, Mr. B asked me to tilt slowly backward with a totally straight body. When I did this during performances, I heard the audience gasp; they felt as if they were witnessing a real disaster, not a staged, choreographed moment. I also felt this effect most intensely. I was like a statue being toppled. As I fell, there was no articulation in my body. (Of course, Mr. B made sure I would be caught.) For me, it was an otherworldly experience. Balanchine liked to startle the audience. And as it turned out, so did I.

The feelings of that first day of rehearsal would stay in my mind and body forever—a freedom from any kind of fear while doing something reckless, feeling the arc of air. Mr. B's choreographic ideas flowed forward—the section was finished in two hours. Of course, we had to work on the mechanics of the piece. The men lifted my legs into splits, hauled me around their waists like rope, and held me high in a towering arabesque. Mr. B asked them to speak very softly to each other so they could synchronize their efforts and make them seamless. Nothing had really prepared me for the new realm of choreography I experienced that day. In that moment, I was born.

I was seventeen, and this was my first principal part. Mr. B had formed an idea and thought that I could best embody it. I had no understudy. I understood that my persona in this dance would be untainted and unobtainable, as so many women were in Balanchine's ballets—and they always wore white. In *Ivesiana*, I also wore white—a leotard, nothing else. The experiences of rehearsing this work in the studio and then performing it on the stage of the City Center were very different. The effect of the choreography and the extraordinary lighting, when combined with the orchestra, was eerie. The five-note trumpet theme seemed to foretell Todd's fate—something already decreed—a sentence spoken by sound, powerful and frightening. He would never receive an answer. The ballet ended with him trailing after the vision of me held aloft. The four men were my spaceship. The movements were so deep inside me, it no longer felt like choreography, but of course it was—Balanchine's.

During rehearsals, Mr. B explained very little. He wanted me to understand his ideas by watching him and listening to the music. He showed me how he wanted me to look, and I looked that way, but I asked no questions, so they were left unanswered.

NOTES

1. Allegra Kent, *Once a Dancer: An Autobiography* (New York: St. Martin's Press, 1997), 19.

2. Bronislava Nijinska (1891–1972), dancer, choreographer, and teacher, began her career with the Imperial Russian Ballet, then joined Diaghilev's Ballets Russes in 1909 with her brother, the

legendary Vaslav Nijinsky. There she performed and choreographed *Les Noces* (1923), to music by Stravinsky, among other works, until her departure in 1925. She moved to California in 1934, where she taught extensively.

3. Kent, *Once a Dancer*, 20–21.

4. *La Sonambula*, with choreography George Balanchine, musical score by Vittorio Rieti, and based on themes from operas by Vincenzo Bellini (including *La Sonnambula*, *I Puritani*, *Norma*, and *I Capuleti e i Montecchi*), was premiered by New York City Ballet (NYCB) on January 6, 1960, at the City Center of Music and Drama, starring Allegra Kent, Erik Bruhn, and Jillana, with costumes by André Levasseur and set by Esteban Francés.

5. Carmen Amaya (1918–1963) was a Spanish flamenco dancer and singer of Romani origin, whose performances were seen around the world under the auspices of impresario Sol Hurok. Anna Pavlova (1881–1931), prima ballerina of the Imperial Russian Ballet, performed in Diaghilev's Ballets Russes from its earliest days in 1909 and toured internationally, both as a soloist and with her own company. Martha Graham (1894–1991) was a pioneering modern dance performer, choreographer, and teacher, whose company toured extensively.

6. Muriel Stuart (1901–1991), an English-born ballerina who danced with Anna Pavlova, began teaching at the School of American Ballet in 1935. She wrote, with Lincoln Kirstein, *The Classic Ballet: Basic Technique and Terminology* (New York: Knopf, 1952).

7. Felia Doubrovska (1896–1981), a Russian ballerina in the Maryinsky Ballet, performed in Diaghilev's Ballets Russes from 1920 to 1929; after dancing in Europe and the United States, she taught at the School of American Ballet from 1949 to 1980. *The Prodigal Son*, choreography by George Balanchine to a score by Sergei Prokofiev (*Le Fils Prodigue* Op. 46 [1928–1929]) and libretto by Boris Kochno, was premiered on May 21, 1929, by Diaghilev's Ballets Russes, at Théâtre Sarah-Bernhardt, Paris, and featured Serge Lifar as the Prodigal Son and Felia Doubrovska as the Siren; NYCB revived the ballet on February 23, 1950, at the City Center of Music and Drama, with sets and costumes re-created by Esteban Francés from original sketches by Georges Rouault; the 1950 cast included Jerome Robbins, Maria Tallchief, and Jillana.

8. Maria Tallchief (1925–2013) was a principal dancer in NYCB from 1948 to 1960 and was married to George Balanchine from 1946 to 1952. Tanaquil LeClercq (1929–2000) was a principal dancer in the NYCB from 1948 to 1956, when she was stricken with polio, and was married to Balanchine from 1952 to 1969. Nora Kaye (1920–87) danced for Balanchine in the American Ballet (1936–1938), danced with the Ballet Theatre (later American Ballet Theatre [ABT]) from 1939 to 1951, and danced with NYCB from 1951 to 1954, then returned to ABT from 1954 to 1959.

9. Charles Ives (1874–1952) was an American modernist composer. *Ivesiana*, with choreography by Balanchine to music by Ives, including *Central Park in the Dark* (1906), *The Unanswered Question* (1906), *In the Inn* (1904–1906?), and *In the Night* (1906), was premiered on September 14, 1954, by NYCB, at the City Center of Music and Drama. The original cast featured Janet Reed, Francisco Moncion, Patricia Wilde, Jacques d'Amboise, Allegra Kent, Todd Bolender, Diana Adams, Herbert Bliss, and Tanaquil Le Clercq.

10. Todd Bolender (1914–2006) was an American dancer and choreographer. He performed and choreographed for NYCB from 1948 until the 1960s; served as artistic director at the Cologne Opera House, Frankfurt Ballet, and the Ataturk Opera House in Turkey; and was the artistic director of Kansas City Ballet from 1981 to 1996.

CATHERINE J. STEVENS

WE DANCE WHAT WE REMEMBER
Memory in Perceiving and Performing Contemporary Dance

Dance presents a challenge for cognitive psychologists. The subject matter of cognitive psychology is the study of mental processes, and until quite recently, those processes have been examined using materials that are largely static, visual, and verbal. Dance, by contrast, unfolds in time and space, is kinesthetic and motoric, and is often nonverbal yet expressive and communicative. In order for us to more fully understand it, therefore, the phenomenon of dance demands a cognitive account that addresses the dynamic and temporal nature of dance that is embodied—in other words, a cognitive account of mental processes that are grounded in action. While cognitive psychology has been slow to recognize this, the universal human capacity to dance, express, feel, and connect through culturally patterned movement is the epitome of cognition that is grounded in the body and in action.

In this essay, I examine one aspect of dance cognition, memory. From the psychological side, we can ask: What is the nature of knowledge and expertise in dance? What role does memory play in practicing and observing dance? In what way is memory for dance similar or different from memory for other complex practices such as language, music, or the recognition of objects? From the dance-practitioner side, basic research on memory may be applied to studio and dance education techniques; methods may be adapted for new students compared with those more experienced and adept; and we can theorize about the fragility and reconstructive nature of memory that may influence dance reconstructions, documentation, dance history, and criticism. To establish the connections that I'm suggesting exist among memory, action, and embodiment, I begin by outlining a few concepts and assumptions from cognitive psychology. Memory is then considered from the perspective of (1) the visual attention of dance experts and novices observing a dance film; (2) novices learning the sequential structure or grammar of a series of phrases of contemporary dance unconsciously or through mere exposure; and (3) mature dancers recalling dance exercises from long-term memory in the absence and presence of associated musical cues. I consider implications of the research for cognitive psychology and for dance and conclude by summarizing some of the emerging and significant topics in research about cognition in dance.

COGNITIVE PSYCHOLOGY: SCIENCE OF THE MIND

Psychology is the science of behavior. Cognitive psychology—one of the many subdisciplines of psychology—is the scientific investigation of thinking or mental processes. Cognitive psychology uses the scientific or experimental method, together with computational modeling, electrophysiology (EEG), and neuroimaging (e.g., fMRI, MEG brain scanning) techniques.[1] The majority of experiments in cognitive psychology since the 1970s have used computers to present experimental tasks to participants and to record their behavioral responses. The processing and storage limitations of early computers meant that the material used in experiments—stimuli—needed to be short, static alphanumeric characters, words, images, or brief sounds. Lengthy, realistic stimuli such as an entire musical piece, a spoken or written story, or a dance work could not be used. Today's greater computer power means that the need for extremely reduced stimuli is changing. These days, continuous response ratings from the audience, or psychophysiological data, such as heart rate and skin conductance, may be recorded by psychologists during presentations of a full piece or long excerpt, and the kinematics and velocity of dancer motion can also be captured and later rendered in 3D.[2] However, constraints on stimuli and tasks still pervade studies that use neuroimaging methods. For example, fMRI scanners produce noise, recordings of the brain are made in sweeps of a few seconds rather than continuously, and movement of the participant in the scanner needs to be constrained. Thus, techniques must continue to evolve to include longer and more real-world or "ecologically valid" materials and tasks for experimental subjects, such as watching a complete or live dance.

Cognition as Embodied or Grounded

One characteristic of cognitive psychology has been its emphasis on the mind and brain at the expense of considering the body as a whole, specifically its actions, motor control, and motor learning. Originally, the mind was viewed as an abstract information processor separate from the body and the environment. Contemporary notions of embodied cognition posit that the human capacity to cognize objects, events, and abstract concepts such as metaphor is subserved by the sensorimotor systems that are used to navigate the world.[3] An embodied cognition view assumes that knowledge is not amodal or propositional but rather grounded in action.[4] This view accords with the close links that exist between perception and action. That is, perception is influenced by actions performed in the past, and actions are influenced by perception.

Studies using fMRI have demonstrated the intimate connection between perception and action. These studies noted that, within test subjects, observing goal-directed action is accompanied by an internal simulation of that observed action, with brain activity similar to the neural activity generated when that action is actually executed.[5] There is also greater activation when the observer has previously performed, and become expert in performing, that action. The oft-cited neuroimaging study demonstrating this effect in humans involved dancers expert in ballet or capoeira viewing short videos of ballet and capoeira. There were greater levels of blood oxygen in the blood vessels of the "action observation network" (AON) in the brains of ballet dancers when they viewed ballet compared with capoeira and, similarly, greater levels of blood oxygen in the AON of the capoeira dancers when they viewed capoeira compared with ballet. A subsequent experiment manipulated the gender specificity of particular ballet movements to demonstrate that male dancers had motor and visual knowledge of typically male movements, such as lifting a partner, but only visual knowledge of conventionally female movements, such as pointe work, and vice versa for the female dancers. Results of brain imaging revealed greater levels of blood oxygen in AON when male and female dancers viewed steps of which they had both motor and visual knowledge compared with only visual knowledge. The results demonstrate that dancers utilize not only their visual but also motor memory. Learning to perform a repertoire of actions impacts the dancer's perception of those actions; action and perception are coupled.

As dance, to our knowledge, has been part of every human culture, dance as a phenomenon holds cultural, evolutionary, and psychological significance. It is of further interest to cognitive psychology, as noted, because dance is embodied cognition par excellence. Explaining the cognitive processes involved in creating, performing, or observing dance also serves as a litmus test for theories of cognition that have concentrated on explaining the way humans acquire knowledge of static, verbal, or visual material. Thus the phenomenon of dance, particularly dance observation and expertise, is of interest to cognitive psychologists and neuroscientists as a tool to probe cognitive and perceptual processes that extend beyond dance. What remains is for researchers to regard similarly other aspects of dance—learning, memory, creation, improvisation, performance—and, where it is of interest, for dance practitioners, pedagogues, and theorists to consider seriously the implications from the science of dance cognition. I return to this latter possibility toward the end of the essay. First, however, I consider the role and nature of memory in dance, define some key terms in the study of memory, and outline three experiments that investi-

CATHERINE J. STEVENS

gated memory processes in observing or reproducing set pieces of contemporary dance.[6]

TYPES OF HUMAN MEMORY

Memory is implicated in all aspects of the many different kinds of dance, including dance as ritual, as social event, or as art. Memory is active when dancers watch a new dance work and learn that work by watching and doing and/or retrieving existing phrases from their long-term memory. Improvisers may seek new material and pathways, striving to avoid or minimize existing movement habits and memory. A dance ensemble and choreographer remounting a collaborative piece from years gone by, wanting to optimize recall, will likely reinstate associated environmental cues, such as music and physical engagement with the original dancers, including those virtually present through videotape documentation. The student of dance, who is learning new movement vocabulary, repeats steps and phrases to transfer the new material from short- to long-term memory. The observer watching a dance may connect it with his or her knowledge of other dance works seen or performed or, looking within that dance, may recognize features of the work and concatenate phrases into longer segments and sections.

Theories of human memory identify three broad categories of memory that can be distinguished by the duration of retention. Sensory memory is short-lived: just some hundreds of milliseconds. Sensory memory refers to very brief retention of visual (iconic) or auditory (echoic) material. Working memory (WM) seems to be a temporary workspace in which material is active while being used, for example, mentally retaining a sequence of ballet steps called out rapidly by a teacher. There are ongoing debates about whether material is lost from WM because of decay or interference. We do know that to maximize the amount of material retained, it is useful to chunk it (e.g., group together numbers of an unfamiliar phone number or connect separate dance steps into a phrase). In young adults, the capacity of WM is approximately four chunks or units that are meaningful within a particular context. For a new dancer, a chunk may be a single new step or phrase, whereas for a more experienced dancer, a chunk may contain an extended motif, a phrase or a series of phrases, or a large section of a work. Long-term memory (LTM) is long-lasting and has seemingly infinite capacity. Information is said to transfer from WM to LTM only after repetition and, ideally, elaboration. The more deeply processed the material (i.e., the more it is connected with existing knowledge), the more likely it is to be retained. Skill acquisition involves learning to segment and eventually chunk complex

90

sequences. The more elements in a chunk, the more material can be held in WM. Contemporary accounts suggest that rather than WM being a separate and distinct neural system, it draws on a temporary activation of, for example, phrases of movement material and a structural analysis of the work already residing in LTM. In other words, WM includes our bringing to conscious awareness knowledge that already exists in a person's long-term memory, such as a particular movement vocabulary or the structure of a work.[7]

Within LTM, theorists distinguish declarative or explicit memory from procedural or implicit memory. Declarative or explicit memory, or "knowing that," refers not only to semantic memory or knowledge of facts and events, but also to episodic memory that tends to have a personal or autobiographical element to it.[8] An example of declarative memory that is semantic would be to recite facts about Martha Graham even though the links to the specific, personal episodes by which the knowledge about Graham was acquired have been lost. An example of declarative memory that is episodic would be declaring a personal memory of one's performance debut. Declarative memory is explicit and available to conscious awareness. Implicit memory, on the other hand, is not available to conscious awareness. Sometimes called procedural memory, implicit memory refers to "knowing how." Procedures such as performing particular dance steps, like grands changements or cabrioles, or moving or responding in habitual ways, are instances that reveal the workings of implicit memory.

Is memory of a particular dance that a dancer has learned implicit or procedural and therefore unconscious? Is it just "muscle memory" that occurs, in a sense, without conscious awareness? To address these questions, I first define a few key terms: kinesthesis and proprioception. Internal sensations when they arise from muscles, tendons, and joints are known as kinesthesis. Such sensations are part of a broader system—proprioception—which includes the body's vestibular system or balance mechanism as well. Proprioception is sometimes referred to as the sense of the position of the body parts in space, while kinesthesis describes the sense of movement of body parts.[9] Muscle memory refers to the broad system of proprioception. Sensors in the muscles, in joints, and in tendons signal muscle length, angles of a joint, and so forth.[10] In muscle memory or proprioception, vision combines with the vestibular system, and experiments reveal that dancers have highly attuned proprioception.[11] Dancers may either consciously or unconsciously remember the proprioceptive signals that tell them about the posture of their bodies, which enables them to return to a particular posture or movement that they have performed before. This "proprioceptive trace" is likely to be what many dancers refer to as muscle memory.[12]

The dancer's memory for movement defies simple classification. For example, the proprioceptive trace may be unconscious, procedural, and implicit, but as I argue in the next section, it can also be explicit and declared in words and/or in movement. There is also declarative (semantic and episodic) memory for dance, including explicit knowledge of dance works and their structure, as well as autobiographically referenced memory for one's own experience learning, performing, and/or watching a particular dance. A defining feature of dance memory is the ability of a dancer to declare knowledge or make one's knowledge explicit and available to others, through movement.[13]

Declaring Knowledge through Movement

A journalist once asked me—as I was waxing lyrical about memory for dance—"What's the big deal? Dancing is no different from running." I think that the journalist's comment was flawed in at least two ways. It misses the technical, creative, communicative, expressive, and emotional elements of dance creation, composition, improvisation, and performance. And it both dismisses the cognitive possibilities of dance and privileges cognitive processes over motor control and planning. I subsequently addressed the issue by considering some dance, like music, visual art, and mathematics, as a kind of language in having a lexicon or vocabulary and a structure or grammar. Although in contemporary dance there is no singular vocabulary and grammar, and choreographers may even eschew them, vocabulary and grammar are useful concepts in explaining the underlying perceptual and cognitive processes in acquiring and representing dance knowledge.

Vocabulary can be a repertoire of steps, phrases, or riffs; grammar refers to the conventions—some based on the laws of physics and others cultural—for the way those steps are sequenced. Michael T. Ullman aligns lexical knowledge with declarative or explicit memory and mental grammar with procedural or implicit knowledge.[14] If we apply this conception to dance, then dance observation, creation, and performance involve both declarative *and* procedural memory. There is an ongoing interplay between steps and phrases and their sequencing and structure. And as often remarked by my colleagues in dance, the art and meaning is not inherent within the steps themselves, but instead is found in the relations between the elements. This is both procedural and declarative memory writ large. If we consider that in contemporary dance ideas for new movement material come from objects, events, or imaginings that are spoken, seen, heard, thought, or felt, then contemporary dance, while largely nonverbal, can be considered a language declared not through words but through movement and stillness of the body. Declared through movement, new ideas are expressed and become visible.[15]

I now consider aspects of long-term memory for dance and discuss three different studies that have used the experimental method. Dance, like music and speech, is not confined to a single modality; it is sequential, unfolding in time.[16] A view of long-term memory that can accommodate the changing and temporal nature of dance and music builds from an assumption that the human brain is sensitive to, and can learn, the statistical structure, that is, the regularities, of different environments. Those environments may be visual, auditory, or multimodal. The learning of structure or regularities is the basis for the ways in which we form expectations about what will happen and when it will happen. Our expectations about speech, music, or dance constitute dynamic knowledge in LTM and can be elicited by either known or novel stimuli.

Long-Term Memory as Expectations

From "mere exposure," that is, implicitly rather than consciously, humans become attuned to the regularities of their environment. For example, infants tune into the sounds of the language to which they are exposed.[17] Similarly, over time and without any formal training in music, children exposed to an environment of Western tonal music demonstrate internalized implicit knowledge of its regularities of melody, harmony, and rhythm.[18] Such attunement or knowledge of statistical regularities is theorized to give rise to "expectations" in long-term memory; expectations are dynamic, changing, and anticipatory, enabling one to predict upcoming objects or events. In the context of music listening, musicologist Leonard B. Meyer and psychologist Jamshed J. Bharucha distinguished schematic and veridical expectations. Schematic expectations refer to a broader knowledge of a form, genre, style, or period (e.g., a waltz, Graham technique, baroque dance), whereas veridical expectations refer to features of a particular piece of music (*The Blue Danube*) or a particular choreographed work (*Swan Lake*). Meyer and Bharucha, and in dance Ivar Hagendoorn, discuss the tension between schematic and veridical expectations as one determinant of interest, engagement, and emotional response in listening to, or watching, a performance unfold.[19]

THREE EXPERIMENTAL STUDIES ON MEMORY AND DANCE

1. Schematic Expectations Guide Experts' Scanning of a Contemporary Dance Film

Knowledge or expectations in long-term memory for a genre or domain, such as dance, are likely to distinguish more experienced and expert observers from those with less expertise. The comparison of groups of participants who possess different levels of expertise is a method used frequently in cognitive psychology and performance science as a way to bring into relief differences in psychological processes. In one experiment, we investigated the idea that experts in contemporary dance have access to acquired schematic (e.g., genre-based) expectations about contemporary dance in a way that novices do not.[20]

How can we measure expectations? An obvious way is to ask people directly what their expectations are, perhaps using open-ended questions, rating scales, a "think-aloud" protocol, or video-cued recall.[21] Unfortunately, these direct methods rely on introspection and verbal description that may return limited or misleading results. While experts and novice dance observers will differ in the language that they have available to describe what is going on, those differences in vocabulary (declarative knowledge) acquired through experience do not necessarily illuminate the cognitive processes and mechanisms that distinguish novices from experts. For example, experts' knowledge of dance may not only be in verbal form but will include proprioceptive traces and postural stability, attuned visual and motor memory, and a specialized action observation network for dance, any or all of which may be less developed in novices. Thus, in researching memory and dance we need to employ tasks and methods that elicit a form of response that elucidates how the diverse effects of more or less dance experience and dancerly knowledge determine these cognitive processes.

The need for an experimental tool to fit specialized dance knowledge was brought home to me in a striking way during our studies of audience response to dance.[22] To our surprise, in response to open-ended and rating scale questions about audience members' individual cognitive and affective responses to a contemporary dance work, there were few differences between audience members with extensive experience in dance and those with little or no experience.[23] We know dance experience and expertise is associated with specialist knowledge, but our word-based survey tools did not elicit this dance-specific knowledge. Hence, we turned to a more indirect but sensitive measure of observer expertise: eye movements.

When we look at or scan a scene, or when we read, we continually make extremely rapid and involuntary eye movements called "saccades," in between which the eyes stay relatively still.[24] The alternations between eye movements and fixations are extremely fast, with humans making about three eye movements per second. When we fixate or focus on some part of a stimulus, our foveal or central vision comes into play, with the fovea being that part of the eye that is good for resolving detail. In contrast to this central vision, peripheral vision is excellent for detecting movement, and it is those features of the stimulus, particularly movement, that determine whether or not a saccade is made. Thus, moving stimuli, such as dances, drive saccades and fixations. In addition to these relatively low-level perceptual processes, knowledge from LTM or expectations also influence saccades and fixations.

Eye movements thus provide subtle but detailed and quantifiable records of aspects of visual attention. Longer fixation times are associated with interesting, puzzling, or complex material and are also influenced by the extent of expertise. Expert radiologists, for example, prioritize attention and efficiently scan X-rays where tumors are most likely to occur, whereas novices scan the images evenly.[25] Fixation time, guided by knowledge, is reduced in experts compared to novices. Therefore, for expert dance observers we anticipated both rapid perception, with LTM guiding perceptual organization, and the tracking of configurations and phrases rather than discrete units. We hypothesized that expert dance observers watching a dance film would fixate on regions of the dance film for shorter lengths of time than novice observers.

To test this hypothesis, we asked four novice and four expert observers to watch a five-minute dance duet film. We also recorded eye movements from the choreographer of the work. The duet was filmed from a single camera angle. Fixations and saccades in response to a 17-second section of the film were analyzed; in this section the dancers worked both together and apart. An EyeLink II pupil-based video-monitoring system recorded eye movement; participants viewed the film twice. As hypothesized, fixation times recorded for expert observers and averaged were significantly shorter than those for novices in both the first and second viewings of the film. Interestingly, the fixation times of novices were significantly shorter in the second viewing than in the first. We interpret these results as evidence for expectations in LTM guiding expert observers' viewing the film. Even after one viewing, the faster fixation times of dance novices suggest that they too have acquired specific (veridical) expectations for the film.

Analysis of the regions that were fixated on by the two groups of participants revealed that experts were more successful than novices at accurately following the dancers' movement. However, experts, novices, and the choreographer all fixated on the background region at times. This is likely to have occurred because the movement of the dancer was then in the movement-sensitive peripheral part of the observer's visual field. Once movement was detected, the eyes could then move quickly to the next region of interest. Fixating on the background, as well as on the dancers, would also be an effective strategy for making visual sense of the dance as a whole when there is more than one dancer and the dancers are working in different spatial locations. Records of the choreographer's fixations indicated she was, as one would expect, the most accurate of all in following, by likely anticipating, dancer movement. Based on the fixation times and regions of fixation, we concluded that acquired schematic expectations enable experts to anticipate movement and recognize bodily and movement configurations, enabling a faster speed of visual processing.

What did we learn from recording and analyzing dancers' eye movements while watching a dance film? First, we identified a method that is sensitive to the knowledge characteristic of dance experts. The method does not rely on knowledge being verbalized or even being available to conscious awareness. Second, while dance expertise likely takes many forms, including types of knowledge—from motor control through composition to recognition of expressive nuance and feeling—measurement of eye movements provides an indirect lens through which we can discern effects of that knowledge and expertise on visual attention. Third, the results provide a fairly gross indication of novice/expert differences, and we interpret these as differences in expectations or knowledge in LTM. Future studies need to investigate the nature of those expectations and to fully test (or refute) the hypothesis. Such follow-up experiments are vital if a comprehensive explanation of expectations in LTM for dance is to be articulated.

What implications can we draw from the study? Based on the evidence we presently have, one obvious implication is that novice observers develop expectations for the dance after just one viewing. This is encouraging for new thinking about the development of dance audiences, as even one exposure clearly makes a difference. This may well be even more important when the structural or spatial elements of a dance are complex. Human cognitive resources—attention and memory—are limited, and complex events or situations increase cognitive load or cognitive demand. For the observer who needs to divide his or her attention in space and time, cognitive demand can be overwhelming. If seeing the dance once or becoming more familiar with the genre can enable the observer to more quickly or efficiently develop schematic expectations for a specific work, then this facility, in conjunction with chunking elements together into phrases and sections (optimizing WM capacity), may help to reduce the cognitive demand, enabling many events and relations to be held consciously in mind at once.

For those dancers, choreographers, and composers who strive to connect and communicate with their viewers, the use of repetition of motifs and of higher-order structuring within a work provide ways to build familiarity and develop expectations in observers. It is likely that this kind of implicit and observational learning has enabled cultures with oral traditions to communicate and share stories, myths, social structures, and identities through music and dance.

2. *Developing Expectations through Mere Exposure in Novice Dance Observers*
The topic of the second experiment was the *development* of expectations for temporal sequencing of dance phrases. Working with dance novices as participants, we investigated the hypothesis that through mere exposure, novice observers of dance begin to learn the regularities or grammar that governs the sequencing of unfamiliar, discrete dance movements.[26]

The idea for this experiment arose from my own experience watching and beginning to learn about contemporary dance. As a researcher, I had the opportunity to watch multiple performances of new dance pieces by Australian dancers and choreographers such as Anna Smith and Sue Healey.[27] I became aware that the more I watched a work, the more I saw. I was able to perceptually organize the choreographic elements of the dance, to make connections over larger time-scales, and to appreciate and understand the work more. Of course the work was not changing; my perception was. We designed an experiment deliberately involving a sample of dance novices, to see if we could capture and quantify this development of familiarity, perceptual fluency, and acquisition of expectations in a controlled laboratory setting. The motivation was to demonstrate under experimental conditions that novice dance observers develop expectations for the sequencing of contemporary dance phrases without intention—that is, through mere exposure.

One paradigm used to study implicit learning involves the learning of an artificial grammar—that is, a grammar that has been invented and is unfamiliar to participants. Participants are first presented with sequences, often strings of letters or tones that conform to the invented grammar. They are then presented with a new series of letters or tone strings and asked to classify whether or not those are grammatical. Learning is said to have occurred when the classification of the new strings is at a level higher than that predicted by chance. The learning is identified as implicit if participants are unable to articulate the rules of the grammar they used to identify grammatical or "legal" strings.[28] We tested for implicit learning, using dance phrases as stimuli, with longer sequences of body-based material serving as the invented or artificial grammar. We deliberately used phrases of movement that, when sequenced together, followed the rules of that grammar but were also discrete phrases that ensured that laws of physics and body morphology could not be used to judge sequence grammaticality. If artificial grammar learning extends to human movement and longer sequences, then a group of participants exposed to examples of grammatical sequences (the exposure group) would be more accurate than those who were not exposed (the control group) in selecting new grammatical sequences in a set of test trials. Further, if the learning is unconscious or implicit, the participants' level of accuracy in the test trials and confidence in their judgments would be unrelated, as they would have selected new sequences that conformed to the grammar without explicitly knowing why, without consciously knowing the rules of that grammar. If implicit, there should be no systematic relationship between whether a response is accurate and how confident the participant is in that response.[29]

In order to demonstrate this, we divided thirty-one adult participants with little experience in dance into exposure and control sample groups. Movements used as visual stimuli in this experiment were characteristic of mid- to late twentieth century Australian contemporary dance. The movements, performed by an expert dancer, were three to five seconds long and, when concatenated according to the rules of the dance grammar, lasted from nine to nineteen seconds. The exposure group saw twenty-two grammatical sequences presented twice in random order. In a test phase, both experimental and control groups saw forty-four previously unseen test sequences presented in pairs. For each pair, participants judged which sequence was grammatical and rated their confidence on a five-point scale (1 = not confident at all to 5 = highly confident).

In the test phase and as hypothesized, the exposure group selected significantly more new grammatical sequences than the control group, 57 percent and 43 percent, respectively. The pattern of accurate responding and confidence ratings revealed no relationship in the exposure or control groups. This "zero correlation" suggests that the learning of the artificial grammar in the exposure group was implicit. The experiment demonstrates that through exposure alone, dance novices can learn regularities of an artificial grammar that govern the sequencing of movements from contemporary dance.

As I suggested above, experimental evidence that novice observers acquire knowledge of an underlying grammar has practical implications for audience development. For example, as choreographers and composers know, the repetition of structure within a dance piece can lead an observer to develop expectations about that structure. Exposure is said to build perceptual fluency, which in turn is associated with a sense of familiarity and heightened *preference* for the movement material.[30] It demonstrates that, just as infants and children implicitly learn the regularities of the linguistic or musical environment to which they have been exposed, so too will adults learn to expect particular relations among dance phrases unconsciously, through mere exposure. Whether within a single work or across a body of dance works by a particular choreographer, familiarity—at least for novice dance observers—"breeds content."[31]

3. Associative Learning and Environmental Cues to Long-Term Memory for Dance

At a dance event in Sydney, Australia, an eighty-year-old woman who had danced professionally in vaudeville some sixty years earlier remarked to me that, while she sometimes forgets why she has gone to the refrigerator, she has no trouble recalling and performing her dance routines from six decades ago. Why is memory for well-learned, complex sequences of human movement so long-lasting? What are the processes by which dance becomes part of LTM, and what cues aid retrieval from memory?

In a third experiment, we investigated long-term memory in mature dance performers.[32] The study was part of a documentation project in which four retired dancers came together in 2007 to reconstruct and document material from Margaret Barr dance-drama technique classes held in Sydney, Australia, from the 1960s to 1980s.[33] As a way to explore which features of the dance environment become part of memory and are possibly shared or distributed across the dancers, we probed long-term memory for seven dance exercises. The dance exercises had always been associated with particular excerpts of music, so the musical excerpt should be a powerful cue to the memory for the exercise. The four dancers had not performed the material for between three and thirty-one years.

Embodied memory for dance takes many forms, including associations between movement and particular features of the dance environment. Those associations become strengthened in the brain with repetition. This kind of associative learning means that presentation of an environmental cue can trigger recall of the associated memory; such associative learning produces context-dependent memories. In a classic experiment, Duncan R. Godden and Alan D. Baddeley gave groups of divers a list of unrelated words to study and memorize either on land or underwater.[34] The participants' recall of the words was then tested in the context in which the words had been studied (i.e., on land or underwater) or in the other study context. Memory for the words was determined to be context-dependent, because recall was significantly greater when the study and text contexts matched (both land or both water) than when they differed (land-water or water-land). These kinds of effects underpin the tendency for dance teachers to vary recall contexts for their students so that good performance ensues without being tied to a particular context or studio.

We documented the amount of material that our four dancers recalled in movement, first on their own and in silence, and then as a group and cued by the relevant musical excerpt. The musical excerpts varied in duration from 50 to 199 seconds. To see whether the movements of the dancers' bodies were necessary for recall, we also had them recall the exercises by moving the limbs, head, and torso of a small wooden mannequin doll in place of their own bodies.

Of the seven exercises, three were recalled in more detail in the presence of the musical cue than in silence. For example, the music associated with the exercise "Simple Arms" elicited movement that was more defined and confident than when it was performed in silence. The music provided cues for counts and timing. Where the dancers had been confused or unable to recall the exercise "Complex Arms" in silence, they began to move immediately and confidently upon presentation of the associated music. Presentation of the music for "The Falls" had the dancers describing or performing the movement and using rhythmical movements of the body to beat time with the music. There were no significant differences between the amount of material recalled when the dancer's body was used and using the mannequin.

In addition to quantifying the amount of material recalled, in this more descriptive and qualitative study we also asked the dancers to reflect on and verbalize their process of recall. Their verbalized approach included recalling an inner voice that described an aspect of the movement; the sound of choreographer Barr's voice in the studio, especially the inflection, prosody, drama, and occasional onomatopoeia of her voice; the importance of music and, in the absence of music, humming or imagining the music; muscular sensations (e.g., thigh-pull) associated with particular exercises; and mood, especially positive feelings for particular exercises, music, and the associated earlier times in their lives. In using the mannequin rather than their bodies, the dancers observed the awkwardness of using the doll—one dancer noted feeling the movement in her body as she moved the doll. Interestingly, when music was presented, all dancers recalled an exercise using the mannequin and were uninhibited in doing so.

Long-term memory for dance is multimodal and associative. In our study, dancers recalled the intonation and timbre of the choreographer's distinctive voice; the social and political context of the time when the material was learned and rehearsed; olfactory features of the studio; and the impact of the dance and the choreographer on their individual personas, outlooks, and lives. Music cued sequential order and, where relevant, timing. Moving the body for recall was preferred by the dancers to moving the mannequin, but perhaps their own body movement was not necessary, as the exercises were recalled with a similar rate of accuracy regardless of whether the mannequin or the dancer's body was the medium.[35]

Implications of this third experiment suggest that memory for dance is not solely movement-based or confined to the brain of an individual. It is multimodal, visual, auditory, motor, and kinesthetic; it is personal, emotional, social, and often distributed among an ensemble of dancers and choreographer. Our future work will pick up on the idea of cognition being distributed among performers and the ways in which creativity and improvisation are distributed across an ensemble.

CONCLUSIONS

These three experimental studies reinforce our confidence that dance is a significant area of research for cognitive psychology as behavior and as universal cultural phenomenon. Present, we believe, in all cultures, dance has deep evolutionary roots. Dance cognition—broadly defined as knowing through the body in motion—is embodied not only in the creator and performer but also, with motor simulation and neural mirroring, in the observer. The more experience in performing particular dance actions someone has, the greater the neural mirroring of those actions when they are observed. Dance knowledge at times is expressed in words, but very often ideas are expressed or declared through movement or stillness of the body, through expressive nuance, and in relations between phrases of movement and among moving bodies. In dance, unlike other forms of art with the exception of singing, the body is the instrument. Creating, performing, and observing dance is multimodal. The perceptual modes include activation and integration across motor, kinesthetic, proprioceptive, visual, and auditory systems. For those new to watching or learning dance, multimodal stimulation is extremely demanding.

Implications

The results of the experiments discussed here speak to the demands on attention and memory in learning and reproducing a set dance. The studies demonstrate the importance of repetition and structure for learning a new language of movement and for strengthening connections and pathways. They also show that different kinds of research tools are needed to study and to elicit multimodal dance knowledge. Finally, the experiments raise questions about acquiring the lexical and grammatical knowledge of a language—whether speech, music, or dance—

and the possibility of a critical or sensitive period during which time the new language is most easily learned.

The Dance-Science Connection

Cultural inventions and forms such as dance, music, and poetry reflect the scope as well as the limits of human perception and memory. For example, if dances or songs are to be passed on (in the absence of a system of notation), then they need to be able to be perceived, that is, distinguished from one another, learned, and recalled. Analyzing the composition, statistical, and structural regularities of dance and music therefore offers us insights into aspects of human perception and memory. I'm not the first to observe that artists have long preceded psychologists with their knowledge—conscious or intuitive—of the processes of perception and memory.[36] Visual artists, for example, understand the properties of light and ways to represent light, depth, distance, and texture. The mechanisms they use in their art may well align with some of the basic perceptual mechanisms in vision. Similarly, world music and dance reflect constraints on perception and cognition, such as the need to utilize rhythm and rhyme as mnemonic devices in oral traditions. Thus, some of the observations made in the psychology laboratory may be old news to artists, dancers, choreographers, and composers. One contribution from psychological experimentation is the gathering of evidence obtained under controlled conditions to support or counter a hypothesized process. Such methods are vital when the underlying perceptual or cognitive processes are not available to consciousness or can be expressed in behavioral but not in verbal form.

Perhaps more exciting are the possibilities offered when cognitive psychologists and artists work together to identify research questions of mutual interest. The past decade has seen intense research on action observation, with perceiving dance recognized by researchers as a heightened and illuminating form of action observation.[37] For example, the Watching Dance: Kinesthetic Empathy project in the UK has laid the foundation for ambitious multidisciplinary research that runs the gamut of investigation from neural pathways to audience response. Close collaboration between artists and scientists is the mission of the Dance Engaging Science interdisciplinary workshops instigated by The Forsythe Company (and facilitated by Scott deLahunta).[38] Questions that can arise include whether a dancer's attentional (and not necessarily visual) focus directs the attention of the audience. Auditory-visual sensory integration may be explored using an actual dance work, and the choreographer's intention may be compared with observer perception. A movement grammar may be developed by a choreographer to test the implicit learning of grammatical structure using more realistic materials from dance. Hypotheses about memory may be applied in the studio to optimize recall in remounting projects, crucial for documentation of endangered dance forms and works.

An increasing dialogue between dance and movement artists and cognitive psychologists will lead to investigations of dance cognition in more naturalistic settings using more sophisticated, artist-informed stimuli. The kinds of topics that are likely to emerge over the coming years include

- studies of the cognitive benefits of dance for child development and learning;
- examining the benefits of cognitive, physical, expressive, and social stimulation from dance in slowing cognitive decline in aging;
- cross-cultural studies of dance perception and cognition;
- the study of extended and distributed creative cognition among choreographers and dancers;
- the importance of social and group processes in learning and recollecting dance;
- the role of personality, empathy, and individual differences;
- integration in perception and memory of dance and environmental cues, such as music, soundscape, expression, speech, studio or other physical surroundings, and other people;
- experiments using theaters that have been designed and wired to record online responses from audience members during live performances, including EEG, heart rate, and skin conductance;[39] and
- investigating aesthetic responses to dance or "neuroaesthetics" using fMRI and MEG.[40]

The impact of research topics such as these will soar as cognitive psychologists and cognitive neuroscientists develop methods that are both more precise and more closely adapted to particular kinds of dance. Relevance for dance studies, at this stage, is in the area of education and learning. A goal of this essay has been to demystify and contextualize the subject matter of cognitive psychology and its methods and sketch general ideas about human memory. As cognitive scientists watch, listen, and learn about dance, the articulation of new research questions that go to the heart of the art form will begin to be within reach.

CATHERINE J. STEVENS

AUTHOR'S NOTE

In memory of scholar, artist, and gentleman Robin Marshall Grove (1941–2012).

Portions of this work have been reported in C. Stevens, H. Winskel, C. Howell, L.-M. Vidal, C. Latimer, and J. Milne-Home, "Perceiving Dance: Schematic Expectations Guide Experts' Scanning of a Contemporary Dance Film," *Journal of Dance Medicine and Science* 14 (2010): 19–25, © 2010 J. Michael Ryan Publishing, Inc. and International Association for Dance Medicine and Science, adapted with permission; T. Opacic, C. Stevens, and B. Tillmann, "Unspoken Knowledge: Implicit Learning of Structured Human Dance Movement," *Journal of Experimental Psychology: Learning, Memory and Cognition* 35 (2009): 1570–77, © 2009 American Psychological Association, adapted with permission; and C. Stevens, J. Ginsborg, and G. Lester, "Backwards and Forwards in Space and Time: Recalling Dance Movement from Long-Term Memory," *Memory Studies* 4 (2011): 234–50, © 2011, Sage.

The research was supported by grants from the University of Western Sydney (UWS) and the Australian Research Council (LP0562687). My thanks to Shirley McKechnie, Mark Gordon, Ruth Osborne, Zoe Ventoura, Kylie Hunter and Alexandra Thearle, Sue Healey, James Batchelor, Tom Hodgson, Garry Lester, Barbara Tillmann, Tajana Opacic, Jane Ginsborg, Lyne-Marine Vidal, Clare Howell, Heather Winskel, dancer participants, volunteer expert and novice observers, and dance industry partners QL2 Centre for Youth Dance, Australian Dance Council (Ausdance), The Australia Council for the Arts Dance Board, and the ACT Cultural Facilities Corporation. Contact details: Kate Stevens, MARCS Institute and School of Social Sciences & Psychology, University of Western Sydney, kj.stevens@uws.edu.au; http://marcs.uws.edu.au; http://katestevens.weebly.com.

NOTES

1. Strengths of the experimental method include the benefit of control where variables of theoretical interest are manipulated and their causal effect on behavior observed and quantified. For example, we could investigate the effect of an aspect of context on memory for a dance. The independent variable context could have two levels: familiar context (e.g., the studio in which the dance was learned) and unfamiliar context (a different studio from where the dance was learned). We could "measure" the effect of context on dependent variables such as the accuracy of performance (precision and quality of the recall or reproduction of the dance) under those two different experimental conditions. While experiment control sounds as if the experimental setting is reduced and rarefied, it actually permits generalization, because the design and sampling reduce confounding extraneous variables, such as the genre and the complexity of the dance that is to be learned and remembered. If these genre and complexity factors are left to chance, then we may find that one group performs better than another not because of the context variable that we have manipulated but because one group memorized a simpler routine or because the routine was from a more familiar genre compared with the other group. The experiment controls such extraneous factors by using a set routine that is in a style equally familiar to all participants. Samples of participants should be large and heterogeneous so that while there will be differences among individuals in the sample (e.g., socioeconomic status including level of education, preferences, IQ, personality, attitudes), such diversity exists in all samples involved in the experiment, and the effect of those individual differences should be similarly distributed, with the effects "washing out" over the entire experiment. Wide sampling also means that results should generalize beyond narrow or specialist groups. In some experiments, characteristics of the participants are systematically varied; for example, dance experience could be

manipulated with two different groups of participants, one with a large number of years of dance training and another with little or no dance training. This kind of approach to experimental design is often used in neuroimaging studies where the comparison of, say, expert and novice dance observers is used to bring differences in patterns of neural activation or connectivity into relief (e.g., Beatriz Calvo-Merino et al., "Action Observation and Acquired Motor Skills: An FMRI Study with Expert Dancers," *Cerebral Cortex* 15, no. 8 [2005]: 1243–49; and Beatriz Calvo-Merino et al., "Seeing or Doing? Influence of Visual and Motor Familiarity in Action Observation," *Current Biology* 16, no. 19 [2006]: 1905–10). Whether differences observed in performance under experimental conditions and/or between different groups of participants are significant can be determined using statistical methods. The replication of experiments and associated significant effects is essential and encouraged. Harold Pashler and Eric-Jan Wagenmakers, "Editors' Introduction to the Special Section on Replicability in Psychological Science: A Crisis of Confidence?," *Perspectives on Psychological Science* 7, no. 6 (2012): 528–30. The initialism EEG refers to electroencephalography. Small electrodes placed on the scalp record electrical brain potentials. The experiment reported in Guido Orgs et al., "Expertise in Dance Modulates Alpha/Beta Event-related Desynchronization during Action Observation," *European Journal of Neuroscience* 27, no. 12 (2008): 3380–84, is an example of EEG in the context of dance and expertise. In magnetoencephalography (MEG), an array of sensors, rather than electrodes, detects changes in magnetic fields produced by electrical activity of the brain. MEG has good temporal resolution, meaning that it can reveal fast-moving neural events in the brain. By contrast, functional magnetic resonance imaging (fMRI) has good spatial resolution, meaning that it accurately measures differences in activity of closely spaced regions of the brain. In fMRI, the scanner acquires images of the brain that indicate regional metabolism. Detecting levels of oxygen in the brain's blood vessels measures brain activity indirectly. Increased activity of a brain region stimulates blood flow to the region that increases the local blood oxygen level. Neil R. Carlson, *Foundations of Behavioral Neuroscience*, 9th ed. (Boston: Pearson, 2014).

2. Roger T. Dean, Freya Bailes, and Emery Schubert, "Acoustic Intensity Causes Perceived Changes in Arousal Levels in Music: An Experimental Investigation," *PLoS ONE* 6, no. 4 (2011): e18591; Corinne Jola, Frank E. Pollick and Marie-Hélène Grosbras, "Arousal Decrease in 'Sleeping Beauty': Audiences' Neurophysiological Correlates to Watching a Narrative Dance Performance of 2.5 Hrs," *Dance Research* 29 (2011): 378–402; Catherine J. Stevens et al., "Cognition and the Temporal Arts: Investigating Audience Response to Dance Using PDAs That Record Continuous Data during Live Performance," *International Journal of Human-Computer Studies* 67, no. 9 (2009): 800–813; and Catherine J. Stevens et al., "Moving with and without Music: Scaling and Lapsing in Time in the Performance of Contemporary Dance," *Music Perception* 26, no. 5 (2009): 451–64.

3. Sian L. Beilock, "Grounding Cognition in Action: Expertise, Comprehension, and Judgment," *Progress in Brain Research* 174 (2009): 3–11.

4. Lawrence W. Barsalou, "Grounded Cognition," *Annual Review of Psychology* 59 (2008): 617–45.

5. Bettina Bläsing et al., "Neurocognitive Control in Dance Perception and Performance," *Acta Psychologica* 139 (2012): 300–308; and Vittorio Gallese et al., "Action Recognition in the Premotor Cortex," *Brain* 119 (1996): 593–609.

6. Emily S. Cross, Antonia F. de C. Hamilton, and Scott T. Grafton, "Building a Motor Simulation de Novo: Observation of Dance by Dancers," *Neuroimage* 31, no. 3 (2006): 1257–67; Cross et al., "Sensitivity of the Action Observation Network to Physical and Observational Learning," *Cerebral Cortex* 19, no. 2 (2009): 315–26; Cross et al., "Contorted and Ordinary Body Postures in the Human

Brain," *Experimental Brain Research* 204, no. 3 (2011): 397–407; Calvo-Merino et al., "Action Observation"; Calvo-Merino et al., "Seeing or Doing?"; Corinne Jola, Angharad Davis, and Patrick Haggard, "Proprioceptive Integration and Body Representation: Insights into Dancers' Expertise," *Experimental Brain Research* 213, nos. 2–3 (2011): 257–65; Corinne Jola et al., "Motor Simulation without Motor Expertise: Enhanced Corticospinal Excitability in Visually Experienced Dance Spectators," *PLoS ONE* 7, no. 3 (2012): e33343; Jola, Pollick, and Grosbras, "Arousal Decrease in 'Sleeping Beauty'"; Orgs et al., "Expertise in Dance," 3380–84; Guido Orgs, Nobuhiro Hagura, and Patrick Haggard, "Learning to Like It: Aesthetic Perception of Bodies, Movements and Choreographic Structure," *Consciousness and Cognition* 22 (2013): 603–12.

7. Nelson Cowan, "The Magical Number 4 in Short-term Memory: A Reconsideration of Mental Storage," *Behavioral and Brain Sciences* 24 (2000): 87–185; Fergus I. M. Craik and Robert S. Lockhart, "Levels of Processing: A Framework for Memory Research," *Journal of Verbal Learning and Verbal Behavior* 11 (1972): 671–84; and Klaus Oberauer, "Design for a Working Memory," *Psychology of Learning and Motivation* 51 (2009): 45–100.

8. Endel Tulving, "How Many Memory Systems Are There?," *American Psychologist* 40, no. 4 (1985): 385–98.

9. Jeremy M. Wolfe et al., *Sensation & Perception* (Sunderland, MA: Sinauer Associates Inc., 2012).

10. Patrick Haggard, "The Dancing Mind," on *All in the Mind* (Radio National, Australia, accessed March 19, 2005, http://www.abc.net.au/radionational/programs/allinthemind/the-dancing-mind/3442236).

11. Eveline Golomer and Philippe Dupui, "Spectral Analysis of Adult Dancers' Sways: Sex and Interaction Vision-Proprioception," *International Journal of Neuroscience* 105 nos. 1–4 (2000): 15–26; Jola, Davis, and Haggard, "Proprioceptive Integration and Body Representation"; Jill R. E. Ramsay and M. Jane Riddoch, "Position-Matching in the Upper Limb: Professional Ballet Dancers Perform with Outstanding Accuracy," *Clinical Rehabilitation* 15, no. 3 (2001): 324–30.

12. Haggard, "The Dancing Mind."

13. Catherine J. Stevens and Shirley McKechnie, "Thinking in Action: Thought Made Visible in Contemporary Dance," *Cognitive Processing* 6 (2005): 243–52.

14. Michael T. Ullman, "Contributions of Memory Circuits to Language: The Declarative/Procedural Model," *Cognition* 92 (2004): 231–70.

15. Stevens and McKechnie, "Thinking in Action."

16. *Modality* refers to the perceptual system that is activated or engaged by a particular task. Vision and audition (hearing) are both modalities. *Unimodal* refers to just one modality, such as vision. *Multimodal* refers to the engagement of multiple modalities. For example, watching dance is multimodal because it engages vision, audition, and motor systems. To say that knowledge is amodal is to assume that knowledge is in a form devoid of features of the perceptual system through which the knowledge was acquired. Propositional knowledge is amodal. *Embodied cognition*, by contrast, refers to knowledge that is grounded in and informed by the perceptual systems engaged in acquiring the knowledge.

17. Denis Burnham and Karen Mattock, "Auditory Development," in *The Wiley-Blackwell Handbook of Infant Development*, ed. J. Gavin Bremner and Theodore D. Wachs (Chichester, West Sussex, UK: Wiley-Blackwell, 2010), 81–119.

18. E. Glenn Schellenberg, Emmanuel Bigand, Benedicte Poulin-Charronnat, Cécilia Garnier,

and Catherine J. Stevens, "Children's Implicit Knowledge of Harmony in Western Music," *Developmental Science* 8 (2005): 551–66.

19. Leonard B. Meyer, *Emotion and Meaning in Music* (Chicago: University of Chicago Press, 1956); Jamshed J. Bharucha, "Tonality and Expectation," in *Musical Perceptions*, ed. Rita Aiello and John A. Sloboda (Oxford: Oxford University Press, 1994), 213–39; Ivar Hagendoorn, "Some Speculative Hypotheses about the Nature and Perception of Dance and Choreography," *Journal of Consciousness Studies* 11 (2004): 79–110.

20. Catherine J. Stevens et al., "Perceiving Dance: schematic expectations guide experts' scanning of a contemporary dance film," *Journal of Dance Medicine & Science* 14 (2010): 19–25.

21. K. Anders Ericsson and Herbert A. Simon, *Protocol Analysis: Verbal Reports as Data*, rev. ed. (Cambridge: MIT Press, 1984); Mary M. Omodei, Jim McLennan, and Alexander J. Wearing, "How Expertise Is Applied in Real-World Dynamic Environments: Head Mounted Video and Cued Recall as a Methodology for Studying Routines of Decision Making," in *The Routines of Decision Making*, ed. Tilmann Betsch and Susanne Haberstroh (Mahwah, NJ: Lawrence Erlbaum Associates, Publishers, 2005), 271–88.

22. Renee Glass, "The Effect of Information and Dance Experience on Psychological Responses to Contemporary Dance," in *Thinking in Four Dimensions: Creativity and Cognition in Contemporary Dance*, ed. Robin Grove, Catherine J. Stevens, and Shirley McKechnie (Carlton, Australia: Melbourne University Press, 2005), 107–21.

23. Renee Glass, "The Audience Response Tool (A.R.T.): The Impact of Choreographic Intention, Information and Dance Expertise on Psychological Reactions to Contemporary Dance" (PhD diss., University of Western Sydney, 2006).

24. A saccade is a rapid, jerky, simultaneous movement of both eyes in the same direction. A saccade directs the eyes to a new location. Eye movements or saccades are rapid, with the eyes moving as much as 500 degrees per second; eye fixations have durations of around 200–300 milliseconds.

25. Harold L. Kundel and Paul S. La Follette, "Visual Search Patterns and Experience with Radiological Image," *Radiology* 103 (1972): 523–28.

26. Tajana Opacic, Catherine J. Stevens, and Barbara Tillmann, "Unspoken Knowledge: Implicit Learning of Structured Human Dance Movement," *Journal of Experimental Psychology: Learning, Memory and Cognition* 35 (2009): 1570–77.

27. Anna Smith (1966–) is a practicing choreographer, educator, and community artist based in Melbourne, Australia. Her works have been presented in Canada, the United States, France, and China, as well as throughout Australia. She is the winner of two Green Room Awards for the choreographic works *Red Rain* (1999) and *Quiesence* (2001). Sue Healey (1962–) is an award-winning choreographer, educator, and dance-filmmaker based in Sydney, Australia. Her creative manifesto speaks to the production of a highly detailed movement language. Experimenting with form and perception, Healey creates dance for diverse spaces: theaters, specific sites, and the camera. Further information is available at http://www.suehealey.com.

28. Dick J. Bierman, Arnaud Destrebecqz, and Axel Cleeremans, "Intuitive Decision Making in Complex Situations: Somatic Markers in an Artificial Grammar Learning Task," *Cognitive, Affective, & Behavioral Neuroscience* 5 (2005): 297–305.

29. Examples of experimental stimuli can be found at http://katestevens.weebly.com/stimuli.html. Individual items of movement material for inclusion in trials of the experiment were selected

so that the position of the dancer in the final frame of each item was maximally different from the starting position in the next item. While the laws of physics and body morphology applied to movement material *within* an item, mismatching the dancer's ending position and starting position *across* items disrupted physical principles and morphology. For example, one item might end with the dancer upstage and prostrate on the floor, and the next item might begin with the dancer downstage and standing. Implicit knowledge is not available to conscious awareness and is not able to be verbalized, unlike explicit knowledge, which refers to conscious, declarative knowledge.

30. Rolf Reber, Norbert Schwarz, and Piotr Winkielman, "Processing Fluency and Aesthetic Pleasure: Is Beauty in the Perceiver's Processing Experience?" *Personality and Social Psychology Review* 8 (2004): 364–82; Karl K. Szpunar, E. Glenn Schellenberg, and Patricia Pliner, "Liking and Memory for Musical Stimuli as a Function of Exposure," *Journal of Experimental Psychology: Learning, Memory, and Cognition* 30 (2004): 370–81; Robert B. Zajonc, "Attitudinal Effects of Mere Exposure [Monograph]," *Journal of Personality and Social Psychology* 9 (1968): 1–27.

31. Opacic, Stevens, and Tillmann, "Unspoken Knowledge."

32. Catherine J. Stevens, Jane Ginsborg, and Garry Lester, "Backwards and Forwards in Space and Time: Recalling Dance Movement from Long-Term Memory," *Memory Studies* 4 (2011): 234–50.

33. Margaret Barr (1904–1991) had a choreographic career that spanned more than sixty years and three continents. Barr was born in Bombay, India, and raised in England, India, and the United States. Receiving her initial dance training from Geordie Graham, she later trained at Ruth St. Denis and Ted Shawn's Denishawn School, and with Martha Graham in New York. Barr's final forty years of practice took place in Sydney, Australia. She described her work as dance-drama because she was interested in both the inherent drama of the body in motion and its ability to create and sustain the human drama of her primarily narrative-based works. There were three interconnected strands in her approach to creativity: technique classes, improvisation, and the creative exploration of the rehearsal process. See Garry Lester, "Galvanising Community: Margaret Barr at Dartington Hall 1930–1934, Part 1," *Brolga: An Australian Journal about Dance* 25 (December, 2006): 39–49; and "Galvanising Community Part 2: Margaret Barr at Dartington Hall 1930–1934," *Brolga: An Australian Journal about Dance* 26 (June 2007): 39–55. Technique classes—the focus of the present study—consisted of a series of set studies performed to the driving rhythms and often deceptively simple melodies of Carl Orff's *Carmina Burana*. This choreographed material explored a broad range of movement dynamics from the elegant simplicity of lyrical studies to the extremes of strong, direct, thrusting sequences. For more on Barr's method see Lester, "Galvanising Community."

34. Duncan R. Godden and Alan D. Baddeley, "Context-Dependent Memory in Two Natural Environments: On Land and Underwater," *British Journal of Psychology* 66, no. 3 (1975): 325–31.

35. The experiment was designed in such a way that on some occasions dancers first recalled movement using their bodies and, on other occasions, first used the mannequin. There was no significant difference in the rate of recall for a dancer using her or his own body or the mannequin, suggesting that repetition was not necessary for recall using the mannequin. While the dancers became more confident using the mannequin over time, recall using the mannequin was as good as using their own bodies. The sample of dancers was very small, which may have contributed to the lack of a statistically significant difference; conducting a similar study with a larger sample is needed to draw a definitive conclusion concerning recall using one's own body versus a mannequin.

36. Jonah Lehrer, *Proust Was A Neuroscientist* (Melbourne, Australia: Text Publishing, 2007); Leonard Shlain, *Art and Physics: Parallel Vision in Space, Time, and Light* (New York: Harper Perennial,

2007); Semir Zeki, *Inner Vision: An Exploration of Art and the Brain* (Oxford: Oxford University Press, 1999).

37. Calvo-Merino et al., "Action Observation"; Calvo-Merino et al., "Seeing or Doing?"; Cross, Hamilton, and Grafton, "Building a Motor Simulation de Novo"; Cross et al., "Sensitivity"; Cross et al., "Contorted and Ordinary"; Jola et al., "Motor Stimulation"; Orgs et al., "Expertise"; Orgs, Hagura, and Haggard, "Learning to Like It."

38. Deirdre Reynolds and Matthew Reason, eds., *Kinesthetic Empathy in Creative and Cultural Practices* (Bristol, UK: Intellect, 2012); http://www.watchingdance.org/; and http://motionbank.org/en /research-2/.

39. Hauke Egermann et al., "Probabilistic Models of Expectation Violation Predict Psycho-physiological Emotional Responses to Live Concert Music," *Cognitive, Affective and Behavioural Neuro-science* 13, no. 3 (2013): 533–53; doi: 10.3758/s13415-013-0161-y; Stephen McAdams et al., "Influence of Large-Scale Form on Continuous Ratings in Response to a Contemporary Piece in a Live Concert Setting," *Music Perception* 22 (2004): 297–350; and Catherine J. Stevens et al., "In the Heat of the Moment: Audience Real Time Response to Live Music and Dance Performance," in *Coughing and Clapping: Investigating Audience Experience*, ed. Karen Burland and Stephanie Pitts (Aldershot, Hampshire, UK: Ashgate, 2014), 69–88.

40. Beatriz Calvo-Merino et al., "Towards a Sensorimotor Aesthetics of Performing Art," *Consciousness and Cognition* 17 (2008): 911–22; and Emily S. Cross and Luca F. Ticini, "Neuroaesthetics and Beyond: New Horizons in Applying the Science of the Brain to the Art of Dance," *Phenomenology and the Cognitive Sciences* 11 (2012): 5–16.

THE STORIES IN OUR BODIES

The other day I was jostled into a memory. Simply walking up a short set of stairs, my body suddenly remembered what day it was. I say it was my body re-membering because that is where I felt it. It was not a thought connected to a date and time. It was not a moment connected to a memory. It was a physical interaction with time—a sudden condensation of time and place. I wondered what this sudden feeling was and then my mind caught up. . . . And then I re-membered.

> *My legs felt strong.*
> *My chest felt heavy, as though it wanted to lie down and rest. I stood, my chest tipped and curved forward. I kept having to pull my neck back into a more comfortable alignment. Then nothing, then the jostling. The ground felt very humus-y and moist, which is maybe not what it actually was.*
> —rehearsal notes 4/7/12; report on dancing while imagining the ground beneath the hundred-year-old gymnasium at Headlands Center for the Arts

I think of the bodies that are no longer here, that from them there is a lateral source of energy that encircles the world, an energy that moves from body to earth and back to body—it connects us to all beings past and present.

> *Slow and steady breathing from the corners of the eyes.*
> —rehearsal notes 4/9/12

Past, present, and future in our bodies.
Current: the moment now, equal to the present.
Future: what will be in a moment and then a moment again.
Future also: when we die we become energy—soil, tree, leaf . . .
Eggs, semen, thought reside as future, possible.
Future generations and future thought held in our very present/current bodies.
Past: who we come from. Who made who. Who held who in whose womb and arms over generations. Whose thought moved your thought to now and beyond. It is simultaneous because it all exists at once. Right now.
The present inclusive of our past pasts and the future, possible.

Time does fold in on itself. Days and days and days and then a day your body remembers. Like my moment on the stairs. Also, other moments I recall: the ice cream I tasted before and then after great-grandma Lena died. Though they are two separate moments, I remember them as one and the memory is wrapped up in a million moments that bring me to my now.

Can I lead this story by letting you know that basketball was my first true love? More than anything I devoted myself to it, to the ball, to the floor, to my team, to my coach. I tried being devoted to other things too—a boyfriend, good grades, friends, but really, I wanted only to play, to be better, to win. We were midseason when great-grandma died and I needed to go. I was asked to go. And this is where my body brings me: to the plane, with my dad. A small plane to Bethel, Alaska. The copilot handed us ice cream sandwiches. We tasted them. We flew. We landed. We stayed with cousins. My dad's cousins. Everyone was cousins! There were days great-grandma was in her house and we were all there too. We drank tea, we talked, her sisters sang. Ceremonies and card games, food and drink, family getting to know one another again or for the first time. We grieved and we celebrated. The weather got bad. We hunkered down.

The words I remember—they were clear and sparse: we touch down in this life, we live to honor, we go, those who remain honor again. There is a right way to live.

My grandpa too, he was there. In ashes. And we let him go into the frozen Kuskokwim. How can I tell you this? In words it doesn't even make sense, all of this history and generation upon generation folded into one time and many bodies. But see, my body, it remembers so much that now, more than twenty years later, it is as if the wind is blowing, my great-grandma is being sung for and we are standing on the frozen Kuskokwim. Me, my dad, my auntie, a cousin, an idling snowmachine, a small bottle of something to pour down . . . and we hardly need to fight back tears because we all cry in front of each other all the time anyway and also because this fierce wind freezes them whole as they come. There are more days. And then we get back on the small plane. The copilot hands us ice cream sandwiches. We taste them and I tuck back into my seat, hear the words great-grandma's sisters sang, feel the wind, my feet on that river and in her house, standing with all my relatives and cry, cry, cry. This sweet melting taste brings me immediately back to the before and brings all moments in between—family, funeral, weather, singing, words—closer. I look over at my dad and he is crying too.

The longing and the pulling. There was an actual pull toward west and also down, like the floor was tipping down, even though, well, maybe it does slope. And there was something in the distance and a knowledge of that distance—a measurement which came in the form of an imagined shot. Bullet traveling. The ground was forest.

—rehearsal notes 4/7/12; report on how it feels to dance in the hundred-year-old gymnasium at Headlands Center for the Arts while imagining the ground of my home in Sterling, Alaska

I mentioned my love of basketball. When I got home from great-grandma's funeral though, something changed. I wasn't played. I sat on the bench. I waited. I practiced. I played as hard as I could. I waited. I sat on the bench. I got angry. I moved to the end of the bench. I got up to get some water from the faucet around the corner near the locker room. My mom was waiting for me. Basketball left me. I did not go back.

A lower feeling, I could name it, for a second: fear. In my solar plexus. And wide, flat land. A river. A Mississippi. I could see it but I did not get pulled to it. A love came forth, a recognition. And lots of dancing. And I realize it is the land where I have done most of my dancing. Moving was inevitable. I wanted to keep moving and it came easily. "God" was pulling toward down.

—rehearsal notes 4/7/12; report on how it feels to dance in the hundred-year-old gymnasium at Headlands Center for the Arts while imagining dancing on the ground at the river flats in Minneapolis, which is where I live now

I think of our bodies as EVERYTHING: our bodies are culture, history, present, and future, all at once. Out of respect for and trust in our bodies and collective memories, I give equal weight to story and image, to movement and stillness, to what I imagine and to what I do not know.

A tipping slope. A whale.
—rehearsal notes 4/7/12 and 3/27/12

This is why I dance and make dances—because the known and unknown is juicy, because dancing brings my cells simultaneously to the past, present, and future. It's a shaking up of what I think I know. It's a transformation. The stories in my body and in our collective memories exist in forms beyond language. And I trust them. I trust in a lifetime of memories that can be passed from one reality to another. I trust the senses. I trust that smell and taste, like the ice cream before and after great-grandma died can conflate time.

When I make dances I rely on this trust. Why this moment now for this arm to raise, for this head to bow? Why, when I think about dancing on the ground below the building I am in, does my chest feel heavy—like I need to lie down onto the ground? What will happen if I do?

I try it. I lie down.

And maybe it's not right—maybe I need to get back up because, of course, there is a mix of form and trust that goes into building this dance. Here is what I have learned so far from my particular mix of form and trust: I acknowledge my ancestors in movement; everything is dance; to think of the ground when I walk on the floor brings me closer to the world; to thank death—to think of death as a cycle; to have ceremony; to pay attention to things, wind, buildings, sound as I head to the studio; to pay attention to animals and plants that I pass or live with; to pay attention to the energies that exist from the lives that have passed; to recognize that we are here now and that we will all be gone one day, too.

With slow and steady breathing.
From the outside corners of the eyes so that your view is wide/expansive.
With all of your senses.
With a willingness to look above, below, to all sides.
With trust and imagination.
—rehearsal notes 4/10/12; on how to watch dances I make; also, I think these are good instructions for life

Our bodies are EVERYTHING. They hold EVERYTHING and they are also the EVERYTHING, possible. Our bodies hold the stories from our lives as well as the stories from our ancestors. Our bodies remember. They know a history we cannot always name. They hold what is good to hold and also what causes pain. They hold consciously and unconsciously. Traumas remain for generations. Sickness comes back to itself. Loves hold tight. I wonder if what our bodies know can become accessible enough to change pattern when needed? To reverse trauma? To leave the possible as a glorious possible? To let some loves lie down and stay? Can this archive of living knowledge, body memory, and experience be of use? Can we learn to trust what our bodies know and remember as real information? Can others learn to respect this information, letting the stories and experiences held in our bodies be of good use to the world? Would it lead to an understanding beyond that which I can grasp?

The whale enters the room, undulates its spine, rolls its huge belly forward, opens its
mouth and water pours over its teeth, out the door, and down the stairs. There is the

113

smell of rain. The whale's soft eye is gazing at everyone in the room. The whale takes a deep breath And then there is the sound of breath. The floor sinks a bit under its weight, creaks, and then There is a sound the world has never heard. The people in the room drop their heads And their shoulders Then their arms, their hands to the floor. They are crawling forward in the sound, each one of them Toward the whale and they want to touch it, they want to remember, they want to hear, they want to rock into that belly They are whispering, they are whispering without knowing they are whispering the ongoing, the everlasting, the forgotten sounds The sounds they forgot Of their mothers. The sounds their mothers made when they first entered the world.

—rehearsal notes 3/27/12

My hands remind me of life another time as I held death. My hands hold a little box and I viscerally remember an entire life. How it felt to hold him—not only HOW, but it was, in that moment, that my hands were holding him again. I could feel the weight of his body. I looked at the box and knew it was not him and yet my hands felt as if they were holding him. And I cared for him in that moment, again. I pet him. I carried him. And his body changed. I could feel all of that again in my hands. I could feel his bones move and his fur—how it got coarser. I could feel an exchange of love between us, and it was a gift. I remember knowing he was giving that moment to me, a last moment to hold him. And all the moments we had shared came through that one last moment—I was feeling memory and he was giving those moments to me. Time was folding in on itself.

There is MATTER that moves back to the earth upon death, but there is ENERGY too, the storied energy of our experiences. What a gift—to give these moments away! Could I do the same? Give my moments, memories, loves, experiences away? Do we choose that upon death? My grandma on my mother's side, she has lost her immediate memory and the connection between her past and her present. But somehow, because we are all still by her side that connection exists. We hold what we know of her and her time and she, somewhere, holds the rest. Though she can't access them all the time, her stories are alive, they exist still in her body, as vital as blood, muscle, bone. They communicate with us. Maybe one day she will gift her memories, her stories to one of us and we'll remember things we thought we had forgotten. Maybe they will pass on as energy somewhere else.

The stories in our bodies; they jostle us from time to time. Come at us from nowhere. They pull us in directions we didn't think we would go. They remind. They teach. I think they rest sometimes, too. I trust them and try to listen to them with all of my body.

III. The Body in the Archive

To rethink the body and the archive is to precipitate change in the nature and existence of both as well as in our understanding of the doubled nature of bodies in the archive. The phrase "body in the archive" refers to both the body of the researcher who enters the archive probing its contents as well as those bodies within the archive that the researcher seeks. Once the archive is entered, neither body is likely to remain unchanged.

There are many bodies in philosopher Michel Foucault's account of body in the archive—bodies of the mad, the military, the sexual, the ascetic, the normalized, the deviant—but among these bodies is Foucault himself. Working for long stretches of time in the various archives of Paris and elsewhere, he described the sensual pleasures, the "feverish laziness,"[1] the sense of delight derived from his research, as well as his drive to "plunge body and soul"[2] into the dust to retrieve the bodied subjects revealed in the archival materials. Eschewing the photocopier as a machine that destroyed the charm of the text, Foucault frequently hand-copied the parchment and rag-paper pages that documented the lives he handled.

Foucault filtered these bodies analytically though the language and rhetoric of files, dossiers, statistics, letters, memoirs, and decrees, but he also acknowledged the intensity of his physical response to their textual ghosts. He was compelled, in part, by his descent through the dusty academic archives to recognize the lived experience represented by the documented accounts of those bodies he touched through paper.[3] Foucault's genealogical approach revealed that *descent*, as a noun comprising the tangled lines from then to now, was completely attached to body.[4] Perhaps, then, *descent* as a verb is bodied as well: the body in the archive is the researcher in descent, her body falling toward multiple origins and in the descent falling into the archive that is our knowing body.

In this part of the book, David Gordon's archive takes the form of "artist's statements" that are frequently demanded by funding agencies and institutions and that prod his memories of the methods and motivations of making or re-making dances drawn from the body of work. Laurajane Smith pairs us, side by side, with visitors as they enter the archive, materialized in her essay as heritage sites serving as cultural and historical "theaters of memory." Sarah Crowner suggests that paintings are archives of bodies in action: paint on the canvas imprinted by the body, whose gestures cover its surface. Nancy Goldner investigates dancers as interpretive bodies by looking at how or if they utilize the archive as they learn to inhabit two historic roles as their own: Giselle and Apollo. Patricia Hoffbauer recalls her preparation for her group performance work, *Para-dice*, drawing from her research and her years as an immigrant and dancer in New York to consider how the marginalized body in performance challenges both the traditional structure of the archive and its exclusionary practices as well as the colonization of these bodies through language, media, and "official" histories.

—Linda Caruso Haviland

NOTES

1. Michel Foucault, "7 January, 1976," in *"Society Must Be Defended": Lectures at the Collège de France, 1975–1976*, ed. Mauro Bertani and Alessandro Fontana, trans. David Macey (New York: Picador, 2003), 5.

2. Michel Foucault, interview, 1977, in *Dits et écrits 1954–1988*, Vol. 1, ed. Daniel Defert and François Ewald (Paris: Gallimard "Quarto," 2001), 372, quoted in Michael Sheringham, "Michel Foucault, Pierre Rivière and the Archival Imaginary," *Comparative Critical Studies*, 8, nos. 2–3 (2011): 237.

3. Michel Foucault, "Lives of Infamous Men," in *Power*, ed. James D. Faubion, Vol. 3 of *Essential Works of Foucault 1954–84*, ed. Paul Rabinow, trans. Robert Hurley (New York: The New Press, 2001), 158.

4. Michel Foucault, *The Archaeology of Knowledge and the Discourse on Language*, trans. A. M. Sheridan Smith (New York: Vintage Books, 2010), 7.

& WE SHOULD LIVE AND BE WELL
Five Artist Statements, 1995–2007

David Gordon's text is the thinking body. His five artist statements collected here speak to the reader about the visceral life of words, their accumulation over time, how words are also gestures. Gordon enumerates the necessity for the long view, of working with performers who shape both process and product. Gordon's writing take us inside the artist's re-purposing of time, how he makes something new from what has gone before. These statements, written for various external reasons, reveal the internal and constant transformation of the artist's mind. Does it matter when — or if — this material becomes an archive? For Gordon it is simply the way things are.
— Bill Bissell and Linda Caruso Haviland

1995, before the middle middle
Some time after the beginning but before the middle middle I begin to acknowledge to myself I am not entirely original. I am not an inventor of dance steps. I am a re-organizer of available movement. I am not an inventor of language. I am only an obsessive re-orderer of words. Rather than have my deficiencies discovered & trounced by others I decide to announce re-use of my own materials boldly & to celebrate my right to enjoy re-appearance & change in context & to revel in how many ways there are to skin a cat. This, however, makes accurate bio life a little complicated & nobody has ever been interested
enough (including me)
to force the issue.

For instance, in 1991, I have a job teaching for 11 wks @ UCLA when *Punch & Judy Get Divorced* surfaces as a wkshp for students. It morphs into a KTCA/Alive TV show w/ music by Carl Stallings & text by me for
2 Punches, 2 Judys, 2 dogs, 2 clowns, 2 devils & 2 babies & evolves into a dance work w/ same music but w/ no text for

White Oak Dance Project w/ Mikhail Baryshnikov as Punch & Valda Setterfield as Judy.

It grows a 2nd act, 1 year later, during another 11 teaching wks @ UCLA called *Life Without Men*. A world of divorced & widowed & spinster Judys live alone together & all the Judys are acted by all the men and women actors of *Punch & Judy Get Divorced* w/ more wkshps & w/ actors from the Mark Taper Forum in LA & later @ The Guthrie Theater in Mpls w/ Guthrie actors & later acts 1 & 2 become a music/theater piece commissioned by American Music Theater Festival & American Repertory Theater w/ new music by Edward Barnes & lyrics written in collaboration w/ Ain Gordon and Arnold Weinstein. So, how much of what I do has how much of how many other pieces in them is a bit iffy to figure.

I can say w/ confidence I improvised dialogue for the 1st time in *Random Breakfast* in 1963 @ the Judson Church & in 1975 in the same concert as *Chair, Alternative 1 Through 5* @ Paula Cooper Gallery was *One Act Play* in which I asked Valda Setterfield to "tell me all about it" & I wrote 6 pages of monologue for her & I stood entirely & patiently still nodding & smiling every once in a while as she told me all about it.

I know that person, I am that dance, circa 2000
Movement is movement & dances are collections of steps (possibly gorgeous) which (once in a while) add up to something greater than their parts. Dances may be glorious reverberating abstractions or eloquent highclass dance/story telling or thoughtful emotion provoking non linear narratives. But, dancing no matter what, always seems to me to be about the people who do it.

Dancers touch each other, avoid each other, take each other's weight, give each other focus or deny it. They dance in unison, in & out of sync, in & out of shared time & space. They pay attention to each other & the power of their attention has dramatic resonance. The social/sensual implications of pairs of people reacting physically to words or music, or words as music, or silence, or the sound of their own footsteps or each others breathing can be recognized & understood. "Oh, I know that person. I am that dancer."

I make dances for the pleasure of meeting the dancers who do them. I spend hours in the studio inventing, reinventing, organizing, reorganizing, agonizing & recognizing valuable movement qualities in others that I do not possess. I take on projects I don't know how to do & I relish the dangerous journey.

Looking past my own text, 2005

End of 2003, having written & choreographed & directed & designed dance & theater for the last many years, I began to
look past my own text. For a couple of years in a couple of
regional theaters I directed plays & recently directed & choreographed a workshop production based on Bertolt Brechts
Roundheads & Pointheads @ Actors Studio where I'm a member.
Turns out the Brecht adventure has been an instigating factor in a new dance journey.

January of 2004 Pick Up Co presented, in collaboration w/
Danspace, a new evening of theater/dance called *Dancing Henry
Five*, based on *Henry V* by William Shakespeare w/ music by
William Walton from his 1940's film score for Laurence Olivier & w/ voice over by Olivier & Christopher Plummer, etc.
In 2003 I studied *Henry V* & French/English history & recordings of the play & the Olivier film & the score & the news of
the US @ war on CNN & BBC & I wrote words to be spoken along
w/ words of Shakespeare (took chutzpah) & I paired recorded
Shakespeare w/ comments spoken live by a 2nd chorus (avoiding,
I prayed, didacticism) re: deficit, war & government shena-
nigan. The French scene & wooing scene, as classic lyric duet
& trio variations, to the music of text conveyed narrative
w/ re-imagined post-modern aesthetic. I used filmic images,
dissolves & wipes physically & reused stage objects including
my folding metal chairs, rolling ladders & painted cloths.

Summer 2004 I worked on Ionesco's *The Chairs* w/ a new translation by Michael Feingold (performed that fall @ Barbican
in London, On the Boards in Seattle & Next Wave Festival @
BAM Harvey). Further investigation of a classic literary
work of historical significance as the jumping off point to
new physical movement married w/ new commissioned music by
Michael Gordon. Valda Setterfield played the Old Woman & I
played the Old Man.

I continue to engage w/ classic theatrical texts & conventions acknowledging integrity of intention (as I understand

it) of the artists. I research politics & economics under which artists worked to produce their art & relate these to contemporary conditions under which I work. I began, recently, to search out translations of Aristophanes *The Birds* & to write dialogue for character of Aristophanes who comments on his own script & being forced, in January of 2006, to collaborate w/ living artists (like me) in dance/theater in NY. Trying to make dance/theater that manages physical & visual & emotional & musical & intellectual relevance to the time in which I exist & to the time in which this art product will exist is an invented task but the "what if" factor, after all these years, is still a driving force.

25 years later, circa 2005 (or 2007)

Movement work I spent my lucky long career making has from
1st Judson Church shows referenced (at times admittedly perversely) ballet & post modern aesthetics, popular & classical
music, film history, current TV, social behavior & politics—
using spoken & visual arts including painted & sculptural objects & insisting everything moves!

Trying Times is created in 1982 after a lucky year of interviews for New Yorker profile by Arlene Croce. I spend eve-
nings at NYC Ballet, seeing Balanchine's *Apollo* many times,
before I realize a virus had entered my brain. The idea of
a muse is a little grand for me but I begin to consider it.
(My company included 3 women who inform my work—Susan Eschel-
bach, Margaret Hoeffel & my wife Valda Setterfield.) I dare
to dream of taking on the Stravinsky score & the mighty reputation of this particular Balanchine ballet.

The next very lucky circumstance is meeting up w/ visual artist Power Booth. We talk & Power designs & paints 4' by 8'
frames, cloths & boards which we called "visual devices" to
avoid the conventional theater term "set" since I am determined they won't "set" still.

This collaborative relationship establishes a precedent for
my new work for years. (Use the actual objects as partners
in rehearsal w/ dancers & actors.) The actual objects make
their way into the next 4 years of actual work as I continue
to take advantage of their decorative power while investigating their meaningful partnering identities. (Last year the
original striped canvas cloths are used as ships & skirts in
Dancing Henry Five.)

My luck continues: David White @ DTW commissions *Trying Times*
and offers a lengthy performance run. Philip Sandstrom, resi-
dent light designer agrees to light the piece. I construct
movement & dialogue for the entire score w/ 1 intermission &
end w/ a mock trial in which Valda Setterfield is my lawyer,

defending me for making dancers talk & having the nerve to bypass my "post modern" credentials. The chutzpah to use this music attracts audience from the many dance worlds & leads to 2 ABT commissions & a commission from the GRCOP of the Paris Opera. I get to use Power's frames some more.

In 2007 DTW is willing to produce the 25th anniversary *Trying Times* in the new larger theater David White built before he left NY. Philip Sandstrom is willing to light the work w/ the lighting system the designed before he left DTW. Power Booth, now a Dean of the Arts, is willing to create new frames, boards & cloths & I admit, uncharacteristically, I'm will-ing to have another go at this piece. I still work, luckily, in the same rehearsal space where *Trying Times* was made & I look at the original record tape & I'm impressed (yes, I am) w/ range of movement, design, response to Stravinsky music & use of dialogue in the fragmented narrative journey that cul-minates in the trial & the music's glorious end.

During the last 2 years I have occasion as a member of Cen-ter For Creative Research (CCR) to spend time at a number of universities discussing a continued absence of dialogue be-tween students of arts disciplines w/ each other in academia & between students of arts disciplines & anybody else in Aca-demia. *Trying Times* is an attempt to pierce art form silos & to pursue positive movement dialogue between aesthetics.

One artist's disintegrating paper trail, 2007

I have begun to assess & catalogue 50 years of photographs,
contact sheets, slides, original negatives, audio tapes (cas-
sette & reel to reel), posters, flyers, mailers, original
typed & handwritten scripts (before I learned to use a lap-
top), costumes (some handmade by me), numerous administrative
files as well as beta & VHS tapes and master tapes (recorded
rehearsal, recorded live performance & created for TV broad-
cast). A majority of these materials are currently housed in
my studio, my company office & two storage spaces.

If I must begin to look back over my shoulder then a fusion
of archeological dig plus first-person rigorous recollection
& critical annotation w/ a contemporary eye would actually
interest me.

I was ambivalent when I received the 1st of 3 NEA American
Masterpiece grants but w/ great frequency (& practicality)
we go where the money is. I watched the original record video
of the 1983 work *Trying Times* (for the 1st time in 25 years)
& chose to remove the color & to project that video during
performance. I located the original dancers for permission
to use their images so the new dancers might perform with the
original cast. Valda Setterfield danced variations on her 25
year old solo with her own projected image. I called it *Trying Times (remembered)* & 6 original cast members showed up in
LA & @ the 25th Anniversary @ DTW in NYC (1982 original com-
missioner). These performers are out there—for now. I would
like to initiate a rigorous video-interview process. Not a
trip down memory lane but a compilation of competing memories—documentation of the true multiplicity surrounding the
ephemeral form of live dance performance.

Old Work as New Work is my name for this process of recre-
ation & its archival relative. I was awarded a 2nd NEA American Masterpiece grant (this time through the NEA Present-
ing Program) to reproduce *Shlemiel the First* (1964). My long
time stage manager revealed his cache of original blueprints,

tapes, programs & notes. We kept new notes as we recast, re-hearsed & readied for Montclair 2010 performance. "Archiv-ing," I now believe, might frequently begin while a work is coming into existence instead of a long time after it's over.

I just received a 3rd NEA American Masterpiece grant for *Dancing Henry Five* (2004). I am gathering related materials together before we begin to recast & rehearse so new per-formers might get a look at the archival history of this work as they approach it's next, newest & possibly final live existence. This will not stop me form radically reworking those parts that need the work.

It's vital to me that the design of this archive be repre-sentative of & compatible w/ original creative impulses. The style w/ which art is documented should, as much as is prac-tically possible, be consistent w/ style(s) in which the art was originally conceived & produced. In this way, at least as long as I am here to facilitate, history is a lively dia-logue between creator & multiple viewpoints of past & present & aesthetics & economics & politics & performers body mem-ory whenever possible rather than one artist's disintegrat-ing paper trail.

THE EMBODIED PERFORMANCE OF MUSEUM VISITING
Sacred Temples or Theaters of Memory?

Heritage can be defined as a form of embodied practice and performance through which we come to understand aspects of the past in the present, so that our sense of the past informs both the present and the plans we make for the future. Such performances may be complex and nuanced or banal and everyday occurrences, but they engage our imagination and feelings and animate practices of personal and social remembering and forgetting.

This definition of heritage stands in opposition to two views of heritage: (1) commonsense understandings of heritage and (2) national and international heritage policy, which defines heritage as those self-evident things or places that represent individual or collective identity and are both inherited and preserved by families, museums, or government agencies. Commonsense definitions tend to assume that these objects have innate and immutable meaning and value while providing limited conceptual space in which to think about how people interact with these places or objects. I argue that these things are not in themselves "heritage," but rather become heritage through the ways that people engage with them. Considering heritage as embodied performances, in which the body physically interacts with certain objects, places, or spaces, reconceptualizes heritage as a moment of action. This action couples embodied emotional and intellectual responses to create and re-create the meaning and value that the past may possess in the present.

Heritage performances inform the processes of negotiating and exploring the cultural, social, and political values that individuals or groups may wish to take from the past and employ in the present, for a range of contemporary needs and concerns. These performances are often, but not inevitably, centered on ways of expressing individual or collective identities or on understanding and perceiving the identities of others. The definition of heritage I am offering here does not negate the importance of protecting sites, artifacts, or places. Rather, I posit that heritage is not "found" but is created through practices and embodied performances of conservation, presentation, and visiting strategies, each of which has important social and political consequences.

Drawing on interviews with visitors to museums and heritage sites in the United States, this essay argues that the heritage practices or the embodied performances of "visiting" exhibitions and sites produce knowledge, emotions, and experiences that individuals use to mediate the meaning of the past. The meanings thus constructed, and embodied by the visit, may be used in a variety of ways to address the contemporary social and political needs and concerns of the performers.

HERITAGE: MATERIAL, INTANGIBLE, OR PERFORMATIVE?

Traditionally, heritage has been defined as material or tangible sites, places, or artifacts that are fragile, nonrenewable, and finite resources, which the current generation must care for and pass on to the future. National and international organizations exist to manage and protect such resources, while history and cultural museums collect and exhibit movable material culture deemed to have heritage value—that is, to be representative of historical, social, cultural, or national collectives. More recently, and certainly since the ratification of UNESCO's *Convention for the Safeguarding of Intangible Cultural Heritage* in 2003,[1] a new category of heritage as "intangible" has been identified, so that recognition can be afforded to cultural and social events, such as those involving music, food, dance, and storytelling, as well as festivals, among other events and performances. This new category acknowledges the embodied nature of some of these events or performances and recognizes that individuals may be identified as bearing knowledge or skills of heritage value.

However, both definitions of heritage are framed by an "authorized heritage discourse" (AHD), which is based on perceptions of heritage that arose in Western Europe in the late nineteenth century, and which has been heavily influenced by archaeologists, art historians, and architects.[2] This discourse establishes a hierarchy of heritage values wherein the tangible or material heritage perceived as representing a nation is regarded as most significant, while intangible heritage, defined by international conventions and other documents as intrinsically "community" based, is defined as possessing less overall or "universal" value.[3] In effect the AHD privileges disembodied heritage; that is, material heritage is often valorized for its aesthetic, historical, or educational values, and it is imagined to consist of objects that will be passively gazed upon by tourists and other visitors. These sites of authorized heritage are defined and stewarded by heritage experts, then placed on national and state or provincial site registers, and sometimes on UNESCO's World Heritage List itself, or collected by local, regional, or national museums. Under the AHD, furthermore, it is only experts who are seen as legitimately engaged in any embodied or active way with material or tangible heritage. Within the heritage studies literature there is a significant body of criticism of heritage activities that step outside of the frameworks established by the AHD; that is, when communities, tourism, and other nonexpert interest groups become involved in utilizing heritage, this literature warns that such use can yield "bogus history," cultish fabrication, or maudlin nostalgia.[4] David Lowenthal notes that heritage is not history, although it can enliven historical study; however, he also disparagingly observes that "heritage is not an inquiry into the past but a celebration of it, not an effort to know what actually happened but a profession of faith in a past tailored to present-day purposes."[5]

Lowenthal makes a number of assumptions here: first, that the past can somehow be understood without reference to the present, and second, that heritage, as engaged outside of authorized settings, consists of a blind, unquestioning, and uncritical celebration. A considerable number of current-day researchers, both within and outside the discipline of history, resist these assumptions, asserting that an objective exploration of the past, uninfluenced by the contemporary context of the researcher, is impossible. History is a subjective process, albeit pursued within specific systematic and disciplinary frameworks.[6] I am more concerned, however, with Lowenthal's second assumption that heritage is simply a form of "faith," because this characterization tends to dismiss both the legitimacy of heritage and its consequences. Heritage performances can indeed be uncritical celebrations, but they can also constitute a critical and mindful negotiation over, and enquiry into, the meaning of the past. Heritage is one way of knowing and understanding the past and its meaning for the present. To understand how heritage can be both a critical and an uncritical inquiry into the past, I return here to my claim that heritage is an embodied performance.

My argument is based on the observation that for something to be called heritage it has to be used. Under the AHD, heritage is often perceived as something that should be left untouched and preserved as it was "found" or collected, or placed in museums so that it may be inherited unaltered by future generations. This practice is underpinned by assumptions that sites and places are inherently valuable and does not recognize the subjective and attributed nature of heritage values. The values and meanings given to material or intangible heritage are subjective and context-specific. For example, heritage sites become significant not because of the events that may have occurred at or around them, but because those events are understood to have meaning and value in the present for understandings of self, nation, and community. I draw on the work of James Wertsch, who notes that we use a range of cultural tools to help us remember and that remembering is an active process that continually reshapes and reworks the understanding of our memories.[7] In short, memories are not something individuals or groups simply "have" and recall, regardless of the social context of that recalling. I have argued elsewhere that nations, communities, individuals, and institutions such as museums use heritage sites and objects to help them remember the past and in that process redefine and renegotiate what the past means for the present.[8]

In a sense, heritage sites and museums become places where remembering (and indeed, forgetting) occurs through the practices we engage in to protect, preserve, and interpret them. Thus, in accumulating museum collections or national registers or lists of important historic places, institutions and governments are themselves making heritage. They are creating a particular representation and interpretation of the past by what they choose to see as significant and worthy of being listed. As Barbara Kirshenblatt-Gimblett notes, the creation and display of museum exhibitions is itself a cultural production and performance of particular cultural meanings.[9] Kirshenblatt-Gimblett draws attention to the performative nature of museum exhibitions and the displaying of heritage sites, arguing that objects and sites are animated by and thus come to perform the knowledge of the curator or interpretative staff. She suggests that displaying or exhibiting frequently transforms what is shown into heritage.

In developing the idea of heritage as performance, I wish to stress that I do not mean the idea of performance as defined by the concept of intangible heritage discussed above, which includes things such as music or storytelling performances (and which informs the AHD). These events may be part of an overall heritage performance, in much the same way as preserving or visiting a historic house is. Rather, in developing the idea of performance, I draw on Diana Taylor's observation that "we learn and transmit knowledge through embodied action, through cultural agency, and by making choices."[10] Indeed, as she argues, embodied practice, such as museum or heritage site visiting, is a way of knowing and exploring new and different ways of understanding, which can serve as a mnemonic practice that facilitates the transmission and communication of individual and social/collective memory. It is, as Raphael Samuel and Jorma Kalela would define it, a way of history making done outside the confines of formal historical disciplines.[11] The way historic sites and artifacts are managed, protected, and exhibited is, as already noted, a performative process.

This idea of performance, however, also allows acknowledgment of "unauthorized" performance, performances that create their own knowledge and understandings that may sit outside, or perhaps even complement, authorized and disciplinary understandings. As Taylor notes, the idea of performance can cover a very broad, and perhaps unhelpful, range of behaviors, both conventional and unconventional.[12]

Considering heritage as a performance, however—as an embodied act of meaning making and knowledge transmission—opens up the possibility that heritage can be used by individuals and subnational collectives or communities to create and re-create their own meanings. The idea of the performative also allows us to bring in ideas of knowledge production that engage directly with subjective ideas of emotion, imagination, and memory. Issues of emotion and imagination have traditionally been dealt with by rationalist forms of understanding, knowledge production, and empirical inquiry in unsatisfying ways and are often dismissed, as Lowenthal has done, as irrational or mindless celebration.[13] As illustrated here, however, imagination and emotion are important elements in the heritage performance.

If we accept that remembering is a creative process, in which new meanings and understandings of the past are continually remade, then it is important to acknowledge, as Emily Keightley and Michael Pickering point out, that this process requires imagination. They developed the idea of mnemonic imagination to identify the dynamic that occurs as people reconstruct and negotiate the past in order to inform the present and future through performative acts of remembering, which are animated by imagination.[14] Performative acts of remembering may be personal (as in the examples in this essay) or they may be collective, as in public acts of commemoration and remembering in which people do not have a personal memory of the commemorated event. They are performative, however, in the sense that a memory does not simply describe something one "has" but something one does: remembering is itself an active process.[15]

Alison Landsberg's conceptualization of "prosthetic memory" also provides an account of performative remembering. Similar to Keightley and Pickering, Landsberg notes not only the importance of imagination but also the role of emotions. She describes the imaginative and emotional encounters that people have with historical narratives in places such as museums, people who may have no firsthand memory of the events discussed but nonetheless take up that narrative as personal and deeply felt memory.[16] In this theorization, the physicality of the objects contained in exhibitions lends a certain sense of "reality" to the secondhand, or prosthetic, memories being created, and the museums become "transferential spaces" that facilitate the uptake of these memories. Importantly, Landsberg notes that these memories will be based on an understanding of difference. They are not "real" in the sense of how those who experienced the events firsthand would feel that reality; rather, they become emotionally real as the space between the historical narrative and the created prosthetic memories is bridged by empathetic emotions.[17]

The issue of empathy is important here. While there has been some criticism of the idea of empathy as a hollow acknowledgment of difference (much like the term "tolerance"), it nonetheless identifies a capacity for acknowledging a connection with another that, if offered and experienced deeply and with sincerity, is key in facilitating the heritage performance.[18] Imagination is central in facilitating the way emotions, and particularly empathy, may be used in cognition. There is now a large and growing literature that argues that emotion, rather than impairing rationality, is actually essential for the exercise of reason, memory, and the development of knowledge and understanding. As Sue Campbell states, "the emotion through which we represent the past is a significant component of recollective accuracy,"[19] as the emotional truth or authenticity of our emotional responses to the past informs the degree of confidence we place in remembering and the memories this process reproduces.[20] In turn, imagination allows the development of linkages between emotions and memories, as well as comprehending the significance of past experiences for understanding present ones. These are processes that are experienced; they are thus embodied performative ways of engaging with the past and making it significant for the present.

What is particularly illuminating is that surveys of North Americans and Australians have revealed a wide public suspicion of and boredom with formal accounts of history, as these surveys continually illustrate that many people associate history with dull and dusty school lessons.[21] However, the surveys have also revealed that individuals retain a deep engagement with the past that is often not associated with formal definitions of history found in universities or museums. Much of the heritage and museum studies literature assumes that people visit heritage sites and museums to learn.[22] However, long-term studies by Smithsonian Institution researchers at a number of their museums clearly indicate that visitors look for and engage with displays and exhibitions that support their "entrance narratives" and tend to leave the museum with these narratives intact; this research questions the idea that people are learning during the visit.[23] If learning is not being done, or at least not being done by all, and if people have both a suspicion of formal history and a deep engagement with the past, what exactly is going on? How is engagement with the past pursued, and what are the outcomes of this engagement?

To answer this, I explore the heritage performance as I have defined it here and as it is played out in performative visits by individuals to museums or other sites of heritage. To do this, however, I do not focus on the performances of the institution or heritage experts, but rather on the embodied performances of visitors to heritage sites and museums, to explore the ways in which individuals engage with heritage.

THE HERITAGE PERFORMANCE: DOING HERITAGE

During the summers of 2011 and 2012 I interviewed 1,141 visitors to sixteen museum exhibitions and heritage sites across the United States (see the following table); these ranged from sites that represented hegemonic national narratives to sites of class history, civil rights, indigenous history, and the history of immigration. These interviews were digitally recorded with the permission of the person being interviewed. Visitors were approached as they were leaving or about to leave the exhibition or site they were visiting. We asked the visitors a standard sequence of twelve open-ended questions (although further questions were asked depending on the site of interview or the individual being interviewed) alongside additional open-ended demographic questions. All interviews were then transcribed, coded for themes emerging out of the responses to each question, and analyzed with statistical and qualitative data software.[24]

A number of embodied performances emerged from the data, which reveal that people use museums and other sites of heritage in quite diverse ways, and that while learning was important to some visitors, it is not as important to most as the literature tends to assume. Seven performances emerged from the data. The first focuses on the management and expression of emotions. Heritage sites and museums become locations in which people find it permissible, or perhaps appropriate or safe, to experience and express or experiment with certain emotions. Certainly heritage sites and museums can be identified as places where people go to feel.[25] Importantly, the performative act of managing or negotiating emotional responses to the past then worked to facilitate and frame the ways in which the next six performances were expressed. Central to these performances was not simply the expression, but also the management, of a visitor's emotion. Certainly the emotions expressed in the performances discussed here were highly varied, but what is more important is that the intensity of emotions also varied. It is useful to identify what I have called "registers of engagement." While it is a simple observation that different individuals will engage differently with a particular aspect of history, and that different heritage sites or museums may engender varying levels of engagement, it is also important to acknowledge that visitors can express different levels of engagement. This is because on the one hand some visitor engagement can be quite shallow, yet counterintuitively, can also carry out important cultural and political work.

Visitor Interviews: US Exhibitions and Heritage Sites

Ellis Island	100
Hermitage, Tennessee	101
James Madison's Montpelier	112
Japanese American National History Museum	38
Lower East Side Tenement Museum	80
Mashantucket Pequot Museum	94
Museum of Work and Culture	18
National Civil Rights Museum	101
National Cowboy & Western Heritage Museum	110
National Museum of American History	
Slavery at Jefferson's Monticello: Paradox of Liberty	100
The Star-Spangled Banner	100
The Price of Freedom: Americans at War	69
Nordic Heritage Museum	14
Rivers of Steel National Heritage Area	20
Yellowstone National Park	62
Youngstown Historical Center of Industry and Labor	22
Total	**1,141**

On the other hand, deep engagement can generate a lot of emotional feeling but does not necessarily go far in developing critical insight. Deep and shallow engagement can also produce a range of conservative or progressive cultural outcomes. However, understanding that visitors express different registers of engagement or display different levels of emotional engagement in the performances they embody is important for understanding both the emotional and intellectual investments that visitors may make in their visits.

The second performance centers on the passing on of family memories and values. Sites and museums were often used for intergenerational communication and could be used by families as the settings or cultural tools by which to pass on familial narratives and social or political values.[26] In the third performance sites were also used as places of individual remembering and affirmation of personal or collective social or political values. The fourth performance found individual visitors also using these spaces to assert, negotiate, or connect personally to familial identity or history. Visitors in the fifth performance very commonly used museums and heritage sites to reinforce what they already knew, understood, or felt about national, regional, or ethnic identity and narratives and the collective memories and values that underpinned them. This performance in particular was carried out in a variety of ways—with deep critical engagement or through banal passive engagement, often expressed by tourists as "having a nice day out."[27] In the sixth performance people used heritage sites and museums to perform recognition of and respect to communities to which they did not belong. This use resulted in quite complicated performances, but it tended to be a very politically engaged and progressive use. It should be noted, however, that this performance did not mean that misrecognition did not also occur in some cases, and indeed misrecognition often underlaid performances in which people sought reinforcement of previously held understandings of other social or cultural groups. Finally, these places were of course also used as educational resources. Although this was an infrequent use, what was being learned when a visitor considered that learning had occurred was not always what heritage experts or curatorial staff may have had in mind.

I cannot here explore all of these performances in detail, but I elaborate on two, recognition (the sixth performance) and reinforcement (the fifth performance). Whatever the specifics of a performance, they all begin with choices: which heritage site or museum will be visited and which aspects of that place or exhibition will be engaged with and which will not. The choice of place to visit signals a particular engagement with the historical narratives the site or exhibition represents. This choice itself often frames the type and meaning of the performance that the visitor then constructs and what will be remembered or forgotten. As an embodied performance it is also framed by emotion, as one person visiting the National Civil Rights Museum in Memphis succinctly noted:

> I don't go to museum for education, I can read material on the Internet or in books, I come for emotional reasons. Coming for education makes no sense. (NCRM61: male, 55–64, health care, African American)

This is a self-conscious assessment of why this person visited, but it defines the strong sense of emotion that people tended to express merely by visiting particular sites or being in the presence of particular artifacts. Sometimes this was expressed as simply making connections with the past and people in it (the fourth performance), which can be seen, for example, in the cases of one visitor to the National Cowboy Museum, Oklahoma City, and another to the Tenement Museum, New York:

> Oh for me, sure, fond memories of my grandfather on horses [starts to cry] anyway but he brought me here. (NC44: female, 45–54, housewife, American)

James Madison's Montpelier, Virginia. Photograph by Laurajane Smith.

That people can endure hard times and how important it is to capture our heritage so it lives on and to show the next generation. It's important to me as stories I heard as a child had no meaning, but seeing this, things now do mean more [*starts to cry*] — Oh dear, I have teared up! (TM4: female, 55–64, retired sales, Jewish American; *Hard Times Tour*)

However, emotions could also be more complex, as the following performance of recognition (sixth performance) illustrates. This occurred at the presidential home and plantation site of James Madison, the fourth US president (see the image above). As a plantation, this is a site with a significant history built on the enslavement of African people. Many of the visitors I spoke to at this site expressed feelings of patriotism and that they were proud to be American; they were thus reinforcing particular nationalistic entrance narratives about the US Constitution and ideas about the "freedom" represented by the American nation. However, one middle-aged woman, who identified as Caucasian American, used the site in a far more complex way. On the site is a railway station that was used to ship people and goods to and from the house (see the next image); there were two waiting rooms, one marked "colored" and the other "whites."

Train station at James Madison's Montpelier, Virginia, 2011. The signs above the two waiting-room doors read "WHITE" and "COLORED." Photograph by Laurajane Smith.

During the interview the woman informed me she had explicitly walked through the colored door, so she could both remember and experience prosthetically what her African American childhood school friend had experienced as a child growing up in the South. She outlined how her experience walking through that door—a performative act—was intense and affecting. She used this action to reflect on racism in her family, which had prevented her from bringing her friend home after school when they were children, and to consider what limitations being white and from a racist family had placed on her friendship:

> I'm a southerner [*sighs*]. We rebelled against our own nation to preserve states' rights. Slavery was a big part of my family's heritage and to see it abolished is a great joy. But to learn how it was conducted, you see very little of that in any other tour you get. This shows you the degrees of slavery and the Jim Crow Museum down there at the train station [*sighs*]. I go through the colored door. I lived that. My dearest friend in high school was a black girl and my mother wouldn't let her come to my house [*sobs*].
> LS: Sorry. I'm so sorry.

Well, but she does now.

LS: She does now?

[Yes ....] This isn't [*unclear, crying*], you'd die to get rid of these feelings to people. I've got my family, some of them they still won't ... Civil War isn't ... I'm only third generation on my mother's side from the war and believe me we were raised to know that we were different and to fight that, coming here helps you do that. (JMM85: female, 55–64, retired teacher, Caucasian American)

This woman made herself uncomfortable so that she could empathize and sympathize with her friend; she then used those feelings to reflect on the need to continue to fight against her regional and family upbringing, to continue to fight against racism. This is a performance of recognition in which the Caucasian southern woman recognizes simultaneously her own privileged and historical background and the history of discrimination experienced by her friend. It is a prosthetic memory, as Landsberg defines it, and the empathy engendered is used to energize action, in the form of the woman reminding herself of the importance of acknowledging and fighting against the negative legacies of her own historical social position. The register of engagement here is deep for this woman, framing an embodied performance in which she physically interacted with the site, and which produced a progressive meaning and outcome.

The next example—of reinforcement (fifth performance)—is also based on a deep register of engagement. It comes from an interview with two visitors to the exhibition on the Star-Spangled Banner, positioned at the entrance to the Smithsonian Institution's National Museum of American History. The performance here is about reinforcing what the visitors both know and believe about the importance of the flag to their sense of national identity:

LS: Does this exhibition have any meaning for contemporary America?

DAUGHTER: I think so. I think it creates a link to the reason we became a country [*crying, interviewee becomes so emotional that she excuses herself and removes herself from the vicinity; it takes her some minutes to collect herself*].

MOTHER: I think it has meaning for the younger generations. ... Just supports my strength for our country even more. The patriotism. (F31 [daughter], 18–24, student; F30 [mother] 45–54, teacher, Caucasian American)

The emotion was deeply felt; indeed, several men in the family had been in the military. This exhibition, and more important their choice to visit it, spoke to and expressed these visitors' deep sense of patriotism. Reinforcement of what people know, feel, or believe often took the form of statements of what visitors considered they were gaining from their visits.[28]

The deep emotional engagement expressed here can, as much as banal or shallow engagement, rehearse what Italian cultural theorist Antonio Gramsci defines as "commonsense" narratives and readings of the past and present.[29] The father of this family, interviewed separately and himself a veteran, when asked what if any meaning the exhibition had for modern America, stated:

> Um, my twenty-one-year-old daughter is bawling like a baby right now because she went through that exhibition, yes. So yes, it does have meaning. You've got to force people to remember. (F32: male, 45–54, self-employed, European Caucasian American)

For him the exhibition was important as an aide-mémoire. He had noted earlier in the interview:

> Yeah, it's part of our history. It's part of our past, and if you don't remember it then bad things will happen again. Yeah, it needs to be remembered.

The statement that he wants to "force" people to remember underlines not only the importance of what is being remembered here for him, but also a sense of urgency or concern about the possibility that other people may forget or not appreciate the importance of this history. This performance is also linked to the importance of the museum as a site of celebration and remembrance; the following person, interviewed at the Pequot Museum, Connecticut, expresses this sense of understanding the museum:

> Museums are, sort of, temples for me, they're a sort of like a holy place of humanity. It's sort of raw; I think it displays the best of our nature. (PM57: male, 45–54, unemployed artist, African and Native American)

As much of the museological literature stresses, museums tend to be perceived by their audiences as "safe" places of authority.[30] Traditionally, they may indeed be defined as "temples" dedicated to the worship of cultural material. So while much of the contemporary heritage and museological literature wants to take us "beyond the mausoleum" and the stultified nature of monumental heritage,[31] the traditional idea of museums and heritage sites as temples continues to have consequences for certain heritage performances centered on seeking reinforcement and authorizing consensus narratives, or "known knowns." What is particularly significant about the preceding quote is that the visitor, himself of African and Native American descent, while observing that museums display "the best of our nature," was standing in a gallery that was discussing the aftermath of European colonization of the Americas, in which issues of dispossession and attempted genocide were difficult to ignore (but yet, as his statement implies, ignored they were). This is because his performance, like that of the family in front of the Star-Spangled Banner, was about reinforcing commitment to particular beliefs (in these cases about either human nature or nation).

CONCLUSION

In these heritage performances, emotional responses to the past were used to affirm and remember particular contemporary and future commitments to fighting racism or celebrating nation, and particular historical narratives and political and social values were created, re-created, and negotiated during and around the visit. These performances demonstrate not only the intellectual but also the emotional and political agency of visitors in creating meaning. Further, these meanings become embodied, and ultimately legitimized in this embodiment, through the emotional and physical experiences of being at particular heritage sites or exhibitions. In each case there was an emotional investment made in particular narratives, and in the values embedded in those narratives, by the choice of what was visited and what visitors chose to remember. There is also a sense of political agency in these performances. In the performance by the woman at the plantation site the political agency and consequence is overt; the family at the National History Museum, in rehearsing their commitment to their patriotism, also perform political agency, although less overtly. To a certain extent this agency is expressed by the father who wants to "force" others to remember, to thus be, think, and feel like himself and his daughter. However, the family's commitment is also to an ideal and a set of values that are authorized by the visit, the depth of their emotional response, the authority of the museum, and the physicality of the flag. The performance here is an authorized one that reinforces hegemonic discourses about the American nation. The woman at the plantation develops an understanding about the past that is not actively provided by the interpretive materials at the site; she is performing her own understanding, and this understanding is validated or made real for her by the depth and nature of her emotional response.

There is also a sense of inquiry and risky exploration in the woman's performance at the plantation, because in walking through that door she is critically examining what the past might have been like for her friend and what the legacy of that past might mean in the present. "Understanding" in these performances is not simply an intellectual exercise, but is reinforced, affirmed, and transmitted through the agency and act of visiting particular places defined as important. The acts that occurred at these places are themselves given legitimacy and strengthened by the physicality of place, the veracity of the emotions they produce, and the occasion afforded by deciding to step outside of everyday occurrences and a specific place. In this sense, heritage sites and museums may be, as Raphael Samuel argues, "theatres of memory" in which particular performances are enacted.[32] As theaters of memory, they may be constructed as temples of celebration and authority to reinforce hegemonic narratives, but they also may be more risky arenas in which to explore and interrogate. However, such places simply serve as the locales or cultural tools to facilitate a performance that is enacted and driven by the agency and contemporary needs and aspirations of the individuals who visit and use them.

NOTES

Demographic information was generated by the visitors at the time of the interviews, and is transcribed as provided in this essay.

1. This convention is an international treaty concerned with defining and protecting intangible heritage, or what had previously been referred to as "folklore." For more information see www .unesco.org/new/en/santiago/culture/intangible-heritage/convention-intangible-cultural-heritage/. The United States is not currently a state party to the convention; see Richard Kurin, "Safeguarding Intangible Cultural Heritage in the 2003 UNESCO Convention: A Critical Appraisal," *Museum International* 56, nos. 1–2 (2004): 66–76.

2. See Laurajane Smith, *Uses of Heritage* (London: Routledge, 2006), 29–34, for fuller discussion of the AHD.

3. For discussion of these issues, see Laurajane Smith and Natsuko Akagawa, eds., *Intangible Heritage* (London: Routledge, 2009).

4. Robert Hewison, *The Heritage Industry: Britain in a Climate of Decline* (London: Methuen, 1987); David Lowenthal, *The Heritage Crusade and the Spoils of History* (Cambridge, UK: Cambridge University Press, 1998); Josie Appleton, "Museums for the 'People'?," in *Museums and Their Communities*, ed. S. Watson (London: Routledge, 2007), 114–26.

5. Lowenthal, *Heritage Crusade and the Spoils of History*, x.

6. Jorma Kalela, *Making History: The Historian and Uses of the Past* (New York: Palgrave, 2012).

7. James V. Wertsch, *Voices of Collective Remembering* (Cambridge, UK: Cambridge University Press, 2002).

8. Smith, *Uses of Heritage*.

9. Barbara Kirshenblatt-Gimblett, *Destination Culture: Tourism, Museums, and Heritage* (Berkley: University of California Press, 1998).

10. Diana Taylor, *The Archive and the Repertoire: Performing Cultural Memory in the Americas* (Durham, NC: Duke University Press, 2007), xvi.

11. Raphael Samuel, *Theatres of Memory* (London: Verso, 1994); and Kalela, *Making History*.

12. Taylor, *Archive and the Repertoire*, 7.

13. Lowenthal, *Heritage Crusade and the Spoils of History*; see also David Lowenthal, "Patrons, Populists, Apologists: Crises in Museum Stewardship," in *Valuing Historic Environments*, ed. Lisanne Gibson and John Pendlebury (Farnham, UK: Ashgate, 2009), 19–31.

14. Emily Keightley and Michael Pickering, *The Mnemonic Imagination: Remembering as Creative Practice* (Basingstoke, UK: Palgrave, 2012), 7–8.

15. Wertsch, *Voices of Collective Remembering*.

16. Alison Landsberg, *Prosthetic Memory: The Transformation of American Remembrance in the Age of Mass Culture* (New York: Columbia University Press, 2004).

17. Ibid., 135.

18. For a discussion of the critique of empathy see Carolyn Pedwell, "Affect at the Margins: Alternative Empathies in *A Small Place*," *Emotion, Space and Society* 8 (2013): 18–26; for a discussion of the political and ethical importance of empathy in the politics of difference see Susan Sontag, *Regarding the Pain of Others* (London: Penguin, 2004); and Anthony M. Clohesy, *Politics of Empathy: Ethics, Solidarity, Recognition* (London: Routledge, 2013).

19. Sue Campbell, "Our Faithfulness to the Past: Reconstructing Memory Value," *Philosophical Psychology* 19, no. 3 (2006): 361–80, 373.

20. See Gaynor Bagnall, "Performance and Performativity at Heritage Sites," *Museum and Society* 1, no. 2 (2003): 87–103; see Smith, *Uses of Heritage*, 158, 218 on this point and applications to heritage.

21. Roy Rosenzweig and David Thelen, *The Presence of the Past: Popular Uses of History in American Life* (New York: Columbia University Press, 1998); Paul Ashton and Paula Hamilton, *History at the Crossroads: Australians and the Past* (Sydney: Halstead Press, 2010); and The Pasts Collective, *Canadians and Their Pasts* (Toronto: University of Toronto Press, 2013).

22. Elaine Hooper-Greenhill, *Museum and Gallery Education* (Leicester, UK: Leicester University Press, 1991); Elaine Hooper-Greehill, *Museums and Education: Purpose, Pedagogy, Performance* (London: Routledge, 2007); John Falk, *Identity and the Museum Visitor Experience* (Walnut Creek, CA: Left Coast Press, 2009); John Falk and Lynn Dierking, *Learning from Museums: Visitor Experiences and the Making of Meaning* (Walnut Creek, CA: AltaMira Press, 2000).

23. Zahava Doering and Andrew Pekarik "Questioning the Entrance Narrative," *Journal of Museum Education* 21, no. 3 (1996): 20–25; and Andrew Pekarik and James Schreiber, "The Power of Expectation: A Research Note," *Curator* 55, no. 4 (2012): 487–96.

24. The software used was NVivo and SPSS (Statistical Package for the Social Sciences).

25. For further discussion, see Laurajane Smith, "Theorizing Museum and Heritage Visiting," in *Museum Theory: An Expanded Field*, ed. Kylie Message and Andrea Witcomb (Oxford: Blackwell Wiley, 2014).

26. This performance has also been discussed in relation to industrial museums in Wales; see Bella Dicks, *Heritage Place and Community* (Cardiff: University of Wales Press, 2000).

27. Smith, "Theorizing Museum and Heritage Visiting"; see also Laurajane Smith, "The Cultural 'Work' of Tourism," in *The Cultural Moment of Tourism*, ed. Laurajane Smith, Emma Waterton, and Steve Watson (London: Routledge, 2012).

28. Smith, "Theorizing Museum and Heritage Visiting."

29. For discussion of banal or shallow engagement and reinforcement see Smith, "The Cultural 'Work' of Tourism."

30. Fiona Cameron, "Moral Lessons and Reforming Agendas: History Museums, Science Museums, Contentious Topics and Contemporary Societies," in *Museum Revolutions*, ed. S. J. Knell, S. MacLeod, and S. Watson (Oxford: Blackwell, 2007), 330–42; Robert Janes, *Museums in a Troubled World* (London: Routledge, 2009); and The Pasts Collective, *Canadians and Their Pasts.*

31. Andrea Witcomb, *Re-Imagining the Museum: Beyond the Mausoleum* (London: Routledge, 2003); and David C. Harvey, "Heritage Pasts and Heritage Presents: Temporality, Meaning and the Scope of Heritage Studies," *International Journal of Heritage Studies* 7, no. 4 (2001): 319–38.

32. Samuel, *Theatres of Memory.*

SIDEWAYS GLANCES
Painting and Dancing

I recently participated in a conversation with an art critic and an artist, in which the critic spoke about the concept of a "crab walk," the artist walking sideways between her studio and her life.[1] The walk was decidedly sideways, moving back and forth between spheres, not forward toward a final conclusion or endpoint. In his example, the critic spoke about the artist moving between her painting studio and the nightclub. He spoke about painting's adjacency, always next to or beside something else, rather than being singular and autonomous — a private experience. An artist made her paintings; a bit later she danced to the nightclub music; and the sideways movement between those two spaces, the blurring when art met life, was where the good stuff happened. This sideways walk might have been the movement between sculpture studio and playground, or between writing desk and the fashion show, or any number of worlds adjacent to where art is made.

I have been wondering lately what can happen when we allow life to get into art and how, in a way, the body can enter into a painting. We tend to see painting as fixed and static. Yet it is a handmade object, and inherent in it is the motion of the artist's body, her muscles and fingers, which activate it. But after it is made, it goes out in the world. How does the body engage with it then? The formal qualities of my painting began to inform an interest in performance, especially dance, with dance's inherent reliance on time and space: How can a painting exist in time and space, as a dancer's body does?

At some point I began to see my paintings as screens or backdrops for an action or event. I started going to contemporary dance performances and having conversations with dancers and choreographers. I dreamed about creating a painting that would become "un-fixed"; its static nature could begin to move without employing special effects or lighting. How can painting, essentially a collection of forms and colors, evolve over time, as dance does?

I proposed some experiments. In an art gallery in Stockholm in 2012 I worked with Anna Pehrsson, a contemporary dancer.[2] She created a dance, her movements echoing the exact forms and shapes in my painting. Her movement went from frozen and still for a moment, then she danced, then froze, becoming still again, the angle of her elbow or leg posing in front of the same angle (or contradicting it) in my painting. In this way she activated the still painting; at the same

Sarah Crowner, *Ballet Plastique*, 2011, oil and acrylic on raw canvas and linen, dimensions variable. Installation view image courtesy Galerie Catherine Bastide, Brussels. (See plate 7 for color image.)

time, the painting stilled her body. It became a conversation between a painting and a body. This also made me consider time and duration. We can view a painting for only a minute and possibly understand it. When it hangs as a backdrop behind a musical performance, how does this "viewing" time — say, forty-five minutes — affect the viewer's experience of the painting?

Another example is an exhibition in Brussels in 2011.[3] My abstract paintings were installed on walls around a low wooden stage. In order to see the paintings on the wall, the viewer had to assume the role of the performer and step onto the stage. Once a visitor decided to look carefully at a painting, he or she was forced to step up on stage, suddenly implicated in a rhythmic action with the paintings as décor.

Now I see that painting is a kind of a medium and is really an archive of all the actions and gestures that surround it: the embodied movements inherent in making the object (cutting, painting, sewing, stretching), but also of the dances around it and in front of it as it exists in the world. Painting can be seen as a threshold or curtain between different life experiences. The painting might "collect" the daily performances of eating dinner in front of it, sleeping under it, dancing around it, or performing it. As it gets older and lives in the world, develops its own rhythms, it becomes an archive of experience, like a body, with its sideways movements, inhabiting the world.

NOTES

1. "Painting in the Present Tense" (conversation at the Walker Art Center with Jan Verwoert [critic], Bruce Hainley, and Michele Grabner, February 6, 2013).

2. Galerie Nordenhake, *Sarah Crowner* (rehearsal), Stockholm, 2012.

3. Galerie Catherine Bastide, *Sarah Crowner: Ballet Plastique*, Brussels, 2011.

LEAP BEFORE YOU LOOK
Honoring the Libretto in Giselle and Apollo

Created almost one hundred years apart—Giselle in 1841 and Apollo in 1928—these two ballets nevertheless have in common two things: they tell a story, and the story each tells is about dancing. Giselle already loves to dance before the curtain rises, and when it does rise she is bounding about the stage with joy. Apollo is not nearly as accomplished a dancer as Giselle. Indeed, he spends much of the ballet trying to harness his body, to control it, to gain mastery of it. Yet these descriptions of the stories are too general to guide a Giselle or an Apollo into the inner sanctum of the ballets' drama. However, there are librettos to flesh them out.

For Giselle there is a written libretto, by Théophile Gautier. In the case of Apollo, there is oral transmission from choreographer George Balanchine to his dancers. In this essay I discuss to what extent the dancers make use of librettos and how that use affects their performance. My model for Giselle is Violette Verdy, and for Apollo, Jacques d'Amboise. Conscious of the dramatic underpinnings of the stories, they both brought added richness to their interpretations.

The first move Verdy as Giselle makes when she steps out of her cottage door is to approach the audience, extend her arms in shy greeting, and smile. Then she begins her circuit of the stage in large jumps. The one thing that seems to be on her mind is enjoying dancing. Only after she completes her tour of the stage does she cup her hand to her ear, acknowledging that she has heard someone knock on her door. Since it's the knocking that brings Giselle out of her house, you might suppose that she'd immediately seek out the knocker. Indeed, that's what all Giselles do. But not Verdy. The most important thing to do, she has written, is to establish Giselle's passion for dancing. Dance first; look second.[1]

Specific to Giselle (1841) is its concept as a ballet about dancing. The conceit belongs to Théophile Gautier. Although he turned to Jules-Henri Vernoy de Saint-Georges, a professional librettist, to work out the details of the story, it was Gautier who first had the idea of creating a ballet based on the Slavic legend of the ghostly Wilis, those "pitiless waltzers," as Gautier described them, who dance men to their death. He encountered the legend in a book by Heinrich Heine and at once sketched out a story for a ballet. Then he scrapped his notes, realizing that he had no experience in writing a ballet. That very night, however, he ran into Saint-Georges at the opera and recounted to him the folktale of

Violette Verdy as
Giselle in *Giselle*,
act 1, with the
Washington Ballet,
1969. Libretto by
Théophile Gautier.
Choreography
by Marius Petipa
after Jean Coralli
and Jules Perrot.
Photograph by
Shirley Nottingham.
Courtesy of the
Washington Ballet
and Violette Verdy.

maidens who die before their wedding day, turn into Wilis, and seduce wayfaring men into a dance of death.

Saint-Georges quickly engineered a libretto that would explain how one particular maiden became a Wili, a transformation that would serve to bridge act 1 with act 2, the Wili scene. Giselle is a young girl who loves Loys. Loys, however, is the name Count Albrecht has given himself to conceal his royal blood, in order to woo the peasant Giselle. Hilarion, a gamekeeper, also loves Giselle and vows to unmask his rival. The neighboring royal party visits Giselle's hamlet, and the Countess Bathilde is so enchanted with the young maiden that she gives her a necklace. They exchange confidences; both are in love. Now Hilarion puts into action his plan of revenge. He reveals Loys to be Albrecht, and when Bathilde sees her betrothed, Albrecht, in the village she extends her hand to be kissed. Albrecht is thus forced to acknowledge his relationship with Bathilde. Giselle sees the kiss, loses her mind, and dies. In act 2, she is reincarnated as a Wili.

Although both men are credited as author, historians agree that it was Gautier who provided *Giselle* with its basic conception and poetic fantasy. Gautier

NANCY GOLDNER

was indeed a poet, and much more. On the opening night of *Giselle*, June 28, 1841, at the Paris Opera, he was persuaded to leave his name off the program as colibrettist because he was too distinguished to share a credit. By the second performance, however, Gautier added his name, realizing that the ballet was a hit.

Joanna Richardson, one of Gautier's biographers, estimates that his writing could fill more than three hundred volumes: novels, short stories, travelogues, plays, and forty years of journalism, mostly criticism on theater, art, and dance. He was one of the original figures in the romantic movement, the themes of which, especially fascination with the supernatural, infuse *Giselle*. Gautier popularized the phrase "art for art's sake" in the preface to his novel *Mademoiselle de Maupin* (1834). "Nothing is really beautiful unless it is useless," he declared.[2]

Through his work as a journalist and his ebullient personality, Gautier came to know everyone who counted in the arts. He chewed hashish with Charles Baudelaire and Honoré de Balzac, and in other ways as well gained the notoriety befitting a romantic icon. Many of his friends remembered seeing him sit on the floor in what Richardson calls oriental style, wearing oriental pants and hair flowing down to his waist. He had numerous lovers, three children, and no wives. Carlotta Grisi, for whom he wrote *Giselle*, was possibly his lover briefly; they remained close friends until his death.

Gautier was honored often, his most precious tribute being the dedication Baudelaire wrote to him upon the publication of *Les Fleurs du Mal* in 1857. Yet Gautier died a disappointed man. He had aspired first and foremost to be a poet, but with no independent income ended up a captive of Grub Street, churning out endless articles and reviews. France rejected him three times for admission to the Académie Française, and only in 2002 was any of his work published by the Editions Pleiade, a series of scholarly books founded in 1931 that has become the seal of the French canon. His most enduring work is *Giselle*, which has been performed continuously for more than 170 years.

Since 1841 much of the ballet has been revised and revamped. More music was added to the score by Adolphe Adam, the ballet's composer. Marius Petipa added his own imprint to the original choreography by Jean Coralli and Jules Perrot. A few small scenes disappeared, and Serge de Diaghilev and his Ballets Russes gave the ballet a new ending when Tamara Karsavina and Vaslav Nijinsky starred in it in 1910, in Paris. Instead of obeying Giselle's bid to take the hand of Bathilde, Albrecht is left alone, desolate by the dead girl's grave. More recently, in 1969 Erik Bruhn directed a production in Sweden that had Giselle fly up to heaven instead of sinking into her grave. And in another production, for Sweden's Ballet Cullberg in 1982, Mats Ek set the second act in an insane asylum. The one element that has become obscured over time is the spirit of Gautier's libretto.

Violette Verdy is the only ballerina I have ever seen who takes Gautier at his word, not only as a librettist but as a dance critic. I saw Verdy dance as Giselle only once, with New York City Ballet (NYCB) dancer Edward Villella as Albrecht, at the Boston Ballet in 1968. I saw it by chance; I happened to be in Boston, visiting friends, and read an advertisement for it in the newspaper. I knew Verdy only as a principal dancer with NYCB, where she danced primarily the Balanchine repertory. Seeing her in *Giselle* would be a change of pace, to say the least. It ended up changing my idea of what the ballet should feel like—indeed, my idea of its very identity.

With Verdy the ballet was not a vehicle for a ballerina; rather, it presented a very moving story told by a compelling actress. In preparation for writing this essay, I also viewed film of the Boston Ballet and National Ballet, as the Washington Ballet was then called, shot in 1969. Verdy's interpretation of the character does not yield a "eureka moment"; rather, the accumulation of choices gives her Giselle unique authenticity. Her decision to leap before looking is the first such calculation that leads one back to Gautier's characterization of Giselle: "Her situation is simple," he wrote. "She loves Loys and she loves dancing."

To love dancing means that Verdy as Giselle dances full out almost all of the time. Her jumps are large and full-bodied. But more important is that the small transitional movements are fully delineated. The smaller movements are what give dancing its luster and energy. The glissades with which Giselle travels to the bench, where she will test Albrecht's love with daisy petals, are fully shaped with a slight spring and pointed feet. Her pointed foot in *coupé* firmly touches her ankle; it doesn't dangle somewhere along the lower leg.

Like Verdy, dancers such as Olga Spessivtseva, Tamara Toumanova, and Galina Ulanova, all of whom I saw on film, show us vibrant jumps. I was extremely surprised by the richness of Spessivtseva's dancing, especially the hearty use of her shoulders and torso, which left no doubt that Giselle was a peasant. I was surprised because the image we have of her as Giselle comes from photographs in act 2, which show an especially soulful line and face.

With all these ballerinas, however, the smaller steps are smudged. Carla Fracci, in many live performances I have seen, blurs all movement except when she dances with Albrecht. She doesn't hold the poses in attitude. Her arms are limp rather than soft. In her solo her torso is static. It's as if she were marking the choreography. Admittedly, I have a personal distaste for halfhearted dancing in any ballet, but it wreaks havoc on the story of *Giselle*. How can she find the energy to lose her mind—it takes a strong spirit to go mad—and how can she summon the courage to save Albrecht from the Wilis in act 2?

As a dance critic, Gautier was drawn to dance because it was—as he wrote in the journal *La Presse* in 1849—"the ideal made palpable."[3]

Gautier was drawn to dancers who were artless, whose gestures had the ring of truth. Again, it's only Verdy who in my experience completely fulfilled that standard, a standard shaped by her observation of Ulanova in the 1950s. I quote Verdy's comments about Ulanova's Giselle at length here because they are so perceptive and appreciative, and because they are a template by which one understands the dramatic architecture of Verdy's Giselle:

> I first saw Ulanova in the late fifties and will never forget the strongly per-sonal impression she made on me. She wasn't pretending to look fragile—which she was not—or strange, or unusual. She was doing it with her own truth, and with such conviction; a dancer of the head as well as heart. Yet though you could see a good head at work there, somehow the intellect didn't get in the way. The reading was completely integrated into what she was her-self. . . . What Ulanova possesses—an essential quality, in my opinion, uni-versal in interpretive dance, and what one rediscovers constantly in all the greatest dancers—is heroism. This heroism—call it grandeur, breadth, pro-fundity [. . .]—is the hallmark of any great interpretation become complete and comprehensible and simple.[4]

Heroism in Ulanova's dancing is intrinsic to everything she does, in every ballet; it is a hallmark of her style, but it has particular narrative relevance in the moment when her Giselle, with the enormous wingspan of her arms, protects Albrecht from Myrtha's demonic power on the cross. Myrtha has met her match, and we know it right from the start of act 2.

Verdy wrote that Giselle has good red blood flowing through her veins, that she is not a sylph or otherworldly creature, at least in act 1. She is shy, but not coy. Early in the first act, Giselle sits down on a bench to count the "he loves me, he loves me not" daisy petals. Verdy simply sits herself down on the bench, and that's all there is to it. Other Giselles primp their dresses to make them espe-cially fluffy, make a point of delicately crossing their ankles, and half anticipate Albrecht's desire to sit down beside them before he makes a move. They have a touch of the coquette, which obscures the fact that Giselle is a true innocent, making more powerful the immense impact of Albrecht's deception on Giselle's heart.

In act 1 Giselle spends much time simply standing or reacting to the events surrounding her: Hilarion's unwanted declaration of love; her mother's constant watch over her daughter; and the entrance of Bathilde, the countess. In all these moments Verdy uses her arms simply, letting them rest by her side; when that's not sufficient to convey her feelings, she moves them gently and with various tilts of her head signaling resignation toward her mother's authority or her rejection of Hilarion, whose passion for her, in her innocence, she does not understand.

Verdy does carry noticeable tension in her neck, however, when she approaches Bathilde's dress to caress it. (My, how she covets that dress!) In fact, so strongly does she want to touch the dress that she ignores her mother's warning as if she weren't there. She responds to her mother's warning about becoming a Wili with similar indifference. Gautier wrote about this: "What young girl of fifteen believes in a story with the moral that one cannot dance?"[5] As close as Verdy's Giselle is to her mother, she can also tune her out.

One reason I am so struck by Verdy's deportment is that it is utterly natural. The other reason is how it compares to other Giselles. Russian dancers especially use codified hand gestures to impart emotion. To show distress, anger, fear, and all related feelings, they bring their hands to their mouths; when they want to show much fear or anger they splay their elbows to the side. Even Ulanova, whose Giselle comes close to Gautier's ideal of artlessness, resorts to this stock gesture. While I always admire the conviction with which Ulanova performs the gesture, it appears as a convention, not as authentic. Only twice does Verdy rely on the gestural crutch: when Bathilde catches her mooning over the dress, and when Bathilde tells her that she is engaged. Even then, Verdy's gesture is gentle, not melodramatic. She saves the drama for the mad scene.

Why does Giselle go mad? Cyril W. Beaumont writes: "Quick temper and poor health might explain her frenzy and her tears, but for madness to result from what at worst is no more than a bitter disappointment proves that Giselle must have been highly neurotic."[6] There is a performance tradition of Giselle being a bit strange, deriving from the Giselle of Alicia Markova; but neurotic?

Interestingly, Gautier offers no reason for this assertion; he takes it for granted that the truth about Albrecht drives Giselle to madness. Verdy noted on this issue: "A maiden's reason lies in her heart. When that heart is wounded, her reason falters." She then added, "Thus it is that Giselle lapses into madness— not the forehead smiting of some disheveled heroine of melodrama, but a gentle madness, sweet and tender as Giselle herself."[7] Later on in her book she iterated that the heroine's madness is sweet, not "clinical."[8]

Violette Verdy as
Giselle and Edward
Villella as Albrecht
in *Giselle*, act 1,
the "mad scene,"
1968. Libretto by
Théophile Gautier.
Choreography by
Marius Petipa after
Jean Coralli and Jules
Perrot. Photograph
by Frank Derbas.
Courtesy of Boston
Ballet and Violette
Verdy.

Verdy's performance of the mad scene is similar to most of the other Giselles
I have seen. She doesn't descend into what seems to me to be, for Giselle, an
uncharacteristic fury, finger-pointing and all, that some Giselles show toward
Albrecht. Even at the height of her madness Verdy keeps the lid on. Nor does
she ascend to the profound moment in Ulanova's mad scene, when she peers
into her mother's face so deeply that she seems to be trying to reclaim her identity in her mother's image. The closeness between Giselle and her mother is in
a flash fully revealed. (And here is the value of film, affording the audience a
more intimate detail of a relationship than could ever be ascertained from live
performance.) The one special moment in Verdy's mad scene comes just before
she collapses and dies. She reaches out to Albrecht, as if trying to speak to him,
and then with her arms softening indicates forgiveness. Thus does Verdy set the
stage as no other Giselle does for act 2.

Gautier would approve, I imagine. He would be appalled, however, by Lynn
Seymour's madness, but here is a case where an unorthodox interpretation

is valuable because it exposes the underpinnings of the story. Seymour was a superb dramatic dancer who in collaboration with choreographer Kenneth Mac-Millan specialized in portraying sexually charged characters, beginning in 1960 with *The Invitation*, about the physical awakening of two adolescents. The dance critic Alastair Macaulay remembers Seymour's radical interpretation of Juliet in the balcony scene of *Romeo and Juliet*, in which she moved like a cat in heat.[9] In *Giselle*, she also brought a sexual dimension to the maiden's mad scene.

Seymour's madness is ugly. At the climax of her delusion, her dancing is messy, almost drunken in its wantonness. She laughs with malice at Albrecht. At a live performance I shall never forget, in a staging by Antony Tudor at the Metropolitan Opera in 1976, when she was a guest dancer with American Ballet Theatre (ABT), Seymour's broken heart showed itself as a broken body, grotesque. And her glances at Albrecht were wildly seductive. Here was a vision of the erotic gone haywire. Perhaps this is what fuels the Wilis' unrelenting energy.

The images that Gautier and Heine use to describe the Wilis and their environment are erotic, and of course the very idea of the dance of death has sexual overtones. Both writers describe the Wilis as being unfulfilled women or virgins of marriageable age. In Seymour's dancing we see what it means to be unfulfilled. The graceful turns ugly, youthful spirit goes berserk, and maidenly passion twists into perversion. Seymour's mad scene is a prelude to the pent-up sexual energy of the Wilis, who destroy the men they desire in nighttime rituals. Needless to say, Seymour kills herself robustly. She plunges the sword so deep into her chest that Hilarion must yank it to get it out.

Many lithographs exist of Carlotta Grisi as Giselle, as well as ballerinas in other romantic ballets. Some of them are derived from paintings. What is striking about all of them is their familiar representation of what a romantic ballerina ought to look like. Chief among the characteristics is an elongated neck, with the head tilted slightly in the opposite direction, which serves to create the illusion of even more elongation. The shoulders are always pressed down, and even when the arms are raised the shoulders stay put. This is anatomically impossible; it's no wonder that some of the lithographs portray dancers in unnatural positions. I think that realism and individuality had no place in the lithographic enterprise. Instead, it produced stereotypical images that probably bore little resemblance to what nineteenth-century audiences saw on the stage.

Nevertheless, these common representations have become the source by which the Wili Giselle now styles herself. She aspires to an extremely elongated upper body. Alicia Alonso found a way to achieve the look even while walking; she said you must walk with your chest forward and your feet trailing behind.

In the adagio passage in act 2, which Myrtha commands Giselle to perform in order to lure Albrecht away from his refuge at the cross, the Russian ballerinas—Natalia Makarova, Natalia Bessmertnova, and current stars Diana Vishneva and Natalia Osipova—raise their arms straight above their heads as their legs extend high to the side into a développé à la seconde.

This use of the arms—straight up rather than rounded—contradicts a basic feature of the continuity of balletic line. This beanpole look is freakish looking, but perhaps that is the point. These lithograph-bound Giselles want to distort supernatural qualities into mannerism. It's no coincidence, I think, that the mannered Wili took hold during the ballet boom of the 1970s, when star dancers held sway. Giselle originally premiered also during a ballet boom, spurred on by the rivalry among the leading ballerinas of that golden age: Marie Taglioni, Fanny Cerrito, Fanny Elssler, Lucile Grahn, and Carlotta Grisi. Yet the critics of that time praised these dancers for their spontaneity and believability as well as their lightness and speed.[10] Unlike contemporary Giselles, they did not have to bear the weight of history, for although the work was an overnight success, it had not yet entered the ballet canon. They could simply dance it.

Many of today's famous dancers care more about projecting Giselle's ghostly attributes than about telling the story. The libretto is not referred to as part of dancer coaching, nor is the cultural context for Gautier's narrative provided to audiences as part of program notes. Giselle is supposed to be about an errant Wili trying to save Albrecht's life. It is a love story from beyond the grave. But because contemporary Giselles are so involved with their incorporeality, they barely look at Albrecht. There is only one moment in the second act when performers consistently express the idea of saving Albrecht: when Giselle rapidly moves away from him in small steps and with her wrist beckons him to follow her. The rest of the time they move in a semi-trance, phantoms hypnotized by their own phantomness.

Although Verdy does not overplay the ghostly condition of Giselle, she adheres to the stylistic qualities of the romantic dancer. She believes that the Wili Giselle of the ballet's second act should have a "weeping willow quality" and that her arms are "wet, heavy, and soft."[11] The wetness refers to the damp, erotic environment of the Wilis' domain, described first by Heine and then iterated by Gautier. In a second reference to romantic style, Verdy at times holds her arms lower than she might in other roles, especially when she jumps. In a third reference, Albrecht does not lift her extremely high in supported adagio; such lifts are too acrobatic, more typical of the Bolshoi in the twentieth century than the more modest nineteenth-century style.

One of the enchantments of Giselle's story is that it poses questions that can't be answered. Does Giselle actually kill herself? Does she die from a weak heart or a broken heart? Who was her father? This question is asked by Beaumont, who, basing his understanding of Giselle's character on Markova, believes that Giselle must have noble blood in her veins because, he writes, "she is sickly and obsessed with a craze for dancing, a strange, elfin creature whose shy, sensitive nature is so different from that of the light-hearted young girls of the district."[12] And who conjures the spirit of Giselle as anti-Wili? This last question would never have occurred to me were it not for several performances I saw of Mikhail Baryshnikov as Albrecht.

After making his entrance and depositing lilies at Giselle's grave, Baryshnikov knelt on the ground with his head in his hands. He was not so much in mourning, however, as he was sunk in profound thought, and so deep was his concentration that he seemed to be the agent drawing Giselle to him as a loving spirit. I've never before been able to interpret the action this way, nor does it follow the libretto. Interestingly, though, it parallels the many ghost stories written by Gautier. In those tales, it is the male narrator who is the active person, who in his desire brings a dead woman to life. One of his born-again women says, in "The Tourist," "No one is truly dead until they are no longer loved."[13] It's a pretty thought, and one can imagine Gautier bringing that idea to *Giselle*—if, that is, he had been writing a ballet story for the twenty-first century. But *Giselle* was written in the nineteenth century, when the ballerina reigned supreme and was, despite the male authorship of the ballet, the active narrative voice. So while Baryshnikov's power as an artist reversed the roles in the story, making the man instead of the woman the catalyst, it was an anachronism. But a truly moving one!

In the conventional *Giselle*, she conjures herself to be Albrecht's dancing mate. Everything the spirit does is intended to show the love she has for him. Verdy shows it nonstop. From the very first moment she appears beside him, everything in her body moves toward him—her torso, her arms, her neck. She doesn't have to look at him for the audience to make the connection; indeed, sometimes the choreography has her moving in the opposite direction or with her back to him, but he is not out of her vision, as it were. Whether the pair can actually see each other is left ambiguous; it's another of the ballet's unanswerable questions. The connection Verdy makes with Albrecht is an act of the dancer's will or imagination; perhaps "psychic energy" is a better phrase. What's remarkable is that in the one live performance and two filmed ones of Verdy that I have viewed, she never once dances alone psychologically.[14]

Another aspect I vividly remember from the live performance is that her feet were extraordinarily turned out, her heels pushing forward toward Albrecht so that her feet as well as her upper body were willing Albrecht to live. Alas, I didn't see this in the films, but I don't doubt my memory.

Those heavy and wet arms that Verdy describes are, frankly, not so evident throughout the act, but toward the end the heaviness takes on extreme resonance. For it is the means by which she changes from a woman saving Albrecht to the more elevated plane of a maternal or mother-earth figure saving us all. Many a Giselle has a maternal moment, when she cradles Albrecht in her arms as he struggles to breathe. Verdy carries the moment forward into the passages before her retreat to the grave. Her ports de bras grow broader, all-encompassing, and her chest becomes higher. And yes, her arms grow heavy, and exalted, with feelings of love. Watching the films, it crossed my mind that Giselle wanted to forgive Myrtha. It's not a far-fetched interpretation, given that Giselle does the deepest ports de bras—the ones that seem to emanate from her solar plexus— standing beside Myrtha. On the other hand, the breadth of her dancing in the second act suggests that she is also bestowing forgiveness on the world around her. She becomes a saint.

And then it's over. Verdy slowly and almost mechanically steps across the stage back to her grave. She is not yet quite dead, though. She pauses just as she passes Albrecht.

Giselle is a hallmark of the romantic age in ballet. In *Apollo*, by contrast, George Balanchine brought the classical technique of Marius Petipa, as developed in the late nineteenth century and into the twentieth century. However different their historical significance, both ballets are enlivened by poetic irony; they are dances about dancing. In *Giselle*, the irony is explicit and literal. In *Apollo*, it is more metaphorical: the 1928 work is about the god's striving for physical mastery, which Balanchine equates with his growth into godhood.

This idea is embedded in Balanchine's choreography. Throughout the course of the ballet audiences see Apollo arch and contract his back, achieve muscular stability, and then lose it as he steps in sequences of arabesque, clenches his fists, and then opens them—a gesture Balanchine said he borrowed from a flickering neon sign advertising gloves in London's Piccadilly Circus. Apollo also comes to master the bodies of the ballet's three muses by dividing them into groupings of one and two, then joining them together as a trio. He partners them one by one, lifts them two at a time, and does an extended pas de deux with his favored muse, Terpsichore.

Perhaps the most important mastery of all comes through Apollo's experimentation with the lute. He takes its measure not only by playing it with varying

Violette Verdy as Giselle and Edward Villella as Albrecht in *Giselle*, act 2, the Washington Ballet, 1969. Libretto by Théophile Gautier. Choreography by Marius Petipa after Jean Coralli and Jules Perrot. Photograph by Shirley Nottingham. Courtesy of the Washington Ballet and Violette Verdy.

degrees of energy—strumming it fiercely as if it were a banjo or plucking it so softly that he must hold it to his ear to hear it—but also by exploring its shape. In how many ways can he hold it? More than we mortals could think of. And what, finally, does the lute mean to Apollo? Does it pose a challenge, or something to be feared? Or does it offer solace, a guidepost for his journey into manhood? When Apollo lurches toward the instrument practically on his knees, he seems to be its supplicant.

"He seems to be"—we are now in the domain of the dancer's interpretation of the choreography. The degree to which Balanchine's choreography reveals a story, or an intention beyond the bare bones of the steps, depends on the dancer's willingness and ability to uncover it for us. With no libretto to guide the dancer's interpretation, *Apollo* over the years has become a ballet with mere glimmers of narrative. Although many Giselles have chosen to ignore major points in the ballet's libretto, at least there is a text available for study.

Igor Stravinsky, who began to compose the music for *Apollo* in 1927, did in fact write a libretto, but not in the conventional format of nineteenth-century opera or ballet. As he did for all of his pieces for the theater, he wrote an out-line of the main action with a time allotted for each event. Just as a writer needs a word length to know how to think about a subject, Stravinsky used specific time lengths to know how to think about his subject. Having received a com-mission from the American arts patron Elizabeth Sprague Coolidge to write a thirty-minute ballet to be performed at the Library of Congress in Washington, D.C., Stravinsky chose the subject of Apollo and three muses.

The ballet was first called *Apollon musagète*, which Stravinsky translated as "Apollo, conductor of the muses." (The music retains this title.) When it was first revived for NYCB in 1951, it was called *Apollo, Leader of the Muses*. Notwith-standing the authority from which the title comes, Apollo is a conductor of the muses only sometimes. In the coda especially, it's the muses who lead Apollo; he must muster all his strength to restrain their exuberance, playing charioteer to his wild horses. And in the most charming moment of the ballet, the muses order Apollo to rest with a clap of their hands. He falls into their hands like an obedient boy.

Stravinsky divided the ballet into two scenes. The first depicts the birth of Apollo, which he said he wanted to be as literal as possible; the second scene is a series of solos, ensembles, a pas de deux, a coda, and an apotheosis, in which Apollo ascends Mount Parnassus and joins his father, Zeus. The composer imag-ined the work as a ballet blanc. This term traditionally refers to a long passage of pure dance in a narrative ballet, in which the dancers wear white dresses. The second act of *Giselle* is a fine example of the ballet blanc. To Stravinsky a white ballet meant choreography stripped to its classical essence. In a more literal meaning of the term, he wanted the muses to be dressed in short white tutus. He had also wanted a fourth muse, but the stage in Washington was too small for an additional dancer. And he had wanted to use a harp and piano, but the orchestra pit was too small. So he composed for a conventionally sized and pro-portioned string orchestra.

This is about all one knows of Stravinsky's extramusical intentions for *Apollo*, although there are extensive notebooks on the method and progress of his composition, stored in archives at the Paul Sacher Foundation's Archive and Research Center for the Music of the Twentieth and Twenty-First Centuries in Basel, Switzerland. The piece premiered in the United States on April 27, 1928, with choreography by Adolph Bolm.[15] It was performed only once. Stravinsky cared little about its fate in the United States because he had already contracted with Diaghilev to produce it for the Ballets Russes. The French *Apollo* was first performed on June 12, at the Sarah Bernhardt Theater in Paris. According to Charles Joseph, rehearsals got under way in January 1928.[16] Stravinsky often invited Balanchine and Diaghilev to his home in Nice while Balanchine was creating the choreography.

In later years, Balanchine remembered Stravinsky's dwelling on tempo, insisting on stately tempos and clear intonations from the strings. But did they discuss the ballet's underlying themes, its many different tones and moods, or for that matter, the idea that Apollo is about the god's mastery of his body? Who decided that Polyhymnia, goddess of mime, would burst into speech at the end of her solo and turn knock-kneed in embarrassment? Or that Calliope, for all her gut-contracting searches for inspiration, would come up empty-handed? Who, in effect, decided that the ballet would have moments of humor as well as grandeur?

In sequencing the ballet's narrative, did the composer and choreographer ruminate on how Apollo's dancing would be largely rough-hewn rather than sleek and supple, the way gods are supposed to be? ("Where did you ever see Apollo on his knees?" an irate critic asked Balanchine, who replied, "Where did you ever see Apollo?") That decision was a practical matter, however, because Serge Lifar, the protagonist, came to the Ballets Russes with unfinished classical training. As he was to do for the rest of his career, Balanchine fashioned choreography to suit the talents—or lack thereof—of his dancers. By default, Balanchine had to collaborate a great deal with Lifar in order to devise steps that would be comfortable for him to do. The task was all the more pressing because Lifar was Diaghilev's lover.

In subsequent years Lifar claimed choreographic ownership of his role. This claim about Apollo might contain a germ of truth. Whoever devised the choreography for the lead role, however, the character was variously described by Balanchine as a "wild youth," a "soccer player," a "rascal," and "untamed." Lew Christensen, the first American Apollo, in 1937, said Balanchine called him a woodcutter, a swimmer, a football player, a god.

A survey of contemporary Apollos reveals the paradox of performing the ballet. For however much its theme, or story, is contained within the choreography, just doing the steps won't get the dancer much beyond the surface. This is true of all of Balanchine's ballets. The choreographer expected his principal dancers to expand on the quality of movement he showed them in rehearsal, to put into visible form his intentions—whether they were musical or dramatic. The dancers who flourished under Balanchine's regime had vivid personalities and creative minds. No matter how abstract a ballet, these dancers seemed to have a story in their heads and a visceral response to the music as they danced. Performance was, above all, an act of the imagination.

This is especially true of *Apollo*. In one case, Balanchine offered a veritable step-by-step narrative guide for Jacques d'Amboise to enhance his performance while preparing him for his debut in 1957. Here is d'Amboise's account of Balanchine's words, recorded in his autobiography:

> "You are born, already grown up. But you are baby, know nothing, and have tantrums. To calm you down, handmaidens bring you music, a lute, and teach you how to play. But you play like a peasant, rake your hands over strings, and use the lute the way a child uses toy. You don't know what to do with it— measure body with it, measure floor, and, like child, you put aside and forget. You leave your toy on the floor. Now, you try to walk to better things, but can't control how you move. You stagger, leap in circles. Finally, on your knees, you beg help from Papa, and he fills you with energy and power, and you become like teenager throwing around energy. You waste it! So Papa says, 'STOP! Go back to your music, and call for muses to come and inspire you.'"

Returning to the lute, Apollo plays, more refined now, and summons the muses of poetry, mime, and dance. [. . .] In sequence, each muse makes a presentation: "The first (Calliope) shows you what she's written, but you don't acknowledge—she has nothing new to tell you. You are a god, already know everything."

The second (Polyhymnia) speaks when she should not, and Apollo admonishes her. The third (Terpsichore) finds favor: "Terpsichore pleases you, and you bless her and dance together. Sometimes you play with her, like dodge game. Then, you take her on your back for nice flying. [This episode has become commonly known as the swimming lesson.] Coda begins, and you dance like thunderstorm, and muses try to hold you back. They want you to practice, ride chariot of sun across sky, and bring sunlight, prophecy, music, and dance to the world. Now, your life as boy is over. Papa says, 'You are grown up. Come up to Olympus to be with family.' The muses try to hold you back, but you make them bow to you, and leave them to ascend to your home."[17]

Of all the Apollos I have seen, d'Amboise gives by far the richest account of the protagonist's journey from baby to god. I base my reading of his Apollo on a film made for Radio Canada Montreal in 1960, with fellow NYCB dancers Diana Adams, Jillana, and Francia Russell as the muses.[18] In scene one he is in swaddling clothes and attended by two handmaidens. As they rock him from side to side, he rolls his head and opens his mouth in a cry. They begin to un-

Jacques d'Amboise as Apollo, with Jillana, Allegra Kent, and Patricia Wilde, New York City Ballet, 1963. *Apollo*, choreography by George Balanchine © The George Balanchine Trust. Photograph by Martha Swope © The New York Public Library for the Performing Arts.

ravel him from the cloth, and he breathes more and more deeply until he has the strength to pirouette himself out of the last of the cloth. He stumbles, frowns as if startled by light. Now the handmaidens present him with the lute. They place his hands on the strings and move his arms up and down. Soon he can draw sound from the lute by himself. His arms fly high at the last of Stravinsky's chords, and he faces the audience calmly.

In his first solo in scene two, Apollo strums the lute ferociously. But in contrast to the power to which he subjects the lute, his steps in arabesque are wobbly, bumpy. His chest sometimes collapses. There's a hint of his being on the alert: Is anyone looking? Placing the lute on the ground, he backs away from it with limping arabesques, then approaches it with arms outstretched beseechingly. He picks it up with tenderness, then as something to take charge of. He plays the lute again, and the muses appear. They dance together.

Sometimes Apollo takes the initiative, the most emphatic example being when he partitions the trio into one and two. Sometimes they dance as equals. At one moment, they appear as his children. The muses stand on pointe in a row; Apollo lunges behind them, and with the most gentle of pushes, sends them into a space that seems vast and theirs alone. They are on their own now. Apollo's

Jacques d'Amboise as Apollo, with unidentified dancer, New York City Ballet, n.d. *Apollo*, choreography by George Balanchine © The George Balanchine Trust. Photograph by Martha Swope © The New York Public Library for the Performing Arts.

arms sink slowly to his sides, bringing a moment of poignancy to this leave-taking. Then, with his first strong port de bras and foot firmly planted on the floor in a turned-out position, he commands each muse to step forward and receive a symbol of her respective art. The young man then seats himself on a stool to watch each perform a solo. He sits with a proud chest. This is the first moment in which he looks like a danseur noble, a god.[19] And the second moment does not come until the end, when he hears the music calling him to Parnassus. His chest again expands; he walks with stately ease, his arms beautifully curved.

D'Amboise does not record what if anything Balanchine told him about Apollo's style of dancing. Should he move like a god, classically? Or like an untamed boy? What makes d'Amboise's Apollo special is that he does not look like a danseur noble except for isolated moments. He does not do polished, controlled arm movements, the ports de bras of conventional classical ballet. His arms just move in a freeform way. His transitions between movements are rough. Some of the off-balance passages in the choreography look genuinely awkward, as if he were about to fall off a horse. When he pushes forward, he

Edward Villella as Apollo, with Patricia McBride, Carol Sumner, and Suki Schorer, New York City Ballet, 1964. *Apollo*, choreography by George Balanchine © The George Balanchine Trust. Photograph by Martha Swope © The New York Public Library for the Performing Arts.

really pushes. The line of his arabesques is askew. He moves like an unseasoned dancer, and by extension an unseasoned god.

Peter Martins and Edward Villella, like d'Amboise both personally coached by Balanchine, also offer important testimony to Apollo's character. Villella says that images flowed out of Balanchine, who coached him in the mid-1960s: to be like "an eagle on a perch, on a rock, looking down from a crag," or "a matador watching the bull go by."[20] Peter Martins reports that after his debut in 1967 at the Edinburgh Festival, where he substituted for an injured d'Amboise, Balanchine criticized him for dancing "too classically" and for "not giving the movement the suggestions of character and imagery that he had built" into the choreography. Balanchine said that the feet should move with "the kind of force needed to punt a football," that the legs should be "shaped to a charged effect. ... There are stabs and mistakes and awkwardnesses, but the movement is to be urgent, not tentative." Martins said of himself, "I had been trying to make everything beautiful and grand, and he demanded shapes that looked grotesque but were packed with energy."[21]

Villella reports, similarly, that Balanchine said to him, "Everybody's dancing like a statue. Apollo is a devil. He's a rascal."[22]

Ethan Stiefel, who danced *Apollo* with ABT in the late 1990s, was not coached by Balanchine but looks like he could have been. Balanchine told d'Amboise that Apollo has a tantrum as a boy god. That bit doesn't show up in the d'Amboise film, but it is there full blast in the Stiefel performance, when he pounds his thighs with his fists as if angry at the lute for not sounding nice. This show of bad behavior is, I admit, unsettling; one sees Apollo as a boy, a youth, but not as an adolescent. Yet it shows that Stiefel thought about the role and understood that it is a radical departure from the standard Greek ideal of grace. There are other wonderful moments, stemming from the notion of Apollo as athlete. He really kicks his legs as if hitting a soccer ball, and in one lovely moment he moves his arm backward as if preparing to throw a baseball. Never does he dance like a statue.

At NYCB, Peter Martins stands as a transitional figure in the performance history of *Apollo*. Based on two films he made in the 1970s, he is most illuminating in the coda, where there's a sense of growing excitement among all the dancers, as if anticipating the ballet's triumphant denouement. Martins himself fairly explodes with energy. His arms fly high as he skids across the stage, and his entire body crunches to a halt. Like Stiefel, he hoists two of the muses in the air with unabashed machismo—look what I can do, his flexed arms proclaim to the audience. And when he hears Stravinsky's chords announcing his destiny, he listens to the music, deeply. Recognition of his future slowly fills his body.

Yet most of the time, unfortunately, Martins resembles the statue that Balanchine warned against evoking. Perhaps Martins can't help it; with his perfectly proportioned body, perfect turn-out, and a classical technique drummed into him as a child at the Royal Danish Ballet, he is the essence of the danseur noble. Even when playing a raunchy sailor in *Union Jack* (1976), he looked like a demigod. And when assaying the awkwardnesses in *Apollo*, especially the pivots in a circle where he sharply bends his front leg and falls backward, he smooths out the jaggedness. In the duet with Terpsichore, he responds to her frisky jumps with his own lunges, but those lunges do not suggest that he wants to play with her, as d'Amboise's do. There's nothing playful about Martins, or youthful. He's simply a gorgeous classical dancer.

Gorgeous dancing is frequently all that's left of *Apollo* now, as we enter the twenty-first century, eighty-four years after its premiere. Balanchine did not help matters when, in 1979, just as Baryshnikov was to make his NYCB debut in the role, the choreographer "decapitated" the ballet, as the critic Robert Garis put it.[23] Balanchine cut the first scene (the birth of Apollo) and altered the ending. Scene 1 is only four minutes and some seconds long, but it is important.

Showing a newly born god, it creates the narrative context for the ballet to come. As performed in most productions currently (2012), *Apollo* begins in medias res, with Apollo poised to play the lute.

Balanchine also had to change the ending for scenic reasons. The prologue features a staircase topped off by a platform on which Leto gives birth to Apollo. Without the birth scene, the staircase would loom over the ballet without purpose, a distraction. So Balanchine arranged another ending. He transposed to the final pose an earlier tableau of the muses, their legs in arabesque arranged like the sun's rays emanating from Apollo. There is no ascent up Parnassus.

I doubt that anyone approves of the changes Balanchine made except Martins, who as the NYCB director has the authority to restore the original. Still, in removing part of the story Balanchine did not remove all of it. It's been up to the post-Martins Apollos to accomplish that. When dancers first learn Balanchine's choreography, the ballet master breaks down each phrase into counts, to ensure accuracy. These dancers in *Apollo* still seem to be relying on those counts, which makes for tidiness but lacks spontaneity. Their movements look studied, seeking the precise shape of each step rather than the larger kinetic impulse driving the choreography. Seeking clarity above all, they seem reluctant to look awkward, unsure, inquiring, untutored. They all move like the "gorgeous Georges" they are. These Apollos include three of George Balanchine's most sensitive and intelligent dancers—Peter Boal, Ib Andersen, and Nikolaj Hübbe—as well as two dancers of the current generation (ca. 2012), Robert Fairchild and Chase Finlay.

It's not for want of information that Apollo's character has strayed so far from its intention, from the narrative brief shaped by Stravinsky or the extensive notes on interpretation of the role offered over time by the choreographer. Balanchine's comments are found in many books. The testimony of Martins and Villella on Balanchine coaching them is also available. And of course there are the films—two of them—of d'Amboise.

Fairchild said that he watched a video of d'Amboise and that the main thing he remembers is d'Amboise being unraveled from his shroud and pirouetting incredibly fast. "His leg wasn't high in passé but it was dancing. [The] most alive thing I've ever seen. A rugged beauty is in d'Amboise. It's not about tendu."[24] Fairchild's words strike me as very perceptive. He understands the difference between dancing that breathes and dancing that is technically proficient.

In the studio Balanchine, and now Martins, drilled the dancers in tendu, believing that this elementary movement of the legs was a foundation for more complex movement. But a good tendu is no cigar. Why, then, isn't there more

Nikolaj Hübbe as
Apollo, New York City
Ballet, 1999. *Apollo*,
choreography by
George Balanchine
© The George
Balanchine Trust.
Photograph © Paul
Kolnik.

of d'Amboise in Fairchild's performance? "*Apollo* is the first time I used video. I
did that because I was insecure. I don't know if I'll watch video again. It puts
too much pressure on me. I loved what he did, but I want to dance as I dance. I
don't want to copy and paste."

Instead of looking at video, Fairchild went right to the source when, in
November 2013, he was coached by d'Amboise. The sessions were taped by the
Balanchine Foundation as part of its Video Archives program. In these sessions
d'Amboise barely mentioned the narrative as it was explained to him by Balanchine. Instead, he focused on the details of movement that would make the
choreography look less classical. He wanted more twisting, more emphasis on
a turned-in leg. "Slide the foot along the floor, don't point it," he said. When
Apollo in his first steps stumbles back, he instructed Fairchild to "let the back
leg hang. Don't do coupé." And he wanted a short stop after each phrase, which
gave the entire fabric of the choreography clarity and poise—indeed, a feeling
of classicism imposed on the anticlassical movement.

Finlay also consulted videos. "Most dancers," he said, "use videos to learn

Chase Finlay as Apollo, New York City Ballet, 2011. *Apollo*, choreography by George Balanchine © The George Balanchine Trust. Photograph © Paul Kolnik.

steps. How they use their head, arms, put their feet on the ground—that's what I was interested in." But his goal was "making it my own."[25]

"Making it my own" is more important to these dancers than incorporating into their performances the best of their predecessors. The same rationale also explains why producers of the classics in other companies present nineteenth-century ballets as if they had just been created. In the case of putting the original choreography onto the stage, they believe that using manuscripts of choreography by Petipa, some of which are held in the Harvard Theatre Collection, would result in an old-fashioned look. Some directors rechoreograph the traditional material of, say, *The Sleeping Beauty*, to leave their own mark.

Rudolf Nureyev and Erik Bruhn produced versions of *Swan Lake* that alter the libretto as well as the choreography. They interpret the character of Prince Siegfried as being out of sync with the culture of the court and burdened by his over-bearing Queen Mother, because he is really homosexual. En route to this scenario, they beef up the Siegfried role by giving him a solo or two in act 1. These neo-Freudian *Swan Lakes* may not be to everyone's taste, but in fact they do little to the overriding theme of the ballet. Once the lakeside act is over, with its long pas de deux for Odette and the prince, *Swan Lake* is firmly returned to the original story. The ballet belongs to Odette, no matter how many solos Siegfried does.

The company most mindful of its legacy is the Royal Danish Ballet and its repertory of August Bournonville, whose ballets have been in continuous performance (give or take several hiatuses) since their creation in the mid-nineteenth century. Yet as experienced and renowned a dancer-turned-director as Nikolaj Hübbe, who grew up with the Danish troupe and was its leading Bournonville dancer until he joined NYCB in 1992 for sixteen years, has updated many Bournonville ballets. One of them is *Napoli*, in 2009. One of his notable additions is to have Teresina and Gennaro, heroine and hero, enter the festivities of the last act on a motorcycle. But this anachronism does no harm to the meaning of the ballet. The more serious change concerns the story. Teresina is not saved from drowning by divine intervention. Instead, Gennaro uses a love token to restore her. To eradicate the Christian values from the ballet is to deny Bournonville his deeply held religiosity. If Hübbe can so blithely misrepresent the character of his artistic father, anything is possible.

Contemporary Apollos do not take personal ownership of the role because they care more about technique than story. I attribute this priority to the influence of Peter Martins. As steward of George Balanchine's company, he seems uninterested in narrative-driven Apollos and thus in dancing that gives priority to ruggedness over classical line. Perhaps it is Martins's influence that kept the distinguished dancers Andersen, Boal, and Hübbe firmly in the danseur noble mold. I write this about Martins based on my experience of his treatment of other Balanchine ballets in the NYCB repertory, which also tends to give short shrift to their dramatic underpinnings. "Just do the steps," is the credo of the company now. It's true that Balanchine used the phrase, but only as a corrective to overwrought acting. Now the phrase is taken as gospel, obliterating the wide middle ground between clean execution of the steps and false emotion.

However little use the *Apollo* videos have been to dancers now assuming the role, they are obviously of immense value to historians and critics. I couldn't have written this essay without them. They record change and the differences individual dancers make to the meaning of the ballet. The same is true of the extant films and videotapes of *Giselle*. Some of them are a mere few minutes long, but a good deal of information can be gleaned from those archival snippets. And of course there is the thrill of seeing a legend, such as Olga Spessivtseva, materialize in flesh and blood.

The kind of archival research that went into the Pacific Northwest Ballet

(PNB) production of *Giselle* in June 2011 is of a different order, for it aimed to arrive at choreographic authenticity.[26] Doug Fullington, on the staff of PNB, and Marian Smith, a dance historian, used three notation scores to uncover information about the original production. One was a manuscript made in 1842 by ballet master Antoine Titus, to help him mount a production of *Giselle* in St. Petersburg. The second was a staging manual made in the 1860s by Henri Justament. And the third was a choreographic notation score by Vladimir Stepanov, recorded at the turn of the century and based on Petipa's version of *Giselle*.[27]

The earlier scores indicate how the action is aligned with the music, while the Stepanov score became the basis for *Giselles* in the West in the twentieth century. This new-old *Giselle* does indeed restore long-lost elements. There is more mime; some of the footwork is daintier, which conforms to the style of romantic ballet; a scene with woodsmen opens the second act (this scene does show up in a few other companies); and the ending is the one the original librettists intended, with Albrecht, at Giselle's bidding, leaving her grave on the arms of Bathilde. (This ending replaces Diaghilev's more romantic conclusion, with the grieving Albrecht alone, condemned to pay the consequences of his sins.)

The irony of the PNB *Giselle* is that the changes affect the ballet hardly at all. There are no extraneous elements in *Giselle*. It is so perfectly constructed, so tight an amalgam of story and dance, that it is impervious to emendations — reasonable ones, that is. The crucial difference between various performances of *Giselle* or *Apollo* is the dancer playing the leading role, her or his sincerity and intelligence. The pursuit of dramatic authenticity, for which historians and performers may go to the archives, is finally about finding one's way to the choreographer's intention.

DRAMATIS PERSONAE

In order of appearance

Giselle ou Les Wilis, choreographed by Jean Coralli and Jules Perrot, was first performed by Ballet du Théâtre de l'Académie Royale de Musique, starring Carlotta Grisi and Lucien Petipa, at La Salle Le Peletier, Paris, on June 28, 1841. The two-act ballet tells the story of Giselle, a peasant girl, who has a passion for dancing. When she finds out at the end of act 1 that Albrecht, the man she loves, is engaged to someone else, she dies of a broken heart. Act 2 is set in a moonlit glade near Giselle's grave, where the Wilis, female spirits who were jilted before their wedding days, rise from their graves at night and seek revenge upon men by dancing them to death. With music by Adolphe Adam and Friedrich Burgmüller, the librettists Jules-Henri

Vernoy de Saint-Georges and Théophile Gautier took their inspiration from Heinrich Heine's *De l'Allemagne* (1835). An immediate success, the ballet was widely imitated throughout Europe. Of all the Paris Opera's productions of the romantic period, it alone has survived. Despite its success, however, *Giselle* did not become a permanent fixture at the Paris Opera, but continued to be performed in Russia. Diaghilev's Ballets Russes reintroduced *Giselle* to the West in 1910.

Pierre-Jules-Théophile Gautier was born on August 31, 1811, in Tarbes, France, and died on October 23, 1872, in Paris. He was a poet, dramatist, novelist, and journalist, as well as a literary, art, and dance critic, who based his observations in sensuous perception, starting from the physical form and vital energy of the individual dancer. He coauthored *Giselle* in 1841 with Jules-Henri Vernoy de Saint-Georges, inspired by a poem by Heinrich Heine, the Slavic legends of the Wilis, and his love for Carlotta Grisi. Gautier's poems typify the art-for-art's-sake movement as early as 1835. This is paralleled by the conception of *Giselle* as a ballet about dancing (dancing is Giselle's passion and the Wilis' form of revenge). He recognized the potential of ballet as a medium of poetic expression and brought six of his libretti to the stage. His dance criticism covered the years 1836–1871. Besides ballet he reviewed popular entertainment and ethnic dance. Gautier was not an analytic critic and barely discussed choreography, but he had a remarkable gift for description of dancers, décor, and librettos. A selection of his reviews, translated and annotated by the dance historian Ivor Guest, was published in 1986 by Dance Books.

George Balanchine was born Giorgii Melitonovitch Balanchivadze on January 22, 1904, in St. Petersburg, Russia, and died on April 30, 1983, in New York. He was a leading twentieth-century choreographer, who developed ballet in the United States and cofounded the New York City Ballet in 1946. Known for his musicality, he worked extensively with composer Igor Stravinsky. Thirty-nine of his more than four hundred ballets were choreographed to music by Stravinsky. *Apollo* was a kind of ballet manifesto for Balanchine, as it set out the terms and predicted the direction of many later masterpieces. Like Stravinsky and Pablo Picasso, Balanchine not only established new modes of expression and standards of execution, but also summed up and interpreted traditional values for contemporary audiences.

Violette Verdy made her debut in *Giselle* with Ballet Rambert at the Mercury Theatre, London, in 1957. Born Nelly Armande Guillerm in 1933 in Pont-l'Abbé, France, Verdy spent most of her career as a principal dancer with

New York City Ballet (1958–1977). She originated many roles in Balanchine ballets, including *Tchaikovsky Pas De Deux* (1960) and *Emeralds* (1967). Upon her retirement from NYCB, she became the first female director of the Paris Opera Ballet; she also served as codirector of the Boston Ballet in 1980. She served as a faculty member in ballet at the Jacobs School of Music at Indiana University from 1996 and was appointed distinguished professor of music (ballet) in 2005. Violette Verdy died in Bloomington, Indiana, in February 2016.

Jacques d'Amboise made his debut in *Apollo*, restaged by George Balanchine and conducted by Igor Stravinsky, with the New York City Ballet at the New York City Center in 1957. Born Joseph Jacques Ahearn on July 28, 1934, in Dedham, Massachusetts, d'Amboise was a principal dancer with the New York City Ballet (1949–1983). His energetic and expansive dancing greatly influenced the image of the male ballet dancer in America. As a dance educator, d'Amboise founded the National Dance Institute in 1976. *He Makes Me Feel Like Dancin'*, a documentary about his work with the National Dance Institute, won an Academy Award and six Emmy Awards in 1984.

Jules-Henri Vernoy de Saint-Georges was born in 1799, and died in 1875 in Paris. One of the most prolific librettists of the nineteenth century, he often worked in collaboration with other writers to conceive vaudeville performances, operas, ballets, and stage plays, including *Giselle* with Théophile Gautier in 1841.

Heinrich Heine was born Harry Heine on December 13, 1797, in Düsseldorf, Germany, and died on February 17, 1856, in Paris. As a writer, he is widely known for his early lyric poetry, which was set to the music of art songs by composers Robert Schumann and Franz Schubert. He developed an interest in Slavic folklore, which he included in his long poem *De l'Allemagne* (1835). According to Heine, Wilis are unable to rest in their graves because they cannot satisfy their passion for dancing, and they lure any young man they meet to dance with them until he falls dead.

Charles Pierre Baudelaire was born on April 9, 1821, and died on August 31, 1867, in Paris. A poet, art and literary critic, translator, and essayist, he was also the pioneering French translator of Edgar Allan Poe. His most famous work, *Les Fleurs du mal* (*The Flowers of Evil*), expresses the changing nature of beauty in modern, industrializing Paris during the nineteenth century.

Honoré de Balzac was born on May 20, 1799, in Tours, France, and died August 18, 1850, in Paris. A prolific novelist, his *La Comédie humaine* presents a panorama of French life in the years after the 1815 fall of Napoleon.

His work influenced many nineteenth-century writers, including Charles
Dickens, Gustave Flaubert, Marcel Proust, and Henry James.

Carlotta Grisi was born Caronne Adele Josephine Marie Grisi on June 18, 1819,
in Visinada, Italy, and died on May 20, 1899, in Saint-Jean, Switzerland.
An Italian ballerina, Grisi was the muse of choreographer Jules Perrot.
Gautier conceived of *Giselle* with Grisi in mind; she had just made her debut
at the Paris Opera in February 1841. After she successfully premiered *Giselle*
in Paris on June 28, she repeated her triumph at Her Majesty's Theatre,
London, in 1842. Grisi embodied the heroine of another Gautier libretto,
La Péri, in 1843, another of her successes. For the following decade she
increased her stature in the Parisian ballet world as well as in London and
St. Petersburg, before retiring in 1853.

Grub Street, in London, existed since at least the eighteenth century on the
margins of the city's literary scene and was famous for its concentration
of impoverished hack writers, aspiring poets, and low-end publishers
and booksellers. The street no longer exists, but "Grub Street" remains a
pejorative term for hack writers and writings of low literary value.

L'Académie française (the French Academy) is the preeminent learned body
that aims to regulate the French language. The Académie consists of forty
members, known as *immortels* (immortals), and new members are elected by
the members of the Académie itself. The body has the task of acting as an
official authority on the language; it is charged with publishing an official
dictionary. Its rulings, however, are only advisory and not binding on either
the public or the government.

Adolphe Adam was born on July 24, 1803, and died on May 3, 1856, in Paris.
He was a prolific French composer of songs, opéras comiques, and ballets
for theaters in London, Berlin, and Paris, including *Faust* (1833), *La Jolie
Fille de Gand* (1842), and *Le Diable à Quatre* (1845). *Giselle*, whose score he
completed in three weeks, remains his biggest success.

Marius Ivanovich Petipa was born on March 11, 1818, in Marseille, and died
on July 14, 1910, in Gurzuf, Ukraine. A preeminent nineteenth-century
choreographer, Petipa dominated the ballet scene of his day. He grew
up in a large family of dancers, receiving ballet training from his father.
He arrived in Paris early in his career, around *Giselle's* premiere in 1841,
in which his brother Lucien danced the leading male role of Albrecht
alongside Carlotta Grisi. In 1847 Petipa was invited to Russia, where his
career blossomed as ballet master and dancer at St. Petersburg's Imperial
Ballet. As a choreographer, his major revival of *Giselle* was in 1884. He

expanded the dance of the Wilis so that it became one of the important dance moments in act 2. He probably also used more pointe work than his predecessors. *Giselle* had passed out of the repertory of the Paris Opera Ballet in 1867 and did not return to the Western stage until Petipa's version was performed by Diaghilev's Ballets Russes in 1910.

Jean Coralli was born Giovanni Coralli Peracini on January 15, 1779, and died on May 1, 1854, in Paris. He served as ballet master at the Paris Opera (1831–1850) and is inextricably linked with the romantic ballet thanks to his collaboration with Jules Perrot on *Giselle*.

Jules Joseph Perrot was born on August 18, 1810, in Lyon and died on August 18, 1892, in Paramé, France. He served as a choreographer at Her Majesty's Theatre, London, and later as ballet master at the Imperial Russian Ballet. He made his first stage appearance at the Grand Théâtre in Lyon. Greatly taken with the dancing of Carlotta Grisi, Perrot became a friend of her family, her teacher, and eventually her fiancé. Together they performed in London, Vienna, and finally Paris, where Grisi and Perrot became acquainted with Théophile Gautier, who worshiped the young ballerina. Gautier presented Grisi with the scenario for *Giselle*. Although Perrot was not at this time an official member of the Paris Opera, he choreographed (without credit) her dances in the ballet. *Giselle*'s success led to an engagement as principal ballet master at Her Majesty's Theatre, London, where Perrot produced the opening performance on March 12, 1842. He himself danced the role of Albrecht opposite Grisi. After this time, Perrot and Grisi separated; she returned to Paris, while he remained in London (1842–1848) before becoming ballet master at the Imperial Ballet in St. Petersburg, where he worked until 1858.

Sergei Pavlovich Diaghilev was born on March 19, 1872, in Selishchev Barracks, Russia, and died on August 19, 1929, in Venice. Diaghilev was a Russian ballet impresario and producer, who founded and directed the Ballets Russes (1909–1929). Diaghilev produced the Petipa version of *Giselle* (staged and revised by Michel Fokine, starring Tamara Karsavina and Vaslav Nijinsky, Palais Garnier, Paris, June 17, 1910), which inspired most twentieth-century productions. He nurtured several outstanding choreographers, including Nijinsky, **Bronislava Nijinska** (born Bronislava Fominichna Nizhinskaya on January 8, 1891, in Minsk, and died on February 21, 1972, in Palisades, California), and George Balanchine, whose *Apollon musagète* Diaghilev produced in 1928.

Ballerina **Tamara Karsavina** was born Tamara Platonovna Karsavina on

March 9, 1885, in St. Petersburg, Russia, and died May 26, 1978, in Beaconsfield, England.

Dancer and choreographer **Vaslav Nijinsky** was born Vatslav Fomich Nizhinskii on March 12, 1889, in Kiev, Ukraine, and died April 8, 1950, in London.

Giselle was performed by the **Royal Swedish Ballet** and staged and revised by Erik Bruhn at the Royal Opera House, Stockholm, in 1969.

Giselle was performed by the **Cullberg Ballet** and choreographed by **Mats Ek** at the Royal Opera House, Stockholm, on July 6, 1982. Born on April 18, 1945, in Malmö, Sweden, Ek was a dancer and choreographer for the Cullberg Ballet (named after his mother, choreographer Birgit Cullberg) from 1973 to 1993.

Giselle was performed by the **Boston Ballet**, starring Violette Verdy and Edward Villella, in Boston in 1968.

Olga Aleksandrovna Spessivtseva was born on July 18, 1895, in Rostov, Russia, and died on September 16, 1991, in New York. She joined Diaghilev's Ballets Russes on tour as early as 1916 and danced opposite Nijinsky. Her stage career spanned from 1913 to 1939.

Tamara Vladimirovna Toumanova was born on March 2, 1919, in Tyumen, Russia, and died on May 29, 1996, in Santa Monica, California. She danced for the Ballet Russe de Monte Carlo and from the early 1940s became a well-traveled guest artist with numerous ballet companies in the Americas and Europe.

Galina Sergeevna Ulanova was born on January 8, 1910, in St. Petersburg, Russia, and died on March 21, 1998, in Moscow. She danced her first Giselle in 1932 with the Kirov Ballet in St. Petersburg, before being transferred by Joseph Stalin to the Bolshoi Ballet in Moscow in 1944. She retired from the stage at the age of fifty.

Giselle was performed by the **London Festival Ballet** and staged by Anton Dolin (after Petipa), starring **Carla Fracci**, in London in 1959. Born August 20, 1936, in Milan, Fracci is an Italian ballet dancer, who started her career at La Scala. In 1959 she appeared as a guest with the London Festival Ballet in *Giselle*, a role she later brought to the Royal Swedish Ballet in 1969 and to the American Ballet Theatre dancing opposite Erik Bruhn in 1970. British dancer and choreographer **Anton Dolin** was born Sydney Francis Patrick Chippendall Healey-Kay on July 27, 1904, in Slinfold, United Kingdom, and died on November 25, 1983, in Paris, France.

Alicia Markova was born Lillian Alicia Marks on December 1, 1910, in London,

and died on December 2, 2004, in Bath, England. She danced in Diaghilev's
Ballets Russes from the age of fourteen (from 1924–1929) and debuted
as Giselle with the Vic-Wells Ballet, in a production staged by Nicholas
Sergeyev, at the Old Vic Theatre, London, on January 1, 1934. In the three
decades that followed she made the role her own. She was the first British
dancer to become the principal dancer of a ballet company. She danced with
the Rambert Dance Company, The Royal Ballet, and the American Ballet
Theatre, and was coounder and director of the English National Ballet.

Lynn Seymour, born Berta Lynn Springbett on March 8, 1939, in Wainwright,
Alberta, was a Canadian ballerina, choreographer, and muse of British
choreographer Kenneth MacMillan for twenty years.

Alicia Alonso debuted as Giselle in 1943 with the American Ballet Theatre,
in a production staged by Anton Dolin, at the Metropolitan Opera House,
New York. Born Alicia Ernestina de la Caridad del Cobre Martínez del
Hoyo on December 21, 1921, in Havana, Alonso is a Cuban ballet dancer,
choreographer, and artistic director, who started her career in New York
with the American Ballet Theatre. After her *Giselle* debut she joined the
company and danced the role until 1948, when she returned to Cuba and
founded Ballet Alicia Alonso (now Ballet Nacional de Cuba).

Natalia Makarova debuted in *Giselle* with the Kirov Ballet, at the Mariinsky
Theatre, St. Petersburg, in 1959. Born Natalia Romanovna Makarova on
November 21, 1940, in Leningrad, she joined the Kirov Ballet in 1959.
She defected to the United States and made her debut as Giselle with the
American Ballet Theatre in December 1970. In 1989 Makarova became the
first Soviet exile to be invited back to dance in her home country. In 2000
she directed *Giselle* for the Royal Swedish Ballet.

Natalia Bessmertnova debuted in *Giselle* with the Bolshoi Ballet, staged by
Leonid Lavrovsky, at the Bolshoi Theatre, Moscow, on November 20, 1963.
Born Natalia Igorevna Bessmertnova on July 19, 1941, she died on February
19, 2008, in Moscow. She was a Russian ballet dancer with the Bolshoi
Ballet (1961–1989).

Diana Vishneva debuted as Giselle with the Mariinsky Ballet at the Mariinsky
Theatre, St. Petersburg. Born on July 13, 1976, in Leningrad, Russia,
Vishneva is a principal dancer with both the Mariinsky Ballet and American
Ballet Theatre.

Natalia Osipova made her American Ballet Theatre debut in *Giselle* at the
Metropolitan Opera House, New York, on June 13, 2009. Born on May 18,
1986, in Moscow, Osipova was a principal dancer with the Bolshoi Ballet

and Mikhailovsky Theatre in St. Petersburg. She joined The Royal Ballet in 2013.

Marie Taglioni was born on April 23, 1804, in Stockholm, and died on April 22, 1884, in Marseille. She was a member of a ballet-dancing family. She began her career at the Paris Opera and gradually developed a rivalry with **Fanny Elssler** (b. June 23, 1810; d. November 27, 1884, in Vienna); they were regarded as two of the great ballerinas of the romantic era. Théophile Gautier went so far as to contrast them in religious terms, Elssler being the desirable and attainable "pagan" dancer and Taglioni the virginal "Christian" dancer.

Fanny Cerrito was born Francesca Teresa Guiseppa Raffaela Cerito on May 11, 1817, in Naples, and died on May 6, 1909, in Paris. She spent much of her career at Her Majesty's Theatre in London, where in 1843 she danced a pas de deux with Elssler, choreographed by Jules Perrot. Earlier that year, she and Taglioni appeared at La Scala, sometimes on the same evening, giving rise to rival bands of fanatical *Cerritisti* and *Taglionisti*.

Lucile Grahn was born Lucina Alexia Grahn on June 30, 1819, in Copenhagen, and died on April 4, 1907, in Munich. A favorite of August Bournonville at the Royal Danish Ballet, she was an outsider when she formally debuted at the Paris Opera on August 1, 1838. Though Gautier was not enthralled by Grahn in his reviews, Perrot eventually included her in a now famous pas de quatre with Taglioni, Cerrito, and Carlotta Grisi, at Her Majesty's Theatre.

Romantic ballets can be seen as reacting against earlier ballets about the gods and goddesses of Greek and Roman antiquity. In their place choreographers drew characters from folk sources, including creatures of the supernatural world, such as the Wilis in *Giselle*. The romantic era in ballet began in 1831 with the premiere in Paris of Giacomo Meyerbeer's opera *Robert le Diable* and its "ballet of the nuns." In this scene, which takes place in an abandoned abbey, ghostly figures cast off their habits and abandon themselves to the sensuous delights of their past lives. The following year, *La Sylphide* (with choreography by Filippo Taglioni and his daughter Marie Taglioni dancing the sylph) brought ballet firmly into the romantic age, because it performed what became a central theme: the conflict between everyday life and a man's vision of the ideal woman. The romantic age heralded the era of the ballerina, who could now embody the ethereal quality of the heroines she played through the technical innovation of the pointe shoe. The era slowly faded in the 1860s, when the locus of classical Western dance moved from Paris to Russia.

Mikhail Baryshnikov appeared in his own staging of *Giselle* (after Petipa) for the American Ballet Theatre at the Metropolitan Opera House, New York, in 1980. Born Mikhail Nikolaevich Baryshnikov on January 27, 1948, in Riga, Latvia, his 1972 Kirov Ballet debut as Albrecht was a turning point in his career. He portrayed the male lead as a warm-blooded youth rather than as the cool, unshakable aristocrat to which Russian audiences were accustomed. In 1974 he defected to the United States and joined the American Ballet Theatre in New York. He danced with the New York City Ballet in 1978 for two seasons before returning to the American Ballet Theatre, serving as its artistic director (1980–1990).

In ancient Greek mythology, **muses** are the goddesses who inspire writers, scientists, and artists. They are represented in storytelling and art by characteristic emblems, poses, and gestures, some of which inspired Balanchine's choreographic choices. **Terpsichore**, muse of dance and song, plays a lyre and accompanies dancers with her music; **Polyhymnia**, muse of sacred poetry and hymns, eloquence, as well as agriculture and pantomime, is serious, pensive, and meditative, often holding a finger to her mouth, dressed in a long cloak and veil; and **Calliope**, muse of epic poetry, holds a writing tablet in her hand. In *Apollo*, the young god selects Terpsichore, personifying dance, over her sister muses.

Composer **Igor Stravinsky** was born Igor Fyodorovich Stravinskii on June 17, 1882, in Oranienbaum, Russia, and died on April 6, 1971, in New York. Noted for his stylistic diversity, he first achieved international prominence with three ballets commissioned and performed in Paris by Diaghilev's Ballets Russes: *The Firebird* (1910), *Petroushka* (1911), and *The Rite of Spring* (1913). In 1928 *Apollon musagète* (now referred to as *Apollo*), the first Balanchine-Stravinsky collaboration, premiered in Paris. After he emigrated from France to the United States in 1939, Stravinsky continued his artistic collaboration with Balanchine until 1962.

Elizabeth Penn Sprague was born on October 30, 1864, in Chicago, and died on November 4, 1953, in Cambridge, Massachusetts. An American pianist and patron of music, especially of chamber music, she started the Berkshire Music Festival in 1916, now housed at Tanglewood in Lenox, Massachusetts.

Adolph Bolm, born on September 25, 1884, in St. Petersburg, died on April 16, 1951, in Hollywood, California. He was a Russian American dancer and choreographer who danced with the Mariinsky Ballet before joining Diaghilev's Ballets Russes (1909–1917). He settled permanently in the

United States in 1917, and in 1928 he choreographed *Apollon musagète*—the first production to Igor Stravinsky's score—at the Library of Congress. In 1933 he founded the San Francisco Opera Ballet, the precursor of the San Francisco Ballet.

Serge Lifar was born Sergei Mikhailovich Serdkin on April 2, 1905, in Kiev, and died on December 15, 1986, in Lausanne, Switzerland. A Russian dancer and choreographer who started dancing with Diaghilev's Ballets Russes in 1923, Lifar was the successor to Nijinsky as the Ballets Russes's principal male dancer—and as Diaghilev's lover. He performed the title role in the French premiere of *Apollo* under Balanchine's direction. After Diaghilev's death in 1929, Lifar was invited to choreograph for the Paris Opera Ballet, which had fallen into decline in the late nineteenth century. After nearly three decades of successful productions and reforms, he retired from the Opera in 1958.

Lew Christensen debuted in the first American production of *Apollo* with the American Ballet, directed by George Balanchine, at the Metropolitan Opera House, New York, on April 27, 1937. Born Lewellyn Farr Christensen on May 6, 1909, in Brigham City, Utah, he died on October 9, 1984, in San Bruno, California. Christensen was a dancer, choreographer, and member of a dancing family that contributed to the establishment of a ballet tradition in the western United States. He directed the San Francisco Ballet from 1952 to 1984.

Diana Adams was born on March 29, 1929, in Staunton, Virginia, and died on January 10, 1993, in San Andreas, California. She was a principal dancer for the New York City Ballet (1950–1963), where she originated many roles in Balanchine ballets, including *Agon* (1957) and *Liebeslieder Walzer* (1960). She later taught at and served as the dean of the School of American Ballet.

Jillana Segreta was born in 1936 in Hackensack, New Jersey, and was a principal dancer with the New York City Ballet (1947–1967), where she originated several roles in Balanchine ballets. She taught at the University of California, Irvine, and is currently the director of the Jillana School in San Diego.

Francia Russell was born on January 10, 1938, in Los Angeles and danced with the New York City Ballet (1956–1961). She codirected the Pacific Northwest Ballet in Seattle (1977–2005).

Peter Martins debuted in *Apollo* with the New York City Ballet at the Edinburgh Festival, Scotland, in 1967. Born October 27, 1946, in Copenhagen, Martins is a Danish dancer and choreographer. He was a principal dancer with the

Royal Danish Ballet (1965–1969), with whom he danced his first Apollo in the spring of 1967. He later joined the New York City Ballet in 1970, where he succeeded George Balanchine as director in 1990.

Born October 1, 1936, in Bayside, New York, **Edward Villella** was a dancer with New York City Ballet (1957–1979). He danced the roles of both Albrecht and Apollo and often made guest appearances with other companies. He debuted in *Apollo* with New York City Ballet at the New York State Theater, Lincoln Center, New York, in 1964. In 1986 Villella founded the Miami City Ballet, where he served as artistic director until 2012.

Born February 13, 1973, in Tyrone, Pennsylvania, **Ethan Stiefel** was a principal dancer with the American Ballet Theatre (1997–2012). He currently directs the Royal New Zealand Ballet.

Union Jack, choreographed by George Balanchine, was performed by the New York City Ballet at the New York State Theater, Lincoln Center, New York, on May 13, 1976.

In Greek mythology, **Leto** is a daughter of the Titans Coeus and Phoebe and the sister of Asteria. In the Olympian cosmology, **Zeus** is the father of her twins, Apollo and Artemis.

Peter Boal debuted in *Apollo* with the New York City Ballet at the New York State Theater, Lincoln Center, New York, in 1985. Born October 18, 1965, in Bedford, New York, Boal was principal dancer with the New York City Ballet (1983–2005) before joining the Pacific Northwest Ballet as artistic director in 2005. He danced the role of Apollo until his retirement from the stage.

Ib Andersen debuted in *Apollo* with the New York City Ballet at the New York State Theater, New York, in 1980. Born December 14, 1954, in Copenhagen, Andersen is a Danish dancer and choreographer who started with the Royal Danish Ballet (1972–1979) before joining the New York City Ballet (1980–1990). He became Ballet Arizona's artistic director in 2000.

Nikolaj Hübbe debuted in *Apollo* with the Royal Danish Ballet at the Royal Opera House, Copenhagen, in 1989. Born October 30, 1967, in Copenhagen, Hübbe trained at the Royal Danish Ballet School and started his career with the company. He was a principal dancer with the New York City Ballet (1992–2008) before rejoining the Royal Danish Ballet as artistic director in 2008.

Robert Fairchild debuted in *Apollo* with the New York City Ballet on tour at the Kennedy Center for the Performing Arts on April 5, 2011. Born in 1989 in Salt Lake City, Utah, Fairchild joined the New York City Ballet in 2006 and is now a principal dancer.

Chase Finlay debuted in *Apollo* with the New York City Ballet at the David H. Koch Theater, Lincoln Center, New York, on May 5, 2011. Born in 1990 in Fairfield, Connecticut, Finlay joined the New York City Ballet in 2009 and is now a principal dancer.

Swan Lake, first choreographed by Julius Reisinger, premiered at the Bolshoi Theatre, Moscow, on March 4, 1877. The score was composed in 1875–1876 by Pyotr Ilyich Tchaikovsky, based on a libretto by Vladimir Begichev and Vasily Geltser. The 1895 revival by Marius Petipa and Lev Ivanov (b. February 18, 1834; d. December 11, 1901, in St. Petersburg), first staged for the Imperial Ballet on January 15, 1895, at the Mariinsky Theatre, St. Petersburg, is the basis for most subsequent productions.

Rudolf Nureyev staged and revised *Swan Lake* for the Vienna State Opera Ballet, starring Margot Fonteyn and Rudolf Nureyev, at the State Opera, Vienna, on October 15, 1964. Rudolf Khametovich Nureyev was born on March 17, 1938, near Irkutsk (Siberia), and died January 5, 1993, in Paris. A celebrated Russian dancer who began his career in 1958 with the Kirov Ballet in Leningrad, Nureyev defected to the West in 1961 while on tour in France. Nureyev danced and choreographed for The Royal Ballet (1962–1976), then became artistic director of the Paris Opera Ballet in 1983, and continued performing until 1992.

Erik Bruhn was born Erik Belton Evers Bruhn on October 3, 1928, in Copenhagen and died April 1, 1986, in Toronto. This Danish dancer and choreographer trained at the Royal Danish Ballet School. His debut with American Ballet Theatre on May 1, 1955, in the role of Albrecht, partnering Alicia Markova, nearly twenty years his senior, caused a sensation. He staged and revised *Swan Lake* for the National Ballet of Canada, starring Lois Smith and Earl Kraul, at the O'Keefe Centre, Toronto, on March 27, 1967. Later he became director of the Royal Swedish Ballet.

August Bournonville, born on August 21, 1805, died on November 30, 1879, in Copenhagen. He was a ballet master and choreographer for the Royal Danish Ballet, for which he created more than fifty ballets over the course of five decades. With a firm foundation in the Danish Biedermeier tradition, Bournonville depicted a harmonious life for a growing middle-class audience. He resisted many of the excesses of the romantic ballet in his work. At a time when European ballet emphasized the ballerina, Bournonville gave equal emphasis to both male and female roles.

Napoli, or The Fisherman and His Bride, choreographed by August Bournonville, was first performed by the Royal Danish Ballet at the Royal Danish Theater,

Copenhagen, on March 29, 1842. More recently, Nikolaj Hübbe directed *Napoli* with the Royal Danish Ballet, starring Ulrik Birkkjaer and Gitte Lindstrom, at the Royal Opera House, Copenhagen, on November 12, 2009.

Vladimir Ivanovich Stepanov, born on June 29, 1866, died on January 28, 1896, in St. Petersburg. He was a dancer for the Imperial Ballet in St. Petersburg. He was the first to base a movement notation system on the anatomical analysis of movement and to use music notes as his basic signs. Stepanov's system had been used to record the Marius Petipa repertory. Interest in this notation system waned as ballet choreography became increasingly complex.

NOTES

1. Violette Verdy, *Giselle: A Role for a Lifetime* (New York: M. Dekker, 1977).

2. Joanna Richardson, *Théophile Gautier: His Life and Times* (London: Max Reinhardt, 1958); and Théophile Gautier, preface to *Mademoiselle de Maupin*, trans. Joanna Richardson (Harmondsworth, Middlesex, UK: Penguin Books, 1981), 39. Although Gautier did not use the phrase "art for art's sake" (*l'art pour l'art*), the preface to this novel was the earliest articulation of the idea that art was valuable as art, that artistic pursuits justified themselves, and that works of art did not require a moral foundation to be considered legitimate—they could even be morally subversive.

3. Richardson, *Théophile Gautier*, 57.

4. Verdy, *Giselle*, 5–6.

5. Théophile Gautier, "Letter to Heine," trans. Cyril W. Beaumont, in *Reading Dance: A Gathering of Memoirs, Reportage, Criticism, Profiles, Interviews, and Some Uncategorizable Extras*, ed. Robert Gottlieb (New York: Random House, 2008), 764.

6. Cyril W. Beaumont, *The Ballet Called "Giselle"* (Princeton, NJ: Princeton Book Co., 1987), 79.

7. Verdy, *Giselle*, 34.

8. Verdy, *Giselle*, 69.

9. Alastair Macaulay, "Ballet Theater Embraces Its Challenges," *New York Times*, July 6, 2012.

10. Ivor Guest, *The Romantic Ballet in Paris* (Middletown, CT: Wesleyan University Press, 1966).

11. Verdy, *Giselle*, 70, 10–11.

12. Beaumont, *The Ballet Called "Giselle,"* 79.

13. Théophile Gautier, "The Tourist," in *My Fantoms*, trans. Richard Holmes (New York: New York Review of Books, 2008), 143–44.

14. This 1969 National Ballet (Washington, DC) production of *Giselle*, available on DVD, costarred Edward Villella.

15. Under Diaghilev's direction, the company rehearsed its early repertory in St. Petersburg but performed exclusively in the West, particularly in Monte Carlo, London, and Paris between 1911 and Diaghilev's death in 1929. In 1928 Diaghilev produced the European premiere of *Apollo* under the direction of George Balanchine, with Serge Lifar dancing the title role.

16. Charles M. Joseph, *Stravinsky & Balanchine: A Journey of Invention* (New Haven, CT: Yale University Press, 2002).

17. Jacques d'Amboise, *I Was a Dancer* (New York: Alfred A. Knopf, 2011), 181–82.

18. New York City Ballet, *La compagnie du New York City Ballet* (Montréal: Radio-Canada, 2007), DVD.

19. Over the last century, the term *danseur noble* has come to designate a male principal dancer who performs at the highest theatrical level, combining grace with technique. Some use danseur noble as the masculine equivalent to prima ballerina.

20. Edward Villella and Larry Kaplan, *Prodigal Son: Dancing for Balanchine in a World of Pain and Magic* (New York: Simon & Schuster, 1992), 146.

21. Peter Martins and Robert Cornfield, *Far From Denmark* (Boston: Little, Brown, 1982), 38.

22. Francis Mason, *I Remember Balanchine: Recollections of the Ballet Master by Those Who Knew Him* (New York: Doubleday, 1991), 253.

23. Robert Garis, *Following Balanchine* (New Haven, CT: Yale University Press, 1995), 77.

24. Fairchild, telephone interview, February 15, 2012.

25. Finlay, telephone interview, February 15, 2012.

26. *Giselle*, directed by Peter Boal, starring Carla Körbes and Karel Cruz (McCaw Hall, Seattle, June 3, 2011).

27. Moira Macdonald, "PNB Turns Old Documents into a New 'Giselle,'" *Seattle Times*, May 28, 2011.

BODY AS SIGNIFIER

When I was first invited to write about the body as archive, I wondered how I could offer alternatives to the mainstream idea that the body serves as a container of historically approved narratives. Body as archive, as a philosophical concept, emerges at the crossroads where "real" culture no longer resides, in cavernous European libraries where scholars toil over postdoctoral research. Challenging the apparatus of the Enlightenment and its established institutional home, this notion reimagines the body as a nonblank slate, on which many histories are inscribed and ready for exploration. It assumes that knowledge exists outside Cartesian rationality and is made available through muscles, bones, energy, and physical motion specific to individual bodies. This concept envisions the performing body as a viable site for displaying knowledge and culture other than that which is archived in Western institutions.

To address these issues, I analyze body as archive in the context of my performance *Para-Dice*, a postcolonial paradisiacal faux lecture that addresses bodies in motion, race, in/visibility, and colonial history. *Para-Dice*, built on different cultural perspectives, extends to dance and the dancing body a critical analysis of the hierarchical processes shaping culture at large and dance history in particular. This hybrid dance theater work attests to my predicament as a transplanted Brazilian artist who immersed herself in the Americanism of New York dance a long time ago.

A twofold perspective that I developed early in New York, when I kept my dancing life separate from my social/cultural encounters, shapes *Para-Dice*. In those early years I trained my body in New York "downtown" dance by day and immersed myself in a community of self-exiled Latin American artists by night. The dancing had no visible relationship to my avid consumption of movies, exhibitions, protests, and talks about Latin American politics and art. This was an experience I missed growing up under the military junta in Brazil from 1964 to 1984, which censored most materials addressing Latin American's art and politics that were considered "subversive" by the military junta.

During those first years in New York I rooted myself in a grid of ideas and people that kept me from consuming the American experience uncritically. I developed a "double consciousness," what W. E. B. Du Bois described as "a sense of always looking at one's self through the eyes of the other."[1]

I read Pablo Neruda and Erico Verissimo and kept the *I ching* by my bed. Graciela Figueroa, the great Uruguayan choreographer who moved to Rio de Janeiro after dancing with Twyla Tharp in New York, told her dancers about the chance-based compositional procedures of Merce Cunningham and John Cage and introduced us to the music and poetry of Violeta Parra, Mercedes Sosa, and Victor Jara. She instilled in me at a young age the need to cultivate a Latin American identity. By inserting myself in a Latin diaspora, my personal history became the foundation on which I grounded my newly Americanized dance universe. Rather than becoming a happy, assimilated immigrant who fully adopted the local culture, I distanced myself from it and asserted my alterity. That choice had nothing to do with a proud nationalism; it was mostly a gesture of self-preservation.

Thirty years later I drew on those early outside experiences to create *Para-Dice*. I foregrounded the straddling of multiple cultures and its effects on my life and body, which I redirected toward the viewers. They became the outsiders, unaware of the language (I referred to them as monolingual while speaking a little Portuguese throughout), the culture, and the cultural references; they were made to feel distanced from the performers' physical experience on stage. Reversing the roles, I patronizingly turned the audience into students, passive observers who were displaced to the margins of a political and cultural history they knew little about. The performance space was transformed into a lecture hall; I turned myself into a foul-mouthed, maniacal professor; and the "students" found themselves transferred into a nineteenth-century imperial European landscape, where they were blamed for their inability to comprehend "others."

I purposefully racialized the performers' bodies as white and other and split the performance space into "civilized" and "primitive," to connect behavior, physical expression, and artistic choice to specific geographic locations, history, and race. In *Para-Dice*, I designated the downstage portion of the stage as the area where the group of trained white bodies spewed clichéd graduate-school language, displayed their physical skills of "trained" dancing, and re-enacted excerpts of the modern dance canon; upstage was where the "multicultural," brown bodies re-created generic scenes from the lexicon of international pop culture.

By arranging the different bits of performance according to the performers' racial identity and spatial location, *Para-Dice* reflected the hierarchical principles that still organize contemporary dance into binaries: white/other, uptown/downtown, experimental/traditional, concept driven/movement driven. Unlike the voiceless, indigenous Other of earlier colonial narratives, *Para-Dice*'s

Alyssa Alpine and Tom Rawe in *Para-Dice* by Patricia Hoffbauer. Danspace Project at St. Mark's Church, New York, November 2013. (See plate 8 for color image.) Photograph © Ian Douglas.

"urban savages" flaunted their bodies, shook their booties, asserted their gender fluidity, and expressed themselves in several languages. They satirized a system of representation that had excluded their testimonies in the past, and re-created iconic pop performances with a parodical revenge. Performers George Emilio Sanchez and Elisa Osborne embraced histrionic stereotypes, discarded their marginal status, and moved into the center of the narrative, making their subaltern bodies impact *Para-Dice*'s overall narrative.[2]

Their presence reshuffled viewers' attention away from the white dancers' "sophisticated" postmodern dancing downstage, and their carnivalesque re-enactments (in skimpy outfits) reflecting US pop culture's fetishizing of Brazilian bodies.[3] Instead of carving out a critical distance between audience and performer, Sanchez and Osborne's self-conscious, over-the-top reenactments purposefully seduced the audience and fellow performers, who desired that outrageousness for themselves.

During research and rehearsal, the white dancers' physicality and choreography, based on my own experience with various New York choreographers, were the most difficult to calibrate as a group expression. Rehearsal guests commented on the white dancers' blandness, their lack of personality, and felt I was misrepresenting them. But only a few were made uncomfortable by the representation of the Others. I wondered if they were reacting to the way I foregrounded whiteness as the unspoken standard for modern dance, if it was my directorial problem, or if indeed there was an actual imbalance in how cultural stereotypes are perceived. After all, one group's caricatured behavior could be considered less entertaining than another's, and all things being equal, postmodern dance's so-called neutrality might not be as much fun—or as funny—as reenacting outrageousness. Some of the performers told me they did not feel comfortable being represented as white; they wanted to wear colorful outfits and share Osborne's performance riff on *Chorus Line*. Being caricaturized as the outrageous Others was not easy either. Much labor went into shaping a physicality that was intended to express both the forced nature of the entertaining bits as well as their ridiculously funny aspects.

As we continued to explore ways cultural difference frames performance and dance, all players eventually embodied a physicality that they did not identify with, experiencing some level of alterity. The downstage white material was characterized by even rhythms; abstract choreography; partnering occasioned by spatial connection, not dramatic relationship; a neutral, self-effacing internal gaze; and an overall attitude that reflected the group's self-sufficient quality. The bits of clichéd stereotypes performed by Osborne and Sanchez included mimicking Anthony Quinn's character from the 1964 film *Zorba the Greek*. They shared the peasant's enthusiasm for dancing that, in *Zorba*, salvaged Alan Bates's emotionally bankrupt upper-class English character, and in *Para-Dice* offered physical alternatives to the humorless white dance downstage. By reenacting the film's teach-me-to-dance excerpt, *Para-Dice* challenged idealized notions of others' so-called natural access to knowledge situated in the (dancing) body and foreclosed to the civilized European (*Zorba*'s Greek identity mirrors "Third-World" stereotypes). The same colonial rhetoric that invented the "noble savage" offered us the narrative in which the body delivers us from cerebral complexities and lets us into our deep buried selves, as illustrated in the Zorba/Bates duet in *Zorba the Greek* and parodied by the Osborne/Sanchez duet.

Instead of neatly resolving the groups' initial irremediable differences, *Para-Dice*'s split structure of upstage/downstage and body/mind eventually reveals their embroiled codependent relationship. The seeming self-sufficiency of the postmodern choreography is unraveled by repetition, and details of its cultural/artistic influence emerge: the loose torso over tap-dancing feet that makes up Tom Rawe's material references Twyla Tharp's exploration of vaudeville and her fascination with the jazz rhythms of black composers like Fats Waller and Jelly

George Emilio Sanchez, Elisa Osborne, and Tom Rawe in *Para-Dice* by Patricia Hoffbauer. Danspace Project at St. Mark's Church, New York, November 2013. (See plate 9 for color image.) Photograph © Ian Douglas.

Roll Morton. The self-involved sensuality of Tharp's interpreter Sara Rudner[4] and the Rudner-like dance phrase performed by Alyssa Alpine reflects traces of show dance inflected with kick-line motifs. If these were not obvious clues, the layering of the choreography with Muddy Water's "Mannish Boy" at the end signaled a history of cultural borrowing, which is emphasized throughout the dance by the onstage appearance of a photograph of African American dancer Arthur Mitchell with Russian American choreographer George Balanchine.

To further explore the "us/them" proposition, I reread anthropologist Claude Lévi-Strauss's *Tristes Tropiques* and sixteenth-century French explorer Jean de Lery's *A Voyage to the Land of Brazil*.[5] I identified the vertigo Lery experienced crossing the Atlantic Ocean with how I felt creating this piece: "Whether you are staggering on shipboard or teetering on the gangplank of the New World experience, you must subject yourself to the risks of vertigo. You must be able to avoid stumbling, and yet must not be afraid of stumbling that will not step . . . [He] must be momentarily out of control: 'sens defaillis et chancelant comme ivrognes.'"

For Lery, stumbling out of his Eurocentric perspective was a sine qua non for absorbing the New World's destabilizing beauty. Similarly, the performers in

Para-Dice by Patricia Hoffbauer. Seated are Elisa Osborne and George Emilio Sanchez; standing, from left to right, are Laura Gilberts, Peggy Gould, and Alyssa Alpine. Danspace Project at St. Mark's Church, New York, November 2013. (See plate 10 for color image.) Photograph © Ian Douglas.

Para-Dice revisited their own cultural histories when performing those stories. The evolution of Osborne's and Sanchez's roles challenged the colonial narrative that placed indigenous peoples on history's margin, moving from exoticized natives to complex characters, offering an easier parable for audiences to absorb and participate in, in the end.

As we finished this performance work, I wondered if we had been successful in fashioning an allegory, based on the old conquest/conquered story, to navigate the instability of contemporary culture. Had we constructed viable alternatives to the archived knowledge of Western museums, libraries, and universities, institutions built to fulfill expectations of those who hoped to achieve an understanding of Western civilization and its storied past? In my ongoing efforts to create alternative paradises, while resisting continuously impending assimilation, I considered the *Manifesto Antropófago* (1928) of Brazilian visionary Oswald de Andrade to inform the conclusion of the dance. Andrade in this work recommends cultural anthropophagy, the proverbial cannibalizing of the colonizer's culture, as the only legitimate political choice for Latin American artists searching for a voice and a body to express their vision. So, rather than dreaming of savages, the artists inhabiting *Para-Dice* found their own internal Wild Man/Woman paradigm. Avoiding predictable mimicry, all performers in *Para-Dice* offered their bodies as archive that displayed the experience of difference.

To conclude my rumination on body as archive, I quote from *Para-Dice's* final text, written by writer/performer George Emilio Sanchez, whose words were delivered by my professorial persona at the end of *Para-Dice*:

> Where do we go from here? How will you get from there to here? Because it is apparent we can no longer remain where we are, as we are. What do questions beg? Questions don't beg; people do. So, I beg your pardon. Pardon me for asking but where lies your paradise? Is it the same place for you and me? Who can live there? Who can remain? . . . What is not in my words reverberates in my experience. What is not in my body is realized in my soul. And what is not entranced in earth is released in paradise.[6]

NOTES

Para-Dice was created in two iterations: phase 1 in 2009–2010 and phase 2 in 2010–2013.

Phase 1—text: Patricia Hoffbauer and George Emilio Sanchez; visual design and film editing: Peter Richards; direction/choreography: Patricia Hoffbauer; performers: Peggy Gould, Patricia Hoffbauer, Elisa Osborne, George Emilio Sanchez. Developed at The Yard, a Colony for the Performing Arts, on Martha's Vineyard under the directorship of Wendy Taucher, and presented at the 92nd Street Y's 75th Anniversary, at Dixon Place, and at Danspace Project at St. Mark's Church (2009–2010) in New York City.

Phase 2—text: Patricia Hoffbauer and George Emilio Sanchez; film editing and design: Peter Richards; screen design: Bryan Fox; set design: Gordon Landenberger; rehearsal assistant: Peggy Gould; performers: Alyssa Alpine, Laura Gilbert, Peggy Gould, Patricia Hoffbauer, Elisa Osborne, Peter Richards, Tom Rawe, George Emilio Sanchez. Developed at the Vermont Festival of the Arts; at Danspace Project; and at the Painted Bride Art Center in Philadelphia; also developed at a residency at Gibney Dance in New York City. Commissioned and presented in New York City by Danspace Project at St. Mark's Church, November 2013. Funding sources provided by Lewis Center for the Arts, Princeton University; Foundation of Contemporary Art; Philadelphia Live Arts Festival residency program; The Yard, a Colony for the Performing Arts; Indiegogo.

1. W. E. B. Du Bois, *The Souls of Black Folk* (Chicago: A.C. McClurg; Cambridge, UK: University Press/John Wilson and Son, 1903).

2. The term *subaltern* here refers to Gayatri Spivak, "Can the Subaltern Speak?," in *Marxism and the Interpretation of Culture*, ed. Cary Nelson and Lawrence Grossberg (Urbana: University of Illinois Press, 1988), 271–313.

3. The white dancers were Alyssa Alpine, Laura Gilberts, Peggy Gould, and Tom Rawe.

4. Sara Rudner, choreographer, dancer, and director of the Dance Program at Sarah Lawrence College, was a founding member of Twyla Tharp's original dance company in 1965. She danced with Tharp for two decades.

5. Claude Lévi-Strauss, *Tristes Tropiques* (Paris: Union generale d'éditions, 1966); Jean de Lery, *A History of a Voyage to the Land of Brazil* [1578], trans. Janet Whatley (Los Angeles: University of California Press, 1992). The Lery quote is used by Whatley in her essay "Impression and Initiation: Jean de Lery's Brazil Voyage," *Modern Language Studies* 19, no. 3 (1989): 15–25.

6. "Entranced in earth" in George's text is a reference to Brazilian filmmaker Glauber Rocha's and Cinema Novo's infamous representative film *Terra em Transe*, translated into English as *Entranced Earth*. This film is mentioned throughout *Para-Dice*, and excerpts of it are used in Peter Richard's film narrative that accompanies *Para-Dice*. *Terra em Transe* is about an Eldorado, a fictitious country in Latin America inundated with the internal struggle for political power.

IV. Performing the Archive

Mining the archive to find history is less about recapturing the past than it is about generating future action. Making a dance is performing one's bodied archive, leading to research in archives of personal or ancestral memory or to external archives of written, oral, or material data. This effort of recapturing may even lead to the archival residues in buildings and places, smells, and sounds. The past is never fully recoverable, and in particular, past human movement compels acknowledgment that every performance of the bodied archive is a supremely present and uniquely different act. The nature of this tension remains unresolved, part of any practice that performs the archive.

If elements of a work are held in recent memory, still palpable or accessible within the choreographer's various archives—notes, notation, visuals, dancers, or her own body—the thresholds of possibility still depend on location, recall, transference, and intent. How to transmit the material depends largely on whether the choreographer intends to replicate the work as closely as possible, or if she views the piece as a living thing, vulnerable to changes bound to occur in her perspective and through generational differences in dancers. Techniques for transmuting and transmitting archived knowledge can range from constructing improvisational movement "scores" that hold within them the possibility of others touching the original idea, to locating and immersing new performers in the geographical and historical milieus that served as initial inspiration for the performance structures.

In the 1950s anthropologist Victor Turner and sociologist Erving Goffman, among others, began to study and frame the social interactions of humans and the "presentation of self" as performances of various sorts.[1] The implication—further developed in other disciplines and in the interdisciinary field of performance studies—is that all of us, every day, consciously or not, draw on and perform our archives of social and cultural choice or coercion, including the bodied and gestural. Artists, however, more consciously conceive, construct, and enact performances, deliberately locating them in the public arena and working to more directly fashion what they make toward aesthetic, social, political, or other desired ends. Nevertheless, intentionally or not, these performances are also extrapolations from the artist's archive of sociocultural as well as dance or movement performances.

Performance is always for another, out there. Learning to dance or learning/relearning a particular dance is an act of trust, taking another's body into your own, receiving an archived life of movement into your own archive. This is true for the audience as well: each one, aware or unaware, perceiving or receiving the performance, adding to his own archive of knowledge.

In this section, in the process of utilizing her archive of performances to create a new work with a group of longtime collaborators, Bebe Miller is struck by the déjà vu experience of having moved together this way before and is reminded that the original instances of making also drew on memories archived in her body and her diaries. Deborah Hay is devoted to the "cellular intelligence" of her body and, over four decades, has developed various practices to lead the dancer to multiple levels of awareness of self, body, space, and time and to transmit her bodied archive to other bodies, either in solo performance projects or in the re-creating of larger works. Jayachandran Palazhy's movement choices in the creation of his work, *AadhaaraChakra—a Dancelogue*, draw on Indian dance and martial arts forms that are both enactments and symbols of bodied history, as well as on the spatial and sensory experiences of the residues of memory in both the architecture and streetscapes of urban India. Jenn Joy engages with Walter Benjamin's account of history and archive, in which the what-has-been collides propulsively with the now, to consider the work of three movement artists, each of whom dips into the archive of memory and body not to retrieve desiccated facts of remembered movement but to bring a live past forward to produce new possibilities of thought or action. Gregory Maqoma understands his body as a repository of various forces, including the histories of his ancestors, which inform his choreographic possibilities, and creates dances that embody history, tradition, arts, society, and politics.

—Linda Caruso Haviland

NOTE

1. Erving Goffman, *The Presentation of Self in Everyday Life* (New York, Anchor Books, 1959). See also Victor W. Turner's examination of social conflict as social drama, beginning as early as *Schism and Continuity in An African Society* (1957) and his continuing influential works, such as *Dramas, Fields and Metaphors: Symbolic Action in Human Society* (1974). His work also evolved, in part, as a result of his friendship with Richard Schechner, theater director and early performance studies theorist, in the 1970s, to include the relationships between social dramas and cultural performances in the theatrical sense (*From Ritual to Theatre*, 1982).

UNTITLED

I have recently finished our company's tour of *A History* (2012), a work steeped in the recall and body memory that was particular to our creative process, but perhaps familiar to other partners engaged in making almost anything over time. Often we—myself, dancers Angie Hauser and Darrell Jones, and dramaturg Talvin Wilks—would find ourselves in a peculiar situation that felt/sounded/ breathed like a studio moment from years ago, an arrangement of our bodies and jokes that suggested we'd been there before. And often, due to Talvin's copious note-taking, we could trace the doppelganger instance. I realized that each of us held our version of that moment in our own train of felt images that receded behind us—or perhaps drove us forward.

This essay offers two such tracks of embodied kinesthetic memory. The dance phrases we remember are shaped by the context of the day they happened, complete with color, light, distraction, and happenstance. Before it is engaged in the phrase the dancer's body carries its own references, triggered by the dynamics and timing of the new movement. The body contains our perceptions as well as the events felt and stored, waiting for retrieval.

RHYTHM STUDIES, 1999

During the winter of 1999 I was a guest artist at Ohio State University, teaching two courses, thinking that I'd have plenty of time to choreograph a new solo. As it was, I didn't get into the studio for six weeks. A theme took shape: the "out-of-rhythm" of my life. I would alternately spend time lying down and staring at the ceiling—an inevitable part of my solo making—and figuring out what I knew about rhythm in as many ways as I could. I have adapted and updated these notes from my journal:

> Listened to Marvin Gaye—got a groove going: directing energy into shape, energy being the key that takes it out of cool posing. Watching the range of it—easy to keep it at same out/high level (not easy—exhausting!); have to remember to listen to how it wants to modulate, without my being tired determining where it goes. Generally that's *up* tempo, and I have to bypass my choreographer-ear that always says stop/rest at the same point of breathless-ness. So is it my aerobic phobia that's shaping my sense of

rhythm or can I go past that point and find a less reliable understanding of *go*? Definitions of funky: I feel my chest/psyche/center commenting on gesture. "Yeah, huh," in sync. Take *that* from foot to foot, change up the weight. Twist it all and ooze, bleat, grimace, undo/delete. There's relief in finding the relationship to the beat. Let it do the work, I'll just comment. Architecture as well as the song. Invention meets time. I don't want to leave rhythm behind, this time.

Saw Billy Forsythe/Frankfurt Ballet[1] last night—a rush of unique movement, energy was nasty, good, great, committed. Bodies solved impossible problems, no congratulations, just kept it up. Choose this! Bend it and kiss it on the lips. Smack into the air. Bite it.

When I'm fooling around to James Brown I see the root back in junior high, learning to funk, to boogie, to dance *outside* of dance class. Can't go back there (won't go back there?); I recognize too much of it, the beat's too easy to follow. All this dance schooling is to get to something I don't recognize, yes? So who do I take with me on this trip? This is similar to the audience question at the Dance and Spiritual Life performance in 1998 when the audience divided—half as art/critical/judgmental, the other half as testifying to the known and familiar.

Am I still stuck in the same place? James Brown is so *old*. But now when I follow his lead and remember what my body knows I get to mess with the kinesthetic I'm recalling. I identify the drop and rebound in the weight, slide the pelvis horizontally in the newer direction, look elsewhere, inhibit the arms, signify nothing. Move the dialogue. Get on with it.

ASMARA, ERITREA, OCTOBER 1999

Prologue

In the fall of 1999 I was invited to Eritrea by Sbrit, the Eritrean National Music and Dance Troupe, to teach contemporary dance and choreograph a piece for an upcoming millennial celebration of African arts and literature. I spent three weeks in Asmara, the capital city, working in a marble-floored villa left over from their days as an Italian colony. The place, the people, the smells, the light— all of it was dimensional and inescapable. I began writing almost immediately, daily, a kind of scribing that I'd not ever done before. Afterward, years later, I began to move, trying to manifest the nature of the encounter rather than re-producing the experience itself. I felt a shift in my understanding of Other: from not-belonging to not-being-accustomed-to, a more inviting and less indulgent self-regard. As one of a generation of African Americans who came of age in the

1950s, my Otherness meter is pretty sensitive and self-propelled. There, it was not useful. What was far more interesting was dissecting the meter and taste of another way of walking, greeting, sitting, and, finally, dancing.

My experiences from this trip eventually became the source material for *Landing/Place* (2005),[2] a work concerning the impact of the unfamiliar against the everyday. In building it I often looked for the import and timing of unexpected events, a loose metaphor for foreign encounters. These notes predate my choreographic strategies of dealing with what I'd remembered and archived.

October 17, 1999
The air is dry, sere, breeze is cool. Buses come in two varieties: long and packed with people, or a van, large sized—the African transit way. Men & women both will look you in the eye—I'm trying to find my way, what is allowed. 2–3 cheeks for kissing, teenage boys walking with a hand draped on another's shoulder. One small boy begging—hand had one coin in it.

I don't know what I'm seeing. I don't know what to read—if anything— into what I see. Jim[3] & I are noticed but nothing more.

Just unpacked, and now pacing the room, I'm not sure why. My body knows I'm somewhere new and maybe that's all it is. Travel puts one in touch with one's basic, fearful self.

October 20, 1999
Wednesday evening. We take a walk past the cathedral on Harnet Avenue, up the hill past the bus station, past the market stalls—high piles of hot peppers, corn, metal, blue plastic bins. Faces streaming by, catchall eyes, brown and wide open. Walnut-colored men, farsighted, leathery. Elegant old men, one loud drunk.

Looking at or for difference is wearying. The best thing is to lose the self-consciousness of being out of place but I can only manage that when I'm tired, and then I am "of the place" and take it in stride.

October 24, 1999
Sunday at the beach, in Massawa:[4] the most beautiful people in the world. A man walks by sluicing his hips slightly forward, finessing the shift of weight through his slight frame, he is naturally fluid. Head is level, eyes too, in the sun. Some B-Boy wannabes pass by the other way with that *bop*, building up to the swagger, transmitted through hip-hop export. Third man, same age as the first, with white caftan and cotton-wrapped head,

strides by, in charge of something, a revolutionary on the move. Four women in various stages of tradition with 40 years spread between them.

Massawa at night: supper outside at an oilcloth-covered table. We sit just out of range of the bare bulbs that light up the better organized tables across the yard that are occupied by straightforward families. After-dinner stroll through town. A garish, happy fluorescence banging out the doorways of local stores, the blaring pale blue light and charcoal grey wash of street life, radio.

Massawa is full of men and boys roaming, on the move. Tsighe[5] gets jostled by a skinny boy who's getting away from some others. I'm thinking it's all fake and check for my passport, but the skinny kid is hovering just out of reach and I can see I know nothing about how far this thing can go. He's scared but not enough to leave his sandals behind, which were tossed in the scuffle.

The ride home: Mountains outlined against a dusty navy sky, terraced traces barely visible, scooped layered land forming valleys and canyons. We come around a risky hairpin and the yellow moon bangs out in the sky, just clearing the hills. The ground gleams copper, more of a warmth than a shine. Lavender & blue begins to fill the air like a solid thing. The land is rounded by evening light.

I'm in Asmara, Eritrea, for three weeks to make a dance with people whose exposure to contemporary work has been limited to six months with Mr. Chang from China, a Finnish teacher who left after two months, and MTV. There are remnants of tendus, several pairs of pink slippers, a try at chaîné turns with hands perched on their shoulders like epaulets. For warm-up, we make a circle with me in the center and I twist, bend, and stretch with their eyes glued on me, following everything I do. This attention is distracting, and I find I've forgotten what comes next. I'm stumped by their wardrobe: one woman comes every day wearing a fine outfit of matching blouse and lounge pants, though she got rid of the black pumps after the first day. Another shows me the stretch factor of her skintight jeans by tugging at her thighs—no problem. The man in chinos and checked shirt seems locked in his skin, or maybe just unsure of what I'm asking him to do, but he continues to show up almost every day. Some take their shoes off, but I leave that up to them. Where do I start forming the idea of dancing out-side of cultural tradition or political propaganda? My usual first step of listening to the body suddenly seems ludicrous and assumes a certain indulgence toward the individual, a political expedience that is unfamiliar in this room. They have no need for irony here, so what will I teach them?

EPILOGUE

A takeaway from the Sbrit company: I'm watching a rehearsal of one of their folk dances, as in "performed for the folks who will read the gestures and know then how to be a citizen." A line of men face front, arms extended almost fully to the side, shoulder height. Their feet dole out a steppy straightforward maneuver, but I'm watching their hands, softly beating the air in time with the uneven, unfunky rhythm. It's a move that's deeply naïve in postmodern terms (What about keeping your shoulders down, sensing your periphery? Nah.), and therefore deeply unfamiliar and incredibly enticing.

I stole this move. It came up in rehearsal five years later: "naïve arms" I called it, accompanied by a breathy panting, small hops in place from foot to foot, eyes widening all on their own. We played with it for hours, trying to identify what the what was, coming down to a disregard of technique, design, and impact in favor of our arrival at a moment of common sensibility. Hard to find, simple to do.

NOTES

1. Most likely this was a performance of *Eidos: Telos* (1995) at the Brooklyn Academy of Music in the Next Wave Series, 2000.

2. *Landing/Place* was commissioned and premiered at the Clarice Smith Performing Arts Center of the University of Maryland in September 2005. Co-commissioners were Bates Dance Festival, Lewiston, Maine; Dance Theater Workshop, and Danspace Project in New York City; and The Wexner Center for the Arts at The Ohio State University.

3. Jim Wood, my traveling partner. We were a mixed-race couple (he is white), an uncommon sight during our stay.

4. Massawa, Eritrea, a beach town on the Red Sea.

5. Unfortunately I don't remember Tsighe's last name; she was a friend of our hosts from Sbrit, someone who had spent time in the United States and who was, for us, a cultural translator of sorts, as well as a friend.

MY BODY, THE ARCHIVE

"Can I transmit a dance to a group of dancers whom I do not know, based solely on the language I have been crafting for forty-five years?" This seemed like a logical development in my working process.

I had actually come to *believe* that I had created a spoken/written language that could convey how to perform my work, despite my suspicions about belief. As a matter of fact, one of my recurring coaching themes is, "You do not have to believe that there is a truth to the question. Just move the question from your head down through your whole body and notice how the sensual impact from the question alters you."

Based on the affinity to my language that seems to have inspired many dancers, including students and professionals, I had come to *believe* that if dancers attend to my questions, using them as tools to engage their awareness in the practice of my work, then they would be prepared to perform my choreography. This *belief* was a solution to participating in a project curated by Ralph Lemon, titled *some sweet day*, at the Museum of Modern Art in New York City in fall 2012. Other commitments already in place prevented me from spending any serious time in New York to work with the cast of twenty-two dancers, ten whom I never met and twelve of whom I had only worked with briefly in the past. In order to choreograph *Blues* I had to take a chance that a method was in place.

This method, not exclusive to me, consisted of writing performance and choreographic directions to the cast, asking them for feedback, to respond with questions, thoughts, or issues. This was all conducted through e-mail and took place for nine months leading up to the public performances at the Museum of Modern Art (MoMA). It was a perfect opportunity to test my *belief* that a method was in place to transmit my work through a language that had been tested, had failed, was redefined and retested, and was refined through coaching and directing hundreds of performers, both students and professionals, since 1970.

I *believed* I could do without the intimate and concentrated process that has served my choreography and the dancers with whom I have worked for the last forty-five years. That *belief* felt real because that is how *belief* works. It is how and why we build religions, skyscrapers, philosophies, prophecies, laws—you name it—and how and why we destroy them. I *believed* I had achieved and articulated a method for the transmission of my work through language.

The dance I choreographed for MoMA was the result of my *belief* that writing might substitute for what actually inspires language: the experience, depth, tone, trust, and absence of fear that drive my teaching and practice. I learned that the transmission of my dances needs my thorough and personal intervention as a choreographer, dancer, teacher, coach, and director. *Blues* was a bitter/ sweet reminder that there is no method to convey my work because my work is a practice. That is all. It is a practice for the choreographer, the dancer, and the audience.

No matter how detailed or broad my language, between the written directions and the dancer unforeseen circumstances and interpretations emerge that cannot be accounted for because my choreographic language deliberately and often omits specifying movement or time and/or space. Not enough sleep, a sudden meaning that a movement provokes, another war, the presence of an audience and the adrenalin that produces, an unpaid bill, a flood, a costume choice, are examples of unaccountable situations. As reflected in past performances of my work, following a period of teaching and coaching and months of practice, those unknowable conditions can be sidestepped in favor of the immersive and elevating experience possible through the practice of performance.

How completely inane my language must sound to anyone not familiar with my working process. Most of the dances I have choreographed in the last fifteen years were followed with a written score based solely on my daily practice of the performance of that dance. At the start of transmitting that dance to others, the prose score was read aloud. At the conclusion of the reading, practically everyone would agree that no one understood anything about the dance or how it could possibly be realized. After the dancers learned the sequence of movement directions that shape the dance, my coaching was under way, and the tools for performing the material were tested, we would read the score again. Suddenly the text would come to life, but only through the experience of the language as it was physically embodied by each individual dancer.

My body, the archive, will not be archived.

JAYACHANDRAN PALAZHY

CHOREOGRAPHING SOMATIC MEMORIES
AND SPATIAL RESIDUES

When we recall a memory, we experience a displacement in space and time. One of my interests as a choreographer is the narrative and emotional implications of this spatial-temporal oscillation. Dance deploys recollection and memory, along with imagination and experience, to create a series of resonances that alter space and time for the performer and the viewer. The cognitive activity of memory is critical to dance, since dance is a creation of the present, not its representation. In my work I strive to bring a variety of experiences to the present through movement and other stage devices.

Accessing memories archived in the body, as well as in architectural spaces and landscapes, is one of the investigations that drive my choreographic research. My practice at Attakkalari Centre for Movement Arts in Bangalore, India, combines mining information and wisdom from traditional performance and body practices, as well as innovative applications from technology and contemporary somatic tools. In this essay, I share insights from NAGARIKA, Attakkalari's seminal research and documentation project on Indian physical and performance traditions, as well as strategies employed in our recent multimedia contemporary dance production *AadhaaraChakra—a Dancelogue*, in order to illuminate some possibilities of how one could choreograph memory archives.

THE BODY IN *KALARIPPAYATTU*
In order to think about somatic and spatial memory differently, we need to look at the human body as well as architecture through an alternative lens, such as the one provided by the research and documentation project NAGARIKA. In focusing that lens on classical Indian performance forms, our effort has been to discover embedded movement principles and body concepts by dissecting, unearthing, and deconstructing the movement vocabulary. These concepts and principles have helped us transform and organize improvised movement sequences.

Research on the southern Indian martial art form *kalarippayattu* showcases differently imagined body movements. In kalarippayattu, movements are conceived of as sections of a larger circularity, whereby the spine, limbs, and other parts of the body organize themselves as part of a circular, continuous motion. Seemingly straight lines, thrusts, and jumps are part of a larger circularity.

200

Moreover, in the kalarippayattu massage that precedes the practice sessions, circularity is viscerally inscribed onto the body through circular strokes radiating outward from the lower back and abdominal areas. Movements are imagined to originate from the lower abdominal core, the root of the navel (naabhi-moola), and return to this center in order to initiate the next move. This notion of the transmission of a vital force (praana) from the navel to the entire body through the nervous system (naadi) is also found in other Asian physical practice traditions.

Kalarippayattu movements represent an integrated system of bodied consciousness, which does not follow the dualistic Cartesian mind/body schema. There is no division between a "thinking mind" and an "acting body"; rather, in kalarippayattu the "body becomes all eyes." The body is conceived as a continuum, a manifestation of the universe, rather than a machine. Thus the kalarippayattu body is able to condense and expand, and at times to transcend its immediate time and space coordinates. Moreover, memory, experience, and imagination become functions of the body, rather than being relegated to the intangible and abstract realms of mind or spirit.

When weapons such as the kettukari (long stick), cheruvadi (short stick), otta (short curved stick), urumi (long flexible sword), dagger, sword, and shield are introduced in the kalarippayattu training process, they are imagined as being extensions of the body. For instance, the practitioner does not simply hold the kettukari in her hand as an instrument to execute a movement. Rather, she engages her lower back and abdomen to initiate the movement, which then travels through her entire back, arms, and eventually to the weapon. Through training and imagination a unique performative body is constructed, which is seemingly able to reach beyond its own physical contours.

In kalarippayattu the body is perceived as a living universe in itself and is viewed as a materialization of the larger universe. In addition, the subterranean physical training arena termed the kalari is also conceived of as a geometric representation of the universe. Deities, teachers, and students are assigned particular spaces linked to cardinal points within the arena. The participation in various rituals and their associated psychological states strongly influence the practitioner as well.

In kalarippayattu training, imagination combined with sensory inputs evokes images for the practitioner and contributes to a layered construction of a body and self, which in turn informs the quality and intention of the movement. Everything practitioners do is bound by their imagined and created universe.

For instance, as one practices the martial art form inside the arena, numerous sensory inputs infuse the movements, lending them a primordial, visceral, and animalistic quality. The scent, texture, and visual qualities of the red mud floor; the herbal oil on the bodies; the sense of being confined in a pit among other bodies; the continuous back and forth pacing in the arena; the intense focus while facing an opponent—all strongly influence the experience of the practitioner. With these sensory inputs, the practitioner learns to move in an economical way, with confined, contained, and concise movements, which can however be expanded through leaps and jumps.

In addition to the imagined spaces and sensory experiences within the arena, images are manifested during the training process. For instance, during the salutation sequence, images of mother earth, the sacred corner, deities, and a lineage of masters are evoked. Many of the movement sequences in kalarippayattu stem from essentialized and abstracted animal motifs (snake, elephant, lion, horse, wild boar, cat, peacock, etc.) that possess a strong earthy undertone. Moreover, the *vaythari* or verbal commands call on animal characteristics and use evocative language to fashion the movement quality, creating particular images for the practitioner. Commands such as *Sarpavativil Amarnnu* (cling to the floor like a serpent), *Parannu Vetti* (fly and slash with the sword), and *Soochikkiruthi* (split legs on the floor, with an upright torso similar to a needle stuck on the floor) are used in kalarippayattu. At times the verbal commands do not correspond to specific body movements; rather, their tone and tempo help guide the shapes, dynamics, dramaturgical intentions, and overall trajectory of the kalarippayattu movement.

Kalarippayattu practitioners access a pool of collective memories. Legends and folklore are passed onto the students as part of the training process. Ballads celebrating the valorous deeds of heroes are sung during seasonal activities such as planting paddy, as well as during daily household chores. Practitioners and the community around them share a universe in which the characters from the ballads are ever present. This universe in turn finds its way into the physical practice of kalarippayattu. Imagination, sensory inputs, evoked images, and collective memories assign a quality to the kalarippayattu movements, which in turn transcend mere empirically physical movements.

SPACE, MEMORY, AND COLLABORATION

Taking cues from our research work in kalarippayattu on the dance production *AadhaaraChakra*, I was interested in the idea of accessing the presence of memory contained in architecture and landscape. How could we capture spatial residues of memory in select sites across India? My strategy was to generate movements by drawing on the sensory response of being in particular spaces and mediate these experiences through choreography and movement exercises. In preparation for the production, a team of eight dancers traveled to and rehearsed in diverse Indian locales.

In North India, the dancers explored both the crowded, noisy bazaars of old Delhi and the expansive solitude of historic sites, such as Humayun's tomb. In southern India they created on-site movements, using wicker baskets and tricycles as props, against the backdrop of the buzzing village markets, amid jasmine sellers and vegetable vendors. The dancers re-created culinary rituals in an old Chettinad house and conducted a dance initiation ceremony in the cool, dark interior of a Shiva temple.

I specifically chose a house of the prosperous banking Chettiar community from the Chettinad region of Tamil Nadu, as its architecture is woven into the fabric of Tamil culture. This merchant community is known for its cosmopolitan outlook and drew materials of its syncretic architecture from its trading partners, including Italy, Belgium, Burma, and Indonesia. The architectural influence played out in the construction of temples as well, which were built by the local patrons from this community. The rituals re-created in both the temple courtyards and the kitchen of the house as part of *AadhaaraChakra* were indicatory of the rich, cultural heritage of the Tamil country. However the rituals were imagined and reconstructed, not precise and particular, thus occupying a space and time in flux.

At each site the dancers dressed in specific attire for improvisation and filming. With the help of the clothing, and by inhabiting the spaces through movement, the dancers were able to temporarily take on qualities that altered their sense of where they were located in time and space. The attire for the dancers consisted of imagined costumes, which were purposely not accurate or precise. We were not interested in using period costumes and instead wanted to invoke a sense of a time past, without the attire being anchored to a specific period. For instance, the female dancers wore a costume with numerous pleats, inspired by the temple architecture of South India, and did not rely on the contemporary *bharatanatyam* costume. The clothes had broad lines and sober colors, subdued and not elaborate. Heavy ornamentation was replaced by simple jewelry made with white silver and black threads. The idea was to invoke an "in-between" spatial-temporal realm that was never fixed, but only suggested. The dancers re-created imagined rituals invoking the initiation rites of *devadasi* (temple dance), and this attire was integral to their imagination and movement. Similarly for scenes in the village markets, the dancers wore simple *dhavanis* (half saris) with long skirts and blouses, which are rarely seen in urban centers today. They were reminiscent of young, outgoing, carefree girls of an imagined past.

During the costume experiments and through improvisation on location, which was filmed, the dancers became more attuned to the subtextual layers inherent in these Indian spaces. While improvising amid urban Indian traffic intersections, for instance, the performers took note of the variety of forms that occupied the space around them, including the urban residents, automobiles, buildings, stray dogs, and even cows. The presence of these beings was worked into the movement sequences as the dancers became more aware of the sense perceptions around them. The movement exercises sensitized the dancers to the complexities of urban Indian spaces. When the dancers came back to the studio in Bangalore, they recalled the layers constructed during filming and further processed them in movement and live performance.

City spaces, especially those in India, are a confluence of the multiple languages, performing art forms, cuisines, customs, and religions of the country. As in other cities, they permit manifold differences and contain multifarious dimensions of time. An ever-present past underlies the city spaces and sometimes ruptures them. For instance, drums in a local traditional ritual procession become juxtaposed with urban shoppers. Or frantic motorbike traffic is juxtaposed with languid, slow-moving stray cows. Individuals in urban India (many of them migrant villagers) also carry within themselves an extraordinary range of information that includes memories of people, places, and events, which vary greatly in their spatial and temporal dimensions.

By traveling and inhabiting multiple locales, the dancers sensed into the "pastness" of the past, but also its underlying presence in Indian culture. Dance creates empathy in the observers through metaphors and the kinetic agency of presence, something that has spiked the interest of neuroscientists as well. The momentary materialization of dance is inextricably tied to its disappearance. Dance plays with the eternal as well as the temporary, and this makes it a particularly rich medium of apprehending knowledge. Through dance, we are able to understand the activity of disappearance, to know the immaterial. In the ephemeral gesture we leave the everyday and encounter the atomization of time.

Multimedia dance production provided a platform for the dancers, music composers, filmmakers, costume-design collaborators, and I to engage with Indian city spaces from the specificity of our own disciplines and artistic sensibilities. The dancers were filmed during their travel and rehearsal in specific locales. The film followed a style that experimented with the idea of a "docu-fictional" travelogue—hence the title "dancelogue" for the production. Even though the film had some figurative qualities such as architectural details, costumes, and movements, these were not connected to an exact time period or location. The film often subverted time and space coordinates by breaking continuity in a series of sequential frames, thus bringing in an abstract, discontinuous quality.

Fictional memories were rendered in color, while the black-and-white images were anchored in the present. Specific images were selected to evoke memories and suggest experiences for the audience. The German composers Sam Auinger and Martin Lutz made use of the soundscapes created from the travels, constructing a score that brought out the spirit of these spaces. Sound motifs, such as the call of the vegetable vendors or the honks of the auto rickshaws, were transformed through artistic mediation. These found sounds were processed and structured to create musical arrangements and in the process were removed from their original function or context.

Our artistic process involved a collection of impressions—spatial, visual, aural, and somatic—that were followed by a mediation and dialogue among the various artists involved in the project. Artistic choices were negotiated in relation to an overall dramaturgy; hence memories and sensory impressions of the various locales found expression through different artistic elements of the production, such as sound, text, image, and movement.

As a choreographer, I am interested in exploring various media such as movement, light, sound, film, plastic sculpture, and digital design, in order to create a world onstage. The same sites we visited yielded differing stimuli for the dancers and collaborators. In the creative process, I looked for signs of how these experiences had evoked reactions or generated significance in each member of the group and attempted to bring these varied existences into the present. For instance, the scenes enacted in the marketplace, railway station, butcher houses, and traffic intersections called out different responses among the dancers depending on their particular backgrounds and the circumstances they grew up in. Drawing on imagination and memory, the dancers used different sources, ranging from popular cinema to novels, paintings, and personal experience. In each of the sites, we then engaged in a short improvisation and arrived at a movement that we "discovered" for that particular space. Some of these movement sequences then found their way into the production.

OSCILLATION: THE TIME AND SPACE FLUX

Inspired and informed by traditional Indian physical wisdom, Attakkalari incorporates contemporary pedagogy experiments with subtle layers of the imagined body and its internal landscapes. This is carried out through a practice of connection, synchronization, and sequential movements of the limbs individually and in tandem with the whole body. Eye focus and breath are often linked to the movements, thus augmenting them by defining their trajectories, directions, and reach. These methods expand the notion of how the body inhabits spaces and how it can reach beyond corporeal contours and extremities. At Attakkalari we simultaneously explore the possibilities to inhabit or suggest multiple layers of orientation, dynamics, and direction, through movement generation and compositional traces of the body—the implication of what the body carries.

Through the multimedia dance production *AadhaaraChakra*, I attempted to rupture and fragment select vignettes of the urban Indian experience. We created a continuous oscillation between the traditional and the contemporary spheres in order to expose a space that somehow resided in between. Both technical strategies as well as body movements fed into this process. For instance, filmed sequences of the dancers performing traditional bharatanatyam were projected onto a specially woven silk backdrop. These contrasted with contemporary live action in the foreground. Along with a layer of contemporary folk music, the classical bharatanatyam *jati* (spoken rhythmic syllables) provided the binding rhythm for the fluctuating conversation between the contemporary and often submerged traditional corporeality. The binding rhythm helped anchor the layers together while creating a tension for the audience, thus revealing the complexity of composite urban Indian identities.

The contemporary movement passages were inspired in part by bharatanatyam and the folk dance form of *thevarattam*, which is performed during social occasions such as weddings and has a martial connection as well.[1] I particularly chose thevarattam, as I was interested in the older devadasi traditions such as *sadir* from the same region and wanted to understand how we could look at temple dance differently.[2] Folk traditions are often relatively easier to adapt and transform due to their flexible nature. By contrast, classical forms tend to be distilled over time into a relatively rigid form with specific aesthetics and conventions.

Another tension was created through the participation of audience members in the performance, thus blurring the lines between the theatrical world and the real world. The "present" of the audience was captured in memory and

1. Rehearsal for *pitié!* (2008) by Alain Platel, in Ghent, June 2008. Mathieu Desseigne Ravel (on left) and Romeu Runa (on right). Photograph by Chris Van der Burght. (See page 24.)

2. Still shots from
Films médicaux
(1904) by Arthur
Van Gehuchten. As
Alain Platel observes,
"the body wants to
express what words
cannot say."
(See page 26.)

3. Philipp Gehmacher and Meg Stuart in *the fault lines* (2010) by Meg Stuart. Video by Vladimir Miller. Museum Moderner Kunst, Vienna, February 3, 2011. Photograph © Eva Würdinger. (See page 55.)

4. Chris Nietveld in *Cries and Whispers*, directed by Ivo van Hove. De Singel, Antwerp, March 16, 2009. Photograph © Jan Versweyveld. (See page 70.)

5. *Persona*, directed by Ivo van Hove. Pictured is Marieke Heebnik. Le theatre de Liege, Liege, Belgium, November 30, 2012. Photograph © Jan Versweyveld. (See page 71.)

6. Berlinde De Bruyckere, *We Are All Flesh*, 2009. Wax, polyester, and steel on wooden plinth, 105 x 165 x 196 cm (41³⁄₈ x 65 x 77¹⁄₈ in.). Private Collection © Berlinde De Bruyckere. This image is of De Bruyckere's sculptural work with the human figure, a portrayal of a "naked body in agony," which Ivo van Hove discusses in his essay. Courtesy the artist and Hauser & Wirth. Photograph by Mike Bruce. (See page 71.)

7. Sarah Crowner, *Ballet Plastique*, 2011, oil and acrylic on raw canvas and linen, dimensions variable. Installation view image courtesy Galerie Catherine Bastide, Brussels. (See page 144.)

8. Alyssa Alpine and Tom Rawe in *Para-Dice* by Patricia Hoffbauer. Danspace Project at St. Mark's Church, New York, November 2013. Photograph © Ian Douglas. (See page 185.)

9. George Emilio Sanchez, Elisa Osborne, and Tom Rawe in *Para-Dice* by Patricia Hoffbauer. Danspace Project at St. Mark's Church, New York, November 2013. Photograph © Ian Douglas. (See page 187.)

10. *Para-Dice* by Patricia Hoffbauer. Seated are Elisa Osborne and George Emilio Sanchez; standing, from left to right, are Laura Gilberts, Peggy Gould, and Alyssa Alpine. Danspace Project at St. Mark's Church, New York, November 2013. Photograph © Ian Douglas. (See page 188.)

11. Alexandre Benois (1870–1960), set design for the garden in act 2 of *Le Pavillon d'Armide*, 1909. Watercolor, ink, and pencil on paper. Howard D. Rothschild Collection on Ballets Russes of Serge Diaghilev: Drawings and Prints, 1907–1956, MS Thr 414.4 (33). Harvard Theatre Collection, Houghton Library, Harvard University. (See page 230.)

12. Michel Fokine as Harlequin in *Carnaval*, Stockholm Théâtre Royal, 1914.
Bibliothèque nationale de France, département Bibliothèque-musée de l'opéra.
Photograph by Atelier Jaeger (Stockholm). (See page 232.)

13. Tamara Karsavina coaching Margot Fonteyn in the role of the Firebird.
Howard D. Rothschild Collection on Ballets Russes of Serge Diaghilev: Photographs
and Scrapbooks, 1909–1975, MS Thr 414.2 (66). Harvard Theatre Collection, Houghton
Library, Harvard University. Photograph by Douglas Elston. (See page 236.)

14. *Schéhérazade*, corps de ballet with duelers. Parmenia Migel, collector; Stravinsky-Diaghilev Foundation Collection, 1912–1989, MS Thr 495 (153, seq. 15). Harvard Theatre Collection, Houghton Library, Harvard University. Photograph by White Studios. © The New York Public Library for the Performing Arts. (See page 240.)

15. Felix Cruz (foreground) and Jeremy Pheiffer in *Them* by Ishmael Houston-Jones in collaboration with Dennis Cooper and Chris Cochrane, PS 122, New York, October 22, 2010. Photograph © Ian Douglas. (See page 275.)

16. Arturo Vidich in *Them*, by Ishmael Houston-Jones in collaboration with Dennis Cooper and Chris Cochrane, PS 122, New York, October 22, 2010. Photograph © Ian Douglas. (See page 289.)

converted to the "past" through three devices. First, audience members were handed *ganjifa* cards evoking temple fortune-tellers. These cards contained poetry that was not specific to a particular event or place and instead dealt with universal themes such as love, death, time, and space, thus prompting the viewers to meditate on the relevance of the words. Poems such as "Since the sun sees with its entire body / How can it view its own rising and setting?" suggested a transcendence of normative conceptions of time and space.

Second, photographs of the audience members (without their knowledge) were taken as they entered the performance venue. The device of the photograph helped convert the present into a memory. These photographs were projected as digital images in a collage on the performance floor and silk screens during the production. Third, the aural Indian street world, with its blaring horns, was introduced into the performance venue, as the dancers began the performance by sounding rickshaw horns. This aural motif was picked up by the sound score and developed into a multiplied musical arrangement throughout the soundscape. Aspects of the audiences' world were interwoven into the performance texture through poem meditation, projected photographs, and an integrated soundscape.

To further enhance the flux, or to create an "in-between" space, we played with the movement principles of classical Indian dance forms. In bharatanatyam, for instance, the eye focus of the dancer is usually based on the principle of completion or resolution, similar to the *tala* system in classical Indian music. Eye focus is used to define and animate space, augment movement, and convey a sense of intention and direction. An experienced viewer comes to expect this sense of resolution, in the same manner that a first-time dance viewer would anticipate the completion of a pedestrian movement such as sitting on a chair. At Attakkalari we attempt to challenge expectations in both experienced and uninitiated viewers. We therefore interrupt the anticipation of classical forms as well as pedestrian movements.

If one extends this idea and couples the principle of eye movement with fragmented, nonstylized movements outside the scope of the bharatanatyam vocabulary, an effect of rupture is created. The audience member expects a particular trajectory, but it is not completed, because of a sudden change in movement. This rupture in eye focus can be further amplified by fragmented spatial orientation originating in and led by other body parts or by the body as a whole. In destabilizing the viewers' expectations based on their experiences, they are forced to attend to the performance and to follow the trajectory of the piece. An imaginary theatrical time, which is not constant, can then stretch and collapse.

This subverts the conventional logic of time and space and affects the viewer in extraordinary ways. The quality of flux, with its spatial and temporal dislocation, suggests the recall of memory alluded to in the opening thoughts of this essay.

At Attakkalari we experiment with movement principles from classical Indian forms in order to present them to contemporary audiences. This experimentation relies on a specifically constructed corporeality, as well as sensitivity to memory, experience, and imagination, in particular spaces. The related and emerging notion of "presence" is an ongoing theme that may resurface in research, experimentation, and practice. The creation and performance of *Aad-haaraChakra—a Dancelogue* is one further exploration in this ongoing journey. Further experimentation will influence my dance creation, performance, and viewing, as it will also illuminate the complex relationship among spatial residues, memory recall, and somatic archives realized through multiple artistic practices.

NOTES

1. Thevarattam (or Thevar-attam) is a folk dance form (*attam*) practiced by the Thevar and Kambalatthu Nayakkar community of southern Tamil Nadu, performed on social occasions such as weddings. It has its basis in martial arts and is traditionally performed by men. The thevarattam costume typically includes a turban and a thin towel tied around the waist.

2. Sadir (or sathir) was primarily a solo dance form performed by the devadasi community in southern India. Devadasi literally means a girl or a woman dedicated to God. Originally performed in temples, sadir eventually moved to the royal courts. In 1932 the Madras Music Academy proposed to do away with the term sadir, because of its association with the then-discredited Devadasi tradition, and rename the dance form bharatanatyam. In sadir performances musicians would traditionally stand behind the dancers and move along with them. Later in bharatanatyam, the musicians remained sitting on stage to accompany the dance. To lend it respectability, so-called upper caste women were encouraged to take up bharatanatyam, and the form was brought from out of temples and royal courts and onto the public stage. For more on bharatanatyam's history and evolution, see Douglas M. Knight Jr., *Balasaraswati: Her Art and Life* (Middletown, CT: Wesleyan University Press, 2010).

TREMULOUS HISTORIES

> It's not that what is past casts its light on what is present, or what is present
> its light on what is past; rather, images is that wherein what has been comes
> together in a flash with the now to form a constellation.
> —Walter Benjamin

> Here is exactly what dancing is, I then told myself: to make of one's body a
> subtracted form, even if immobile, of multiple forces. To show that a gesture is
> not the simple result of a muscular movement and a directional intention, but
> something much more subtle and dialectic.
> —Georges Didi-Huberman

To dance is to whisper: a release of memories secreted in fascia and bone. The body contains its own dark archive of conflicting desires and dreams, often glimpsed only in moments of awakening; this is a dense terrain that is as much physical as emotional as psychological. To encounter dance as so many whispers, so many images, reveals a contingent and tremulous idea of archive and of history.

"(History arrives only when we don't know what has happened. Only when we forget. Only when people disagree on what has happened. That is why a theory of history must always come into being at the same moment as history itself)."[1] Inscribed in the final pages of *The Motion of Light in Water: Sex and Science Fiction Writing in the East Village* (1988), Samuel R. Delany's parenthetical statement responds to a previous comment, in which he claimed that if we know what has happened we exchange history for mythology. This constant slippage, as history, myth, memory, dream, and cultural event touch, becomes the structuring tension in Delany's elliptical narrative and also speaks of the subjective (embodied, and for Delany, explicitly sexual) pressures exerted upon any easy understanding of history, or for that matter of archive.

Delany's constellating discourse evokes that of the distinctly different yet strangely connected (in obsessive investments and attraction to the speculative, if not in shared personal experiments) archivist Walter Benjamin. Benjamin writes about the machinations of history contained in images—not stories, but images. He describes history coming apart in images as so many phantasmagorias, both perceptual and ideological. Against the "feeling of vertigo" specific to a nineteenth-century model of history, Benjamin argues again and again for a more archaeological relationship to history, one that would not only seek prosaic and magical objects in the loam but note the material conditions of their occurrence as so many messages and perhaps almost mystical prescriptions for the present.[2] As readers of these images, we become witnesses, involved even if only coincidentally, critically complicit in the machinations of evidence and event. If we ignore his urgent plea, we use history as Emmanuel Levinas has condemned it, as a "blinding toward the other."[3]

This is also to note that history becomes essential in moments of proximate crisis, as Benjamin anticipates the end of his own life, a life he tragically takes on the border so as not to fall victim to someone else's torment or perhaps finally giving into his own, as the angel is thrown backward by the rush of air into the ruins even as he stares into the distant horizon. (Or at least this is the way Benjamin writes of the angel of history pictured in *Angelus Novus* [1920], the naïve drawing by Paul Klee that hung in his apartment.) The work of this image, what he will call a dialectical image, is deeply relational. Is it too much to say we are touched by it? He was, deeply. Perhaps under the influence of Benjamin's suspended angel we transpose a visceral language to the theoretical peregrinations that collect around the archive. Inside this tremulous movement of choreographic image, dance rather than document encounters history as constellating presence.[4] Presence, that is, as image—a shimmering picture evoked by the work/performance/dance/sculpture—including its auratic implications.

I understand Benjamin and Delany asking us not only to read the many archives and fragments they offer, but explicitly to witness them as well. In this moment of witnessing, we enact an impossible temporal and spatial convergence, generating a more reflexive involved approach to content and interpretation: a process of critical intimacy.[5] Critical, not as a degree zero of negativity or an evacuation of content, but as a mechanism of creative thinking that attends closely to the material, political, emotional, technical, and aesthetic qualities of a dance, a text, an image.[6] Theoretically and methodologically, critical intimacy structures the constellation of the artists discussed in this essay, my affinity and proximity to their working processes; I remain seduced by the archives they address and invent.

CAST SHADOWS

Blue illuminating darkness, the dancer hesitates on the threshold of the Museum of Modern Art's (MoMA's) gallery and garden, watched over by August Rodin's harshly modeled *Monument to Balzac* (1898). Eyes closed, his hands float along his hips, pulling his torso into a slow undulating dance: ankle shifts, knee bends, hips sway, shoulders roll, a mute serpentine. Without crescendo his repeated movements intensify their meditative quality; this is signaled only in the distraught expressions lining his face. In Rodin's shadow cast by patina and stone, the dancer, Trajal Harrell, appears even more precarious, yet never tentative, his choreography conjuring the ghosts of Tatsumi Hijikata, Marguerite Duras, and Alain Renais, as so many aesthetic and emotional interlocutors.[7] Here the ghosts begin to gather. In the interstices of *Used, Abused, and Hung Out to Dry* a concept of choreographic archive breaks away from the notion of an archive aligned with dusty boxes or static recitations of repertoire or mimetic imperative, to instead imagine a messier convergence of influences and events.

Dressed in black knee socks and a stained burgundy black dress, Harrell calls on the violently subversive gestures and interior sensations of Hijikata's *butoh*, a dance form conditioned by the wretched disfiguration of bodies, of landscapes, even of piles of bodies turned into agonized, writhing, ash-covered terrain in the wake of Hiroshima. Of course, as Harrell undulates under blue light on marble there is no texture, no visible landscape as such, just an accumulation of slowly ascending compositions and decompositions of movement, in which he appears at moments ecstatic, unrecognizable, in pleasure, in agony. Yet as choreographer Faustin Linyekula reminded us a few weeks earlier in this space after performing his own *What Is Black Music Anyways . . ./Self-Portraits*: "[To perform] in the Congo is about clearing a space of rubble and not only physical rubble. Then the colonial heritage of the proscenium theater is a blessing. The possibility of clearing space here [MoMA] is the opposite. The space is cleared already. . . . Oh no, even in the white box you have rubble. I come in with my own obsessions and build from there . . . invent them. . . . The work is the same story over and over."[8] There is much ideological, historical and aesthetic rubble lying under these pristine museum floors. Staged in the threshold between the lobby, sculpture garden, and main stairway, *Used, Abused, and Hung Out to Dry* calls attention to MoMA's architecture as critical interstice and interlocutor; museum as archiving machine or apparatus, if we were to borrow language from Gilles Deleuze or Giorgio Agamben.[9] A Deleuzian machine might allow us to imagine an accumulation of effects as these many performances, traces, ghosts, footsteps, and children's cries circulate, modern aspirations buried under marble dust coming together in the thick air surrounding Harrell's swaying dance.[10] And yet Agamben's apparatus confers a more distinctly ideological picture in which the force of the archive as apparatus is the determining condition under which we come to see Harrell's dance against so much now-invisible rubble.[11]

Following Michel Foucault across time and thought, Agamben argues that an apparatus works through a mechanism of capture; it both invents and conditions the ways in which organisms live. And yet, against the tightly encoded Foucaultian power he critiques, an Agamben apparatus (*dispositivo*, if we translate back to the Italian) allows a small sliver of agency through a generative process of subjective becomings. He names a few possible examples: "web surfer, the writer of stories, the tango aficionado, the anti-globalization activist."[12] These subjects connect through their abilities to shape-shift identities, narratives, and politics, yet what is most strange (perhaps a tic in the translation) is that he does not include a dancer of the tango but an aficionado, one who knows something about tango, which seems an important elision of the agency wrought through and in the moments of dancing, a quite literal technique of moving subjectification from one image to another image, and to another and another and on and on.

Turning to Georges Didi-Huberman, another philosopher also seduced by dance, yet this time by the dancer dancing flamenco, illuminates an alternative to these strictures of subjectification, a possible series of exits, in the dance of Israel Galván. Following Friedrich Nietzsche's affiliation of dance with flight, innocence, light, verticality, and silence, Didi-Huberman imagines not only a virtuosic escape from ground, from thinking, from gravity, but rather a virtuosity of stillness generated only in relation to movement. Describing Galván as a bird of prey suspended in air, Didi-Huberman writes that the dancer is not "rending the air" but somehow holding immanent movement in stillness.[13] In this text, Didi-Huberman returns to a concept from his *Confronting Images: Questioning the Ends of a Certain History*, speaking of the rend in the image witnessed in the torn flesh of Christ's hands.[14] Through his detailed attention to these exquisite tears, he breaks with iconographic and psychoanalytic interpretations of image to identify an immanent and often paradoxical power in the hands of the subject. In the earlier text, *rending* powerfully resists the imperatives of representation (as an apparatus of image capture) and its discourse, and now in relation to dance it is not that the bird is tearing at the air, but rather that it hovers within this surround that is never only movement or stillness but always multiple. So while perhaps the action has shifted from tearing to suspension, Didi-Huberman stills asks us to focus on the in-betweens of flesh and hole, bird and air, flight and immobility. What is, he asks, "the right distance (*sitio*) between beauty and the wound?"[15] Beauty and the wound, always both suspended, a site or location implying stillness, the aftereffect or anticipation of a rupture along the aesthetic horizon.[16]

To move, "to dance or to bullfight"; these are the processes by which one might "multiply oneself."[17] To clarify, these movements of multiplication do not constitute an endless dissemination of identities, but rather evoke the multiple solitudes emanating from the solo dancer dancing that I witness in the arrested gesture as image. "Air and *carne*. The dancer's knowledge and non-knowledge."[18] All of these pairings construct a dialectical tension, a both/and, that evokes a complicit attraction between violence and the beautiful. Of course the aesthetic, as a categorical mode of subtraction, always enacts its own rhetorical vengeance on appearance. Yet there is something even darker at work in Didi-Huberman's duet of air and meat or flesh, bullfighting and dancing. (I cannot escape the thought of Hemingway's brutally succinct portrait of the animal-human pas de deux par excellence.[19]) Always where desire hovers, movement contains a re-pressed violence.

"Why are they so damaged? And why do they not speak?" Prescient questions asked by a child watching Eiko and Koma's *The Caravan Project* in the same transitional space at MoMA where Harrell will also perform.[20] Are these not the questions Didi-Huberman asks as well? Against the prohibitive status and impossibilities of speech surrounding histories contained in images, might dance reveal a different way of understanding these archives (of images, of movements) as deeply connected to our present, at least at the level of consciousness?[21] Isn't this the urgent work of dance or of art, to make demands on our conscience?

Witnessing *Used, Abused, and Hung Out to Dry* after *The Caravan Project*, I sense Eiko and Koma as ghosts dancing behind Harrell's more austere presentation. Painted white and wrapped in twisted rags, Eiko and Koma slowly, at times even imperceptibly, crawl into and out of the folds and depths of their trailer, vehicle, or grave, conjured from flaking white plaster, clay, broken tree limbs, grass, dried leaves, and mounds of dirt. In contrast to the minimal effects of Harrell writhing at different velocities under a square of blue light, Eiko and Koma explore the durational effects of slowness, becoming part landscape, disappearing, fragile, tenuous, always closely guarded by MoMA security.

In distinct ways Harrell and Eiko and Koma mine the histories of Hijikata's *butoh*. Eiko and Koma (whose work often is referred to as *butoh*, a category they vehemently reject) studied with Hijikata, while Harrell's interest is more contemporary, sourced through document and technique. Both Eiko and Koma and Harrell invent what Harrell describes as a "third possibility" as their choreographies imagine a convergence of disparate geographies and histories in the now of performance.[22] *Used, Abused, and Hung Out to Dry* follows Harrell's series *Paris Is Burning at Judson Church (XS, S, M (Mimosa), L, XL, Jr., Made-to-Measure)*, initiated in 2009, that responds to the question: "What would have happened in 1963 if someone from the voguing ball scene in Harlem had come downtown to perform alongside the early postmoderns at Judson Church?" Each of the individual works weaves an "impossible history" from these two disparate scenes and Harrell's contemporary critique of pop culture and conceptual dance; Used, Abused, and Hung Out to Dry adds Hijikata to the mix.[23]

Dramaturgically, one of the symbols crossing many of Harrell's works is that of the photograph, or at least the frame of photograph as rectangular platform upon which the dancers will move. As in Used, Abused, and Hung Out to Dry, when Harrell performs his solo (the second section of the work) within the blue light, he calls out to the three white platforms placed on the front of the stage in Antigone Sr./Paris Is Burning at Judson Church (L).[24] Following Harrell's explanation of the work to the audience and performer Thibault Lac's melancholic anthem "Hit Me Baby One More Time" (sung by Lac to a standing audience), Ondrej Vidlar, in suit jacket, white shirt, and shorts, walks to his platform and slides to turn, a smooth choreography to the duration of Fred Alpi's "One Man's Luck Is the Other Man's Pain." He exits as Stephen Thomson dances, slowly, flying as if to fall in black suit, until Rob Fordeyn begins his own kinetic off-balance turns, jumps, and runs in place to Tori Amos wailing "Cornflake Girl."

To suggest that these platforms act as photographic frames is not to make static the many shades of exquisite dancing, but rather to call out to the qualities of black against white and as many or more modulations of gray that haunt the works as part of the costume design, the staging, and the shifting identities of the performers themselves. Harrell's choreography is seductively gorgeous, yet always critically incisive in the ways he forces disparate narratives to tear each other apart, in effect queering the too-static historical frames and locations of something called Judson, something called voguing, and something culled from the tragic melodrama that is Antigone. So when he turns his attention to Hijikata in the darkness of the museum at night, he invites all these images to join him on stage in a new, internecine dance.

We are told to take off our shoes and sit along the edges of a square taped on the floor, which demarcates the stage. We wait, and continue waiting, until we hear a faint approach of sneakers running on stone, jumping, shifting fabrics brushing against each other, and dancers breathing; then the sound breaks as Harrell and Lac enter through the main lobby, thrashing arms, spinning, and voguing in chic, diaphanous robes before crossing into the square. This restrained staging—audience as periphery and two piano benches containing props, book, and microphone—forms the set that the performers will enter and exit from. Later we are invited to dance, asked by other audience members chosen by the dancers to stand along the edge and move. Performer Niv Acosta extends his hand; I accept, self-consciously dancing, laughing. We return to sit: lights out, silence.

Facing one section of the audience holding a microphone and book, Mina Nishimura tells us that the title of the piece has changed. It is no longer *Used, Abused, and Hung Out to Dry*, but has been renamed *Hiroshima mon amour*. Forget the film and the script, she insists.[25] And yet I cannot.

> HE: You saw nothing in Hiroshima. Nothing.
> (*To be used as often as desired. A woman's voice, also flat, muffled, monotonous, the voice of someone reciting, replies.*)
> SHE: I saw *everything. Everything.*
> [...]
> SHE: Like you, I too have tried with all my might not to forget. Like you, I forgot. Like you, I wanted to have an inconsolable memory, a memory of shadows and stone. (*The shot of a shadow, "photographed" on stone, of someone killed at Hiroshima.*) For my part, I struggled with all my might, every day, against the horror of no longer understanding at all the reasons for remembering. Like you, I forgot.[26]

If we understand history as always coded by ideology, written only in fragments and visions, a compendium of sutures against amnesia, then what might it mean to demand forgetting, or rather to acknowledge a quality of forgetting that opens to a different mode of witnessing and memory? This is perhaps what Nishimura incites in her disavowal of the book she holds in her hand and the script from which the dialogue quoted here is taken. In the scene, the two lovers—a French woman and a Japanese man—lie in a hotel bed in Hiroshima, bodies passionately entwined. The film conveys their words over a montage of fragments: his smooth skin, a child's blind eyes, her fingers gripping his shoulder, ghastly figures of the now unrecognizable dead, a cat walking along an empty street.

In *Images in Spite of All*, Didi-Huberman describes the image as the "eye of history."[27] His meditation on four photographs shot in the gas chambers at Auschwitz argues against any easy rejection or obfuscation of what is given to be seen, even if it seems impossible to comprehend. He describes these images as "breathless," evoking a visceral condensation of past that implicates the present, and reminds us that "to remember one must imagine."[28] Even when we look into these documents with their blacked-out corners and out-of-focus figures in the distance, we must see the conditions under which they were taken as part of the images, as part of their history, as the most extreme conditions of torment and destruction placed on the body. In spite of all this, we must feel and sense these urgent qualities, something much stronger than ghosts, within and emanating out of the photograph.

In the present of this witnessing as imagining, we might dance, wail, and tremble in the surround of our forgetting, and perhaps we remember something else, akin to what is seen in the dark behind a blindfold. Harrell includes this image, too, as David Bergé sits elegantly dressed on a piano bench, blindfolded, watching the performance unfold. This choreographic archive reveals the lie at work in vision, proposing instead that to see these images of history as necessary in and of the present we must acknowledge blindness; to experience we must forsake transparency and linger in the murky depths.

ICONOGRAPHY TREMBLES

SoloShow begins in stillness. Choreographer Maria Hassabi balances on the edge of a black rectangular platform angled toward the audience entering the darkened space.[29] Her legs are crossed, and her left hand rests on her knee. Dressed in creamy beige pants and a translucent tank top, her skin seems almost indistinguishable from the fabric. Spotlights illuminate half of the platform so that it almost disappears into the black theater. She uncrosses her legs and turns away from the audience, one leg propped up on the platform with her arm resting on it, the other draped off the edge. She takes her arm from the knee and places it behind her, fingers stretched as if carrying the weight of her upper body as she leans back. As she looks down, her tendons strain as her neck extends. The poses are long, almost too long, almost long enough to bore us. Her chest lifts and lowers as she breathes, and the sound score, a crush of white noise cut with fragments of conversation and an occasional song lyric, fills the space. The performance continues for almost an hour as she carefully changes from one position to the next, executing a choreography of excruciating transition that moves slowly across the platform.

SoloShow is choreographic inhabitation and association, a series of postures appropriated from photographs from art history and pop culture, performed by the solo dancer on her "public-address platform."[30] Taken out of their original context, the postures call attention to the difficult physicality of female representation—the ways in which the woman's body is displayed and in this moment of display contorted and disfigured across time and media. Each posture reveals a slightly different composition of her body, and the transitions highlight her micro-attention to anatomy as historically contingent. Her exquisite slowness requires a virtuosic attention to balance and weight as she slides, lifts, shifts, turns, bends, arches, extends, and collapses into each new position. Leaning back on the edge of the platform, she slides her legs parallel to the platform's edge and lifts them off the surface so that they hover suspended, trembling. She pauses. She arches her head, casting an anamorphic confusion as her chin juts toward the sky. She pauses.

Against iconography's assumption of transparency, that images can be interpreted as text representing something from the real, SoloShow calls attention to what is not visible or legible as representation through her difficult inhabitation. Hassabi questions the ways that a specific body—her body—transforms these gestures back into images to reveal the historical and aesthetic imperatives at work in the positions themselves. If, as scholar Francis Barker writes in The Tremulous Private Body, "the body has certainly been among those objects which have been effectively hidden from history,"[31] what Hassabi translates is the discrepancy between the disappearances of the female body within iconographic code as she becomes recognizable only as a series of poses or identities (muse, whore, queen, witch, odalisque) through the reappearance of her body on a minimal stage. This distance between code and corporeality is, as Barker describes, perhaps less about body than about a kind of "bodiliness," a "system of liaisons which are material, discursive, psychic, sexual, but without stop and center."[32] Barker's relational body is modernity's body, cauterized in seventeenth-century flames; it is private and supplemental, a body that tightly contains and restrains desire, disease, and corporeal excess but at the cost of its own division.[33] As he moves between text and image, Barker seeks to uncover the "tremulous" relationship between this new subject and its disconnect from the body. Hassabi's SoloShow excavates the gaps between corporeality and textuality, between anatomy and image, as her trembling, virtuosic body contorts against the imperatives it paradoxically seeks to embody. The choreographic force of her gestures reveals tension, strength, and fatigue performing an archive in the throes of a mimetic crisis.

And where does Hassabi leave us? Trembling on the threshold of understanding, yet still captured by the machinations underlying her poses. Through its intense embodiment of image at the point where it breaks down, the work complicates our contemporary relationship to image, rejecting an argument that there is nothing but image and that everything falls into image. In a sense, the work moves us closer to a concept of image as a "dissemblance" or rupture in the either/or of the visible and sayable of representation, which Jacques Rancière condemns in *The Future of the Image*.[34] Rancière goes even further, returning us into the realm of blindness and forgetting, when he proposes a "flesh or substance" of image that "has become the active, disruptive power of the leap—that of change of regime between two sensory orders," between "the chaotic force of the great parataxis" and the "phrasal power of continuity."[35] Moving back and forth through Jean-Luc Godard's *Historie(s) du cinema* (1998),[36] Rancière attempts to release the dialectic from the dialectical image, in effect searching for an auratic, shimmering image. He seeks mystery and paradox simultaneously, such that through this consciousness of images we also come to understand history as always "heterogeneous" and multiple. And yet even as he attempts to write his way around Godard's provocative political work, the cinematic limitations hover.

DANCING A CATALOG, AGAIN

In a photograph the dancer appears in silhouette, backlit through the doorway with the receding Manhattan skyline in the distance. This door opens onto a rooftop studio filled with cardboard boxes and the faint trace of a crack across the gray concrete floor. This concrete crevasse between dancer and photographer/choreographer is Richard Serra's *Untitled* (1976). It is no longer mentioned as one of the permanent installations on the PS1 Web site, nor is it open to the public. What once was an artwork is now a repository for detritus from past exhibitions, surrounded by shadows and mildewed brick.

Captured by choreographer DD Dorvillier during a site visit to PS1, the photograph anticipates her still-in-process works *Diary of an Image* and *A Catalog of Steps*, which premiered at Danspace Project in May 2014. In these works Dorvillier returns to her personal repertoire to distill gestures and movement sequences that will be reconfigured and performed by other dancers. Composing a choreographic retrospective of all new works, Dorvillier evokes a darker, more violent subtext from these contingent fragments of earlier dances. In one fragment seen during a rehearsal with students from P.A.R.T.S.,[37] Serra's *Untitled* becomes a tenuous boundary as the dancer thrashes in a dim corner, tearing off her jacket and throwing it to the floor, bending over to untie her boots, and then pausing abruptly to look off to the side. Her frantic actions appear rushed, messy, then interrupted, as if she is anticipating a response or attempting to escape from herself, her clothes, or someone nearby. Even in this brief fragment, danced by a younger, more frantic, and less fluid dancer than Dorvillier, I glimpse the tensions played out in an earlier, untitled piece from 1995.[38] In the first version,

Dorvillier and Mark Ashwill stage an erotically charged pas de deux of loose release and contact improvisation, only to fall into a more dangerous exchange of submission, weight, and capture. Ashwill lies on the floor, arms and legs spread, as Dorvillier jumps and turns over him, her body a knife landing in the negative spaces between his limbs; she ties him in duct tape; he jumps, thrashes alone in the spotlight; she arches to collapse, standing, swaying to fall onto the floor in a back bend, boots stomping on the floor to pull her up. The intensity of their choreography echoes the dark, energetic anarchy of punk and hard core (movements in close proximity to their own work at that time) and the then not-so-distant riots in Thompson Square Park.[39]

To dance these fragments again—as cipher, as refrain—touches on so many tremulous histories that bleed into the personal, emotional, political, and aesthetic simultaneously. In this moment, the magical shimmer of image calls out to us as witnesses to ask how we see and experience the darkness of the past conjured in the present. Our encounter with a choreographic archive doesn't always entail a vehement scream; instead, it often whispers if we listen closely to the precarious stories woven along the frayed edges of gesture and movement. Our bodies imagine to remember, desire an urgent pressure against amnesia.

NOTES

The epigraphs that open this essay are from Walter Benjamin, *The Arcades Project*, trans. Howard Eiland and Kevin McLaughlin (Cambridge, MA: Harvard University Press, 1999), 462; and Georges Didi-Huberman, *Le Danseur de solitudes*, excerpts in *Solos and Solitudes*, ed. Jenn Joy and Noémie Solomon, trans. Noémie Solomon (New York: Danspace Project, 2013), 6.

1. Samuel Delany, *The Motion of Light in Water: Sex and Science Fiction Writing in the East Village* (Minneapolis: University of Minnesota Press, 1988), 543.

2. Benjamin, *Arcades Project*, 14. Rather than imagining history as a causal line of events leading toward an inevitable end, Benjamin wants to use another model of thinking about history, one that requires a more active approach to seeking out events and stories and objects from the past, considering their context, but also asking what questions these pose for us in the present. Particularly in his later writings, Benjamin's texts take on an almost mystical quality.

3. Jacques Derrida, "Violence and Metaphysics: An Essay on the Thought of Emmanuel Levinas" [1967], in *Writing and Difference* (Chicago: University of Chicago Press, 1978), 94.

4. To evoke the dangerous terms of presence is not to return, I hope, to the hysterical cries issued by Michael Fried around its manifestation in literalist (i.e., minimalist) sculpture, nor is it to return to the problematics of "liveness" as the structuring dead end witnessed in some trajectories of performance studies. Rather, it is to ask what these works (live or on video) offer as evidence of another approach to archive that includes a close attention to events of the past but performs them as necessary for the present as well, imagining, as Trajal Harrell suggests, a third possibility as a lens to look back and to the future.

5. The term *critical intimacy*, as I use it here, came out of a conversation with choreographer Tere O'Connor and Ryan Kelly about ways of thinking through criticality in relation to dance, specifically O'Connor's recent work *Secret Mary* (2013), in which Kelly performs.

6. Thank-you to Bill Bissell for seeing this; my writing is deeply indebted to Theodor Adorno's work on aesthetics. Writing against a model of aesthetics as a transparent interpretative matrix that seeks to analyze and understand art, Adorno constructs a dense paratactic writing, through which he strives to reveal the paradoxes within each artwork as a trajectory for other modes of thinking. As he writes of this processual quality: "Artworks' paradoxical nature, stasis, negates itself. The movement of artworks must be at a standstill and thereby become visible." Adorno, *Aesthetic Theory* [1970], trans. Robert Hullot-Kentor (Minneapolis: University of Minnesota Press, 1997), 176.

7. Harrell's work also harks back both in its location and content to Ralph Lemon's series *Some Sweet Day*, curated with Jenny Schlenzka in the MoMA atrium, October 15–November 4, 2012. Harrell participated as a dancer in Jérôme Bel's *The Show Must Go On* (2001). As he claims, he was the first male ballerina. Other artists involved were Steve Paxton, Faustin Linekula, Dean Moss, Kevin Beasley, Deborah Hay, and Sarah Michelson.

8. Faustin Linyekula, post-performance conversation, Museum of Modern Art (New York, 27 October 2013).

9. Gilles Deleuze and Félix Guattari, *Anti-Oedipus: Capitalism and Schizophrenia*, trans. Robert Hurley, Mark Seem, and Helen R. Lane (Minneapolis: University of Minnesota Press, 1983); Giorgio Agamben, "What Is an Apparatus?" [2006], in *What Is an Apparatus and Other Essays*, trans. David Kishick and Stefan Pedatella (Stanford, CA: Stanford University Press, 2009).

10. Deleuze's thinking, what he refers to as a *practical philosophy*, is always accumulative. Thus a "Deleuzian machine" would be a joining of disparate parts, objects, and affects to generate something else. He imagines these affects as so many parts in play rather than symptoms that must be repressed, erased, or solved, as a psychoanalytic model might propose.

11. Agamben's concept of the apparatus breaks with the schizo-model of Deleuze's machine to propose a set of conditions that are deeply ideological, that constrain and restrain our experience and thinking. An apparatus is not only responsive to but also a generative determinant of our experiences and relationships.

12. Agamben, "What Is an Apparatus?," 14–15.

13. Georges Didi-Huberman, *Le Danseur des solitudes* (Paris: Minuit, 2006), 5.

14. Georges Didi-Huberman, *Confronting Images: Questioning the Ends of a Certain History* [1990], trans. John Goodman (University Park: Penn State Press, 2005).

15. Didi-Huberman, *Le Danseur des solitudes*, 7.

16. Thank-you to Noémie Solomon for her excellent translation of the excerpt of *Le Danseur de solitudes* and for her explanation of these impossible-to-quite-translate parentheticals.

17. Didi-Huberman, *Le Danseur des solitudes*, 7.

18. Ibid.

19. Hemingway's fascination with bullfighting as a metaphysical performance of violence and or ritual is detailed in *Death in the Afternoon* (1932) and also makes an earlier appearance in *The Sun Also Rises* (1926).

20. *Used, Abused, and Hung Out to Dry* and *The Caravan Project* were commissioned as part of the MoMA exhibitions *Performing Histories: Live Artworks Examining the Past* (September 12, 2012–March 8, 2013),

curated by Sabine Breitweiser and Ana Janevski, and *Tokyo 1955–1970: A New Avant-Garde* (November 18, 2012–February 25, 2013), curated by Doryun Chong. *The Caravan Project* ran January 16–21, 2013, at MoMA and has also been performed in 1999 and 2011. *Used, Abused, and Hung Out to Dry* premiered at MoMA February 13–14, 2013. It was choreographed by Trajal Harrell and performed by David Bergé, Trajal Harrell, Thibault Lac, and Mina Nishimura.

21. I wonder about how these works, perhaps together with the series *Another Sweet Day* (2012), curated by Ralph Lemon and Jeny Schlenzka, ask questions of race or black music. Or what it means to see Okwui Okpokwasili dressed in a bunny suit, lying in the corner of the MoMA atrium, crying at the beginning of Ralph Lemon's duet *Untitled* (2008), as a middle-aged white woman rudely interrogates a black security guard for doing his job. Or even Simon Starling's exhibition *Red White Blue* at Casey Kaplan Gallery in 2009, which asked questions about sculptor Henry Moore's relationships to Cold War politics, financing, and the double agent Sir Anthony Blunt.

22. Trajal Harrell conversation with author, New York, October 12, 2012.

23. Ibid.

24. *Antigone Sr./Paris Is Burning at Judson Church (L)* premiered at New York Live Arts, New York, on April 25–28, 2012. It was choreographed and directed by Trajal Harrell and performed by Rob Fordeyn, Trajal Harrell, Thibault Lac, Stephen Thomson, and Ondrej Vidlar, with sound design by Harrell and Robin Meier; set design by Erik Flatmo; costume design by Harrell, in collaboration with the performers; lighting design by Jan Maertens; production management by Bob Bellerue; production assistance by Michael Hart; and dramaturgy by Gérard Mayen.

25. Alain Resnais's film appeared in 1958 with a script written by Marguerite Duras.

26. Marguerite Duras, *Hiroshima Mon Amour: A Screenplay* [1960], trans. Richard Seaver (New York: Grove Press, 1961), 15, 23.

27. Georges Didi-Huberman, *Images in Spite of All* [2003], trans. Shane B. Lillis (Chicago: University of Chicago Press, 2008), 30.

28. Ibid.

29. *SoloShow* premiered November 12–15, 2009, at Performance Space 122 in partnership with PERFORMA 09. The piece was conceived as part of a diptych with *Solo*, a performance that premiered September 29–October 4, 2009, at Performance Space 122 in partnership with Crossing the Line. Both pieces were choreographed and performed by Maria Hassabi and featured lighting by Joe Levasseur, clothing by ThreeAsFour, dramaturgy by Marcos Rosales and Scott Lyall, sound score by James Lo, and set design by Scott Lyall and Hassabi.

30. Maria Hassabi, conversation with author, Brooklyn, New York, July 30, 2010.

31. Francis Barker, *The Tremulous Private Body: Essays on Subjection* (Ann Arbor: University of Michigan Press, 1995), 9–10.

32. Ibid.

33. Ibid., 57, 58.

34. Jacques Rancière, *The Future of the Image* [2003], trans. Gregory Elliot (London: Verso, 2007), 7.

35. Ibid., 46.

36. Godard worked on *Historie(s) du cinéma* for almost ten years; the film became his critique of cinema and its effects on the twentieth-century. Stretching over eight sections, the film is mostly accumulated from excerpts of other cinema and audio, emphasizing the multiple valences of *histories* as both history and story.

37. P.A.R.T.S. is a training program for contemporary dance and theory based in Brussels, founded in 1994 by choreographer Anne Teresa De Keersmaeker of Rosas and Bernard Foccroulle, director of the national opera De Munt/La Monnaie.

38. Performed at the Movement Research benefit, Judson Church, New York, in April 1995. It was created and performed by DD Dorvillier and Mark Ashwill, with music by Michelle Nagai, Cristina Dorvillier, and Cheb Mami and costumes by DD Dorvillier.

39. Mark Ashwill was also part of Missing Foundation, an industrial anarchist band that performed in the late 1980s and early 1990s. Their tag was sprayed in the East Village, an upside down martini glass inscribed with the dates 1933–1988, juxtaposing the rise of Weimar Germany with New York City under Mayor Ed Koch. Here again the aura of Benjamin returns.

EXIT/EXIST — EMBODIMENT

My work has been about the embodiment of history, tradition, arts, society, and politics. It treats the body as a moving portrait that continues to find transitional points in tradition and language and that evolves in finding creative translations for unfamiliar and familiar elements. In this writing I delve deeper into my recent staged work Exit/Exist as a point of departure to further understand and interpret the body as an archive.

I focus on my ancestral past: Chief Maqoma, a nineteenth-century warrior who fought to maintain Xhosa cultural traditions of the Eastern Cape in the face of colonial dispossession of land and cattle. This story has seen a family torn apart and a new generation (in myself) making peace with it, finding relevance in this piece of history in the now. In my integration of traditional and contemporary dance vocabulary, I attempt to reflect on who we are, where we come from, and how all of these facets, past and present, inform our personal and collective identities today. Finally, I look at how the body is able to archive and restore personal legacy, creating a distinctive identity.

THE BODY ARCHIVE

In many places in the world, people feel that political pressure defines cultural identity in ethnic terms and cultural diversity in political terms. Cultural identity, however, cannot be defined in terms of race and ethnicity alone. It is a complex subject and is complicated further by such factors as gender, class, generation, sexual and religious orientation, and the tension between tradition and modernity. The body becomes the temple that preciously archives these complexities, and they become visible when the artist chooses to bring them out for public consumption.

As artists, we often see things through our personal histories, with their parts rooted in convention, and they become subject to the change we desire. These histories come to include reflections on what inspires us to take that first step of discovering their complex nature. Through such reflections I believe we become the mirror to the society we represent, and as a result we become political and our identities are formed. With political consciousness, we become aware of who we are, and some knowledge of self and place creates a possibility for a discourse; in my case, the body becomes the principal communicator, informed by many experiences.

My work fuses mud huts, the Internet, and various dance forms; all of these make up my form, a cultural cocktail. In my quest to express my true identity, I allow my intuition to be the driving force, the adrenalin that is set in a particular register, which I find difficult to pin down to one word or description. When I reflect and try to make meaning, to find words to describe the movement aesthetic my body exudes, the only word I can come up with is *architecture*: the landscape that continues to evolve and change, closely related to the earth and affected by its deteriorating nature; a collection of identities, acknowledging the many centuries of social and political heritage. The intuition frees me, and it leaves me with a bittersweet feeling and contradictory emotions. My work is grounded—it gives in to gravity, getting closer to the earth—but at the same time I am consumed with the feeling of taking flight, an escape to the world of the unknown or perhaps the world that my ancestors traveled, embedded in their DNA, my inheritance.

THE ARCHITECTURE OF MOVEMENT

In the challenging world of contemporary dance—particularly in terms of what is called "conceptual art," in which execution of the work is regarded as subsidiary to the idea or concept behind it, and in which even the term *conceptual art* must rely on words rather than art to define itself to the viewer—traditions become meaningless, and the very nature of art, particularly the power of the visual and the motional, becomes secondary.

History, however, tells us something different. When our ancestors performed their rituals, dancing around a fire till dawn, they used rocks and burned sticks to draw on cave walls what they were seeing while in a trance; memory, intuition, and consensus were the driving forces. Our ancestors relied on driving the body to an extent of reaching that point of total submission to the unknown.

When I created Exit/Exist—a contemporary dance work that looks at the history of my ancestor, Chief Jongusobomvu Maqoma, a Xhosa warrior who was born in 1798 and died in 1873 under mysterious circumstances in isolation while being held as a political prisoner on Robben Island in Cape Town, South Africa—I became aware of the danger of being trapped within the parameters of conceptual art.

In my research for the work, I realized that both oral and written history were not enough for me to be able to create a true reflection of my interest in the subject of displacement and colonial disposition. I needed more than a history page to walk my ancestor's path and rediscover part of my own story in his, the story that I carry within myself. That needed vigorous training in Xhosa tradition, culture, and customs, to embody them fully. After I spent days and nights of movement practice in traditional Xhosa dances, dancing in the mountains of Eastern Cape, what emerged was the same concept, only different. I was living the story, no longer telling it but reliving the memory through the visual form, by my body. A sense of ownership emerged; the foundation was stronger to start building the walls for the architecture to come to life.

I realized when I started performing the work that the body can only reveal what it has learned, and new information always triggers what lies underneath, in the body archive. In creating Exit/Exist I realized that escaping the urban city life and stepping on the redness of the earth of Eastern Cape, smelling the ocean and the fresh breeze of the mountains, instantly separated the theory of the subject from the practice of it. The interesting development is when all the information and ideas start to collaborate and, without making concessions, manage to reach an agreement, creating a new language. A formidable work emerged. Every performance creates new transitional entry and exit points. Every performance becomes a memory, and when the lights go off and the curtain falls, a new history is written.

IN CONCLUSION

My experience of working with history and the body made me believe strongly that one cannot write the dance with ideas only; some degree of movement understanding of the subject is needed. The body is often eager to experiment with the unknown to better reveal what it has learned. With time, such practice becomes a form, a personal movement style, creating fresh expressions. As we grow older, the body matures, and we become more and more trusting. Before anyone can see the work, we have the opportunity to live it, feel it, and experiment with it. In essence we become the first witnesses, and if we connect with and understand what the body is communicating, then the work is ready for public consumption. As creators, when all is achieved, we trust that what has been preciously archived will be revealed with honesty every time an opportunity is given.

V. Afterlives and Transformations

Every performance has an afterlife, whether as a brief memory or as one that is retained through image, notation, written text, or transmission from one body to another. Willful extension of a work beyond its original instantiation in performance forces us to attend to both the archiving and retrieving of this afterlife, raising questions not only of motives, expectations, and methodologies but also just what it is that we have brought back to life.

While varying from culture to culture, the transient materiality of dance and other bodied performance forms has presented multiple challenges to dance's place in the archive throughout most of Western history. Exactly notating or finding a perfectly compatible technical medium to record and preserve a dance, for example, may always elude completion. And there is the problem of time; in a sense there is nothing to preserve, as each dance unfolds and is swallowed whole, almost instantaneously, by the past. We may choose to identify and champion performance in both its liveness and its brief life and dismiss any effort to record or document. We may argue, instead, that the past has not vanished but rather is brimming with power or the potential to reframe the present and the future. Or we may recognize some value in prolonging the life of a performance, work, or genre and investigate technology, objects, events, and writing that enable us to continue considering the work after its first instantiation. Time resolutely ignores all philosophical stances, detaining any original in the past, releasing only traces, shards, and shadows into the present.

The rethinking in the last few decades about archive and bodiedness compels reconsideration of the afterlives of archived materials, be they memories, historical facts, bodied works, or performances. If we consider both the bodies *in* the archive and the body *as* archive, we also have to attend to the implications of our decisions to enter the archive. If we choose to prolong the life of a performance beyond its instance of performance, no matter the format or platform, we must continue to contend with issues of what gets saved, why, and how, as well as the relationship of power to these decisions, and we must apply the same set of cautionary questions to retrieval and reenactment. Furthermore, we cannot ignore the impact of technology on both body and archive and how their natures and functions may be extended or morphed in ways yet inconceivable.

Dances dug out of the archive are far more vulnerable to "slippage" than works in other art forms that are captured in visual media or that can be substantially notated with symbols or text. Decisions rest on whether this slippage is regarded as a loss or as an opportunity to reengage the work in its new cultural and historical milieu. Expectations of returning to a complete or authentic original are impossible to fulfill, as every retrieval or reconstruction is to some extent an act of intentional or accidental transformation.

In this section Marcia B. Siegel, while embracing a view of restaging dances that acknowledges the vitality of historical change, asks us to also pause and consider what is lost when we cannot find in the archive the work as it originally existed. Jennifer Monson conceives of the dancing body as an archive not only of past movement and dance histories but also of ongoing and ephemeral or changing relationships with nature, which she captures and retains through improvisational archiving practices and transfers to data shareable through performance and media. Thomas F. DeFrantz offers a compelling study of a work retrieved from the intensely personal and political bodied archive of a choreographer and reset a quarter of a century later with dancers whose own bodied archives are shaped by different sets of racialized, sexualized, and politicized aesthetic imperatives. Mariana Ibañez and Simon Kim consider the body's physiognomy, proportions, and sensate corporeal capacities as the basis for the performance-based criteria that inform their architectural designs of performance spaces. André Lepecki critically engages with the work of choreographer Ralph Lemon, focusing on Lemon's collaboration with Walter Carter from 2003 to 2012 and investigating the implications that emerge when choreographers explicitly approach the dancer's body as embodiment of history.

—Linda Caruso Haviland

PAVILION OF SECRETS

The Ballets Russes de Serge Diaghilev made its debut on May 19, 1909, at the Théâtre du Châtelet in Paris, preceded by a well-attended *répétition generale* on May 18.[1] Leading off the program was Michel Fokine's *Le Pavillon d'Armide*, a sumptuous fantasy ballet that had premiered at St. Petersburg's Imperial Theater a year and a half before. Considering that this ballet inaugurated a twenty-year revolution in ballet and the entire arts world, we might want to know exactly who danced what on those historic nights.

There is no definitive account of who performed in the debut. To publicize the season, Diaghilev relied heavily on projected appearances of the already famous Anna Pavlova, for whom Fokine choreographed the title role of Armida. However, as an independent artist Pavlova was booked to tour several other cities until halfway through Diaghilev's season. A beautiful but undistinguished dancer, Vera Karalli, headed the cast of *Pavillon* at the *répétition generale*. Apparently it was Tamara Karsavina who danced Armida on the official opening night, but even this is a deduction. Two close associates of Diaghilev, Serge Grigoriev and Boris Kochno, assert that Pavlova appeared on opening night, but other sources, including the encyclopedic Cyril Beaumont, report that she didn't arrive in Paris until the end of May. Karsavina ascended to stardom in these first performances, not as Armida but as the partner of Vaslav Nijinsky in the "Fire Bird" (the renamed "Blue Bird" pas de deux from *Sleeping Beauty*, incorporated into the divertissement *Le Festin*). It was Nijinsky who stunned the audience in *Pavillon*. His sister, Bronislava Nijinska, has described his performance in detail, but even this sensational debut was described differently in retrospect by Karsavina.[2] Ballet history is littered with casual scraps of information, unexamined for so long that they have become engraved, as if the latter-day writers had actually seen what they describe.

The difficulty of ascertaining the most basic facts about a hundred-year-old ballet is only a foretaste of what it would require to establish the identity of the ballet itself, or any ballet from Diaghilev's extraordinary career. Serge Diaghilev's twofold reputation as an impresario is not in doubt. For twenty years he marshaled the financial and administrative wherewithal to operate the company, and he masterminded the ballets by putting together the exceptional cre-

Alexandre Benois (1870–1960), set design for the garden in act 2 of *Le Pavillon d'Armide*, 1909. Watercolor, ink, and pencil on paper. Howard D. Rothschild Collection on Ballets Russes of Serge Diaghilev: Drawings and Prints, 1907–1956, MS Thr 414.4 (33). Harvard Theatre Collection, Houghton Library, Harvard University. (See plate 11 for color image.)

ative artists to execute his ideas. But the ballets themselves vanished the moment they were born. Virtually no one is alive today who took part in the Ballets Russes enterprise. Whatever filmed footage exists provides little idea of the productions, given the limitations of moviemaking technology prior to 1929. Every other form of documentation requires translation of some kind to simulate an original stage event. The many eyewitnesses and participants have left differing accounts. The Ballets Russes became a scholarly industry, a popular legend, and an ongoing reference point from which the ballet repertory is descended. Its significance is not in doubt, but its accomplishments are as elusive as myth.

In collaboration with Diaghilev's handpicked composers, librettists, and designers, five choreographers were responsible for most of the ballets produced by the Ballets Russes: Michel Fokine, Vaslav Nijinsky, Léonide Massine, Bronislava Nijinska, and George Balanchine. With the exception of Nijinsky, who was overcome by mental illness after making only four ballets, these artists consolidated international careers after the death of Diaghilev and the closing of the company in 1929. They all associated themselves with successor Ballet Russe companies as choreographers and ballet masters.[3] Teaching, choreographing, and heading American-based companies, they instilled their aesthetics into

Tamara Karsavina
in *Le Pavillon
D'Armide*, 1918.
© 2016 Curatorial
Assistance, Inc./
E. O. Hoppé Estate
Collection.

American dance. The Diaghilev-era ballets lived on, in conditions that approxi-
mated their original impressiveness to varying degrees.

But the productions whose originals had prompted extreme reactions of eu-
phoria or outrage often failed to evoke rapture when seen in revivals. Faded
productions were blamed—unspectacular dancing, dated styles, lost choreographic information, ill-advised updating—but the same revivals could also
inspire adoration, perhaps fueled by nostalgia or wishful expectations. Critical evaluation often depended, in the words of Lincoln Kirstein, on "mori-
bund criteria and rosy memoirs."[4] Current ballet criticism seems to have boiled
down to a casual consensus that we needn't—can't—recover the originals. We
should simultaneously believe in the mythological originals and the imperfect
but clouded versions of them in current repertory. Today these ballets remain a
subject of fascination for dancers, critics, scholars, and even audiences. When

Michel Fokine
as Harlequin
in *Carnaval*,
Stockholm
Théâtre
Royal, 1914.
Bibliothèque
nationale
de France,
département
Bibliothèque-
musée de l'opéra.
(See plate 12 for
sepia image.)
Photograph by
Atelier Jaeger
(Stockholm).

they're brought back before the public, they can only suggest something that's lost. Yet the allure of the Ballets Russes remains undiminished.

Michel Fokine, Diaghilev's first choreographer (1909–1914), established the fame of the Ballets Russes in its first years. His works became legendary, yet the ballets aren't stable as they have come down over the years. In this essay I examine their paradoxical nature as they are remade and how they have come to inspire approval and controversy. Even though these restaged ballets are accepted as compromised and sometimes inauthentic artifacts, the mystique of the Ballets Russes has increased. I don't dismiss the restaged and reconstructed ballets or the immense literature that has grown up around the originals; they comprise the history. But I do suggest that this history tells us much about ballet that we have not explored and less about specific ballets than we think we know. Here

I examine some of these manifestations, looking into the gulf between present and disappeared productions, to see how dance history invents itself.

FOKINE AND THE INHERITANCE

What is singular but not deeply analyzed about the Ballets Russes choreographies is that they could be defined by dance steps, movement styles, compositional patterns, and the dancing of the artists who created them. These elements have eluded credible descriptive writing. Instead, eyewitness accounts tend to stress narratives, disguises, and metaphorical flights of fancy. Unless it is scrupulously guarded, the dance element slips away immediately, in imperceptible increments. Choreographic notation gives us the steps of many seventeenth- and eighteenth-century ballets, but the *idea* of those ballets has resided largely with the music and the story. We understand that the nineteenth-century work of great ballet masters like August Bournonville, Marius Petipa, Jules Perrot, and Jean Coralli will have been reshaped by subsequent hands. The accepted practice of rechoreographing ballets further diminishes any hope for the preservation of the oldest choreographic entities.

The choreographer assumed a crucial position during the Diaghilev era. The Ballets Russes choreographers occupied a predominant role in the creative process; their individual styles became synonymous with the ballets. Either they didn't remain with Diaghilev long enough to assert their ownership, or for various other reasons the ballets fell out of their hands. Fokine claimed that not a step was changed in his ballets as long as he supervised productions, and his heirs have worked to maintain that standard. In his *Memoirs* he recounts the lapses and betrayals that befell his highly successful works after he left the company in 1912 (he returned very briefly two years later).

Les Sylphides, choreographed as *Chopiniana* in Russia before the advent of the Ballets Russes in Europe, has become a staple in the modern repertory. Fokine claimed that "I have never changed anything in this ballet," after ruefully describing the inadvertent liberties dancers took with it from the beginning and how they had to be reminded of its stylistic imperatives. Of *Carnaval* he said, "I have never changed a single movement in it." Without assigning responsibility, the omnivorous English critic Cyril Beaumont recounts how the delicate fabric of this ballet frayed during the 1930s. Years after the fact, Fokine recalled the Polovtsian Dances from *Prince Igor* as performed over the years: "The changes made by others are most painfully endured by me." When he wasn't on the scene to coach the dancers, "the style no longer retained its meaning, and the dancers began to add their own designs." He went out of his way to counter what he considered the wrong interpretations writers made of *The Firebird* and lamented how even the original production fell short of his ambitious scheme. In the wake of a 1921 Ballets Russes performance of *Firebird*, he renounced "responsibility for the senseless distortions that have taken place in my absence, and without my consent." Despite his vociferous disclaimers, Fokine's ballets have changed. The public has no choice but to accept approximations, expedients, and loose interpretations of *Schéhérazade*, *Firebird*, and other Diaghilev-era works as if they were the famous originals.[5]

Michel Fokine, as the first of Diaghilev's great choreographers, authored the ballets that secured the fame of the Ballets Russes and launched the company's mystique. Although the ballets are gone, the music and designs Diaghilev shrewdly commissioned from important artists can still be experienced as separate artifacts: *Schéhérazade*, *Firebird*, and *Petrouchka* are staples of the symphonic repertory, and Léon Bakst's exotic costume designs and the romantic settings of Alexandre Benois can be seen in museum collections and are reproduced in books. But Fokine's choreography is a thing we surmise from static images. Hundreds of photographs, mostly posed, give us the glamour and the drama of the ballets. Nijinsky crouches like a panther in *Le Festin*. Ida Rubinstein, encrusted with jewels, faints backward voluptuously in *Schéhérazade*. An imperious Karsavina, in feathers and long blonde braids, gazes past her shoulder in *The Firebird*. Fokine himself, as a mischievous Harlequin, sneaks up on someone outside the camera frame in *Carnaval*. But what were the moves that precipitated these poses and followed them? What animated the ballets, if not the choreography? It's precisely the choreography that falls out of the equation.

Even in its first appearances, the choreography sometimes slipped away despite Fokine's strenuous efforts to protect it. Fokine's domination of the Diaghilev repertory lasted only five discontinuous years. When *Schéhérazade*, *Firebird*, and other works passed from his hands, he couldn't prevent changes being made. His work was adapted and imitated even before it left the Ballets Russes stages, and he himself directed revivals in Europe and America, presumably making his own adaptations when necessary. In his memoirs, completed and published posthumously by his son Vitale in 1961, Fokine vouched for the continuing authenticity of his ballets, except where they couldn't withstand an implacable evolution. Some of his signature works became implanted in the repertories of far-flung post–Ballets Russes companies, where they grew their own hybrid personalities. Alexandra Danilova commented in her memoirs about dancing the Firebird with the de Basil Ballet Russe, which she joined in its early days, around

1934: "I had danced Lopukhov's *Firebird* at the Mariinsky and Fokine's version in the Diaghilev company. Both were based on the same story, but Lopukhov's was modern, while Fokine's choreography was much more classical. In the de Basil company's production, there were a lot of blank spots in my role, because no one exactly remembered Fokine's choreography. So I used to mix the two versions, adding some Lopukhov steps here and there, and they blended very well. No one seemed to notice." [6]

After his death in 1942, maintenance of Fokine's work fell to others. The Fokine Estate Archive was established on an undisclosed date in the early 2000s.[7] Before establishment of the Berne Convention and subsequent US legislation protecting ownership of creative work, Michel Fokine had registered his ballets for copyright in Paris. According to the Estate Archive, Fokine's works are still under copyright and are subject to its permission for public performances. In addition to authorized productions, the Archive stipulates: "Any 'versions' of Fokine's works are still subject to the copyright, due to the fact that a version … is by its nature, a derivative of the copyright." Wielding these legal weapons, the Estate Archive has controlled exposure to Fokine's work in North America, preventing the public from judging for itself whether a given production is convincing or misguided.

THE DANCERS' ROLE

The fame of the early Ballets Russes ballets relied heavily on the gifts of the dancers who created them: the incomparable Nijinsky, Pavlova, Karsavina, Adolph Bolm, and a succession of younger dancers. It's a truism in the dance world that dances associated with important performers can never be re-created. Filmed records now can demonstrate the progression of stylistic and interpretive liberties imposed by dancers, even if the producing company doesn't inform the audience what those subtle modifications were or who made them. Through the widespread practice of learning a ballet from films, the idiosyncrasies and faulty memories of great stars tend to be copied and exaggerated by later generations of dancers and absorbed into the "original" version that is produced on stage. These evolutions, whether or not intended by the choreographer, cannot credibly be traced on film before about 1960.

Modern-day modifications by dancers, even when they have access to the authorized Fokine repertory, can pitch a ballet into psychological ambiguity. Superficially, the antagonistic pas de deux of *The Firebird*—between the naïve Ivan Tsarevich and the exotic bird he sees in the forest—is a fairly conventional-looking duet. It's up to the dancers to signal that they're not engaged in a con-

235

Tamara Karsavina coaching Margot Fonteyn in the role of the Firebird. Howard D. Rothschild Collection on Ballets Russes of Serge Diaghilev: Photographs and Scrapbooks, 1909–1975, MS Thr 414.2 (66). Harvard Theatre Collection, Houghton Library, Harvard University. (See plate 13 for sepia image.) Photograph by Douglas Elston.

ventional love scene. When the steps have been preserved adequately, the man holds and balances the woman, and she tries to escape him, turning and pulling away. This isn't a significantly different vocabulary than the "white" pas de deux in *Swan Lake* would have if it were modernized. We learn that some kind of seduction isn't taking place from the way the dancers perform it. Margot Fonteyn, who probably created the most convincing Firebird accessible to us, learned the role in 1954, from Diaghilev's longtime régisseur Serge Grigoriev, from Liubov Tchernichova, and from Tamara Karsavina, the original Firebird. Fonteyn's performance with Michael Somes as the Tsarevich was preserved in a 1959 film. It's now considered definitive, but other dancers have had their own ideas.[8]

When the Firebird first appears, she dances alone, establishing her affinity for the air in a series of jetés. Fokine insisted in his memoirs that even though the Firebird's initial solo was full of jumps, it contained no virtuosic technicalities—staples of the ballet lexicon like battements, ronds de jambe, and entrechats—and no preparations or turnout. Arms weren't to take the familiar classical positions, but were to be used expressively, in accordance with the narrative.[9] Still, dancers in contemporary productions insert multiple pirouettes, overextended balances, and jerky, birdlike arms. Some dancers simulate a bird quality with quick changes of the gaze or arms that flap in segments. Fonteyn uses her arms in distinctive ways. In the solo, her wing/arms wave successively, with the hands floating free. At pauses in the musical phrase, her arms hit exact positions, with the hands fluttering as if to emphasize her stillness. Pursued and momentarily trapped by the Tsarevich, she loses her free, "natural" relation to the air; her arms become stiff, lifting from the shoulders in one unit with only the forearms and hands working. Her head tilts back, and her upper body strains away from the Prince's grasp. Her energy seems to drain away as she struggles against him, until, pinned to the floor on one knee, she thinks of the magic feather that will persuade him to release her.

Fonteyn seems to have resisted the generic smiles and pouts that constitute standard classical ballet personification of emotion, a practice even more common today than it was in the 1950s. She said her guiding thought about the Firebird came from Fokine by way of Karsavina: "Here is no human emotion." Indeed, in the 1959 film Fonteyn gives a chilling performance. She couldn't be mistaken for a yearning princess. She's like some prehistoric animal that has only self-preservation in mind. In the second-act pas de deux of *Swan Lake* on the same Royal Ballet recording, she is again partnered by Michael Somes (and an anonymous Benno); the interaction between the dancers contrasts sharply with *The Firebird*, though the action is similar. Here she yields to him, allowing him to pin her arms close to her body, an echo of the crossed-hands gesture signifying that she's the prisoner of the evil Rothbart. When she does unfold her legs, they expand into the air, in tandem with her arms. Later in the dance she rests against him, curving her whole body along his. Instead of plunging freely into the air, as in the Firebird's solo, her arms seem to be seeking an embrace, begging to be rescued by the benign prince who would possess her in a new if romantic confinement.[10]

Dancers often try to appear fierce in this role, notably Royal Ballet principal Leanne Benjamin, who recorded *Firebird* in 2001 with Jonathan Cope as the Tsarevich.[11] Benjamin treats this as an acting opportunity, a contemporary interpretation. She inserts occasional dramatic moves to indicate a struggle—extreme backbends, shoulders that try to shrug away from his grip—and the camera moves in on her exaggerated facial expressions.

THE STEPS HAVE MEANING

Fokine's modernism was founded, in part, on the idea that movement could be expressive without relying on the coded gestures of classical ballet. While crossed hands, the ballet mime indication of imprisonment or captivity, were a sign understood by ballet choreographers and audiences, Fokine also used the whole body expressively to indicate emotional states. Having seen and been impressed by Isadora Duncan early in his career, his work from around 1910 exhibits her influence. He didn't often resort to Duncan's inventive lyricism, but he deplored the strictures of classical ballet for indicating character and was often criticized for it. As popular as his ballets were with audiences, they didn't satisfy those who would preserve tradition. According to André Levinson, one of the chief critical defenders of classical ballet, Fokine "sacrificed the forms of abstract movement for expression, pure dance for pantomime."[12]

Now, a century after the schism opened up between proponents of expression and "pure dance," the fine points of dramatic interpretation are no longer high priorities. Dancers are celebrated for their technical skills and their physical beauty. Character and stories are a matter of suggestion; the audience can read them in, or not, in modern choreography. The dancers need only become emblems of codified desire and repulsion, without past histories or cultural implications. Dancers now don't have classes in acting; there's little time for workshopping choreography, digging into motivations, or even researching past performing precedents. According to Meredith Daneman, when Monica Mason of the Royal Ballet took over the role of the Firebird in 1978, she had to beg Fonteyn for coaching advice, which she got in one brief rehearsal.[13] Eventually, whatever Mason knew was probably passed on to Leanne Benjamin. Fonteyn's image, via Karsavina through Mason and whoever came in between, emerges in Benjamin's own portrayal as a woman mortally afraid of being seduced, not a brittle creature with an inborn antipathy toward men. These discrepant images may not change the effect of the whole ballet, but it does matter whether the Firebird is an active or a passive player in her first encounter with the Tsarevich.

The Firebird, along with most of the early Diaghilev ballets, was performed at a time when the revolutionary arts of the fin de siècle were at their height. Art nouveau, visionary utopianism, symbolism, theosophy, synesthesia, cubism, and the early gestures of constructivism were all churning around the ballets and the art fanciers in the audience. Magic transformations and revelations could be effected in the theater of the time; they were, indeed, a big part of what made dance theater appealing. Fokine was well aware of the cosmic implications of the fairy tales he appropriated and/or adapted for The Firebird, Petrouchka, Le Dieu Bleu, and other exotic early pieces. Firebird's final scene depicts the wedding of the Tsarevich and the Princess, in a grand processional with no dancing, the Firebird presiding over all. The Firebird symbolizes not only the survival of the folk, as Petrouchka does, but the "natural" or primitive force that legitimizes the ongoing power of the monarchy. A significant part of Diaghilev's audience was composed of Russian expatriates, members of the elite classes who had fled the revolution and looked back on the days of the Russian aristocracy with nostalgia. Dance historian Sally Banes elaborated this reading of The Firebird in her book on female dancers.[14]

As concrete as Fokine was about his steps being meaningful in themselves, he wasn't unaware that the audience was expecting to read something more into the productions. Music historian Richard Taruskin, a dance outsider and hence no dedicated protector of reputations, has pointed out that Diaghilev cannily incorporated made-up folk material into ballets like The Firebird in order to please the French taste for féerie and exoticism. With Igor Stravinsky's Firebird and Petrouchka, the Ballets Russes brought important composers into the production process and elevated ballet from its status as a "handicapped form of opera" to the art form of the future.[15]

RUSSIAN EXOTICISM

Fokine's Ballets Russes ballets fell roughly into two categories: the classical (Spectre de la Rose, Carnaval, Les Sylphides) and the exotic (Schéhérazade, Firebird, Cléopâtre, Le Dieu Bleu, the Polovtsian Dances from Prince Igor), with Pavillon d'Armide

Schéhérazade, corps de ballet with duelers. Parmenia Migel, collector; Stravinsky-Diaghilev Foundation Collection, 1912–1989, MS Thr 495 (153, seq. 15). Harvard Theatre Collection, Houghton Library, Harvard University. (See plate 14 for sepia image.) Photograph by White Studios. © The New York Public Library for the Performing Arts.

neatly encompassing both modes. Apart from the acclaim earned by the principal dancers in all of these works, it was the exotic ballets, with their lush music and designs, that had the greatest notoriety and the most popular appeal and that seem the least recoverable in something close to their original form. Their stories and designs gave them immediate appeal, but was there any choreography?

Schéhérazade may not have exemplified Fokine at his most innovative, but it's probably the best known of his early ballets, and certainly the most notorious. With a story put together from tales of the Arabian Nights, courtesy of composer Nikolai Rimsky-Korsakov; its lush harem décor by Bakst; and its scenes of transgressive interracial liaisons and an emergent sexual liberation, *Schéhérazade* created an uproar when it premiered, and in revivals it has continued to represent the mystique of the Ballets Russes.

Schéhérazade had only two notable dance sequences, if we can rely on first reports: the trio of Odalisques who provided entertainment in the opening scene and the "orgy" in which the harem wives engaged in forbidden dalliance with the Shah's slaves. Serge Grigoriev, Diaghilev's ballet master, reported that when Fokine began to choreograph the Odalisques, he placed the three dancers on the floor and instructed them to "use only their arms and heads and the upper halves of their bodies." They were "eventually allowed to rise and continue the number in more orthodox fashion." This loose description suggests pretty torso undulations and Grecian-maiden groupings, very much like the interpretive dancing of Isadora Duncan, as well as the exotic temple dancers imitated by Ruth St. Denis.[16]

It was the "orgy" that aroused the most feverish response. As filmed by the Kirov Ballet in 2002, after the slaves are let out of their cells, they pair off with the wives; for a long interval they sit together on the floor, entwining and stretching their bodies in simulated ecstasy while Zobeide and the Golden Slave (Svetlana Zakharova and Farukh Ruzimatov) dance a highly erotic version of the duet Fokine added two years after the premiere.[17] When we try to imagine what Fokine choreographed for this outrageous scene, we find the most graphic description given by the American critic H. T. Parker following the Ballets Russes's Boston performances in 1916. The slaves and sultanas finally join, relates Parker, "into the heat and whirl of the long winding lines of flying figures, the swift, sudden concentrated circlings, the colorful confusion of tossing arms and twisting torsos, the glowing sweep and the mounting frenzy of passion released and unsated ... the figures outflung for a single instant only to be engulfed at the next in the vortex of the whole."[18]

To the English critic Cyril Beaumont the orgy reached its peak just as the Shah and his companions returned.[19] But the musical pause and unraveling took place *before* the return of the Shah, according to Grigoriev.[20] The dance for "the various groups of dancers woven in with a number of individual moves" reached a tremendous climax when "having combined all the different groups into one, [Fokine] used a pause in the music suddenly to halt them, and then, while accelerating the pace still more, as it were to unravel this human tangle." Some descriptions separate the group dance from the spectacular solo dancing of Nijinsky, although he apparently danced this in the midst of the slaves and harem girls, creating a vortex for the whirlpool of passion that Fokine was constructing.

One of the most lucid accounts of the ballet's choreographic design is given by the music critic Robert Lawrence. With excerpts from the musical score to illustrate his description, Lawrence brings out some important information that others neglect. *Schéhérazade* evoked a furor in the first seasons among musical followers, who resented the fact that Fokine disregarded Rimsky-Korsakov's

Arabian Nights scenario and omitted the composer's third movement entirely. Lawrence implies that the ballet gained coherence from this tightening. Ida Rubinstein, the original Zobeide, wasn't a dancer, and a romantic duet might have seemed inappropriate. Fokine reported in his memoirs that Rubinstein's tall, sensuous body and Nijinsky's short, "unmasculine" appearance were ill-matched for a pas de deux. When Fokine acceded to his critics two years later and reinstated the third movement, he made a demi-classical pas de deux for Tamara Karsavina and Nijinsky, creating, Lawrence thought, a distracting contradiction in style.[21]

H. T. Parker had seen *Schéhérazade* many times in Europe since 1913, and he thought little had changed by the time of the Ballets Russes's 1916 American tour.[22] Though newcomers to it proclaimed that it had lost its "'inherent' sensuality and savagery," Parker made the startling observation that "the piece and performance have long enjoyed a fictitious reputation on the unctuous tongues of old men, and in the shocked whispers of maidens."[23]

The Shah returns to the trap he has set for his subjects and commands his soldiers to cut down all the offenders, which they do, again in mime and, in some revivals, using their scimitars like daggers. The Golden Slave dies (but not in every production), in Nijinsky's astonishing paroxysm of spins and a shoulder stand with his legs quivering in the air. During the massacre, the Kirov film focuses on Zobeide and the Shah as he deliberates whether to forgive her. This last dramatic encounter is depicted many different ways but doesn't involve any dancing. Fokine, invoking his theory that storytelling should be carried out in dance, resorted to very few mime gestures, but he wrote clearly about what was happening dramatically at the end of the ballet. In the last few moments, Zobeide pleads for her life, swearing her love for the Shah. He's on the brink of forgiving her when his brother, angry at this show of weakness, steps on the Slave's body, inflaming the Shah's rage again and provoking him to order his soldiers to execute Zobeide. In his memoirs, Fokine coyly sidestepped the question of just how Zobeide dies, although he described in some detail how she repents her infidelity and begs to be forgiven. She dies anyway. Dancers in different productions interpret the denouement differently. Zobeide frequently escapes the soldiers' swords by stabbing herself.

In *Schéhérazade*, the motivations of the main characters can affect the way we view the whole plot. Is it a story of a doomed illicit love, or of a woman of conscience who must submit to her husband's will? Does it matter to the ballet's integrity whether Zobeide is a dutiful wife or a fallen favorite? What prompts the substitution of suicide for the execution of Zobeide? To have the heroine kill herself inserts another element of sensationalism in an already inflamed scenario, but what is the motivation for this? Does Zobeide really love the Shah, or would she rather not face life without her lover? These are questions answered only by the dramatic intentions of the dancers and their directors.

The conservative critic André Levinson, no fan of Fokine's work, thought the choreographer was engaged in "the pseudo-dramatization of ballet," and that eroticism substituted for dancing in *Schéhérazade*.[24] This assessment probably underwrites the steaminess of some representations made for a latter-day popular audience. In a composite of excerpts from Ballet Russe de Monte Carlo performances, filmed between 1948 and 1952 by Victor Jessen, the Zobeides wear platform shoes throughout the ballet. Andris Liepa even filmed *Schéhérazade* as a cinematic narrative, with generous close-ups on furtive glances and seductive bodies.

CLASSICISM AND NOSTALGIA

Notwithstanding his great success with the exotic ballets, Fokine didn't abandon the classical aesthetic entirely. Before the Great War, he had at his disposal a company of superb dancers trained in the Russian imperial schools, and he used their skills in the idyllic representations of *Les Sylphides*, *Le Spectre de la Rose*, and *Carnaval*. They concentrate on character portraits instead of elaborate plot devices and scenic effects. Fokine's classical ballets (sometimes referred to as romantic) have been distilled into standardized versions. Perhaps they were less subject to fashion; they could be transposed from their original productions to situations in which none of the original casts or décors could be retained.

Les Sylphides has been passed from one company to the next in typical word-of-mouth succession. A few performance photographs have supplied the ensemble designs that serve as the backup to the variations of the four principal dancers. These—originally Karsavina, Pavlova, Alexandra Baldina, and Nijinsky—were often photographed solo, in studio poses that can't be relied on for an exact record of the ballet. The most we can get from this type of documentation is a sense of the period, and that is precisely what escapes the dancers of today—perhaps not only the dancers, but the audience as well. In *Choura*, the memoir Alexandra Danilova wrote with Holly Brubach, the dancer spoke about *Les Sylphides* as a staple of the de Basil Ballet Russe repertory: "*Les Sylphides*, which many people now find rather boring, was a favorite with the audience. But *Les Sylphides* today is a different ballet completely. The steps are the same, but dancers no longer understand the style; they don't know how to project the mood it requires, an air of lyrical detachment."[25]

Les Sylphides, Ballet Russe de Monte Carlo, undated, photographer unknown. Image retrieved from the Library of Congress, https://www.loc.gov/item/ihas.200181816/.

A certain suspension of disbelief is needed to reestablish the aura of naïveté surrounding the ballets of the early nineteenth century that were Fokine's proto-types, but unlike *Giselle* or *Coppélia*, *Les Sylphides* has no story line to engage us, no specialty variations to show off dancers' personalities, no manufactured folk-lore, no engaging characters or comedy. We're asked to accept this low-key representation of a mood, a community of ethereal sprites. The choreography in many guises can be readily seen on YouTube. According to Ballet Alert! contributor Alexandra Tomalonis, the editor of several dance publications, a different version exists for every company Fokine visited in his roving post-Diaghilev career.[26]

By the time of its Paris premiere in 1909, *Les Sylphides* had already undergone considerable recrafting. It first surfaced in St. Petersburg as *Chopiniana* the previous year, with a quasi-narrative plot based on ideas inspired by the music, five short pieces by Frederic Chopin orchestrated by Alexander Glazunov. Only a month later, students gave a performance in which its plot had been abandoned and its period costumes exchanged for the long white muslin dresses of the early nineteenth century. The musical selections had also changed by the time Diaghilev presented *Les Sylphides* in Paris. The ballet's two-year gestation exemplifies the trend to abstraction followed so often in the twentieth century by George Balanchine and others, in which a narrative ballet, with its period trappings deliberately submerged and altered, became a plotless spectacle of pure dancing.

Balanchine brought the evolution of *Les Sylphides* to a controversial if temporary halt with his production of *Chopiniana* for the New York City Ballet (NYCB) in 1972, staged by Danilova. The idea was to reveal Fokine's choreography by eliminating the "sentimental" long tutus and orchestral music. New York City Ballet presented the work in white tunics, accompanied by a solo piano. Critical reaction was mixed. Arlene Croce called it "an experiment in distillation which failed." In response to the adverse press, Danilova insisted the time had come when costumes were unnecessary. "There was the pure art of Chopin and pure choreography of Fokine."[27]

Directors of *Les Sylphides* are confronted with reestablishing three things: the steps, the group patterns, and the overall style that characterizes the dance. Like most traveling choreographers, Fokine adapted his work to the dancers at hand, and *Les Sylphides*, a repertory staple, probably changed in large and small ways. In his memoirs, Fokine recalled what he called the "glorious" cast of principals at an undated performance after the Paris premiere: Pavlova, Karsavina, and Olga Preobrajenska, partnered by Nijinsky. He described the individual qualities of each dancer, celebrating Pavlova's elevation, Karsavina's "rare romanticism," and Nijinsky's "personification of a poetic vision." Adjusting whatever he'd done before, Fokine made the most of Preobrajenska's "exceptional sense of balance." But Preobrajenska had shortcomings — she was apt to embroider her part in performance. "After dancing the Prelude exactly as I had created it," Fokine wrote, "she repeated it for an encore entirely differently." He insisted on "the inadmissibility of improvisation in my ballets," which were conceived as unified concepts, not as a series of numbers. Yet in the next paragraph, he described appreciatively how each of the women contributed her own ending to her variation.[28]

The style of *Les Sylphides* is hard to codify in a way that can be taught. The audience either wants to be overtaken by a magical effect or not. Balanchine's NYCB made atmospheric productions obsolete over the years, cultivating an audience for his brilliant, pragmatic choreography. But even NYCB, particularly after Balanchine's death, has resorted to the escapist attractions of the nineteenth century. Danilova's revisionist *Chopiniana* hasn't remained in the repertory, but it wasn't meant to capture the romantic period. Stripped down, it was tailored for the literal attitude of the NYCB dancers.

Some in the audience will find any plausible *Les Sylphides* bland and styleless. Films can give us a way to study in detail what escapes us in the theater. In a

1991 performance by the Kirov Ballet, Konstantin Zaklinsky faultlessly does the male solo, with its complicated air turns, but looking at the YouTube version, we can see that his dance seems to have stops in it, perhaps a result of Zaklinsky's rather stiff plié. Mikhail Baryshnikov, with American Ballet Theatre in 1984, looked much smoother, his legato pliés moving him without hesitation across the music. He could, on the other hand, become utterly still in his relevé poses, anchoring the swirling ensemble behind him. Baryshnikov and the rest of the cast (ABT principal dancers Marianna Tcherkassky, Cheryl Yeager, and Cynthia Harvey) used consistently slow gestural changes of the arms to create a floating quality.

Watching the ballet in the theater, we might not isolate these individual qualities at all, and even the dancers may not have made conscious choices to use them. *Les Sylphides* is so emphatically an ensemble ballet that an otherworldly atmosphere can be created by a corps that responds together to the music.

ESCAPIST DREAMS

Le Spectre de la Rose (1911) represents another facet of Fokine's ability to establish diverse worlds on the stage. The original, like all of Fokine's ballets, was a perfectly balanced fusion of design, music, and dancing. A miniature, not a spectacle, this duet between a dreamy young girl and a disembodied spirit (Karsavina and Nijinsky) is set to a musical vignette, Carl-Maria von Weber's *Invitation to the Dance* (1819), and inspired by a poem of Théophile Gautier published in 1838. The poem's narrator speaks to a virginal dreamer in the voice of a ghost, the wilted rose she has worn throughout the evening, saying it doesn't regret its death because it's had the good fortune to be worn on her breast. In the ballet, the girl returns from the ball, removes her cloak, and settles into an armchair, where she falls asleep, remembering the ball and perhaps the young man who presented her with the rose. The Spectre appears in a window and summons her into a waltz. Then he leaps out of the window and vanishes. When all these elements are assembled, the ballet can create a bygone atmosphere of naïve reverie.

Like most metaphors, this simple scenario has been re-created in different ways. It's been done on huge stages with virtually no scenery and performed by dancers who can't act or can't master its classical reinventions. Perhaps the most convincing latter-day performance of the ballet, though admittedly not a true replica, was given on the Metropolitan Opera's one-hundredth-anniversary gala program, on May 13, 1984. The Spectre was ABT guest star Patrick Dupond, and the girl was the ninety-one-year-old movie star Lillian Gish.[29] She dreams in the chair as he leaps and conjures around her, doing most of the original

Spectre's solos. The production omitted all the duet sections, and Gish never left her chair until the end. But if re-creating a classic can actually bring back the idea of the original, this performance evoked the spirit of the Rose in a new way, as an old woman reflects on youthful romance.

Who or what does the Spectre represent? Fokine calls him a spirit, a hope, something intangible, but not in the conventional sense a cavalier.[30] The program note by Philip Ralph, for the Paris Opera Ballet's recording of the piece, suggests a more pragmatic and less naïve encounter.[31] To the girl, the Rose represents a specific lover, and their dance together in her dream is "ecstatic." Historian Grace Robert describes a character of much more innocence, in keeping with the music and Léon Bakst's period setting of the girl's boudoir. She "has come home tired from her first ball. In her hand she carries a souvenir, a red rose."[32] Whether the Spectre is a real suitor whom the girl remembers in a dream or a generalized idea of romance, the essence of the ballet seems to lie in the girl's innocence, in the imaginary person she pictures as her lover: a benign seducer or a nonthreatening androgyne.

Fokine said there were no displays of virtuosity in the ballet, but he did choreograph Nijinsky's many pirouette enchaînements and his dramatic exit through a French window, which came to dominate the ballet. This final leap is usually executed as a conventional grand jeté, although Robert notes that "the leap was done originally as a saut de chat, executed with the forward leg bent," which enhanced the illusion of flight.[33] (We don't know if Robert actually saw Nijinsky do this, or if this was from some latter-day interpretation.) Audiences and critics seized on this final leap as a magical effect, and no choreographer could have made a better climax to this romantic encounter—but Fokine was ambivalent about it. It had been "overplayed," he wrote, as if the acclaim poured on Nijinsky had ruined the dignity of the whole ballet. Perhaps it was a structural mistake on Fokine's part, one prompted by an abrupt change in the music. The audience is never prepared for Weber's tiny coda, in which, after the Spectre has lofted away, the girl awakes from her reverie and wonders about the rose that has slipped from her hand. As Fokine ruefully retells it, "When [Nijinsky's] dance ended, everyone automatically raised hands, ready to applaud."[34]

Many performances of Spectre have been posted on YouTube. To my knowledge they haven't been compared in great detail, but they differ in large and small respects, ranging from technical adaptations to individual interpretations of the characters. Credits are hard to come by, unless a particular YouTube entry has been posted from a commercial DVD. Two versions can be seen from the Paris Opera Ballet, with different casts; in one, the girl uses various mime gestures to help the audience understand that she knows she's been dreaming. In one uncredited version, purportedly Faroukh Ruzimatov and Altynai Asylmuratova, she "acts" a girl in love with exaggerated facial expressions, and he does less complicated enchaînements than other Spectres. He throws a kiss to the air before leaving, merely skimming her brow rather than kissing her. The depth of the girl's dream can differ greatly. In one Kirov cast, the Spectre (probably Igor Kolb) behaves like the danseur noble in a conventional pas de deux; the girl acts half awake, half intoxicated.

One of the most convincing interpretations of the Spectre was given in 1976 by Mikhail Baryshnikov with ABT.[35] Baryshnikov learned the ballet from André Eglevsky, who got it directly from Fokine in private sessions. In his book about his repertory, Baryshnikov says he "tried to deepen the ballet's dramatic implications . . . the spiritual and erotic notions of 'roseness.'" He finds this combination of the spiritual and the sexual inherent in the steps and style of Fokine, which Baryshnikov sees as "a kind of broken, soft harmony."[36] Marianna Tcherkassky, his partner in the 1976 Wolf Trap performance, falls asleep at the beginning with a small smile on her face. The Spectre appears and gestures her out of her chair without touching her. They dance together, Tcherkassky still smiling and still dreaming. The Spectre holds her upper arm, caressingly, as they dance in tandem. When the first theme of the music returns, she opens her eyes; they dance together again, but Tcherkassky still seems to be asleep. She looks at him but perhaps doesn't see so much as feel his light touch. In his airborne variations, Baryshnikov seems to be holding back on his prodigious technique, keeping a calm, protective focus on the girl he is chastely seducing.

In a Kirov Ballet performance recording, the relationship between Igor Kolb and Zhanna Ayupova is less an erotic encounter than that of a teacher and pupil, or a danseur noble and a ballerina.[37] Standing behind her in their first duet, he supports her by holding her wrists, lightly but securely; he steps back in a wide fourth position to give her space. Kolb makes a lot of the Spectre's curling arm gestures. At a climactic moment in the music after their second duet, she suddenly "sees" him, and they face each other more directly than before. After a brief skipping circle together around her chair, she subsides into it; he's on the floor at her feet. Through all this, they both seem to be conscious of an audience, even when they're wrapped up in the vision of each other.

Le Spectre de la Rose has probably been in the repertory of the Paris Opera Ballet continuously since the death of Diaghilev in 1929, but one can't know what small interpolations were made by Serge Lifar during his tenure as artistic director and ballet master of the company (1930–1944). In the first and most satisfying of the Paris Opera recordings, both Claude de Vulpian and Manuel Legris seem nearly natural, not self-consciously giving a performance.[38] De Vulpian takes most of the overture to establish the girl's dreamy, sensitive character. She gazes out the window where the Spectre is to appear, as if she catches his perfume before he's entered the room. (In most other versions, the lights don't come up on stage until after the overture.) When he does appear, she's asleep in the chair. After his first brief series of leaps and turns, he stands behind her as if conjuring her to rise and dance. When they do dance together, he doesn't grasp her arms at all, but simply extends his own, so she can rest her arms on them. They both move slowly, as if breathing to the pulse of the music's rhythm. At a moment when the music changes to a new theme, she "sees" him, but in the solo sequence that follows, although she's addressing where he's standing, she doesn't look directly at him. This may be an illusion of the camera work, but the effect is that she doesn't actually see him in the room with her; that is, she doesn't ever fully awaken from her dream. He remains a specter.

THE SEARCH FOR AUTHENTICITY

Are all these varied interpretations to be considered *Le Spectre de la Rose*? As far as the audience is concerned, they are. The recorded Kirov performance carries the copyright of the Fokine Estate Archive, as all Fokine performances presumably now do, whether or not they have been approved by Isabelle Fokine in person. How can the many versions be so different? In an extraordinary 1997 British-made TV special, *Fighting Over Fokine*, Isabelle Fokine coaches dancers in three early Fokine works, *The Dying Swan*, *Spectre de la Rose*, and *Prince Igor*, with interpolated comments from critics and former dancers.[39] She is very specific about the steps, timing, and dramatic interpretation of each action, and very confident that she holds the template for reproducing the authentic ballets. She informs an (invisible) interviewer that she has consulted all possible sources for information, chiefly her father, Vitale Fokine, who worked with his father on restaging the choreographer's works in the post-Diaghilev years. But, says ballerina Irina Baronova tartly, "Michel Fokine died on the 27th of August 1942. [Isabelle Fokine] wasn't even born then, was she?" Baronova says she learned the ballet from Karsavina and intends to pass it on to later dancers. In other words, how can there be a more credible source than word of mouth?[40]

Critics and dancers in this film represent very different views of how these ballets should be preserved. Debra Craine, dance critic of the London *Times*, was interviewed after seeing two entirely different interpretations of *The Dying Swan* in London. One of them seemed very correct and classical; the other, taught by

Isabelle Fokine, was highly dramatic throughout. Craine thinks the dramatic version of *The Dying Swan* that she saw seemed more true to Fokine. In *Fighting Over Fokine*, as Ms. Fokine rehearses Faroukh Ruzimatov and Anastasia Volochkova in *Spectre*, she assigns a specific motivation and timing to virtually every phrase. Judith Mackrell of the *Guardian* holds that striking original performances can't be re-created, but that if contemporary dancers can be taught the original steps, and if they understand the ballet's historical provenance, some flavor of the original can be captured. The senior critic Clement Crisp of the *Financial Times* feels there's little point in trying to recover works of this vintage, especially those choreographed for the special qualities of the original dancers; we should just be satisfied with the memory of the dancers on whom the roles were created.

The ballet world takes little notice of the fact that Diaghilev produced operas even at the height of his company's ballet repertory. After his successful first Paris season of operas (1908), Diaghilev decided on a bill combining opera and ballet for 1909. The ballets were so successful that the focus of the enterprise switched to ballet, but when the Ballets Russes made commitments to appear in operas, as it did during its post–World War I engagements in Monte Carlo, ready-made ballets could be transported back into the operas from which they came or could be newly created to fulfill operatic commitments. *Prince Igor* constituted the second act of Alexander Borodin's opera, with the great Russian baritone Feodor Chaliapin singing the role of the Khan in 1909 and featuring Fokine's choreography in the opera's Polovtsian Dances. The *Dances* were then extracted and performed as a separate short ballet, partly in the interest of economy.

Fokine called *Prince Igor* one of his most important works. He may have undertaken some ethnographic research into tribal dances, but, as he confessed: "I came to the rehearsals with Borodin's music under my arm. This comprised my total armament."[41] His creative focus was on featuring the ensemble as an expressive unit, and the audience's response to the frenzied conclusion testifies to his success. *Prince Igor* as a stand-alone ballet remained a staple of the Ballets Russes repertory for many years, along with *Schéhérazade* and *Les Sylphides*. After 1929 it was carried forward into the Ballets Russes's successor companies by former Diaghilev dancers and made its way to many other companies worldwide through Fokine's extensive travels. A 2002 Kirov performance has been recorded, along with *Schéhérazade*, *Spectre*, and *Firebird*.[42]

In *Fighting Over Fokine* Isabelle Fokine coaches the corps de ballet of the Kirov at the London Coliseum prior to performances in 1997 of *Polovtsian Dances*. Unlike Ruzimatov, Volochkova, and Yulia Makhalina, with whom Ms. Fokine works on *Spectre de la Rose* and *The Dying Swan*, the women of the Kirov corps are resistant. Rumbles of discontent are heard as Fokine begins her cleanup of what has been performed for years by the company. "Must we do it like she says?" one dancer asks. After a contentious rehearsal, in which Isabelle Fokine fails to connect with the Kirov corps, let alone convince them to change their notion of the dances to reflect her instructions, the company announces in a note at the end of the film that due to lack of rehearsal time it was permitted to dance *Prince Igor* its own way. On the Kirov recording released in 2002, Isabelle Fokine is not credited with any role in the production. But the Fokine Estate Archive lends its copyright, dated 1919 — although the ballet was first created in 1909.

This Kirov performance oddly resembles scenes from other Fokine ballets of the early Diaghilev period, chiefly the monsters in *Firebird* and the orgy in *Schéhérazade*. Fokine had hit upon a formula for building a great emotional climax by combining unison groups of characters, dressed in different ethnic costumes and dancing characteristic rhythms. In the *Polovtsian Dances*, each group has a soloist in its midst, to allow for a more virtuosic representation of the musical theme while the group executes simpler steps. The Kirov performance incorporates Borodin's vocal chorus, with the singers standing solemnly around the dancing area. The dancers, relieved of Isabelle Fokine's insistent corrections, look energetic but emotionally passive except for their leaders' manufactured smiles.

CONCLUSION

This consideration of early Fokine ballets only hints at the many questions surrounding the innovative achievement at the heart of the Ballets Russes's reputation. Ballets in recall may boil down to a connoisseur's preference for specific performances and performed moments, but the audience doesn't care about or even recognize the fine points of choreography and performance. Ballets survive in the general audience's memory as a total image — a look, a style, an overall impression — and sometimes as a climactic feat that has been mythologized by writers, like Nijinsky's supposed phenomenal leap at the end of *Spectre de la Rose*. This overall memory is often very unspecific, but very definite. Either a revival matches it or it does not. This is why revivals of doubtful accuracy can succeed, why misguided details of a revival can be overlooked if the style or the mood is right.

We haven't developed sophisticated means of analyzing or writing about ballets or implemented scholars' opportunities to study live productions in any depth. We judge revivals intuitively, rather than comparing them structurally.

Videographer John Drummond writes this about *Les Sylphides*: "Although the many versions I have seen have all contained fundamentally the same movements, the different nuances can tremendously affect its capacity to involve and move an audience, preventing it from becoming a slightly faded museum piece."[43]

Over the last several decades, opinion among scholarly researchers has held that no performance can be repeated. Following from this is the idea that there's no such thing as repertory, or indeed a canon of masterpieces. Maybe we aren't even allowed a pantheon of great artists who have produced great works. In ballet, the nineteenth-century classics draw big audiences and are hence well enough known by the audience to be retrofitted and deconstructed for popular new productions without being endangered. Yet the Diaghilev repertory, and also much of the other new ballet of the twentieth century, is invisible. Since the death of Robert Joffrey, no formidable impresario has appeared in America to honor that body of work and keep it before the public in respectable form.

While I believe performing artwork has to change and theater works have to be refreshed in performance, I also feel a great respect for the achievements of artists in the past. We have to have something before us to honor the creative work of artists, and in dance this means the live performances that try to retrieve the unremarked details of choreography, the craft, the inspiration, and the spirit of soloists and ensemble that made these works original.

Epilogue: The Unanswered Questions

WHAT IS A REVIVAL?

- What did the ballets actually look like? Only by experiencing what occurred in a theater can we determine the nature of the innovation for which a ballet is known.
- Should today's revivals of these ballets strive to approximate the originals? What concessions can be made to contemporary factors: the need to attract audiences; economic necessity; or the bodies, skills, and sensibilities of contemporary dancers?

ESTABLISHING THE BASELINE

- How has the ballet's reputation been established? Today, choreography can be decently documented on film or video. A century ago, this method was not developed enough to represent a ballet adequately. The identity of any Fokine ballet is compounded of studio photographs; costumes, sets, and designs that have been fortuitously preserved; and scores, notes, and other written documents. Also present are nostalgic memories plus insider and outsider contemporary critical accounts.

All of this material needs to be carefully verified and evaluated, especially when it represents conflicting or ill-defined information.

- Both Ida Rubinstein and Tamara Karsavina danced successive, "original" versions of the pas de deux in *Schéhérazade*. Karsavina's version is the basis for most productions of the ballet today. Rubinstein was a movement-theater artist and not a ballet dancer, so her performance was not considered definitive by the ballet community.
- How important is it to the ballet's survival to sort out relatively minor discrepancies, such as the dispute between Isabelle Fokine and the Kirov Ballet corps about whether a particular hopping sequence occurs on the right or the left foot?
- Many dancers claim they are performing roles exactly as taught to them by the creators or direct inheritors of those roles. Yet there remains an unavoidable gulf between this type of source information and the personalities, language, and talents that separate two such performances.
- Ballets are often talked and written about in metaphorical terms. Often they *are* metaphors, and the audience, unfamiliar with the ballet, is prompted to see the metaphor as identified in the literature or the program notes. A case in point: Florence Clerc, who staged the 2010 Boston Ballet revival of *Les Sylphides*, researched the ballet primarily by looking at photographs of Nijinsky, Pavlova, and Karsavina and a pre-1950 film of the ballet performed by the Mariinsky Ballet. She thinks of the ballet as a dream, an immaterial substance without flesh. It's unclear how she conveyed this idea to the dancers, but the revival was a big success.[44]
- Exactly what documentation exists of the original performances, and how close is it to the choreographer's evolved intention and the intentions of the team of cocreators? What changes did Fokine and others make to the ballets after their initial performances, and for what reasons? If these changes can be identified, how important are they to the permanent entity that is the ballet?
- How should these documentations be interpreted? As blueprints for revivals? Or as templates for reconstructions? Presently, there are few formal ways of training people to read, interpret, analyze, and teach

ballets from the diverse source materials that comprise the "scores" for these "lost" dances. Every documentary source, including word of mouth, contains interpretive interventions. Any film incorporates choices of camera angles and distance from the performance, lighting and placement of the dancers within the recording space, and how or whether the film is edited. These and many other options are up to the filmmakers, sometimes without consulting the choreographer. Colors fade; fabrics rot; and designs often are extremely fanciful and have to be adapted to the realistic demands of performing, but the designs may survive while the costumes and sets don't. A dance score, even one written in a codified system such as Stepanov, Laban, or Benesh notation, requires the notator to make choices about what to include or omit.

- Was it Fokine's practice to leave a régisseur in charge of his ballets when he left town? What instructions were these deputies given about the essential elements to be taught? Have these instructions survived?
- How much interpretive leeway can be given to performers before the work is distorted? How much interpretive necessity can be invoked before the ballet becomes frozen?

Revivals are often evaluated by insiders and originators of the roles and by their disciples. These judgments are questionable for a variety of reasons: porous memory, personal rivalries, nostalgic enhancement, even political ambition. But they're given extra weight because they come from the horse's mouth.

HISTORIOGRAPHY, OR RECORDING THE EVENT

The training that professional critics receive seldom addresses the question of how to balance personal reflection against the creation of a historical record and how to write so as to incorporate and acknowledge both these perspectives.

- How does a writer read the subtexts of history and memoirs, and how does she or he counteract or put into perspective the personal allegiances and rivalries of those who have contributed to the record? What did they all have at stake?
- How do researchers take account of the political and aesthetic pressures of those times and of our time?
- What is the context of the original choreography? In Fokine's case, for example, not enough has been written about the influence of Isadora

Duncan on his work (he denied any), or of Stanislavsky, Meyerhold, Goleizowsky, war, revolution, exile, and modernism in the arts.

- How much information should the company producing a revival/ reconstruction provide to the audience about when and how the production came about?

DRAMATIS PERSONAE

In order of appearance

Choreographer **Michel Fokine** was born Mikhail Mikhailovich Fokin on May 5, 1880, in St. Petersburg, Russia, and died on August 22, 1942, in New York. He was the primary choreographer for Diaghilev's Ballets Russes from 1909 to 1914.

Le Pavillon d'Armide, restaged by Michel Fokine, was performed by Diaghilev's Ballets Russes and starred Vera Karalli, Mikhail Mordkin, and Vaslav Nijinsky. It premiered at the Théâtre du Châtelet, Paris, on May 19, 1909.

Anna Pavlova was born Anna Matveyevna on February 12, 1881, in St. Petersburg, Russia, and died on January 23, 1931, in The Hague.

Vera Karalli was born Vera Alexeyevna Karalli on July 27, 1889, in Moscow, and died on November 16, 1972, in Baden, Austria.

Tamara Karsavina was born Tamara Platonovna Karsavina on March 9, 1885, in St. Petersburg, Russia, and died on May 26, 1978, in Beaconsfield, England.

Author **Cyril William Beaumont** was born on November 1, 1891, and died on May 24, 1976, in London.

Ballets Russes régisseur **Sergei Leonidovich Grigoriev** was born on October 5, 1883, in Tikhvin, Russia, and died on June 28, 1968, in London.

Boris Kochno, librettist and author, was born on January 3, 1904, in Moscow, and died on December 8, 1991, in Paris.

Dancer and choreographer **Vaslav Nijinsky** was born Vatslav Fomich Nizhinskii on March 12, 1889, in Kiev, Ukraine, and died on April 8, 1950, in London.

Le Festin, choreographed by Michel Fokine et al., was first performed by Diaghilev's Ballets Russes at the Théâtre du Châtelet, Paris, on May 19, 1909.

Dancer and choreographer **Bronislava Nijinska** was born Bronislava Fominichna Nizhinskaya on January 8, 1891, in Minsk, and died on February 21, 1972, in Palisades, California.

Ballets Russes choreographer **Léonide Massine** was born Leonid Fedorovich Myasin on August 8, 1895, in Moscow, and died on March 15, 1979, in Weseke bei Borken, Germany.

Lincoln Edward Kirstein, cofounder of the New York City Ballet, was born on May 4, 1907, in Rochester, New York, and died on January 5, 1996, in New York.

Danish choreographer and ballet master of the Royal Danish Ballet **August Bournonville** was born on August 21, 1805, and died on November 30, 1879, in Copenhagen.

Choreographer, ballet master, and dancer with the Imperial Russian Ballet **Marius Ivanovich Petipa** was born on March 11, 1818, in Marseille, France, and died on July 14, 1910, in Gurzuf, Ukraine.

Jules Joseph Perrot, ballet master at the Imperial Russian Ballet, was born on August 18, 1810, in Lyon, and died on August 18, 1892, in Paramé, France.

Giovanni Coralli Peracini, ballet master at the Paris Opera, was born on January 15, 1779, and died on May 1, 1854, in Paris.

Les Sylphides, choreographed by Michel Fokine, was first performed by Diaghilev's Ballets Russes, starring Anna Pavlova, Tamara Karsavina, Alexandra Baldina, and Vaslav Nijinsky, at the Théâtre du Châtelet, Paris, on June 2, 1909. The original scheme of *Les Sylphides*, as well as its evolution beyond the 1909 Paris premiere, is recounted in Beaumont, *Complete Book of Ballets*, 565–67.

Carnaval, choreographed by Michel Fokine, was first performed by Diaghilev's Ballets Russes, starring Vaslav Nijinsky, Tamara Karsavina, and Michel Fokine, at Pavlov Hall, St. Petersburg, on February 20, 1910.

Prince Igor, choreographed by Michel Fokine, was first performed by Diaghilev's Ballets Russes, starring Adolph Bolm, Sophia Fedorova, and Elena Smirnova, at the Théâtre du Châtelet, Paris, on May 19, 1909.

The Firebird (*L'oiseau de feu*), choreographed by Michel Fokine, was first performed by Diaghilev's Ballets Russes, starring Tamara Karsavina, Michel Fokine, Alexis Bulgakov, and Vera Fokina, at the Théâtre National de l'Opéra, Paris, on June 25, 1910.

Schéhérazade, choreographed by Michel Fokine, was first performed by Diaghilev's Ballets Russes, starring Ida Rubinstein, Vaslav Nijinsky, and Alexis Bulgakov, at the Théâtre National de l'Opéra, Paris, on June 4, 1910.

Petrouchka, choreographed by Michel Fokine, was first performed by Diaghilev's Ballets Russes, starring Vaslav Nijinsky, Tamara Karsavina,

Alexander Orlov, and Enrico Cecchetti, at the Théâtre du Châtelet, Paris, on June 13, 1911.

Painter and scene and costume designer **Léon Bakst** was born Lev Samoilovich Rosenberg on May 19, 1866, in Grodno, Belarus, and died on December 27, 1924, in Paris.

Artist, art critic, and historian **Alexandre Benois** was born Aleksandr Nikolaevich Benua on May 3, 1870, in St. Petersburg, and died on February 9, 1960, in Paris.

Performer **Ida Rubinstein** was born Lydiya Lvovna Rubinshtein on October 18, 1885, and died on September 20, 1960, in Vence, France.

Dancer **Alexandra Danilova** was born Alksandra Dionisievna Danilova on November 20, 1903, in Peterhof, Russia, and died on July 13, 1997, in New York.

Dancer **Adolph Bolm** was born on September 25, 1884, in St. Petersburg, and died on April 16, 1951, in Hollywood, California.

Swan Lake, originally choreographed by Julius Reisinger, was performed by the Bolshoi Ballet and starred Pelageza Karpakova and A. K. Gillert, at the Bolshoi Theatre, Moscow, on March 4, 1877. Most subsequent productions are based on the 1895 revival by Marius Petipa and Lev Ivanov, first staged for the Imperial Ballet on January 15, 1895, at the Mariinsky Theatre, St. Petersburg.

Margot Fonteyn, principal dancer with England's Royal Ballet, was born Margaret ("Peggy") Evelyn Hookham on May 18, 1919, in Reingate, England, and died on February 21, 1991, in Panama City, Panama.

Dancer **Liubov Tchernichova** was born Lyubov Pavlovna Chernitseva on September 17, 1890, in St. Petersburg, and died on March 1, 1976, in Richmond, England.

Dancer **Michael Somes** was born on September 28, 1917, in Horsley, England, and died on November 18, 1994, in London.

Dancer **Leanne Benjamin** was born on July 13, 1964, in Rockhampton, Australia.

Dancer **Jonathan Cope** was born in 1963 in Crediton, England.

American dancer and choreographer **Angela Isadora Duncan** was born on May 26, 1877, in San Francisco, and died on September 14, 1927, in Nice, France.

André Yacovlev Levinson was born on November 1, 1887, in St. Petersburg, and died on December 3, 1933, in Paris.

Choreographer **Alexei Ratmansky** was born on August 27, 1968, in Leningrad.

Former Royal Ballet dancer **Monica Mason** was born on September 6, 1941, in Johannesburg. *The Firebird*, revived by The Royal Ballet, starred Mason and was performed at the Royal Opera House, Covent Garden, London, on April 6, 1978.

Composer **Igor Stravinsky** was born Igor Fyodorovich Stravinskii on June 17, 1882, in Oranienbaum, Russia, and died on April 6, 1971, in New York.

Le Dieu Bleu starred Vaslav Nijinsky, Tamara Karsavina, et al. and premiered on May 13, 1912; *Le Spectre de la Rose* starred Vaslav Nijinsky and Tamara Karsavina and premiered on April 26, 1911; *Cléopâtre* starred Ida Rubinstein, Anna Pavlova, Tamara Karsavina, Vaslav Nijinsky, Michel Fokine, and Alexis Bulgakov and premiered on June 3, 1909. All were choreographed by Michel Fokine and performed by the Ballets Russes at the Théâtre du Châtelet, Paris.

Composer **Nikolai Andreyevich Rimsky-Korsakov** was born on March 18, 1844, in Tikhvin, Russia, and died on June 21, 1908, in Luga, Russia.

Dancer and choreographer **Ruth St. Denis** was born on January 20, 1879, in Somerville, New Jersey, and died on July 21, 1968, in Los Angeles.

Dancer **Svetlana Zakharova** was born on June 10, 1979, in Lutsk, Ukraine.

Dancer **Farukh Sadullaevich Ruzimatov** was born on June 26, 1963, in Tashkent, Uzbekistan.

Critic **Henry Taylor Parker** was born on April 29, 1867, and died on March 30, 1934, in Boston.

Polish composer **Fryderyk Franciszek Chopin** was born on March 1, 1810, in Żelazowa Wola, Poland, and died on October 17, 1849, in Paris.

Russian composer **Aleksandr Konstantinovich Glazunov** was born on August 10, 1865, in St. Petersburg, and died on March 21, 1936, in Paris.

Dancer **Olga Preobrajenska** was born on February 2, 1871, in St. Petersburg, and died on December 27, 1962, in Paris.

Dancer **Konstantin Zaklinsky** was born on May 28, 1955, in Leningrad.

Dancer, choreographer, and actor **Mikhail Nikolaevich Baryshnikov** was born on January 27, 1948, in Riga, Latvia.

Former American Ballet Theatre principal dancer **Marianna Alexsavena Tcherkassky** was born on October 28, 1952, in Glen Cove, New York.

Former American Ballet Theatre principal dancer **Cynthia Harvey** was born on May 17, 1957, in San Rafael, California.

Composer **Carl Friedrich Ernst von Weber** was born on November 18/19, 1786, in Eutin, Germany, and died on June 5, 1826, in London.

Pierre-Jules-Théophile Gautier, coauthor of the libretto for the ballet *Giselle* (1841), was born on August 31, 1811, in Tarbes, France, and died on October 23, 1872, in Paris.

Dancer **Patrick Dupond** was born on March 14, 1959, in Paris.

Best known for silent film roles, movie actress **Lillian Gish** was born on October 14, 1893, in Springfield, Ohio, and died on February 27, 1993, in New York.

Dancer **Altynai Asylmuratova** was born on January 1, 1961, in Alma-Ata, Kazakhstan.

Dancer **Igor Kolb** was born on June 6, 1977, in Pinsk, Belarus.

Dancer **André Eglevsky** was born on December 21, 1917, in Moscow, and died on December 4, 1977, in Elmira, New York.

Dancer **Zhanna Ayupova** was born on October 12, 1966, in Petrozavodsk, Russia.

Dancer and choreographer **Serge Lifar** was born Sergei Mikhailovich Serdkin on April 2, 1905, in Kiev, Ukraine, and died on December 15, 1986, in Lausanne, Switzerland.

Dancer **Claude de Vulpian** was born on December 29, 1952, in Paris.

Dancer **Manuel Legris** was born on October 19, 1964, in Paris.

The Dying Swan, choreographed by Michel Fokine, was first performed by Anna Pavlova at the Mariinsky Theatre, St. Petersburg, on December 22, 1907.

Dancer **Irina Mikhailovna Baronova** was born on March 13, 1919, in Petrograd, Russia, and died on June 28, 2008, in Byron Bay, Australia.

Dancer **Anastasia Volochkova** was born on January 20, 1976, in Leningrad, Russia.

Singer **Feodor Ivanovich Chaliapin** was born on February 13, 1873, in Kazan, Russia, and died on April 12, 1938 in Paris.

Dancer **Yulia Makhalina** was born on June 23, 1968, in Leningrad.

Robert Joffrey, the cofounder of the Joffrey Ballet, was born Abdullah Jaffa Bey Khan on December 24, 1930, in Seattle, and died on March 25, 1988, in New York.

DIAGHILEV'S BALLETS RUSSES AND ITS OFFSHOOTS

Director(s)	Company Name	Years & Location	Major Choreographers
Diaghilev	Les Ballets Russes de Serge Diaghilev (aka Diaghilev's Ballets Russes)	1909–1929. Founded in St. Petersburg by Serge Diaghilev. Touring company outside Russia; based in Monte Carlo, 1922–1929. Company disbanded on Diaghilev's death.	Michel Fokine; Vaslav Nijinsky; Bronislava Nijinska; Léonide Massine; George Balanchine
De Basil & Blum	Les Ballets Russes de Monte Carlo (aka The Monte Carlo Ballet Russe)	1932–1935. Founded by Col. Wassily de Basil, René Blum, and Serge Denham. Based at Casino Theatre in Monte Carlo (Théâtre de Monte Carlo). De Basil and Blum/Massine split. Joint venture ceased officially in 1935.	Léonide Massine; Balanchine; Fokine; Nijinska
Blum & Massine, Denham	Ballet Russes de Monte Carlo	1938–1962. Founded by René Blum, Serge Denham, and Léonide Massine in Monte Carlo. US touring company based in New York after 1939. Blum died at Auschwitz in 1942; Massine and Denham led company until 1962.	Massine (1938–1942); Balanchine (1944–1946)
De Basil	Les Ballets Russes de Colonel W. de Basil	1934–1937. Founded by Col. Wassily de Basil.	Fokine; David Lichine
	The Covent Garden Russian Ballet	1938–1939. Founded by de Basil. Presented by Educational Ballets Ltd., directed by Victor Dandré.	
	Original Ballet Russe	1939–1948. Reestablished by de Basil. Touring company in Europe, the Americas, and Australia. Last performance, Palma de Mallorca, November 6, 1948; revived briefly after de Basil's death, 1951–1952.	

NOTES

1. *Répétition generale* designates a dress rehearsal open to the public, usually on the night before the official premiere.

2. Cyril Beaumont, *Michel Fokine and His Ballets* (New York: Dance Horizons, 1981), 44.

3. See "Diaghilev's Ballets Russes and Its Offshoots" for more on the lineage of the Ballets Russes.

4. Lincoln Kirstein, "Sour Gripes: A Gracious Postscript," in *Ballet: Bias & Belief*, ed. Nancy Reynolds (New York: Dance Horizons, 1983), x.

5. Cyril Beaumont, *The Complete Book of Ballets: A Guide to the Principal Ballets of the Nineteenth and Twentieth Centuries* (New York: G. P. Putnam's Sons, 1938), 574–75; and Michel Fokine, *Memoirs of a Ballet Master*, trans. Vitale Fokine (Boston: Little, Brown, 1961), 134, 137, 157, 169, 174.

6. Alexandra Danilova with Holly Brubach, *Choura: The Memoirs of Alexandra Danilova* (New York: Fromm International Publishing Company, 1988), 124.

7. For more on the Fokine Estate Archive, go to michelfokine.com.

8. *The Royal Ballet*, dir. Paul Czinner (Hollywood, CA: Bel Canto/Paramount Home Video, 1959). Videorecording.

9. Fokine, *Memoirs of a Ballet Master*, 168.

10. Fonteyn quotations are from Meredith Daneman, *Margo Fonteyn: A Life* (New York: Penguin Books, 2004), 304–7.

11. *The Firebird & Les Noces*, performed by The Royal Ballet (Heathfield, East Sussex, UK: BBC/Opus Arte, 2001). DVD.

12. Joan Acocella and Lynn Garafola, eds., *André Levinson on Dance: Writings from Paris in the Twenties* (Middletown, CT: Wesleyan University Press, 1991), 64.

13. Monica Mason/Firebird material is from Daneman, *Margo Fonteyn*, 305.

14. Sally Banes, *Dancing Women: Female Bodies on Stage* (London: Routledge, 1998), 99–100.

15. Richard Taruskin, *Music in the Early Twentieth Century: The Oxford History of Western Music* (Oxford: Oxford University Press, 2009), 151.

16. S. L. Grigoriev, *The Diaghilev Ballet: 1909–1929* (London: Dance Books Ltd., 2009), 33.

17. *The Kirov Celebrates Nijinsky*, performed by Kirov Ballet (West Long Branch, NJ: Kultur, 2002). DVD.

18. Olive Holmes, ed., *Motion Arrested: Dance Reviews of H.T. Parker* (Middletown, CT: Wesleyan University Press, 1982), 101.

19. Beaumont, *Michel Fokine and His Ballets*, 61.

20. Grigoriev, *The Diaghilev Ballet*, 36. For another account from New York in 1916, see H. T. Parker, "The Unclouded Russians," in *Motion Arrested: Dance Reviews of H.T. Parker*, ed. Olive Holmes (Middletown, CT: Wesleyan University Press, 1982), 94–103.

21. Fokine, *Memoirs of a Ballet Master*, 155–56; Robert Lawrence, *The Victor Book of Ballets and Ballet Music* (New York: Simon and Schuster, 1950), 398.

22. Fokine had left the company at this point, and Adolph Bolm acted as ballet master in keeping Fokine's popular works in the Ballets Russes repertory. American audiences had heard of them and seen the imitations produced by Gertrude Hoffmann (b. Catherine Gertrude Hayes, May 7, 1885, in San Francisco; d. October 26, 1966, in Los Angeles) and her company in their tours of the States.

23. Holmes, *Motion Arrested*, 100.

24. André Levinson, *Ballet Old and New* (New York: Dance Horizons, 1982), 41.

25. Danilova, *Choura*, 126.

26. Comment on *Les Sylphides*, Ballet Alert! Ballet Discussion Forums, April 4, 2002, balletalert .invisionzone.com/index.php?/topic/4498-les-sylphides/.

27. Arlene Croce, *Afterimages* (New York: Knopf, 1977), 265; Danilova quotation from George Balanchine and Francis Mason, *Balanchine's Festival of Ballet* (London: W. H. Allen, 1978), 612–16.

28. Fokine, *Memoirs of a Ballet Master*, 130–31.

29. Metropolitan Opera, "*Le Spectre de la Rose*—Patrick Dupond and Lillian Gish!" (YouTube, January 29, 2010, youtube.com/watch?v=BstrKHbR2e4).

30. Fokine, *Memoirs of a Ballet Master*, 182.

31. Philip Ralph, "Program Notes," in Paris Opera Ballet, *Paris Dances Diaghilev* (Electra Nonesuch, 1992). Videorecording.

32. Grace Robert, *The Borzoi Book of Ballets* (New York: Alfred A. Knopf, 1946), 301.

33. Ibid., 304.

34. Fokine, *Memoirs of a Ballet Master*, 182, 181.

35. *Baryshnikov: Live at Wolf Trap*, directed by Stan Lathan (Kultur, 1976). DVD.

36. Mikhail Baryshnikov, *Baryshnikov at Work: Mikhail Baryshnikov Discusses His Roles* (New York: Alfred A. Knopf, 1976), 141–43.

37. *The Kirov Celebrates Nijinsky*.

38. *Paris Dances Diaghilev*, performed by Paris Opera Ballet (New York: Elektra Entertainment, 1992). Videorecording.

39. *Fighting Over Fokine*, directed by Gerald Fox (Ovation/NVC Arts, 1997). DVD.

40. The Fokine Estate Archive holds Fokine's own films, notes, and choreographic scores, but it does not make this inventory public or allow individual researchers to study what it contains. For all her specificity, Baronova's memory erred on this date. According to reference sources, Fokine died on August 22, 1942. Isabelle Fokine was born in 1958.

41. Fokine, *Memoirs of a Ballet Master*, 148, 150.

42. *The Kirov Celebrates Nijinsky*.

43. John Drummond, *Speaking of Diaghilev* (London: Faber & Faber, 1997), 319.

44. Florence Clerc, interview with author after Boston Ballet rehearsal, February 1, 2012.

JENNIFER MONSON

ARCHIVING INDETERMINATE SYSTEMS
OF ECOSYSTEMS AND IMPROVISATIONAL
DANCE STRATEGIES

In my project *Live Dancing Archive* I propose that my dancing body itself is an archive, not only of past movement experiences but—primarily—of the ongoing and ephemeral relationships of specific ecosystems. By dancing in various kinds of landscapes, my body accumulates an experience of the dynamics and interdependencies of environmental systems, an experience that becomes a kind of data or knowledge (rather than expression). In the creation of the project I activate the perceptual research practices I have developed over two decades of work, primarily dancing outside, to further document the ways that places, experiences, ecological systems, and states live in the dancing body.

In 2000 I began work on a series of environmental dance projects, including the multiyear BIRD BRAIN Project, which followed the migrations of gray whales, ospreys, ducks, and geese (2000–2006), and the *iMAP/Ridgewood Reservoir Project* (2007), a yearlong project on the border of Brooklyn and Queens that tracked seasonal changes, a project that also served as a catalyst for community organizing to save the reservoir's natural habitat. The *Mahomet Aquifer Project* (2009) offered performances in farmers' markets in Champaign County, Illinois, and utilized an Airstream trailer, which served as a mobile gallery for a video of three-dimensional images of the aquifer and other educational materials. SIP *(Sustained Immersive Process)/Watershed* (2010), a collaborative interdisciplinary project with a composer, architect, and dancer, investigated New York City's watershed. We presented twenty-eight performances to a limited number of audience members along NYC's waterfront. As a result of these projects I felt my dancing had absorbed a vast body of information that held a way of communicating the complex and ephemeral nature of landscape.

I was looking for inherently improvisational archival methods that can adapt to present conditions and, in this case, respond to a sense of location and immediacy. I was interested in using several different approaches to cataloging the documentation, based in my improvisational dance practices, as a way of responding to the challenges of archiving the complex elements of these durational dance projects: their multiple formats, the ephemeral forms of improvisational dance, and the dynamic flux of ecosystems. As a result, *Live Dancing*

Archive consists of three interrelated components: an evening-length solo performance, a three-hour video loop, and a digital archive.

The performance, choreographed out of set and improvised material derived from the BIRD BRAIN *Osprey Migration* (Fall 2002), references impermanence, adaptability, and indeterminacy in ways that are specific to dance and not accessible in other modes of archiving. It holds the lived experience of the dancing body as archive of spaces, relationships, and experiences of the migrations and other environmental phenomena. The video functions as an immersive, durational, and contemplative experience to convey and draw out the context and relationship of the various components of the BIRD BRAIN *Osprey Migration* project. These included the research and the public engagement activities, such as workshops, panels, and performances, as well as other ambient and community experiences we had camping along the route and interacting with the public. The digital archive provides a platform on which the various modes can interact and be experienced by the viewer in relation to each other. For example, once the user has selected a video clip, she or he can find related journal entries, photos, publicity documents, and so forth to provide context for each of the archived objects.

The digital archive is designed to be browsed in an improvisational manner that might juxtapose different categories of objects or events based on random searches or the viewer's line of interest. In *Live Dancing Archive* the digital archive also provides context for the other two components of the project: the live performance and video installation. Ideally, the digital archive will allow the data to be repurposed and imagined for other users, for example, ecological historians or environmental educators. I hope that in compiling this material in a variety of formats it will serve artists, educators, ecologists, environmental scientists, and others as a model for the intersections of art (specifically dance) with environmental research.

Throughout the creative development of *Live Dancing Archive*, the perceptual and sensory practices and choreographic processes I had developed over the previous decade functioned as a way of regathering, organizing, and producing knowledge about the transmission of meaning and knowing between what is human and adjacent to human. Accumulating the environmental knowledge through dance occurred through the repetition of specific choreographic practices that had developed alongside scientific research of the various phenomena each project investigated. For instance, in the BIRD BRAIN *Gray Whale Migration* (Spring 2001), research into the navigational strategies of animals led to the development of specific exercises that activated all five senses to navigate through space with dancing.

Navigation and orientation are concepts drawn from migration that lend themselves easily to dance investigation; animal navigation strategies include listening, seeing, and smelling, as well as imagining the ability to see polarized light or tuning ourselves toward celestial navigation, wind direction and speed, and changing tidal and daylight hours. Adapting these navigational strategies into our dance research profoundly shaped our approach to dancing and moving through all of the different locations. The weeks of dancing under all kinds of conditions with a filter highly attuned to sensory experience provided us with ways of perceiving and understanding the systems we were moving with and through and being moved by. And in this "being moved by" we absorbed or collected the spatial, temporal, and energetic movement of these various systems.

At the time of the BIRD BRAIN Project, I was primarily interested in our direct relationship to the scientific information we were encountering through conversations with biologists and environmental educators. I was keenly focused on developing a research methodology through dance that was influenced by both scientific methods and the embodied experience of migrating with the animals. I was also deeply aware of the metaphorical connection to human migration, especially along the Pacific coastline from Mexico through California to Canada. Through each of the migrations, the movement between the scientific and the cultural/political realms was an important process for shaping the body and creating space for what is between the human and adjacent to human. Each of the environmental phenomena I was researching was being shaped by human actions, whether in the act of restoration or habitat construction, in the planning and development of urban recreational sites, or in the design of infrastructures that would serve the vast residential and industrial needs of New York City.

I want to use archival practices to document, as well, the choreographic development of my work over the past decade. I have expanded my own notions of nature, wilderness, and body through the practice, and I hope to make those transformative developments transparent in the archive. In *Osprey Migration* I began to question the choreographic strategies I had used in *Gray Whale Migration*. I became aware of my own romantic notion that the body could become part of the environment and felt slightly uncomfortable with the choreographic choices I had made in *Gray Whale Migration*, which were based on integrating ourselves into the environment and becoming a vehicle to heighten the audiences' own experiences of the landscape and tune them into their own navigational approaches.

In *Osprey Migration* I started to work with the concept of "location" as a way of addressing the artifice and aesthetics of an experimental dance event happening within a much larger environmental context. Through the concept of a "location," each dancer generated a space or location through her dancing that another dancer would then join and inhabit. Through this "score" the dancers had to imagine the various systems and conditions that they wanted to include in each of their locations and then adapt to the new information provided by the other dancers as they joined in. This framework helped us to imagine, create, and adapt to each other and to the actual physical locations we were dancing in with much more agency then we had accessed in the *Gray Whale* creative practice. In my own experience, creating a location in dancing, while at the same time learning about and researching with local specialists and inhabitants the different locations we were passing through, helped me build more complex movement scores. It was almost like creating an entire world, influenced not only by imagination but also by the actual spaces I was both inhabiting and dancing in while also creating a dance in and for.

We also worked with the concepts of transition, arrival, and departure, constantly creating and negotiating that in-between place as a state of movement but also of comfort and home. Could moving be the space of arrival, the space of being at home? Is that the experience of other creatures that migrate? These are just a few examples of the creative practices I developed and am reencountering in the archival process of performing *Live Dancing Archive*. I developed many other research methods for each of the other phenomena I investigated.

As we know, we cannot completely restore complex ecosystems. We can only approximate the conditions that help organisms to thrive. The situation is similar with these dances, and that is why in part I am so drawn to the concept of an improvisational score. It proposes a framework in which to re-create and reimagine a present that can rely on a dynamic past and look toward a moving future. Dancing in landscapes that were sometimes brutally and sometimes gently shaped by human activity and desire rearranged my own approach to choreography and the scales on which time and space developed in my dancing body.

I am always aware of what is absent when I am performing *Live Dancing Archive*, as I am also aware of the loss of certain places or conditions of the landscapes I have come to know. The archive provides us with a place to see what is missing; it holds an inherent desire to open a space for an experience of absence. For me dancing has the potential to create new places while acknowledging the dynamics of loss and change. We can't hold onto dance, just as we will not be able to hold onto seasonal patterns we have come to think of as permanent as they shift with climate change. Dance gives us a thread to follow and the tools to sense and feel backward and forward simultaneously.

THOMAS F. DEFRANTZ

THEM
Recombinant Aesthetics of Restaging Experimental Performance

Them, a work created in 1985 by choreographer Ishmael Houston-Jones with collaborators Dennis Cooper (text) and Chris Cochrane (music) and restaged in 2010, offers a compelling case study for the consideration of the body as archive. This essay explores the unusually rich nodule of information contained by Them to consider queer theory, critical race theory, and shifts in the creative biographies and public profiles of experimental performance artists in collaboration across thirty years of making work. The essay suggests new ways to think about the under-documented experimental dance performance communities operating in New York City in the 1980s; the myriad ways that race, sexuality, and masculinities circulated in those communities; and the political economies that made way for the immensely successful restaging of this work in 2010.

Them occupies an important, small space as a remnant of experimental dance performance from New York in the 1980s. The work was created by three "outsider" gay artists, men whose separate efforts held notable, but circumscribed, currency in their areas of expertise at the time. The work expressed volitional force as an exemplar of experimental creativity at once multidisciplinary and enlivened by live performing bodies improvising together. It demonstrated an awkward community of tenuous masculine connection. Them came and went fairly quickly after its original string of engagements, disappearing like other improvised works of the era that seemed to hold little value for audiences outside a tight circle of connoisseurs.

The reconstruction of Them in 2010, and its continued touring through 2014, limns a different picture of how experimental work matters across time and its attendant audiences, performances, and locations. Buoyed by the aggressive and corporately modeled publicity machine of New York–centric performance art of the twenty-first century, Them received wide publicity in 2010 before and after its re-premiere. Journalistic dance writing centered on its process, historical resonance, and achievement as an AIDS-era work concerned with identity and the body. The work toured internationally on a vibrant itinerary at notable venues, including Paris, Berlin, and Utrecht. The displacement of Them from a string of small, gala-styled performances in the 1980s to international touring in recognized venues in the 2010s demonstrates the most obvious shift in scale surrounding experimental performance work. By 2010 the reconstruction of a lost work of art from twenty-five years before satisfied curiosity about its content and form, even as it proposed older strategies of performance that held shifting streams of relevance in the context of later social and political circumstances.

THE BODY REMEMBERS, AND IT REMINDS

A grainy film of the first workshop of *Them* from 1985 suggests a do-it-yourself experiment with men's bodies, contact improvisation (CI), velocity, noise, and indeterminacy.[1] Its opening images vibrate in murky black-and-white oscillation. The sound of distortion threatens to overwhelm an electric guitar riff struggling to come into sonic clarity. Someone—a youngish man dressed in a T-shirt and loose pants, in casual, everyday clothes someone might wear at home—walks in circles, searching for what to do next. He seems to wonder *how* to do that next thing. Distortion wins out, and the sound dissembles as the dancer heaves and careens into awkward movements of distress. The archival film itself oscillates more, and the image dissolves and recovers periodically. Watching this early film, we can't really see the dance. As if to reveal the fractured quality of any reconstruction project, it seems important to note that we can't really see what happens in the studio space at PS 122, where the first performance of *Them* took place.

A film from 1987 of the larger ensemble version of *Them* confirms the dance theater aspirations of its development. Performing in Toronto, Canada, now eight performers inhabit the work: six dancers, the musician, and the poet-narrator. The work feels more grand and expansive. It takes up more space in the theater, and the archival film of this version allows us to see more of its compositional strategies. Now the dancers seem to respond more to the tone of the stories told by Cooper, suggesting the harsh, fleeting encounters of men seeking sexual contact. These men find violence and indeterminacy along the way. The wages of being *Them* bring casual death and disappointment in the act of trying to be with someone else. But even with a better filmed referent, *Them* confounds. Even here, in this incomplete and decidedly partial documentation of the performance, the work is at once raw and complicated, in part because of its resistance to narrative or compositional clarity.

BEGIN WITH THE BODY AND WHAT IT SEEMS TO BE DOING

Reflection on the 1985 film: The improvisation is about what makes sense now, to me, in relationship to you, now. It's not about a technique or an organized way to tell this particular story for the ages. The improvisation answers what it is for us to engage this

A scene from *Them* at PS 122, New York, 1985. Pictured left to right are Chris Cochrane, Ishmael Houston-Jones, Donald Fleming, and Jonathan Walker. Photograph by Dona Ann McAdams.

thing together, now. Dancer Donald Fleming is long and lithe, with an upward curve to his gestures; Houston-Jones tends to explore more urgent downward-directed weight. As the two confront each other, Houston-Jones does most of the chasing. But they don't touch or actually reach each other in this first foray. Composer Cochrane enjoys the various ways he can play with farting, overprocessed sounds that deny tenderness. At first Fleming resists dancing and mostly allows himself to perform aborted physical impulses. As he works through an improvised solo to guitarist sounds offered up by Cochrane, his movements become more and more dancerly. He becomes willing to perform moves that look like "dance." He tries to achieve a trancelike, liminal state, moving with harsh arcs and forcing his curving body to answer the brittleness of the guitar. Houston-Jones watches from the background in an off-balance sort of cruising attitude, moving slowly, seeming to be at once titillated and unsure.

Fleming's longish solo from the first iteration of Them seems to be about looking for the least likely physical gesture to come next. This sort of creative "breaking of habit" can be very difficult for dancers to achieve. After all, habit is what allows us all to move through the world. Physical habit might be recognized as the mode of motion that allows us to get from here to there, to walk briskly or run, or to climb stairs without thinking. Dancers take technique classes daily to train their physical habit into reliable physicality. But Fleming works to dance outside of habit: to create physical articulations that are queer to himself and, by extension, to those of us viewing his performance. Throughout, he never appears too far away from a sense of being hurt or abject. The small gestures and impulses he performs demonstrate an embodiment of a continual sort of abjection, and as we watch, they seem to tilt toward a manifestation of physical death. The death of moving outside of habit.

Upon his move to New York in 1979, choreographer Houston-Jones began exploring CI as a mode of generating movement. By 1985 this mode of physical suggestion spoke to his intertwined aesthetic and political concerns as a young, mixed-race, gay artist. By the time *Them* premiered, he had chosen elements of the CI form that spoke to him: the blank refusal to capitulate to any known movement sequence; the intransigent resistance to flowing, familiar gestures; and the idiom's allowance for unlikely partners to dance together without any assumption of unison complicities of motion. For Houston-Jones, CI allowed the arrival of an unexpected grotesque, one always shifting moment to moment and encounter to encounter. And CI explicitly resists the comfort of physical habit. This form within a kind of formlessness enlivened Houston-Jones's creative willingness to explore and to create works that answered unspeakable dimensions of gay life under siege in the first years of AIDS in New York.

Contact improvisation developed during the neoliberal political moment of privatization, famously forwarded by Ronald Reagan's economic policies. The neoliberal turn assumed that citizens might be best suited to create their own structures of support—social and economic—in lieu of extensive governmental coordination and oversight. Paradoxically, neoliberal policies shift responsibility for well-being onto the citizen, without reference to differing entry points to economic or social exchange. Contact improvisation fits into a neoliberal rhetoric of democratizing dance by seeming to allow any who would engage its form access to its expressive and social potential. In reality, though, CI lives in the world, and the world remains bound to concerns of race, gender, class, and sexuality. Contact improvisation was mostly practiced by heteronormative middle-class white men and women, who used the form to express their very personal attitudes about seemingly apolitical vectors of embodiment, including skin, weight, gravity, touch, and velocity. Contact improvisation always had queer people of color among its number, but its engagement seldom reached outside of the detheatricalized moment of its "jams." It may have spoken to the world in many ways, but it seldom spoke *of* the world at large in a way that acknowledged gay and racialized presence.

Working with improvisation allows the collaborating artists to imagine *Them* as a living, breathing response to the shifting landscape of outsider gay life. Physical and sonic improvisations by Cochrane provide counterpoint to the fixity of oblique narrations of death and desire read aloud by Cooper. The bodies of the composer/musician and the choreographer/dancers demonstrate human resources that allow them to persevere. Their performance of unexpected responses to the moment of performance both reflect and model our own sense of possibility at the rise of HIV infection and death from AIDS.

TIME AND IMPROVISATION: QUEER THEORY

> Queerness is a structuring and educated mode of desiring that allows us to see
> and feel beyond the quagmire of the present.
> —José Esteban Muñoz

Improvisation forms the warp and woof of Them. The gestures of the performing bodies in motion are realized as a queer sort of body behavior, one that materializes outside of any regular motions of dance or dance theater. Because the inventory of movements—the physical lexicon of the work—becomes manifest improvisationally, in the creative exploration of the moment, the work is inherently queer in the most everyday sense, as a realization of a desire to do something unusual.

The work is also "queer" in its most obvious twenty-first century articulation of the concept, as dance that offers up nonnormative sexuality as a center of its operations. Queer theory, which found its way into college classrooms and then mainstream discourse in the 1990s, concerned itself with the anxiety generated when desire, sex, and the portrayal of gender don't necessarily match. For example, men who look butch and macho, like motorcycle gang members, might desire sex with others who look like them or with feminized, cross-dressing men who live public lives as women. The queer space between this powerful, socially circumscribed triumvirate of sex, desire, and gender allows for strangely eroticized behavior and response to gesture; queer acts typically feel unusual, precocious, and sexy. Houston-Jones and his collaborators mine the possibility of a creative structuring that resounds outside of "straight time." The work operates differently from the richly detailed postmodern dances of the early 1980s, dances like those of Garth Fagan or Bill T. Jones, which explored order and predetermined gesture created with compositional scrutiny. In Them, the various scenarios are meticulously designed by the choreographer but filled in by the collaborators according to the moment. Most important, the work utilizes CI to tell a story of queer sexuality and abjection, a story that is concerned with age and location, and in some ways, race.

> Hope along with its other, fear, are affective structures that can be described as anticipatory. —José Esteban Muñoz

Where the late queer theorist José Esteban Muñoz seeks hope in his depiction of a queer utopia, Houston-Jones mines fear as both a compositional strategy and a structuring device for the work. Anxiety and fear permeate the dance in each of its iterations. When the performers strike attitudes of repose, a nagging desire always fills the air. Little of romance or tenderness finds its way into the exchanges between the men of Them. Rather, stillness operates as triage for the next encounter.

Reflection on the 1985 film: Now the two dancers lunge and grasp at each other, chasing and indicting each other while trying not to touch. Chasing and wanting, but not touching. Running and wishing, but rarely receiving. Are they afraid? Would something bad happen if they were to touch? They try to read each other's energy, but they also seem to try to miss each other. Again, that fear? Full of force—and something like anger?—They push toward contact. They collide, one succumbs, and they wrestle to the ground, into darkness.

Working with fear or anxiety as a trope for gay male performance might raise some questions of stereotyping around the representations of queer bodies in Them. But Houston-Jones counters the prevalence of anxiety and nervousness with a sweaty, industrial masculinity that feels patently raw, a little bit dirty, and very funky (as in smelly). In calling on working-class or alienated male youth identities for his dancers, Houston-Jones constructs Them as simultaneously threatening and titillating to the art-house audiences that witness its events.

Academic discourses of queer performance often focus on "failure" as a trope that helps us recognize queer. Queer includes gestures that don't quite add up. These nonnormative, mismatched attempts to succeed that ultimately fail are to remind us of how fragile anything like "normal" might be and how difficult it is to remain "normal." Houston-Jones explores failure as an inevitable physical by-product of improvisation, and he encodes failure to operate as a structuring concept for the way in which his male performers resist emotional intimacy. Throughout the work, physical encounters fail, and conventional theatrical dancing also fails. Importantly, the work offers no utopian vision of gay sexual practice. When Muñoz writes that "utopia is always about the not-quite-here or the notion that something is missing,"[2] he underscores the notion that utopia

Ishmael Houston-Jones, Chris Cochrane, and Jonathan Walker in *Them*, PS 122, New York, 1985. Photograph by Dona Ann McAdams.

is a speculative and aspirational category of being. It doesn't quite exist, but it is crucial to consider in its ambition to inspire social change.

Them points toward no alternate, "better" future; it focuses instead on spaces of abjection and dystopian fear. The fear and anxiety of *Them* portray an inability to sustain care or empathy among men. Even in a series of tableaux of three entangled men in physical contact, their shifting poses and forceful scrutiny of each other suggest a nervousness tempered by "dis-ease." Sometimes the men touch, but the touch doesn't seem to actually do anything in particular or linger past its moment. Physical touch on the stage appears like the impermanent touch of sex that Cooper continually describes in his narration.

MEMORY AND ABJECTION: CRITICAL RACE THEORY

> To make dances from a place of melancholy abjection is to wield power of immense proportion.
> —David Gere

Them suggests a remembering of pain and mistrust, of hurt inspired by a sense of outsiderness, and of death as the wage of men having sex with men. In some ways, its totalizing sense of abjection speaks to gay failure as a norm and reminds us of similar cautionary tales of real life told by disenfranchised artists of color through the ages. While *Them* has little to say about race in particular through Cooper's text or Cochrane's music, its overwhelming affect conveys a bitter tongue well practiced by a global cohort of black artists speaking to cir-

Felix Cruz (foreground) and Jeremy Pheiffer in *Them*, PS 122, New York, October 22, 2010. (See plate 15 for color image.) Photograph © Ian Douglas.

cumstances of white control. The work feels *hard* as it deals with personal in-abilities to act within stigmatizing social circumstances. Paralleling the lim-ited social and economic mobility that most African Americans encounter, Houston-Jones's gay archetypes have little hope and can seemingly do little more than they already do in the world of *Them*.

Remembering pain and cycling its wages into creative ensemble effort is a basic practice of black art. Work in this mode mines suffering toward an end of renewal and recovery. It tends to conceive of remembering as a revitalization of social possibility. In this, Houston-Jones visits territory familiar to Leroi Jones's seminal performance work *Slave Ship* (1967), an experimental play with music and movement that told of the horrors of the Middle Passage. *Slave Ship* featured improvised musical structures that were considered avant-garde when it was created. It imagined theater comprised of the moaning sobs of captives in the hold — realized in a darkened space that allowed no exit for its audience. *Slave Ship*, like other radical black performance art, including Eleo Pomare's dance theater work *Blues for the Jungle* (1966), forced its audience into difficult corners of complicity and empathy. These works made black bodies *strange* to their mostly white audiences. They built upon unexpected nuances of aggressive behavior that spilled over the boundary between audience and performer. Radical black dance theater works like these, and Katherine Dunham's staging of a lynching in *Southland* (1951) a decade earlier, confirmed the possibilities of enacting contemporary dystopia as a strategy for the creation of provocative, difficult, progressive performance.

In staging the bullying and hostility common to punkish gay life in the 1980s, Houston-Jones and his collaborators refer to these earlier works that engage critical race theory at their core. Like the three works mentioned above by Jones, Pomare, and Dunham, *Them* assumes a community that recognizes itself, already in motion, even if that community's gestures are circumscribed by an offstage, controlling protagonist. Where the earlier works assume an offstage, racist, white mainstream that constrains the gestures of the community onstage, *Them* adds a dimension of sexual dissidence to the challenges of racist interaction. *Them* refers obliquely to an offstage, heteronormative mainstream that would deny its characters the social agency to love, admire supportively, or rejoice in a shared identity politic. *Them* arrives as dissident evocation of a world rendered without resource to calm.

Reflection on the 2010 film: The they of Them are not particularly raced, but they could be. Is this what the beginning of racially mixed progressive expression might have looked like in the 1980s—this sense of ease without racialized ontology or a possibility to be alongside each other in this space of East Village gay/queer? Wasn't it enough that these men made choices outside of a pressing Yuppie mainstream that seemed to want everyone to join the banking industries of the day? Reagan's neoliberal tilt seemed to circumscribe a crass, tiny space for young people of color to join the fray of "I'll get mine first" economic participation. But Houston-Jones's world of grungy gay men seems little interested in hierarchies of race or class. Here, though, black presence capitulates to white essence. Black presence might be resolutely humanitarian at its core of creation through the violence of the Middle Passage and forced enslavement. The white essence of Them realizes a somehow chic, devil-may-care nihilism.

Reflection on the 1985 film: Cooper's text offers an unsentimental recitation of the deaths that came unexpectedly and too soon. It also presents a string of personal, first-person stories that detail young life full of desire for more, and more varied, sex. These stories, voiced against bleeding sounds of Cochrane's electric guitar, predict a searching sequence in the dance of men cruising each other in a narrow passageway of light. This cruising section includes familiar interactions of attraction and unsurety: sizing up others in anticipation of a physical encounter, enjoying the unknown pursuit. Somehow, this sequence feels meditative and almost delicate, animated by something that relishes being unsure and slightly mistrustful. The thrill of discovery—that the guy whom you cruised, cruised back and is also interested in you—gives way to an excitement of possibility. The men try to disguise their desires while letting enough be known to entice a partner. The sequence accelerates, though, into a frenzy of sound

and motion and a sense of trying to exceed the tenuous relationship and the sound score—
jumping onto the wall and trying to move and dance outside/beyond the work somehow. We
hear the sound of audiotape moving backward. Finally the men touch and embrace in motion,
but it is a sort of wrestling, fighting touch. They move to a bed and tear into a demonstration
of confusing, angry, unloving sex. This is encounter without emotional intimacy, a fantasy
encounter of relationship bound by power established in the crucible of the cruising.

A bat and a bed: two prominent props from the original production. An object of violence and an object of intimacy and repose. The first version of the
work had no phantasmagoric ending, no bleeding goat carcass. As a scrappy
sort of chamber dance for five performers, the first production betrayed little
of its forthcoming grand dance theater ambitions. Later, of course, the additional prop of the dead goat would transform the performance content, and
Them would become a classic of its time.

Reflection on the 1987 film: Musically, Them develops a mature identity of sonic motivation
across its various iterations. From his opening riffs, Cochrane plays like a shaman
summoning the ghosts on his guitar and with his many electronic setups. He begins at a
fever pitch that sounds of noise, offered as a prelude to variegations of sonic assault and
an occasional meditative respite. By 1987 Cooper stands at the side of the performance
space, rather than sitting at a table as he had in 1985. The larger cohort of dancers looks
emphatically like the discarded youth of suburbia. They seem to be a gang of kids in ugly,
ill-fitting gear that makes everyone seem very ordinary and anti-aspirational. Cooper reads
the opening text—which has changed little from its earlier iterations—but now the dancers
touch each other. These encounters—improvisations of manipulating but holding—seem to
be about failed relationships, or at least about trying to be in a relationship rather than just
physical contact. The dancers hold their energy close to their bodies in this section, and we see
postures of intimacy that show what it looks like without, somehow, being intimate. After
all, intimacy doesn't belong in this work. The movement accelerates into a sort of searching
and jumping/falling thing, much more dancerly and explicitly about dancing than in the
1985 version. They fall. They keep falling. They keep touching without affect or tenderness.
But they do allow themselves to touch faces, to hold bodies, and to physically resist each
other. Is this queer corporeality? Does it resound more than it might because we know that
its creators are men who have sex with men?

> Simple pleasures and affections are far away. In Houston-Jones' outlook the
> bullying, clamorous, brusque, torn-up aspects of . . . relationships are intrinsically
> knotted up with our passion and tenderness and need. . . . [B]ut our rough human
> grace is overwhelmed by frustration and defeat. — Burt Supree

THOMAS F. DEFRANTZ

SOUNDS OUT OF TIME: GENDER THEORY

Houston-Jones has described the work as operating on three parallel streams of music, movement, and text. The creative pathways opened by each of these idioms are not intended to intersect, comment upon, or even support each other so much as to exist and emerge simultaneously, with each influencing the other organically by the nature of its presence. This complex method of assemblage assumes three coherent, self-contained entities unfolding in time. In this, Cochrane, Houston-Jones, and Cooper excel. The musical score can be appreciated on its own merits as an exquisite exploration of unexpected soundscape: screaming electric guitar riffs and farting electronic sounds mix with recordings of birds and children playing in a schoolyard. Indeed, Cochrane created a digital recording of the score on CD that stands up extremely well as an independent listening experience. Cooper's text for *Them*, similarly, rivals that of some of his most celebrated literature.

Houston-Jones's choreographic score is composed of several compelling scenes of action that allow the performers to execute a range of methodological approaches. Contact improvisation duets that morph into wrestling, a sequence of improvised postcoital tableaux, a dramatic improvisation around strategies of cruising, and a mysterious bedroom encounter of domination demonstrate four approaches to practice found here. The bedroom encounter threateningly places one man at the will of another, as he is repeatedly pushed down onto the bed to be physically topped. The dominating man climbs atop him and adjusts his hair, caresses his face, then rises to repeat the action again and again. This sadistic sequence suggests a perverse titillation in the masochistic act of domination. Taken together, the varied sections demonstrate a confident creative structure, one that values diversity of approach in staging provocation.

The body is a fragile and gendered archive, one rendered by social circumstance as well as intellectual, spiritual, and physical activity. In *Them*, the body is rendered as innately eroticized and sexualized. It appears as a process in motion always concerned with its physical capacity and fragility. While the dancers of *Them* grunt, sweat, and wrestle through physical encounters, Cooper's text recounts the body's ultimate instability and the ever-looming prospect of death that approaches us all. The bodies in motion onstage act as counter-report to the litany of deaths that hover at the edge of the stage space. This disturbing—and productive—tension among text and body, body and music, and text and music propels the experience forward.

278

The body as archive suggests knowledge outside of the limitations of language. Houston-Jones's reliance on improvisational structures allows this "looking outside of words" to be amplified in terms of gesture and dancerly motion. Many cultural and literary theorists have specified the ways in which language and writing circumscribe gender. Jacques Derrida, among others, writes persuasively on the ways in which textuality, based largely on linear binaries, appears as masculine, while movement might suggest an essential feminine outside of obvious, everyday systems of power and control. Derrida's concept of "incalculable choreographies" exists in an always-shifting consideration of gender and sex that reaches beyond any sexuality, reaching for something outside of the everyday.[3] Casting the body as archive, we underscore the impossible infinities of knowledge. What we did, and how and why we did it, are stored within the body's entire memory. But we tend to rely on language to share that information with others. And yet the body already knows what it has done even when there are no words that come easily to share that knowledge.

Cooper's text arrives at the edge of an emergent punk gay literature of the 1980s that placed nonnormative sexualities alongside violent excursions of self-doubt. Cooper's poetry and fiction hold volitional force as exemplars of homosexual literature written without reference to mainstream concerns of social propriety. His text for *Them* places stories of casual sex and unexpected death alongside poetic flights of fancy detailing a wish to belong to a larger group. The confident, evocative, and nonsequential text stabilizes the larger production with an unblinking yearning for life bound by young, casual sex. Indeed, as the musical and movement performers make choices in response to the emerging moment of the production, Cooper's text varies little from venue to venue in terms of its content. Thirty years later, Cooper's outsider, punk-tinged text aligns well with queer articulations of twenty-firstcentury nonnormative sexualities.

While Cooper's text fits into a lineage of homosexual or gay letters, Houston-Jones's staging of gay gesture finds a more limited cohort in terms of dance performance. In the mid-1980s audiences witnessed few theatrical works expressing gay male corporeality as an everyday sort of occurrence, meaning those not bound by melodramatic portrayals of homosexuality as pathology. Dance historian David Gere reminds us that Tim Miller and John Berndt's performances *Live Boys* (1980) chronicled that couple's everyday navigations of gay life in New York City at the time, including reference to a "mysterious skin fungus" that Berndt developed.[4] *Them* arrived at the beginning of work that responded to the emerging AIDS crisis as well as to outsider gay sensibilities.

> Homophobia is very much the same—this idea of exposure, of something bad
> happening just because of who you are.—Gia Kourlas

Same-sex nomenclature and identity politics shifted from the mid-1980s to the 2010s. After the millennium, young men were as likely to claim a "queer" identity as a gay or homosexual one. The change in naming coincided with a large-scale shift in both the visibility of nonnormative sexuality and an ease with which young men might consider a spectrum of sexual identity and experience. The 2010 cast of *Them* included self-identified queer and straight performers, alongside the mature, gay creative artists. Queer identity in the 2010s surely enjoys a lower stigmatization than gay identity did in the 1980s. By 2010 there may even have been something "chic" about appearing in a work tilted toward queer and homosexual identities.

Reflection on the 1987 film: The stories have so much sense of quotidian melancholy, an abiding sense of "this is just what the day is," that makes it all seem tawdry. When one performer starts to bang the bed repeatedly with the bat, I wonder, "Is this internalized homophobia? Are we being invited to witness the self-hatred that can come with being gay in a straight world?" But when the bully character chases the others around the space, we know that this sort of violence circumscribes the lives of the characters. The bully chases him, and Houston-Jones falls and rolls; he survives. The work trades in dystopia but also demonstrates a fact of surviving the ineloquent moment. These moves, these tableaux of gay presence, remind me of a sequence from filmmaker Gus Van Sant's My Own Private Idaho (1991), when two young male hustlers have sex with an older client. Van Sant edits this sequence as a series of almost-frozen tableaux, as slightly moving, breathing bits of stillness, captured in melancholic pause. This gesture in the film and in Them seems to make gay men more present in the world somehow. "I wish I had taken a photo . . ." the narrator reads, and I think, yes, if only to confirm that the thing I wondered at actually happened; that I, and these men, were here at some point. But it is all ephemeral and goes away soon: these lives, these moves, and these sexual drives.

This shift in sensibility from "gay" to "queer" underscores a large shift in how *Them* might be received in the 2010s and beyond. After the millennium, scores of choreographic works dealing with same-sex identities and nonnormative sexualities found their way to audiences in the United States and Europe. Some works about global epidemics and holocausts were realized and experienced by artists and audiences interested in dance that might suggest possibilities for social movement. *Them* was both a remounting of an older work from a time of heightened confusion and anxiety and a singular work created by collaborators still concerned with performance as a valuable mode of identity expression. While the impulse for these artists to revisit the themes and methods of *Them* might have remained consistent across twenty-five years, the context for viewing or participating in this work changed mightily over time.

As Houston-Jones and dance writer Danielle Goldman have both noted, dancers for the reconstruction of *Them* explored expansive ways to approach the movement requirements of the work.[5] Many of the new performers had undertaken advanced dance training that might have included explorations in CI. Even the performers who had little or no performing experience before being cast in *Them* had been exposed to the sight of men dancing together intimately. While Houston-Jones felt it was important to include a range of movement experiences among his 2010 cast, the performers shared a gung-ho willingness to experiment as movers working in proximity to each other and ideologies of same-sex desire.

The 2010 dancers were generally younger than Houston-Jones and his collaborators had been in the 1980s. This generational displacement contributed to a sense of naïve optimism within the reconstruction of the work, an optimism that might have felt more akin to curiosity than anxiety in live performance. In general, the reconstruction of the work felt more like a playful exploration of structures of moving rather than an urgent invention of forms tailored to a particular story and its telling.

This may be the largest challenge of reconstructing a work of experimental theater: the fact that an urgent, inciting moment that inspires the collaborative creation may come and go, leaving only the trace of urgency in its wake. The moment that produced *Them* was characterized by worry and confusion, with gay men falling ill without any seeming pattern. The 2010 reconstruction occurred amid a popular culture nostalgia for the 1980s, as well as academic reconsiderations of early creative responses to AIDS.

Of course *Them* in the twenty-first century can't raise the socially provocative concerns that its performances brought forth in 1986. The space for politically motivated dissent does not rightly exist in the venues where the most recent performances toured. Presentations at the Pompidou Centre in Paris or as part of the Tanz im August festival in Berlin suggest an accommodation to the contemporary circulations of live art. The current restaging exists as a show that, like other shows, certainly speaks from a particular point of view, yet like other shows, it can be enjoyed and forgotten in short order. Because of this shift in time, the reconstruction turns *Them* into an evening's diversion. In this circulation, the restaging closes off its original potential for radical discovery and political excitation.

The homosocial physical world of *Them* makes little space for women. Cooper's references in the text remind the performers and audiences that women do populate the world beyond the pursuit of sexual encounter portrayed on stage. But *Them* capitalizes on masculinist privilege to exclude ideologies that arise outside of its narrowed field of vision. While the 1980s productions reflected a still-novel staging of masculinity performed by a cohort of male performers, by 2010 the casting of only men in the work inspired criticism. In 2010 Houston-Jones commented on his casting and the shifts of time: "The piece is poetic not didactic, but it is about certain experiences that are male. Dennis was writing about his memories of himself and others as males. The inspiration for the dances was mine (and Jonathan Walker's and Donald Fleming's) as male. Surely any number of female and transgender performers we know could perform the scored improvs of the dance beautifully. But that isn't the point of view of the piece."[6]

Here Houston-Jones confirms that the work has its own ambitions, and those are not entirely attendant on everyone. One of the ways that *Them* functions as an outsider, and therefore politically progressive, work, might be that it speaks for those who cannot or will not. It speaks for those young men who feel maligned and passed over by social stigma. *Them* can't be about mainstream or middle-class gay life. It can't tell of reciprocal emotional lives or successful compromise among partners. It gains its representational force as a testament to life outside of convention and also outside of widespread visibility. Houston-Jones describes the work to be about "urban roughness," and says that it is "non-pastoral" in its motivations, while Cochrane opines that *Them* exists in relation to "suburban white gay stuff too," an important nod to the grungy, slightly soiled ennui that permeates the air here. *Them* also makes male queer black presence manifest, in Houston-Jones's physical presence and authorial command of the project. *Them* portrays a ragtag, uneasy community of outsiders who commune by their erotic desires. These characters include the overly aggressive character wielding a bat and hitting pennies against the back wall of the performance space and a bully who chases others with his bat even as he lies down with them for sex. The bully, the young "twinkie," the eager pup, the temporary wolf—these types emerge in response to the requirements of the physical score. Building on the differences among the assembled cast, *Them* demonstrates a variety of gay/queer identities that form and collide as young men convene.

WHY RECONSTRUCT?

Them is one in a trio of works Houston-Jones created concerned with AIDS, the other two being *The Undead* (1990), an evening-length theatrical piece, and *Unsafe/Unsuited (A High Risk Meditation)* (1995), an improvised trio with Keith Hennessy and Patrick Scully. But *Them* emerged early in the chronology of recognizing HIV infection. Its ambivalence and urgency reflect the randomness and insecurity of the early 1980s. The choreographer tapped autobiography as a resource for his structural choices in order to highlight how the personal is inherently political, especially for an African American experimental choreographer:

> In *Them*, especially, I was working out parts of myself, working out fears of disease, violence, and death, trying to find a way of dealing with those issues for myself. That's how autobiography lets the audience in. I don't want to make hermetic work, but I don't know how to make political work that's not personal: I'm trying to show myself as a human being facing these big issues—and sometimes failing. In my life, as well, I sometimes fail to deal with these issues—but I'm not afraid to do that publicly.[7]

When the creative trio discussed the reconstruction in interviews in 2010 and 2012, they agreed that the work was never intended to be "about" HIV or AIDS, but those circumstances impacted what came forward in its creation. In sourcing their own experiences in the world, along with their still-emerging creative processes as artists, the personal became politically engaged, and the work offers something up close and particular, gay, dissident, and punkish to its audiences. But the creators weren't always comfortable with how audiences and critics received the work. According to the trio, in its first iterations, some gay media "didn't like the work" and termed it "nihilistic." They wondered that "everyone has to become examples of the problem or the community" at issue in creative work, and Cooper especially contended that the work, like much of his work, we might assume, explores "personal agony" rather than connections to groups of people. They also acknowledged the changes in audience response over time. Cooper noted that the "controversial work . . . seems sweet now," in the context of live art and experimental choreography circulating by 2012.[8]

Reflecting on the genesis of the reconstruction, Houston-Jones noted that the project was a commission from PS 122 artistic director Vallejo Gartner. Houston-Jones thought it could resonate in 2010 and enjoy a longer life amid the reclaiming of various dance and fashion trends from the 1980s. By 2010 the work had landed in the marketplace of chic, decidedly experimental work

THOMAS F. DEFRANTZ

Unsafe/Unsuited (A High Risk Meditation) with Keith Hennessy, Patrick Scully, and Ishmael Houston Jones, PS 122, New York, 1995. Photograph by Dona Ann McAdams.

that intended to demonstrate still-vital approaches to creative process. In Paris, *Them* was programmed alongside *Teenage Hallucination*, a visual art show at the Pompidou Centre curated by Gisele Vienne and Dennis Cooper. At the Tanz im August festival in Berlin, the "largest annual festival for contemporary dance and performance in Germany," *Them* enjoyed a brief, sold-out run. In these contexts, *Them* performs the work of progressive nostalgia, asking its audiences to consider the urgent masculinist dystopias of the 1980s from the safe vantage of twenty-first-century dance theater.

The three artists recognized that all of the original cast members—twelve dancers in all—are still living, but something about having fresh-faced, younger artists perform the work seemed important to its revival. After all, the handing down of stories across generations matters here, as we consider reconstruction and restaging. The task of sharing the work with a group of young performers fulfilled a basic human need to disperse ideas and ideologies among others. But some elements of *Them* became difficult to convey across landscapes of time: cruising, for example, is not a practice of the young in the twenty-first century. In a public question-and-answer session in Paris, one of the dancers noted that he and his cohort "didn't have these problems" of HIV and intensive social stigma, so he found it somehow instructive to connect with older artists and learn about their struggles. Another dancer confirmed that he felt distanced from his collaborating elders, even in the use of *gay* rather than *queer*. *Them* connected its new cohort of artists, but not without the consequences of noting differences among its generations.

The reconstruction of *Them* pushed buttons for its collaborators. The work deals with events torn from their memories of surviving a terrible time, and its reconstruction landed, uneasily, amid conversations about the economies of experimental dance, hierarchies of ageism, and diminishing resources for the arts in general. In a strong critique of the politics of its reconstruction, New York–based performance artist Lindsay Drury opined that she didn't think of Houston-Jones as "an artist who is seeking to make a history text of himself, especially while he is very much alive." In response, he wrote, I "really care about how my work is seen and that it is seen and remembered."[9] In some ways, within the contexts of late capitalism and twenty-first-century live art production, *Them* could do little more than answer the curator-driven need for controversial, experimental works that build upon flashpoints of traumatic historical narratives. Even as an unwilling example of early creative responses to AIDS, the reconstruction brought forward the embodied maturity of noted experimental artists performing live alongside sweaty, young, male performers to fit this bill.

Reflection on question and answer session in Paris, 2012: In a (literally) white room with fifty people assembled, the three collaborators sit at a table to answer questions about their work. We are in the basement of the Pompidou Centre in Paris. It seems a strange place and time to talk about a performance work made many years ago in New York City. But maybe this time and place have no more strength than that time and place might have had. A line separates the collaborators at the table from the audience. A sign placed along the line reads, "Do not cross." Is this the world of Them? Do not cross?

Writer Lucas de Lima noted the complexity of re-creating a work bound by a historical moment rent with fear: "Flanked from different sides of the room by the older men who conceived *Them*, the young dancers become children of a perversely reproductive nostalgia. A nostalgia not for the AIDS epidemic, to be sure, but rather for the act of youthful yearning itself: a yearning then, if not so much now, pronounced and produced through the taboo and risk it carried."[10] De Lima points to the nostalgic turn that produces desire, whether the physical terms of that desire persist or not. In some ways, the reconstruction of *Them* surely explores the performers' need to be onstage, to be viewed in practice and in public.

Portrait of Chris Cochrane, Ishmael Houston-Jones, and Dennis Cooper. Photograph by Christy Pessagno, 2010.

Reflection on interview in Berlin, August 16, 2012: The men seem to get along and like each other, of course. They are survivors. They don't agree on everything, though. Dennis is the "smart" one because he has words at his command. He also seems the most skeptical to use everyday language to describe the experience of their collaboration. Ishmael defers amid the group, but not when it comes to his making movement with other people—then he is the boss. Chris, who seems so strangely needy at times onstage, seems even more so in person. Yes, we realize that you are a sonic inventor and a genius at creating those sounds and this performance. Do you think we don't notice you? We surely do recognize your brilliance. Together, we four find our way through a conversation. Several times I think, these guys don't seem very gay at all. I wonder if this is part of how they work together well. After spending the tiniest bit of time with them all, and even more with Ishmael alone, I think that they would hate that I could say this. And I wonder if they would be glad that I could think so, too.[11]

> I thought about love. I think I confused what they did with it. But my belief made the day great. I think I decided to make that my goal—to be like them. I put such incredible faith in the future that I sobbed a little I think. —Dennis Cooper, in *Them*

HOW CAN WE SEE THEM NOW?

Reflection on performance in Paris, 2012: In a duet sequence from the first version of the work, Donald Fleming pushes Houston-Jones onto the mattress, climbs on top of him, and presses his hands into his mouth. They rise and begin again. The climbing on top feels aggressive, invasive, and violent. Again and again they almost kiss or embrace, but

Fleming pushes Houston-Jones onto the bed and straddles him, moves his head about, and they rise again. Jones is again pushed down and straddled by Fleming. Again and again, up and almost kiss, then a push and down again. Ultimately indeterminate, the sequence enacts a repetition without resolution—no ending to this cycle of attraction and repulsion. Houston-Jones seems passive and soft, somehow yielding. Fleming demonstrates hardness and unrelenting domination. Does it matter that white man Fleming lords over black man Houston-Jones? In the 2010 reconstruction, African American dancer Niall Noel Jones performed the role of the aggressor. Are we to rethink the terms of racialized representation in the age of Trayvon Martin's murder? How could we not?

Reflection on performance in Berlin, 2012: We are a mostly middle-aged white European audience of some 250 or so. At an eye-level evaluation, we are a maybe 15 percent women, 10 percent young (presumably queer) men, and 100 percent educated art audience. We are mostly gay. The sold-out performance begins with the hush of expectation. Ishmael Houston-Jones enters the space, which is littered with performers in the wings and along the edges.

Cochrane's sound rises as a blindfolded young man is manipulated by the mature dance artist. The music gets bigger and bigger—is it overwrought?—and Houston-Jones becomes captivated by its scale. He performs his solo of nervous-system interruptions, slapping his face fifteen times before stopping his own hand to leave the space. His dance is a question, and the rest of the work will offer its answer. This performance seems quite sure of itself. It wants us to consider how sad and hard it might be to be queer, or to have been gay as HIV infection and death from AIDS took over the landscape of New York life. In all, the work feels like something of a ritual procession of its own volition by now: an act that will allow the performers to excise something around nostalgia and an absent futurity. In an interview the morning after, the guys tell me that the work "enacted a resonance" as its restaging brought together people who had been there in the 1980s, to assemble again and reflect on the twenty-five intervening years. Of course I wasn't there, then, and neither were many of us in the audience now, in Berlin 2012, but we did indeed feel the yearning of this performance, to answer a need to allow this sort of queer masculinity and presence to continue into this space and time . . .

Across the years—from 1985 to 1987 and then to 2010 and 2012—Them remained consistent in its compositional ambitions.[12] Watching films of its productions side by side, we note the familiarity of gesture and similarity of their emphases. This "family resemblance" has to do with the presence of the creators in all versions of the work; Cochrane, Cooper, and Houston-Jones have participated in every performance of Them. The ability of the work to remain recognizable to itself and an attendant audience also has to do with the subtle clarity of the compositional technique at work in the sonic, literary, and corporeal processes that produce its contents. Finely crafted, in each of its three streams of invention (music, text, movement) the work withstands shifts of venue and cast. What has changed across time is the refinement of its theatrical gestures. Sequences take shape within a logic of the theatrical event; scenes begin to feel like the "earlier scenes" and the "later scenes" of the evening. This relates most importantly to the sense of inevitability of its ending. The 1987 and 2010 productions both included final scenes with the animal carcass and the inspection of lymph nodes as endings for Them. In 2010 and 2012, the performers all knew that whatever happened along the way in the structured improvisations, these scenes would land on their audience with burning representational force.

Reflection on the 1987 film: Houston-Jones appears on the bed wearing boxer shorts, a backward shirt that looks like a hospital gown, socks, and a blindfold. He carries a dead goat. He presses it against the bed and himself. One blindfolded and the other already dead, they cannot see each other or understand the nature of each other's presence. He hugs the goat close to his body and twitches with it. The encounter is a silent scream of despair and remorse, desperation and sublime grotesquerie. Again, it is somewhat difficult to see what happens here in this archival film. It is surely hard to watch.

Reflection on performance in Berlin, 2012: Arturo Vidich enters the space, blindfolded and in a semblance of a hospital gown, led by another performer who carries a goat carcass. Deposited on the dirty mattress, Vidich and the goat wrestle, seeming to sputter in despair at their shared misfortune. Blood seeps across his body and onto the sheets. He puts the goat over his head as if it were a mask, or as though its interior could relieve this unrelenting degradation. Flailing under his large, weighted body, the animal carcass is difficult to see. The action of this segment is indecipherable and unpalatable.

Them ends with a gesture-based theatrical coda rooted in a physical realism not seen earlier in the work. The men stand nervously looking into imaginary mirrors that direct their gazes toward the audience, searching for lumps in their lymph nodes, feeling tentatively at their necks, armpits, groins. In this state of personal vulnerability made public for the stage, a death figure in black moves among them, wrestling them to the ground and immobility one at a time. Some go fairly easily; some resist and struggle until they succumb. A portion of the text repeats, with a difference—read now by one of the younger dancers before being taken up again by Cooper. This ending surprises us in its shift of aesthetic ambition; the realistic pantomime of the moment of awareness of mortality seems overwrought. But then, these direct gestures anchor the physicality of the

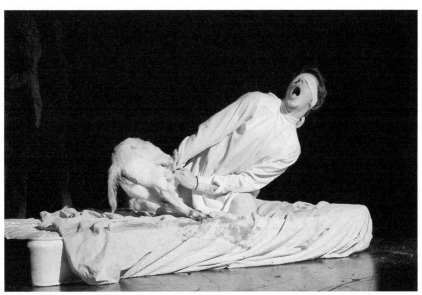

Arturo Vidich in *Them*, PS 122, New York, October 22, 2010. (See plate 16 for color image.) Photograph © Ian Douglas.

work in a way that the text and music already have. As viewers, we might appreciate the clarity of gesture and affect that this section provides. This sequence also confirms that the work is something of a play, more akin to "dance theater" than abstract postmodern dance or CI. *Them* concludes confidently, aware of its theatrical and cultural ambitions and capacities.

> Queer dance is hard to catch, and it is meant to be hard to catch—it is supposed to slip through the fingers and comprehension of those who would use knowledge against us. But it matters and takes on a vast material weight for those of us who perform or draw important sustenance from performance. Rather than dematerialize, dance materializes. Dance, like energy, never disappears; it is simply transformed. —José Esteban Muñoz

Reflection on performance in Berlin, 2012: These are grungy people in grungy sorts of scenes. The goat carcass suits the work because it is also ugly and decrepit, sort of phantasmagoric and horrible. (While short in terms of duration, this sequence holds huge impact. Audience members always leave during its performance.) The goat sequence seems longer in the reconstruction. It seems more important somehow in this later version.

We hear children's voices playing outdoors as the men check their lymph nodes. The voices add an actual sense of innocence and possibility to a work bereft of seeming alternatives. This sequence goes on for some time—longer than the dance with the goat—and the embodied manifestation of abjection and queer death digs into the sense of the entire event yet again. They don't go lightly to the floor; . . . they kick and scream, they resist even as they fail.

And in this, I wonder if the work has a moral compass that tilts toward a puritanical, cause-and-effect sort of ethic. The answer to the unmitigated sex becomes these murders. The anxiety of queer life now, reflecting back on gay life of twenty-five years ago, ends with defeat and disenfranchisement. There is no outside of this outsider effort to resist conformity.

Visual art theorist Bill Seaman's "recombinant poetics" draws on a metaphor of cellular regeneration to emphasize how new meaning making happens as participants intermingle "their mind-set with the interpenetrating fields of the media-elements that shift in meaning in relation to constructed context and dynamic action."[13] Focusing on the intermingling that inevitably troubles our relationships with materials encountered, new and old, Seamen asserts that "the participant conceptually projects meaning across the entirety of the ongoing experience."[14] If we consider the young performers as the "participants" in the reconstruction process, we can surely appreciate the many ways in which their presence changes *Them* on a molecular level. *Them* shimmies and shifts, taking on an aggressive, hyperbolic resolve to achieve a husky, curious, youthful masculinity that arrives newly minted after the millennium.

And what of the body as archive here? For Cochrane, Cooper, and Houston-Jones, their bodies comprise the inevitable archive that allows the work to exist. Their experiences as mature artists saturate the latter-day performances of *Them*, and through their continued performances they consider their bodies to be indispensable to its realization. The younger bodies become a different kind of archive, one that still searches for ways to confront the rich array of information contained by the dance's structure. The younger bodies are interchangeable (indeed, dancer injury and unavailability have forced last-minute shifts in casting for the project at times). The younger bodies know things that the older bodies don't; they know more about CI technique, maybe, but less about the fizzy physical thrill of gay cruising or the torturous weightiness of everyday abjection amid the inexplicable rise of HIV infection. No single body, or generational group of bodies, has all the answers to the work. In concert, they ask the question, "How can we shift together, in dynamic action, to create an archive of physical responses to experiential truths of gay life in New York in the 1980s? What does our physical recombination produce?"

We note with interest the following story in the *New York Daily News* in 2014: "For the first time since the HIV epidemic exploded more than a generation ago, AIDS is no longer one of the top 10 causes of death in the city, the city's top health official said Thursday."[15]

And men—they—still have sex. They still mourn an ineffable desiring that will not abate.

They still die. And we watch them.

NOTES

The epigraphs, in order of appearance, are from José Esteban Muñoz, *Cruising Utopia: The Then and There of Queer Futurity* (New York: New York University Press, 2009), 1; Muñoz, *Cruising Utopia*, 3; David Gere, *How to Make Dances in an Epidemic: Tracking Choreography in the Age of AIDS* (Madison: University of Wisconsin Press, 2004), 122; Burt Supree, "Men with Men," *Village Voice*, December 23, 1986; Gia Kourlas, "Ishmael Houston-Jones: The '80s are back with *Them*," *Time Out New York*, September 20, 2010; and Muñoz, *Cruising Utopia*, 81.

Interviews were conducted with Ishmael Houston-Jones on February 29, 2012, in Paris; August 18, 2013, in New York; and July 14, 2014, in Durham, NC.

1. "Contact Improvisation is an evolving system of movement initiated in 1972 by American choreographer Steve Paxton. The improvised dance form is based on the communication between two moving bodies that are in physical contact and their combined relationship to the physical laws that govern their motion—gravity, momentum, inertia. The body, in order to open to these sensations, learns to release excess muscular tension and abandon a certain quality of willfulness to experience the natural flow of movement. Practice includes rolling, falling, being upside down, following a physical point of contact, supporting and giving weight to a partner.

Contact improvisations are spontaneous physical dialogues that range from stillness to highly energetic exchanges. Alertness is developed in order to work in an energetic state of physical disorientation, trusting in one's basic survival instincts. It is a free play with balance, self-correcting the wrong moves and reinforcing the right ones, bringing forth a physical/emotional truth about a shared moment of movement that leaves the participants informed, centered, and enlivened." Steve Paxton, "A Definition," *Contact Quarterly* 4, no. 2 (Winter 1979): 26. See also Ann Cooper Albright, "Touching History," in this volume.

2. Muñoz, *Cruising Utopia*, 118.

3. See Jacques Derrida and Christie V. McDonald, "Choreographies," in *Bodies of the Text: Dance as Theory, Literature as Dance*, ed. Ellen W. Goellner and Jacqueline Shea Murphy (New Brunswick: Rutgers University Press, 1995), 141–56.

4. Gere, *How to Make Dances in an Epidemic*, 4.

5. See Danielle Goldman, "Improvised Dance in the Reconstruction of *Them*," in *Oxford Handbook of Critical Improvisation Studies*, ed. George E. Lewis and Benjamin Piekut (Oxford University Press, 2015).

6. Lindsey Drury, "Response: Lindsey Drury on Ishmael Houston-Jones, Dennis Cooper and Chris Cochrane's *Them*, with a Reply from Ishmael," *Movement Research: Critical Correspondence* (October 20, 2010).

7. Marc Robinson, "Performance Strategies: Marc Robinson, Ishmael Houston-Jones, John Kelly, Karen Finley, and Richard Elovich," *Performing Arts Journal* 10, no. 3 (1987): 31–55, 36.

8. See David Velasco, "Ishmael Houston-Jones: 09.26.10," *Artforum* (September 26, 2010), http://artforum.com/words/id=26489. Interview with Ishmael Houston-Jones, Chris Cochrane, and Dennis Cooper, Berlin, August 16, 2012.

9. See Drury, "Response."

10. Lucas De Lima, "Infectious Nostalgia in Ishmael Houston-Jones, Dennis Cooper and Chris Cochrane's *Them*," *Montevidayo*, January 16, 2011, http://montevidayo.com/2011/01/infectious-nostalgia-in-ishmael-houston-jones-dennis-cooper-and-chris-cochranes-them/.

11. Interview with Houston-Jones, Cochrane, and Cooper, Berlin, August 16, 2012.

12. Filmed versions of the 1985, 1986, and 1987 performances of *Them* are held by the New York Public Library of the Performing Arts, Dance Division. *Them*, videotaped at PS 122, New York, May 12, 1985. Performed by Ishmael Houston-Jones, Dennis Cooper, and Chris Cochrane, with Donald Fleming and John B. Walker. Available at Performing Arts Research Collections—Dance (*MGZIA 4-7553); *Them*, videotaped at PS 122, New York, November 28, 1986. Performed by Ishmael Houston-Jones, Dennis Cooper, Chris Cochrane, Barry Crooks, Donald Fleming, Julyen Hamilton, Daniel McIntosh, and David Zambrano. Lighting by Carol McDowell. Available at Performing Arts Research Collections—Dance (*MGZIA 4-7534); and *Them*, videotaped in performance at the Du Maurier Centre, Toronto, Canada, as part of the Harbourfront Festival, in 1987. Performed by Ishmael Houston-Jones, Dennis Cooper, and Chris Cochrane, with Barry Crooks, Almon Grimsted, Benoît Lachambre, Daniel McIntosh, and Brian Moran. Available at Performing Arts Research Collections—Dance (*MGZIA 4-7545).

13. William Seaman, "Recombinant Poetics and Related Database Aesthetics," in *Database Aesthetics: Art in the Age of Information Overflow (Electronic Mediations)*, ed. Victoria Vesna (Minneapolis: University of Minnesota Press, 2007), Kindle electronic ed., loc. 1644.

14. Ibid., loc. 1646.

15. *New York Daily News*, March 13, 2014.

FURTHER READING

DeFrantz, Thomas F. "To Make Black Bodies Strange: Social Critiques in Concert Dance of the Black Arts Movement." In *A Sourcebook of African-American Performance: Plays, People, Movements*, edited by Annemarie Bean, 83–93. London: Routledge, 1999.

Houston-Jones, Ishmael. "On Burt Supree." *Movement Research Performance Journal: Heroes and Histories* 6 (Spring/Summer 1993): 5.

Houston-Jones, Ishmael. "Performance Strategies." *Performing Arts Journal* 10, no. 3 (1987): 36.

MARIANA IBAÑEZ AND SIMON KIM

NEW BODIES, NEW ARCHITECTURE

The body has a long tradition as the primary agent in the design and occupation of our buildings and cities. Our physiognomy, proportions, and sensate corporeal agencies that process external phenomena, internalizing them as stimuli and cognition, are the performance-based criteria for the spaces we design. From the harmonies of the Vitruvian figure and its contemporaneous drawings of body as basilica, to the augmentation of human geometries at the Bauhaus and by Le Corbusier, the human form has been architecture's metric.

In his *Triadic Ballet* (1922), Oskar Schlemmer extended, as well as limited, the human body's range of actions through the use of devices and costumes. Schlemmer put on stage a new construct of human kinesiology, created amid the automation generated by industrialization and the Werkbund movement. The use of diagrams and notation systems implemented at the Bauhaus by Schlemmer and László Moholy-Nagy provided graphic interfaces through which to design these new performances. For example, the *Sketch for a Score for a Mechanized Eccentric* by Moholy-Nagy integrated human performance, sound, and lighting in a single diagram.

As one of the primary reference points for the design and production of architecture, the body and its capacities of motion provide order and function to architectural space and structures. Notation of design is a feature shared by choreography and architectural design, utilized in both for its preservation and realization. Within the domain of ballet and other theater dance forms, architecture has conventionally focused on the production and design of stage sets, environments in which the performance occurs. The drawing and design of the building or the set are held in its collection of materials—its archive—and within the experience of performers and audience.

While a dance can be preserved in notation, the performed event can only linger in the viewer's memory. Because its primary medium is the body, the experience of the dance is ephemeral; only recently have new technologies been able to record it significantly as moving images. New technologies, however, can extend human performance into digital signals that may be interpreted in computation and reenacted in variable output.

With the widespread use of personal computers and accessible robotics,

293

the past thirty years have yielded various models of proportioning and part-to-whole systems. If Schlemmer drew the human form within abstract geometries and mechanized its movements, the cyborg body is freed from physicality and type. This freedom makes possible the body's ability to participate in an evolving series of different and variable formats and forms. The ubiquity of technology is not exclusively an external condition. As the surface of the body is potentially altered or enhanced by technology, its transformations can also be absorbed within (e.g., implants or other internal additions) or expressed as anomalies on the exterior. These anomalies can be visible, producing changes in symmetry, proportion, composition, or any other enhancements that wearable computing can provide. These anomalies may also be invisible. Such transformations can augment the body's occupation of time and space, allowing us to see farther, be stronger, hear formerly inaudible sounds, and so forth.

In her now classic essay, "A Cyborg Manifesto: Science, Technology, and Socialist-Feminism in the Late Twentieth Century," Donna Haraway speculates that fusions of technology with bodied and social dimensions of the human, such as gender and race, will not only radically shift the boundaries of these identifiers but also contribute to the reinvention of power and social structures.[1] In Haraway's scenario, bodily enhancement is an option, but there are other possibilities that might facilitate more fundamental transformations. If our capacity to communicate with other agents—human as well as nonhuman—is developed, the human body and the architectural body become analogous. For designers, this cross-linking of disciplines, devices, and human limits allows for an open and flexible merger of systems that previously were locked in place with static, inert geometries. This technological cyborg in architecture allows human occupancy to dynamically manifest change in real time, as required.

Our first work with dance was a collaboration with two co-choreographers in conjunction with a university robotics lab and kinematics group that engage in team research and projects bringing together engineering, design, and computing.[2] This production was generated around the synthetic idea of the human-nonhuman agency of dance. This transmediated performance was a shared and collective expression among humans, robotic appendages, and wearable devices. All of these agents and the relationships manufactured among them were considered to be equal participants in the dance. The normal hierarchy of human performers, with tools or props in service to them, was replaced by a network model in which the dance comprised the relationship of modular robots and humans performing together. The aspect of performance in which humans are normally given the primary focus was shifted to be shared with the mechanical and digital performers on stage. The robotic arms were called "the divas" for their exasperating tendency to refuse to work or to respond in expected ways.

The first rehearsals included a reading and a discussion of Haraway's essay, as well as serial, experimental interactions of performers with several machines devised to be worn or to behave in particular ways. One "wearable" device emitted smoke based on proximity sensing; another read the acceleration and positioning of the dancer, using a sensor found on many smartphones, and relayed and translated that information to interactive geometries projected onto surfaces of the performance area. Other machines could roll and crawl. This series of rehearsals evolved into a laboratory in which the unique physical space of the theater, once a church meeting room, as well as the interplay of human and machines, yielded a hybrid of choreography and architecture. The limits of wireless signal transmission became the limit of human movement; the range of motion of the body's joints became the degrees of freedom for the servomotors.

For this performance, architectural design and choreography overlapped; we designed the sensitivity of the interaction and responded to the speed of human movement. We then had to create meaningful and communicative exchanges for the audience, who could only experience the moment of performance itself. There would be nothing left in steel and glass as a referent. The choreographers would likewise need to respond to the behavior of the nonhuman performers. The dancers practiced and drilled so that their movements became the lingua franca of the digitally stimulated movement. The stage set also became simplified to a desk and a cubic formation of robot arms that came to life only with human interaction. Movement and kinetics were driven by the synthesis of human dancer, digital geometric dancer, and robotic linkage dancers, but only in the space and duration of the event.

In this scenario, in which human bodies and architectural bodies are analogous, traditional disciplines undergo a shift. Architecture as a stable, inert collection of geometric material becomes a continual condition of difference and reordering. Body, architecture, and environment are all part of a multiagent system that promotes exchange. It is in the space and time of the event that this exchange takes place. All of the digital signals could be stored and replayed—the linkages would flex, the polyhedra could swivel and flutter—but without the collective, there would be no meaning.

NOTES

1. Donna Haraway, "A Cyborg Manifesto: Science, Technology, and Socialist-Feminism in the Late Twentieth Century," in *Simians, Cyborgs and Women: The Reinvention of Nature* (New York: Routledge, 1991), 149–81.

2. Immersive Kinematics, a research group directed by Simon Kim and Mark Yim, aims to integrate robotics, interaction, and embedded intelligence with architecture. The Modular Robotics Lab (ModLab) is a research group within the Mechanical Engineering and Applied Science Department at the University of Pennsylvania, under the supervision of Professor Mark Yim.

ANDRÉ LEPECKI

CHOREOGRAPHIC ANGELOLOGY

PART I: CRITIQUE OF FLOW, ACTIVITY OF ANGELS

In a letter dated February 23, 1793, Friedrich Schiller called upon his experience of watching an English country dance to describe what an ideal free society should look like, and moreover, how it should move:

> I know of no better image for the ideal of a beautiful society than a well-executed English dance, composed of many complicated figures and turns. A spectator located on the balcony observes an infinite variety of criss-crossing motions which keep decisively but arbitrarily changing directions without ever colliding with each other. Everything has been arranged in such a manner that each dancer has already vacated his position by the time the other arrives. Everything fits so skillfully, yet so spontaneously, that everyone seems to be following his own lead, without ever getting in anyone's way. Such a dance is the perfect symbol of one's own individually asserted freedom as well as of one's respect for the freedom of the other.[1]

In Schiller's project of an aesthetic state (Aesthetischer Staat), the uninterrupted, apparently "spontaneous" flow of this particular dance demonstrated the possibility of a perfect society just as it expressed the ideal degree of freedom one could hope to achieve in it. It is telling that such an ideal of freedom could be properly represented by dancers performing and sustaining unimpeded, free-flowing, fluid movement. Schiller's image has fixed itself as central to the political and aesthetic imagination of the West; bodies engaged in ongoing, fluid motion become exemplary of an ideal body politic. As Paul de Man writes: "The Schillerian aesthetic categories, whether we know it or not, are still the taken-for-granted premises of our own pedagogical, historical, and political ideologies."[2] Versions of this kind of choreography appear even today as vivid emblems of a desired society.[3] In this sense, Schiller's description has perversely fixed dance as subservient to some dubious aesthetic-political ideals of aligning danced movement with (the illusion of) an ongoing fluid circulation of bodies, moving without impediments and without collisions across a populous yet magically uncluttered space.

Within half a century Schiller's image became an aesthetic imperative and a philosophical-political cliché in regard to movement. As Hillel Schwartz has demonstrated, between 1840 and 1930 flow emerged as a pervasive concern in the arts, science, pedagogy, and industry. Flow mobilized ideology, pedagogy, aesthetics, politics, and technology informing and being informed by scientific discourse, particularly physics. The articulation between a moving toward modernism in dance and an increased capitalist implementation of free-flowing movement became the grounds for a new, supposedly efficient and healthy, normative subjectivity. Schwartz called this supremacy of flow "the new kinaesthetic" for the twentieth century: a century-old process of activation and reification of flow as the great rescuer of both subjects and nations. Its political-kinetic order was conjoined: "fluid movement flowing out of the body center" as expression and promoter of "sincerity" (both social and psychological) and of "health" (individual and national).[4] The physics of flow became the template through which a whole system of incorporations could be framed as socially, clinically, and aesthetically ideal.

A few consequences ensued: from this image of flow as social ideal a corresponding, symmetrical, and parallel image of repression, censorship, and tyranny as blocking or antiflow emerged. Indeed, even the most clear-minded of philosophers seem to have fallen into this political-kinetic dichotomy predicated on the physics of flow coming from the seventeenth and eighteenth centuries. Gilles Deleuze, in an interview in the mid-1980s, described the essential difference between Left politics and Right politics as a difference predicated on the latter's main objective of always "blocking movement."[5] In an interview also in the 1980s, Jacques Derrida equated a feminist revolution with a dance that "would not lag or trail behind its time"—indicating once again that the aesthetic-political ideals, once linked to choreography and dance, remained close to Schiller's image of a flawless evolution of fluid bodies in space, without bumps, stumbles, tripping, delays, or blockages.[6] In many ways, this is indeed so; tyranny and repression aim at restricting *certain* movements. But in the logic of our neoliberal times, strict control and harsh discipline promote widespread "interpassivity"[7]: a constant motion in previously established and monitored streams of "networking," in which "logistics" imposes smooth circulation so that capital may profit from its harnessing of flow.[8] Within this logic, we find that the highest degree of conformity is to succumb and to serve a physics of flawless flow that both precedes and forecloses one's political, historical, and aesthetic agency: notably, one's capacity to opt for a different kind of movement.

Among all this praise of flow an intriguing text—which one of its most astute readers, Paul de Man, has directly linked to Schiller's influential musings on the merits of English dance—appeared as a stumbling block: first, because it historically announced "the new kinaesthetic" almost verbatim some three decades before its clear articulation, and second, because it denounced in lucid and deep ways the pitfalls of a sociability and a dancing subservient to flow. I am referring to Heinrich von Kleist's *Über der Marionettentheater* (*On the Marionette Theater*, 1810).[9] At face value, it seems that this short text had a simple, single, point: to affirm how puppets and animals are superior dancers compared to humans, since both achieve a "naturalness of movement" that relieves them from "the exertions of the dance" and from those humanly unavoidable moments of "rest," which, as one of the characters in the text tells us, "are clearly not part of the dance."[10] As we will see, Kleist's notion of flow as grace seems to have replicated the ideals of physics in the classical age, as historiographed by Michel Serres. But Kleist's ironic verve (which Paul de Man does not cease to emphasize) opened up the possibility of reading his parable as a possible stab against Schiller's project of affirming flow's hegemony over choreographic, political, and aesthetic imagination. Kleist identified movements immanent to humanity not as flow, but as *exertion, hesitation, affect,* and *persistence.* Exhaustion, to make flow stumble and to infuse dance with resting, only to start it again, is what Kleist called "History."

In this essay I am proposing a political-choreographic critique of the still strong notion of flow as dance's—and sociality's and economy's—privileged identity and goal. I do so aided by two quite different philosophers—Walter Benjamin and Michel Serres—who at certain crucial points in their ouevres considered the importance of standstills, of blockings, of viscosity as essential for a renewed understanding of how movement relates to the notions of political agency and history. Since what unites their very different analyses is one very particular figure, I have titled this essay after it: angelology, the science of angels.

My proposal is that through Serres's and Benjamin's divergent understandings of angels and their kinetic-historical (and in Benjamin at least, political) functions, some of the recent and quite extraordinary work by choreographer Ralph Lemon and his collaborator Walter Carter may be assessed politically. I propose that their collaboration, spanning the years 2003–2010, succeeded in escaping the still operative Schillerian physics of fluid, unimpeded movement flow as political-aesthetic ideal and embraced a kind of critical viscosity, what Fred Moten has called, with regard to Lemon's work, "the blackness of physics."[11]

My hope is that, through Michel Serres's critique of a physics of flow as essentially "anti-historical," through Walter Benjamin's image of "angel of history," and through Ralph Lemon's and Walter Carter's black physics of choreographic angelology, a renewed political-aesthetic choreographic paradigm may emerge, attentive to the force derived from viscosities and blockings, from non-fluid hesitations, to those elements Kleist saw as being so deeply constitutive of the human. This kind of dance—exhausting because endlessly persistent, hesitant because it knows that to move is to co-complicate what only illusion offers as smooth ground, body, or history—this choreography of standstills allows for something called history to actually take place and for something called dance, as Ralph Lemon and Walter Carter perform it, to open spaces, inflect times, and persist in and as history.

PART II: ANTIHISTORY FLOWS, THE GENERIC DANCER, AND THE NEW PHYSICS

> Physics' ideal implies the suppression, the erasure, the scrubbing, of history.
> —Michel Serres

Physics

Perhaps what Michel Serres writes about the advent of physics as a modern science, from the late seventeenth to the late nineteenth centuries, could also be applied to the founding and consolidation of that newly developing art of embodied physics: choreography. Perhaps, as Serres demonstrates, the suppression of history by physics as a precondition for its enunciation of universal laws of motion governing bodies also constituted choreography's ideological substratum, more evident as the latter became increasingly focused on the propulsion and display of body in and as unimpeded flow, what Hillel Schwartz called "new kinaesthetics."

If choreography, like physics, is an antihistorical discipline, the success of choreography as a new technology of transmission, expression, propagation, and preservation of movement as flow would require a substantive change in the relationship between dancer and dance, a change revealing the point of articulation among subjectivity, embodiment, historicity, and scientific reasoning. Under the antihistorical ideal of the new science of physics, choreography systematized dance as an art of transmission of physical forces. By doing so, it redefined the image of the dancer under two main *affects*, which in turn would redefine the dancer's ideal professional, corporeal, psychological, and personal qualities. Those affects were a capacity to absorb and introject any movement coming from an exterior (authorial) source/force and a capacity to repeat those movements, not only exactly, but upon demand, undistorted, anytime, anywhere. This dancer had absolute capacity for reception, absolute capacity for retention, and absolute capacity for expression, but managed under an imperative to move and be forged in this new fusion between a *memory impervious to history* and an *obedience introjected as free will*. Rather than being perceived as historically grounded *sources* of movement, the implementation of choreography as art of motion, as physics aestheticized, required turning dancers into antihistorical *vehicles* for movement.

As vehicles for flow, as vehicles in flow, dancers started to be treated, perceived, and self-perceived less as experiential agents or critical sources of their own mobility (i.e., as subjects endowed with historical consciousness, able to include and transform their movements because of their experiencing of historicity) and more as passive and ideally neutral media, through which the whole antihistorical physics of movement traversed. In order to serve flow, dancers had to become as fluids, which were treated in the seventeenth century by the new physics of Isaac Newton and W. G. Leibniz as "eternally virgin wax tables, even if continually traversed [by physical forces]."[12]

Neutral media, traversed by movement, of which they became mere vehicles—such were the components of the "ideal dancer" under the antihistorical, and yet scientific, new physics coemerging with the new choreographic regime. By 1810 the ideal dancer was the object of a fine analysis and a few ironic stabs and commentary by Kleist in his *On the Marionette Theater*, a parable on the fate of human dancers once they fall prey to an aesthetic discipline subservient to "the laws of motion." As is well known, the main thesis of the text was "how consciousness could disturb the natural grace of man," thus making beasts and marionettes superior dancers.[13]

Certainly this ideal dancer remained a fantasy, a horizon. However, this does not mean this fantasy would not act as both telos and emblem of a kinetically bound choreographic impetus, organizing the field of possible compositions, regimenting perceptions, disciplining bodies, harnessing forces, and reconditioning the relations between movement and the management and activation of bodies serving movement. Under such impetus, the dancer's task, the choreographer's ethics, as well as the public's perceptual regimes, revealed their mutual co-confinement and complicity with physics' project and became a major impediment in imagining dance as the experiencing of history.

Angels

> Solids are also, evidently, a medium of propagation. But, in relation to fluids, they are, also, a place of preservation.
>
> —Michel Serres

Because in this ideal-fantastical mode of imagining and implementing choreographic production the reception, storage, and expression of movement by a dancer should take place with zero distortion or noise, it follows that the dancer's memory must also be trained, plied, carefully selected, and certainly disciplined so as to be absolutely faithful in regard to the instructions it receives. The dancer's particular form of memory must be, just like the episteme informing the classical physics that forms it, both absolutely reliable in terms of keeping track of movement information and absolutely impervious to history—or rather, absolutely *immune to the effects of historicity*, if we understand the latter as a critical-perceptual awareness regarding the effects of social, historical, cultural, racial, and economic forces upon the formation of subjectivities, corporealities, discourses, and their performances.

It is in the work of the dancer that the constitutive paradox of physics becomes clearest: universal laws of motion imply an absolutely (meta)stable medium for motion, but one in which, *even if time passes, history leaves no mark*. Under this antihistorical physics a choreographic ideal emerges: dancers must be absolute servants of the authorial memory they store without distortion, buffered as they must be from the critical effects of experiencing history. It is under this particular fusion of semiotic obedience, ahistorical memory, and noiseless performance that the dancer becomes, literally, *angelical*. I use both the adjective, angelical, and the noun, angel, in their most traditional sense to signify a *perfect messenger*: one whose relationship to the message is absolutely devoid of authorial agency, a performer's interpretation, or simple semiotic distortion. The angel is that being who perfectly serves perfect transmission. Angel: ideal transmitter, noiseless medium, absolute servant.

Serres has written a whole philosophy of angels predicated on this notion (motion) of an ideal being who serves the purpose of being the carrier of a transmission without noise: "The angels are the messages; their very body is a message. . . . We are talking about *delivery people*, relational bodies."[14] What Serres tends to neglect in his celebratory angelology, in which angels work just as ideal dancers—that is, as servants of flow—is the fact that angels, like ideal dancers, are transmitters of someone or something else's messages.[15] They are indeed "delivery people"—but absolutely flawless in their labor, as they efficiently flow toward their destinies, perfectly delivering what has to be delivered: the master's message, the master's will, undistorted. This is why, for Serres, angels are embodied metaphors, in the etymological sense of metaphor as transportation.

Choreography as antihistorical physics is thus a perfect partner to an angelology of perfect servants. Choreography as the physics of affectless and compliant "delivery people," "whose body is a message," reinforces and displays as spectacle a whole philosophical, scientific, semiotic, and hierarchical system predicated on the specific labor of "delivery people" who, because they must perfectly store and perfectly deliver their (authorial) messages, must remain absolutely immune to the effects of historical experience or consciousness. They are movers without agency, speakers without voice, whose trajectories cannot deviate from the logistics of flows. Dancers as angels, as servants of messages, live in a temporality that cannot partake of historical time lest critical introjection and incorporation of experiencing (i.e., historicity) shake their confidence in the smooth physics of perfectly transmitted motion as message.

Serres posits that modernity's space, but also the space of our contemporaneity, completely coincides with "angel space," made of "messengers, the systems of mailmen, of transmissions in the act of passing or the space through which they pass."[16] It follows that we can also define both spaces as *choreographic space*. What is contemporary subjectivity to do within this hegemony of choreographic angelology but to wish to become also a perfect "delivery person?" In other words, it would become a mix of being for movement and being for transportation, both cargo and passive agent. The perfect angel becomes a delivery person under the antihistorical impetus of a physics that propels the logistics of permanently dispatched subjects as cargo as clear messages. This is the ideal dancer's image under the physics of angels, the choreography of antihistorical dancers.

Flow

> And yet he believed that even the last trace of human volition to which he referred could be removed from the marionettes, that their dance could be transferred completely to the realm of mechanical forces and that it could be produced . . . by turning a handle.
> —Heinrich von Kleist

It is indeed this fantasy, this fantastical construction of the body of the dancer as angelical being, that informed Kleist's *On the Marionette Theater*, one of the more persistent narratives on the dancer's burden under the choreographic regime. This often quoted and endlessly interpreted short text, written a year before Kleist took his own life in a double suicide, is a treatise on the relationships among intention, expression, history, antihistory, affects, subjectivity, and a certain ideal physics of flow.

The verdict of *On the Marionette Theater* is well known: the human body is not capable of graceful dance since it is filled with too many affectations. Psychological life, vanity, subservience to representational conventions, and personal as well as aesthetic expectations all prevent the smooth delivery of movements, the alignment between humanity and physics. But in animals and in marionettes, the flow of movement is unimpeded; thus these beings express nothing other than the transport of flow itself. The marionette expresses a movement whose source clearly transcends it (the puppeteer's intentions or commands, transmitted purely in a physical manner by the propagation of physical forces through strings), while the animal expresses a movement whose source is apparently immanent, interior; but since it is of the nature of the animal to be *in* nature *and* to be *of* nature, this immanence is tied (immediately and forever) to the transcendental plane of God *as* nature, of God *as* physics. Marionettes and animals benefit from that particular characteristic that binds the mechanical with the beastly: a nonhistorical nature, which extracts them from consciousness and, most important, from self-consciousness. Through their shared lack of affectation and shared lack of historicity, puppets and beasts are perfect dancers because they are perfectly angelical: pure transporters, delivery laborers faithfully committed to the perfect propagation of a movement that is not theirs. In other words, puppets and animals execute, display, and transmit—but do not *perform*.

Humans, as they stand stuck among the divine, the animal, and the machine, can only expect to dance affectedly, in other words, without fluidity, without grace, without that "natural disposition of the limbs" typical of physics. The problem is that as much as they may want to yield to choreographic angelology, it is always a specific *he* or a specific *she*, in a specific *situation*, who dances. Someone is always the one who is performing, and performing is always the brutal activation of a precariousness that reveals that to dance even the most exact of scores is always to experience physics as deep historical turbulence. Arrests, returns, hesitations, viscosities, affect, desire, delirium, and imbalance are historicity's other names.

Work

> To work today is to be asked, more and more, to do without thinking, to
> feel without emotion, to move without friction, to adapt without question,
> to translate without pause, to desire without purpose, to connect without
> interruption.
> — Stefano Harney and Fred Moten

The consolidation of the understanding of transmission and movement via
agents who are simultaneously messengers, media, and messages represents
nothing other than the consolidation of choreographic angelology as hegemony—what Harney and Moten have called "logisticality": the recent transformation in the system of subjectivation in current capitalism where what matters
above all is the smooth circulation of goods, "to free the flow of goods from
'human time' and 'human error.'"[17] Their notion of logisticality mirrors both
choreography's and angelology's production of a population endowed with the
capacity to store memory but asked, even compelled, to rid themselves of the
capacity to critically embody, experience, and express history's effects upon
memory: "Logistical populations will be created *to do without thinking*, to feel
without emotion, *to move without friction*, to adapt without question, to translate
without pause, to connect without interruption, or *they will be dismantled and dis-
abled as bodies.*"[18]

If "logistics wants to dispense with the subject altogether,"[19] it is also true
that it wants to dispense with a certain kind of body altogether, get rid of a certain critical-historical or agential-historical way of embodying *experientially* or
consciously. Angelology as logisticality founds an affective-disciplinary choreographic regime under which the dancer (the subject in motion) must be content
to be metaphor, pure transportation, a translator-translation endowed with the
inhuman task of never disremembering, of never misplacing the memory of a
movement demand, of never losing a stored sign or mark.

Either one succumbs to the antihistorical physics of choreographic angelology and becomes a logistical being—a member of a people condemned to
perpetually move according to an image of movement as endlessly perpetual,
becoming a subjectivity always ready to deliver without pause, reflection,
thought, questioning, or interruption what has been dispatched for (the always
urgent) delivery—or one faces dismemberment and exclusion. Ironically, it is
in the capacity to experience the violence of literal or figurative dismemberment
and exclusion that one may actually discover the historical experience of em-

bodiment, of racial and gendered histories and experiences, and thus use that violence as a countermove through which another kind of historical, or critical-historical, embodiment may erupt.

Incoherence

> The fluid potential of the paradisiacal body cannot be restored; the fall cuts humans off from fellowship with angels.
> —Karma deGruy

> A fluid does not preserve any mark, any impression: neither air of my trajectory, nor water of my swim. . . . Thus, a fluid has no history because it has no memory. It is not a stockpile of preserved marks.
> —Michel Serres

Serres demonstrates how the new physics postulated "a world whose continuity assured coherence," but only if that world was "a world without solids."[20] If Serres tells us that classic physics sees the coherence of the world emerging from the antihistorical condition of fluids, Kleist shows us something extraordinary taking place. For Kleist, it is not so much the air that does not preserve any trace or vestige of a body's trajectory. It is the puppet, or the beast, that also does not preserve impressions or vestiges. Kleist's description of a puppet's relation to the movement transmitted to it, namely how a puppet expresses movement fluidly, exactly, isomorphically, and only as long as movement is being transmitted to it, ceasing to express it as soon as "the emission [from the puppeteer] stops," reveals how, for Kleist, even if a puppet is a hard solid, choreographically, it must behave as a fluid: "Fluid elements . . . are wax tablets, eternally virgin, even though continually traversed."[21] In other words, a puppet is not a thing, but an amnesiac propagating medium for the fluid expression of forces that traverse it. Kleist calls these forces "the puppeteer's soul," and they propagate through the strings and puppet as if these were a fluid, revealing the puppet as a medium "voluble and silent as much as we would want."[22] Just like a fluid, puppets have "no history, because there is no memory." Neither are they "a hoard of preserved marks," archival beings. This is the case for the animal as well, since in it this "hoard of preserved marks," this hard archive, also does not exist. The animal has no memory beyond the moment in which it is included. This *instantaneous* memory turns the body into "momentary spirit" or into "a spirit without memory," to use Leibniz's expression in describing fluids. This is why Kleist envisions the animal as lacking memory, history, and forever excluded from any possibility of having one, since the animal is fully within the plane of total movement.²³

Thus, if "continuity" is that which assures the world's "coherence," it follows that what is incoherent in the world is that interference called "the human." Incoherent interference is humanity's other name. The human is a "hard thing" (une chose dure), an impediment, a rent in the plenum. It is also a blocking of the universe's continuous, coherent flow. This blocking is not due to a physical attribute but rather to historicity as the active, necessary experiencing of affects and affectations. As de Man writes: "The text indeed evokes the puppet's dance as continuous motion. A nonformalized, still self-reflexive consciousness—a human dancer as opposed to a puppet—constantly has to interrupt its motions by brief periods of repose that are not part of the dance itself. They are the parabases of the ironic consciousness which has to recover its energy after each failure by reinscribing the failure into the ongoing process of a dialectic."²⁴

This peculiar dialectic process, which reinscribes failures or fissures as the human task before the choreographic-angelic imperative of flow, rescues memory from its passive role to an active modality of historical experience, historicity. Historicity or humanity: synonyms naming a critical interruption of flow, an altogether different task for choreography, one informed by, and activating, historical consciousness *as performance*. Be it personal, be it civilizational, be it even theatrical in the sense that a dancer acquires and produces history through rehearsal, through repetition, historical consciousness is above all both antilogistical and antiangelical—because it is, above all, sticky. Historicity's viscosity produces a fundamental crisis in the choreographic fantasy of the dancer as metaphor, as angel, as pure subject for transportation, as affectless delivery person. It is because history is allowed to stick as memory and to make memory stick that another kind of movement performance may erupt to free choreography from its participation in the logistics of angelology. Slippery, viscous, critically hesitant, fully affective, agential, and unconcerned with the imperative to deliver without distortion, this is movement whose performance disturbs the fantasies of choreographic angelology, of antihistorical choreographic logisticality. It follows that historicity, historical consciousness, and the embracing of the experiencing that "the movement of things will not cohere"²⁵ allow the dancer to find for herself a work less as angel and more as agent. Here an inevitable crisis of flow, a crisis in the fluidity of flow, is introduced by the nonangelical dancer, correlative to a crisis in the dancer's subjectivity as crisis in and of the project of choreographic (authorial) primacy.

If the dancer still wants to aspire to any kind of angelical qualities—for instance by refusing to be mere messenger or transporter, mere "delivery person" within the violence of logisticality and yet truly embrace that other aspect of the angel's labor, to become a true "relational body" and add to her dance the critical marks of the labor of her memory, the labor of her transporting, and the effort of her delivering—then the dancer has only one option: to do so as an angel of history. This is Walter Benjamin's angel. But this is also Ralph Lemon's and Walter Carter's angel.

PART III: BLACK VISCOSITY, ANGELS OF HISTORY, AND PERFORMANCE'S TASK

> An imperative is implied here: to pay attention to (black) performances since it is left to those who pay such attention to re-theorize essence, representation, abstraction, performance, being.
> — Stefano Harney and Fred Moten

> Later, charged with the blackness of physics, its extralegal social surrealities, in search of conceptual thaw having survived the river's violent floes and squalls, its seizing distancing, but drawn to the river of the river of rivers, Lemon began a long series of residencies in itinerance.
> — Fred Moten

History

In the opening minutes of How can you stay in the house all day and not go anywhere? (2010) choreographer Ralph Lemon sits alone on a white plastic chair, stage right, facing the audience. Behind him a large screen projects images of a very old black man, Walter Carter, whom Lemon calls his teacher, going about some mundane, as well as some improbable, tasks: climbing into a jittery, homemade spaceship; slow dancing with his wife in a crowded living room; walking in a forest wearing a sparkly-silvery astronaut costume. Sometimes the sequences in which Walter appears are cut by scenes from Andreï Tarkovski's Solaris (1972) or Yazujirô Ozu's Late Spring (1949). The video and Lemon's monologue last about twenty minutes. This is what Lemon reads to his audience, early on:

> Solaris came out in 1972. Thirty years later, in 2002, while in Mississippi researching for Come home Charley Patton, I met Mr. Walter Carter. Purportedly the oldest man in Yazoo City, Mississippi. Fifty years or so shy of being a full-time slave. But he was an ex-sharecropper, carpenter, gardener . . . his longest job was planting cedar trees.

We began a creative discussion about our whereabouts, our bodies, our
  belief systems, and mortality, through the most ineffable of languages,
  his and mine.

[*little pause*]

(When I first met Walter he showed me some juke joint dances, dances he
  had danced when he was 18 or so, old dances formed on the spot of his
  memory at that moment. I think he had not done them since he had
  done them 80 years before. And, at the moment he was dancing the "one
  step," the "two step," the "slow drag," he was remembering them and
  dancing them, on the spot.)

[*short pause*]

Walter and Edna, who they are and what they represent, cannot be staged.
  It is a symbolic exchange. Perhaps they are (memory) avatars, collapsing
  past present and future time.[26]

A choreographer, sitting, reading, reminisces about someone he calls his
teacher, his collaborator, his friend, someone who, the choreographer tells us,
"likes to hear about God." The choreographer also remembers and evokes the
illness and death of his partner, Asako Takami, with whom he watched Ozu's
and Tarkovski's films in the months preceding her death. In a kind of response
to his centenarian teacher's likings, the choreographer anchors his musings on
personal loss, time lost, and time regained by reading from Walter Benjamin's
1940 essay *Thesis on the Philosophy of History*—the last manuscript to be completed
by the German philosopher, just two months before his suicide, escaping the
German invasion of France. Lemon reads from the opening paragraph of the
often-quoted thesis IX. By doing so, he confronts his dance, his dancers (Djédjé
Djédjé Gervais, Darrell Jones, Gesel Mason, Okwui Okpokwasili, David Thomson, and Omagbitse Omagbemi), his teacher Walter Carter, his collaborator
Edna Carter, and his audience with the gaze of a very particular angel. As the
large video projection shows Walter Carter in a silvery spacesuit climbing up
into a homemade spaceship, Lemon reads about what the German philosopher
called, after a drawing by Paul Klee, *Angelus Novus*—literally, the new angel. What
does it mean for a choreographer to read about an angel of history, as he evokes
the work of 102-year-old Walter Carter, with whom Lemon activated old dances,
as well as uncharted futures? Lemon reads:

The angel would like to stay, awaken the dead, and make whole what has
  been smashed. But a storm is blowing in from Paradise; it has caught in

his wings with such a violence that the angel can no longer close them. The storm irresistibly propels him into the future to which his back is turned, while the pile of debris before him grows skyward. This storm is what we call progress.[27]

Because what frames and activates the quotation is a dance piece, we are thus, right from the start, before a kind of Kleistian variation, where all the main elements structuring *On The Marionette Theater* reappear, even if recast: a choreographer's dancer who is also his master and his collaborator and who likes to hear about God will be told a story by his pupil, who is also his choreographer and his collaborator, about a new angel whose wings are bound—just like a puppet's limbs are tied to their strings—to the winds of a storm "blowing in from Paradise." Because this storm is called "progress," the name of the new angel, whose flight is partially directed by the storm's force, can only be angel of history.

Similarly to Kleist, once paradise has been blown open by humanity's fall, there is no coming back. To be human is to endure the storm of history. But this is also where the parallels between Kleist's and Benjamin's evocations of movement in the plenum of living, movement in regard to historical agency, start to diverge. Because what Benjamin, Ralph Lemon, and Walter Carter show is that *even the angelical is subjected to the forces of history*. Angels appear less as delivery people, delegated performers, or perfect messengers flowing above the fray of human affairs, and more as inescapably subjected to, and acting upon, the effects of history. In this, angels of history are a para-human category. Their task is to remind us that even if we are inescapably bound by the powerful winds of history, our task is to "set sail"—and to find within that apparently overwhelming propulsion occasions for deviations from the apparently inescapable route. The angel of history may not be able to close his wings, but perhaps he may be able to slightly reset them so that his backward motion may lead to another place. Perhaps.

This reverberating partnership between historical storm and the fleeting witness of its wreckage turns the angel from delivery person, perfect servant, or passive carrier of someone else's message into a new kind of dancer. His body stands as the fibrillating membrane of historical experience, both border and articulator of past, present, and future. The angel of history dances the impossible sutures and constitutive ruptures of historical time.

Minor

> That country, that broken body, is black. That crossed, broken border is also a
> broken vessel.
> —Fred Moten

How can you stay in the house all day and not go anywhere? is an altogether different conception of choreographic angelology, sutured together by Ralph Lemon, Walter Carter, Edna Carter, Walter Benjamin, and all the others in the ensemble. This is an angelology taking place in history thanks to Lemon's choreographic project with a dancer who is a centenary man, who is also a memory avatar, who is also the choreographer's master, and who performs the experience of his memory once this is activated by a true encounter. Thus, within the extraordinary amount of work cocreated by the two, we find Walter Carter performing dances he had not danced in eighty years—such as in *Derelict Architecture* (2006), the single-channel video in which Walter appears dancing alone on a rickety stage inside a ruined, roofless, empty theater in downtown Yazoo City, Mississippi. Black dances, dormant as cold cinders, are momentarily reactivated as a mix of memory and historical experience.

Walter's frailty is his strength. His dance emerges in its essential force, and what truly matters is the resurfacing of dance through the avatar of memory, scrambling past, present, and future in the ruination that builds the South. We enter a qualified, very specific, Kleistian situation, inflected by blackness as much as by Jewishness and are thus mobilized by a double history of violence and its historical movements. These movements are inflected by a doubling of living in fugitivity alongside the possibilities or impossibilities in which choreography can weave a time warp between pastness and futurity through a reconfigured notion of the dancer as reconfigured minor angel.

Performance

> The Southern question of travel makes a joyful noise and moves slowly in
> awareness. Now we can speculate on the relay of our common activity, make a
> circle round our errant roots. Dancing is what we make of falling. Music is what
> we make of music's absence, the real presence making music underneath. I'm
> exhausted so my soul is rested.
> —Fred Moten

Lemon's lesson from his work with Walter Carter is that a dancer as memory avatar collapses past, present, and future times into a new formation of temporality. In this new formation, motions are less the order of flow than an order of a certain kind of interference that is so human as to reconstitute the whole category of the angelical. We may call this interference performance, but only as long as performance is understood to be equivalent to "a chronopolitical act"— referencing the reconsiderations of temporality in Afrofuturism (of which Lemon's project would be a particular, if quite delicate, expression).[28]

The dancer becomes an active, interfering agent in this formulation: a being who fully embraces the viscosity of memory, the viscosity of futurity, the ephemeral precariousness of the present. The dancer works on the threshold of another kind of choreographic formation, in which precariousness and ephemerality are experienced and lived less as a sorrow regarding time passing than as the condition of matter, demanding two very specific affective responses: persistence and a will to return. To persistently interfere in and to constantly reactivate *material ephemerality* (ephemeral only because imprinted, ephemeral only because stored, ephemeral only because mnemonic); these are the conjoined tasks of the dancer as *angelus novus*, in this case the new angel or (black) angel of (minor) history. By performing these tasks again and again, a whole reconfiguration of the very category of the angelical takes place, a whole reconfiguration of the physics of dance takes place, one that simultaneously undoes and redoes Kleist's parable. This undoing that does something else is the performance of a certain more political, certainly historical, understanding of the choreographic.

Ephemeral

> A Talmudic legend has it that angels are created—a new one every instant and in uncountable cohorts—just to cease their hymn right after they have chanted it before God, and dissolve into the void. May the name of this magazine, *Angelus Novus*, signify that it achieves such actuality, which is the only true one.
> —Walter Benjamin

How remarkable that a perfect performance would require a singular being whose entire existence coincides perfectly, in absolute adherence, to its execution. To repeat the hymn of godly praise means to create an altogether new being dedicated exclusively to that hymn. Ephemerality here is not really about a time that passes or a performance that passes in time, but rather about a performing body that must be radically destroyed so that performance may remain intact; indeed, it may be impervious to passing into history, passing through history. As the Talmudic interpreter Todros Abulafia wrote in 1879 in his *Otzar Hakabad*, ephemerality here entails the endless production of bodies so they may endlessly be "disappearing like sparks on coal" in order that the same performance may take place.[29] Ephemerality's aftermath is not a memory of what has just happened. It is the antihistorical, endless piling up of extinguished bodies, cold cinders fully consumed by their single performance.

At first sight then, this is all profoundly disturbing regarding the possible hope both for the angel's agency and for finding agency in the dancer's work— as well as for the very idea of dancing performance's ephemeral urgency. Cohorts upon cohorts of uncountable numbers of bodies are discarded as each performance finishes. Cohorts upon cohorts of uncountable numbers of more bodies are born to deliver the same exact performance: repetition without variation; reproduction without differentiation. So both the plane of expression and plane of immanence may be one and the same before the face of the transcendental.

And yet if there is all this infinite violence—the violence of a life being consumed by the monomaniacal task of executing a perfect performance to praise a "master"—it is because the master perceives the deviant potential always embedded in performing. The master (dance master, god, or choreographer) perceives that even in the most dedicated delivery person there is always lurking an infinite danger: the danger of error, of botching the song, and the danger of deviation from the master plan.

It would have been conceivable to imagine one sole angel repeating the same one song eternally. And yet the fact that uncountable angels must be eternally produced and destroyed for just one song, that nothing can remain after the performance except a void filled with dark matter, that no repetition may ever be performed by any one angel, indicates the always lurking risk of repetition in itself, and the will to persist, bringing even to the most perfect of beings the turbulent risk of difference—of variation, of modulation, of erring—whether willed or accidental (if it is even possible to make such a distinction), whether a major variation or most minute.

Difference interferes. It is interfering matter. It interferes with matter. Thus, the most dangerous risk is not that of failing to perform, but of discovering in the sameness of the repetition the potential for variation, metamorphosis, invention. In other words, of finding differing derivations. The risk lies at the moment repetition opens up the possibility for a double transgression of the plane of the divine: the advent of historical consciousness and the activation of memory's imperfections. This is how the path to agency is carved: persistent repetition as survival of experience.

Disorientation

> Survival *disorientates history*.
> —Georges Didi-Huberman

A black angel of history performs his choreographic task of minor angelology: to disorientate history. Disorientating history scrambles the arrow of ephemerality that is heading toward a telos of disappearance and death. Disorientating history turns angels-messengers into archival agents—in the sense that Michel Foucault described the archive as being not "a storehouse" nor "the library of all libraries" but as "the system of formation and transformation of statements," which moreover "establishes that *we are* difference."[30] Kleist put history on a biblical path. The beginning and the end of history correspond to a circular path from absolute divine knowledge back to it. In between, human history is itself disorientation, interference, incoherence. This is why, if Kleist took his own theology seriously, there could only be poor human dancing. But this is also why only this poor dance—half broken, never fluid, incoherent, rushed by the crescendo of dying, fully aware of the materiality of ephemerality (whose other name, as Eleonora Fabião writes, is "precariousness"[31])—is politically powerful. It can politically interfere in history's course: "It is the unfinished accomplishment of a victory that finished accomplishment takes away."[32]

In the single-channel video *(the efflorescence of) Walter* (2008), we see Walter Carter going through different chores: digging a hole on the ground, smashing a porcelain white rabbit with a brick, placing an empty plastic cup under the rain to fill it with water, spreading a white paste (Crisco shortening) on a blue porcelain jar. As he digs the large hole, archaeologist of black matters' remains, his spade picks up three black vinyl LPs. All are intact. Carter grabs them, walks up to two nearby, rickety wooden shacks, and throws the records about on the ground, as if sowing the land. When he is done, he stands and then stoops—his task unfinished, yet accomplished.

Toward the end of the video Walter appears inside a room with a large window, standing by a workbench. He turns on a single lightbulb and places on top of the workbench shards of broken black vinyl LPs. With silver duct tape, he patiently proceeds to put the shards together, not always able to fit them perfectly but persisting in trying to mend what has been smashed. Broken records kind of mended, *kindly kind of mended*, by an angel of history, by centenary black hands of a centenary black dancer whom his choreographer calls angel of history and who knows how to both remember the distant past and how to forget the barely present. Walter's particular modes of remembering and forgetting are ethical and "chronopolitical acts": performance. Restored records as broken wholes, perhaps to be set spinning around their centripetal/centrifugal hole, without which nothing spins out, nothing may be preserved, nothing may be set into motion, no recording can resurface as ephemeral re-presenting of a persistent slice of the past. Black physics—seeped into broken records. The question that is activated by the mending hand and reactivated dances of Lemon's master, Lemon's dancer, Walter Carter, is *how to get time to work for dance.*

Matters

> There's one other thing that I know, that really matters, that Walter knows really matters, that if his body invokes one thing, only one thing, it is *the crescendo of dying.* He's that wildly alive.
> —Ralph Lemon

Every day a new angel; every day a new body. But this is bullshit. There is only this one body, persevering in insisting, to return every day. Yet one does not come back every day as a new body. One has to keep something of the past as much as one has to forget something of the past in order to perform this crucial return, this stubborn hanging on, despite, or perhaps thanks to, the crescendo. Forgetting is what makes the body all return, as long as it is synthesized through the viscosity of labor. "I ask Walter [Carter] what he thinks about the work we are doing all the time. And he says that he doesn't care, literally 'I don't care what this is.' If I ask him the next day what he did the day before he won't remember, but he will always say: 'It's fun.'"[33] Here again we return to the minor angels, to those creatures whose performance fuses with labor in unthinkable heat so that they may perform their only life labor song in praise of their sole master. For these minor angels, their mission is their performance, their only life, their only time—but a time filled exclusively by that which in actuality truly matters: absolute ephemerality of a labor life created for the sole purpose *of singing* for and before their master-creator. Ephemerality here is not a category of time as much as a category of existence, an existence in which the labor of performance is perfectly aligned with the persistence to perform. We can only think here of Georges Didi-Huberman's insight: "Time does not just flow: *it works.*"[34] Belaboring, time elaborates itself as labor, as work, working through whatever is worked through it. In the time of the black angel of history, the sparks of performance do not simply vanish into black coal, along with a single life. This is a particular angel who belabors time and ephemerality, one who moves toward a particular kind of work called survival: history's disorientation.

After spending a whole day working with Ralph Lemon on a series of short scenes and variously performing Lemon's movement scores and tasks, the choreographer asked Walter what he had done that day. "'I can't remember,' he answered. And then, 'a man and his chores, something like that.'"[35] Later, in his opening monologue in How Can You Stay in the House . . . , Lemon tells us, in a similar vein: "On the other hand, a few minutes after we had turned off the camera Walter had already forgotten that any of this ever happened. His brilliant critique."

"I can't remember," and yet, still going through the chores of performing, or reperforming, of learning and memorizing, of enacting, and forgetting, and remembering, and forgetting and inventing and returning to do it again, all day long. Not to remember, the most brilliant critique: forgetting as the repetitive, radiant performance of history's black angel and its black physics.

Black spark = immanent expression of a performance's singularity. Black cinder = the piling up of deaths and radical forgetting after each performance. Between them, the crescendo of dying is the wild vibration that kicks life into the choreography of a man's chores: choreographic angelology regained, through "the unfinished accomplishment of a victory that finished accomplishment takes away."[36]

Zone

> And in this zone, gap, void, where they diligently want to follow the rules but can't—that is where I want this work to live and flourish.
> —Ralph Lemon

In the zone, the South zone, the black zone, a black angel in silver spacesuit walks about. Walter, in the active worlds of solids. Around him, all is rust, dirt, and yet all is functioning, since exploitation ceaselessly reproduces its own history. Today as yesterday, as two centuries ago: different machines, same exploitation. Today as yesterday, as two centuries ago: different bodies, same resistance. This derelict South and its scarred ground open the single-channel video 1856 Cessna Road (2012). This is the landscape where Walter Carter as time traveler and memory avatar walks about breaking the rules that supposedly should regulate his pace, manner, and existence. His hesitations, quasi-stumbles, and persistent actions map the many ruptures, fissures, cracks (on the land, on bodies) produced by history in what should be—in the ideal fantasy of logistical capital, Schillerian dances, and physics dream—just smooth surface for flow. Walter bumps against bumps, solid force against brutal reality. Michel Serres points out that all that is solid "has a history" and as such "escapes the exact sciences."[37] Choreography as black physics, then: escaping the exactitude of exact sciences, performing a fugitive opening to another solidity of movement, releasing choreography and its subjects from the false promises of flow.

AUTHOR'S NOTE

This essay was subsequently developed for a chapter in my book *Singularities: Dance in the Age of Performance* (Routledge, 2016). In the current essay I am mostly concerned with developing a critique of flow, inspired by the collaborations between Ralph Lemon and Walter Carter. In the version I created for *Singularities* (subtitled "Remembering Is a Hard Thing"), I shift my attention to the obdurate qualities of historical remembrance that Lemon and Carter's collaborations also entail. Thus, each version supplements the other by offering a different emphasis on what I consider the main traits of choreographic angelology: (a) choreographic angelology proposes a political ontology of movement predicated on cuts and interruptions and (b) choreographic angelology insists on the dancer's choreopolitical task to treat historical memory not as ephemeral but as hard matter. Subjacent to both traits is the question of racial blackness and its particularly political physics.

NOTES

The epigraphs, in order of appearance, are from Michel Serres, *Hérmes II, L'Interférence* (Paris: Les Éditions de Minuit, 1972), 80; Serres, *Hérmes II*, 80; Heinrich von Kleist, "On the Marionette Theater" [1810], in *German Romantic Criticism: Novalis, Schlegel, Schleiermacher, and others*, ed. A. Leslie Willson (New York: Continuum, 2002), 239; Stefano Harney and Fred Moten, *The Undercommons: Fugitive Planning and Black Study* (Wivenhoe, UK: Minor Compositions, 2012), 87; Karma deGruy, "Desiring Angels: The Angelic Body in Paradise Lost," *Criticism* 54, no. 1 (Winter 2012): 120; Serres, *Hérmes II*, 78; Harney and Moten, *The Undercommons*, 49; Moten, *The Little Edges* (Middletown, CT: Wesleyan University Press, 2015), 19 (emphasis added); Moten, "The Case of Blackness," *Criticism* 50, no. 2 (Spring 2008): 201; Walter Benjamin quoted in Gershom Scholem, *Benjamin et Son Ange* (Paris: Rivages Poche, 1995); Georges Didi-Huberman, *L'Image Survivante* (Paris: Les Éditions de Minuit, 2002), 85; Ralph Lemon, "Four Years Later," in *Planes of Composition: Dance, Theory and the Global*, ed. André Lepecki and Jenn Joy (Calcutta: Seagull Press, 2009), 276 (emphasis added); and Lemon, *How can you stay in the house all day and not go anywhere?* (2010). All quotations from Serres's *Hérmes II*, Scholem's *Benjamin et Son Ange*, and Didi-Huberman's *L'Image Survivante* have been translated by the author.

    1. Paul De Man, "Aesthetic Formalization: Kleist's Über das Marionettentheater," in *The Rhetoric of Romanticism* (New York: Columbia University Press, 1984), 263.

    2. Paul De Man, "Aesthetic Formalization: Kleist's Über das Marionettentheater," in *The Rhetoric of Romanticism* (New York: Columbia University Press, 1984), 263–90, 266.

    3. See Andrew Hewitt, *Social Choreography* (Durham, NC: Duke University Press, 2005).

    4. See Hillel Schwartz, "Torque: The New Kinaesthetic of the Twentieth Century," in *Incorporations*, ed. Jonathan Crary and Sanford Kwinter (New York: Zone, 1992), 73, 79.

5. Gilles Deleuze, *Negotiations: 1972–1990* (New York: Columbia University Press, 1995), 127.

6. See Jacques Derrida and Christie McDonald, "Choreographies," *Diacritics* 12, no. 2 (Summer 1982): 66–76, 66.

7. See Claire Bishop, "Delegated Performance: Outsourcing Authenticity," *October*, no. 140 (Spring 2012): 91–112, 108.

8. See Stefano Harney and Fred Moten, *The Undercommons: Fugitive Planning and Black Study* (Wivenhoe, UK: Minor Compositions, 2012).

9. See Heinrich von Kleist, "On the Marionette Theater" [1810], in *German Romantic Criticism: Novalis, Schlegel, Schleiermacher, and Others*, ed. A. Leslie Willson (New York: Continuum, 2002), 238–44.

10. Ibid., 239–40.

11. Fred Moten, "Hard Enough to Enjoy" (paper presented at Conversations: Among Friends, Museum of Modern Art, New York, fall 2012). Published in Moten, *The Little Edges* (Middletown, CT: Wesleyan University Press, 2015), 19.

12. Serres, *Hérmes II*, 78.

13. See Kleist, "On the Marionette Theater," 242.

14. See Michel Serres and Bruno Latour, *Conversations on Science, Culture, and Time* [1990] (Ann Arbor: University of Michigan Press, 1995), 119 (emphasis added).

15. See especially his book *Angels, A Modern Myth* [1993] (Paris: Flammarion, 1995).

16. Serres and Latour, *Conversations on Science, Culture, and Time*, 119.

17. Harney and Moten, *The Undercommons*, 87–99, 91.

18. See ibid., 91 (emphasis added).

19. Ibid., 87.

20. Serres, *Hérmes II*, 67–68, 69.

21. Ibid., 78.

22. Ibid.

23. The animal introduces the question of velocities, since it anticipates a human's movement. This anticipation can be said to be a parallax effect: it is not so much the animal that is ahead of time, but the human's viscosity of being, its hardness, that slows it down, within the plenum. The human is belatedness, more than the animal is anticipation and foreseeing.

24. De Man, "Aesthetic Formalization," 287.

25. Harney and Moten, *The Undercommons*, 93.

26. Ralph Lemon, *How can you stay in the house all day and not go anywhere?* (performance text manuscript, Brooklyn Academy of Music, 2010), n.p.

27. Walter Benjamin, "Essays on the Philosophy of History" [1940], in *Illuminations*, ed. Hannah Arendt (New York: Schocken, 1969), 257. These are the immediately preceding lines from Benjamin's essay, not read by Lemon during his monologue: "A Klee painting named 'Angelus Novus' shows an angel looking as though he is about to move away from something he is fixedly contemplating. His eyes are staring, his mouth is open, his wings are spread. This is how one pictures the angel of history. His face is turned towards the past. Where we perceive a chain of events, he sees one single catastrophe which keeps piling upon wreckage and hurls it in front of his feet" (257).

28. See Kodwo Eshun, "Further Considerations of Afrofuturism," *CR: The New Centennial Review* 3, no. 2 (Summer 2003): 287–302, 292.

29. Abulafia, cited in Gershom Scholem, *Benjamin et Son Ange* (Paris: Rivages Poche, 1995), 108.

30. See Michel Foucault, *The Archaeology of Knowledge*, trans. A. M. S. Smith (New York: Pantheon,

1972), 130, 131 (emphasis added). For a reading of dance, body, and archive in relation to Foucault's theories see André Lepecki, "The Body as Archive: Will to Re-Enact and the Afterlives of Dance," *Dance Research Journal* 42, no. 2 (Winter 2010): 28–48.

31. See Eleonora Fabião, "History and Precariousness: In Search of a Performative Historiography," in *Perform, Repeat, Record,* ed. Amelia Jones and Adrian Heathfield (Bristol, UK: Intellect, 2012), 121–36, 134. "If 'ephemerality' denotes disappearance and absence (thus, predicating that at a certain moment, something was fully given to view), 'precariousness' denotes the incompleteness of every apparition as its corporeal, moving, constitutive condition."

32. Fred Moten, "The Case of Blackness," *Criticism* 50, no. 2 (Spring 2008): 177–218, 204.

33. ovguide.com/video/ralph-lemon-the-efflorescence-of-walter-922ca39ce10036ba0e115ae24 860b55 f.

34. Georges Didi-Huberman, *L'Image Survivante* (Paris: Les Éditions de Minuit, 2002), 320.

35. Lemon, "Four Years Later," 276.

36. Moten, "The Case of Blackness," 204.

37. Serres, *Hérmes II,* 73.

CONTRIBUTORS

Ann Cooper Albright is chair of the Dance Department at Oberlin College. She is the author of *Engaging Bodies: The Politics and Poetics of Corporeality* (2013) and *Choreographing Difference: The Body and Identity in Contemporary Dance* (1997), among other works, and coeditor of *Moving History/Dancing Cultures* (2001) and *Taken By Surprise: Improvisation in Dance and Mind* (2003). She has served as president of the Society of Dance History Scholars, is founder and director of Girls in Motion, an after-school program at Langston Middle School in Oberlin, Ohio, and codirector of Accelerated Motion: Towards a New Dance Literacy.

Bill Bissell is the director of the Performance program at The Pew Center for Arts & Heritage. His writing has appeared in *Continuous Replay: The Photographs of Arnie Zane* (1999) and *Dance Now*. He previously served as residency and education manager for Dance Alloy in Pittsburgh, Pennsylvania; prior to that he was a choreographer and performer. Bissell holds an MFA from the Tisch School of the Arts at New York University and an MA from California State University, Fresno.

Bonnie Bainbridge Cohen is a movement artist, researcher, educator, therapist, and developer of the Body-Mind Centering® approach to movement and consciousness. She founded The School for Body-Mind Centering® and is the author of *Sensing, Feeling and Action* (1994). Her work has influenced the fields of dance, bodywork, yoga, body psychotherapy, infant and child development, and other body-mind disciplines. Her work has influenced the application of somatic research to training practices in performance.

Linda Caruso Haviland is associate professor and founder of the dance program, and Alice Carter Dickerman Chair for the Director of the Arts, at Bryn Mawr College. She performed with ZeroMoving Company in Philadelphia; her scholarly research has included engagement with Philadelphia dance artists, including oral and video documentation, and researching the rise of a professional class of dancers in turn-of-the-twentieth-century Philadelphia. She holds an EdD in dance and philosophy from Temple University.

Sarah Crowner is an artist living and working in Brooklyn, New York. Recent exhibitions of her work include a solo show at Casey Kaplan Gallery, New York, and inclusion in *Repetition and Difference*, a 2015 exhibition curated by Jens Hoffman and Daniel Palmer at the Jewish Museum, New York. Crowner's work is held in the collections of the Museum of Modern Art, New York, and the Walker Art Center, Minneapolis.

Thomas F. DeFrantz is professor in the Department of African and African American Studies, Theater Studies, and the Program in Dance at Duke University. He is also director of SLIPPAGE: Performance, Culture, Technology. He is the author of *Dancing Many Drums: Excavations in African American Dance* (2002) and *Dancing Revelations: Alvin Ailey's Embodiment of African American Culture* (2004), among other works. In 2013 he helped to found the Collegium for African Diaspora Dance.

Barbara Dilley designed the dance/movement studies program at Naropa University. From 1960 to 1975 she performed with the Merce Cunningham Dance Company, Yvonne Rainer, and Grand Union. During that period she formed her own ensemble, Natural History of the American Dancer: Lesser Known Species, which explored structured improvisational forms that she continues to teach. She recently published *This Very Moment: Teaching Thinking Dancing* (2015), a memoir and handbook. Dilley is a graduate of Mount Holyoke College.

Nancy Goldner is a dance writer and critic. She is the author of *Balanchine Variations* (2008) and *More Balanchine Variations* (2011), and her dance criticism and essays have appeared in *The Nation, Christian Science Monitor,* and *Raritan,* among other publications. She was a member of the editorial board of the *International Encyclopedia of Dance* (1988). Under the auspices of The George Balanchine Foundation, she has lectured across the nation on the ballets of George Balanchine.

David Gordon is a writer, director, and choreographer. A founding member of Grand Union and Judson Dance Theater, Gordon has performed with Yvonne Rainer and James Waring and has made work for the American Ballet Theatre and the Guthrie Theatre, among others. His projects include *United States* (1988–1989), *Uncivil Wars: Moving with Brecht and Eisler* (2002–2009), *Dancing Henry Five* (2004), and most recently, *Archiveography* (2015). His longtime collaborator is dancer and actor Valda Setterfield.

Tomie Hahn, a performer, an ethnomusicologist, and a writer, is a professor and director of the Center for Deep Listening at Rensselaer Polytechnic Institute, Troy, New York. She is the author of *Sensational Knowledge: Embodying Culture through Japanese Dance* (2007). Hahn is a performer of *shakuhachi* (Japanese flute) and *nihon buyo* (Japanese dance), as well as a practitioner of experimental performance. Musician Curtis Hahn is her longtime collaborator. Tomie Hahn received her PhD in ethnomusicology from Wesleyan University.

Deborah Hay is a choreographer, performer, and writer. She began her career in the 1960s with the Judson Dance Theater. Recent work includes a 2015 collaboration with Laurie Anderson for the Cullberg Ballet, Stockholm, and *Blues* (2012), performed at the Museum of Modern Art, New York. She has also participated in Motion Bank, a project of the Forsythe Company. Hay is the author of *Lamb at the Altar* (1994) and *My Body, the Buddhist* (2000).

Patricia Hoffbauer is a dance artist originally from Brazil. Her works include *Para-Dice* (begun in 2010), commissioned by Danspace Project, New York, and *The Architecture of Seeing* (2006), with writer-performer George Emilio Sanchez, a longtime collaborator. She also performs in the works of choreographer Yvonne Rainer. Hoffbauer is an assistant professor in the Open Arts Department at Tisch School of the Arts, New York University, and has taught dance at Hunter College and Princeton University.

Mariana Ibañez, an architect from Argentina, is on the faculty of the Massachusetts Institute of Technology School of Architecture and Planning, having previously taught at the Graduate School of Design at Harvard University, and the Graduate School of Architecture at Columbia University. Her collaborations with artists include projects with Grace Kelly Jazz and Opera Philadelphia; her architectural work has been exhibited at the Museum of Modern Art, New York. She is a graduate of the Architectural Association and worked with architect Zaha Hadid. She is also part of a partnership with Simon Kim called IK Studio.

Emily Johnson is an artist who makes body-based work. Originally from Alaska, she is of Yup'ik descent and creates work that considers the experience of sensing and seeing performance. Her dances function as installations and include the trilogy *The Thankyou Bar*, *Niicugni*, and *SHORE*. Johnson is a Doris Duke Artist and has been a fellow at the Robert Rauschenberg Residency, the Institute for Advanced Study at University of Minnesota, and Williams College.

Jenn Joy cofounded Collective Address, a choreographic research space in Brooklyn, with Kelly Kivland, has taught sculpture at Rhode Island School of Design, and is critic in sculpture at Yale University. She is the author of *The Choreographic* (2014); her writing has also appeared in *DANSE: An Anthology* (2014). Joy served as contributing editor to *BOMB* magazine, curated *Conversations without Walls* (2011–2014), and coedited *Diary of an Image* (2014) and *JUDSONOW* (2012) for Danspace Project in New York City.

Allegra Kent joined the New York City Ballet in 1953 and served as principal dancer from 1957 to 1981. She created roles in works by choreographers George Balanchine and Jerome Robbins, including *Ivesiana* (1954), *Bugaku* (1963), and *Dances at a Gathering* (1969). Kent has coached dancers and is the author of *Once a Dancer . . .: An Autobiography* (1996). She studied ballet at the School of American Ballet, New York, after early training with Bronislava Nijinska and Carmelita Maracci in Santa Monica, California.

Simon Kim, an architect, is an associate professor at PennDesign and codirector of the Immersive Kinematics Research Group at the University of Pennsylvania. Kim has published papers on robotics and multiagent interaction and has collaborated on several shows with artists, theater groups and performers, such as The Dufala Brothers and Pig Iron Theatre Company. His work has been exhibited at the Institute of Contemporary Art, Philadelphia. He is a graduate of the Architectural Association and worked with architect Zaha Hadid. He is also part of a partnership with Mariana Ibañez called IK Studio.

Ralph Lemon is a choreographer, writer, visual artist, and curator, and the artistic director of Cross Performance. His many works include *Four Walls* (2012) and *The Geography Trilogy* (2001). Lemon is the author of *Come Home Charley Patton* (2013), and his *Meditation*, a visual art installation, is in the permanent collection of the Walker Arts Center,

Minneapolis. As a 2014 Annenberg Fellow at the Museum of Modern Art, he curated *Value Talks*, a series of "performance essays."

André Lepecki is associate professor in performance studies at Tisch School of the Arts, New York University. He is the author of *Exhausting Dance: Performance and the Politics of Movement* (2006), and *Singularities: Dance in the Age of Performance* (2016) and has edited several anthologies in dance and performance theory, including *Of the Presence of the Body* (2004) and *Dance* (2012). An independent curator, Lepecki has created projects for the Museum of Modern Art, Warsaw, and the Hayward Gallery, London, among others.

Gregory Maqoma, a dancer, choreographer, teacher, director, and writer, was born in Soweto, South Africa. His recent works include *Rain Dance* and *Exit/Exist*. He founded the Vuyani Dance Theatre in 1999 and has collaborated frequently with James Ngcobo on theater productions such as *Master Harold and the Boys* and *Songs of Migration* (with Hugh Masekela). Other collaborations include working with the London Sinfonietta and choreographer Akram Khan.

Bebe Miller first performed her work at Dance Theater Workshop, New York, in 1978, and formed the Bebe Miller Company in 1985. The Company's latest work, *A History* (2012), premiered at Wexner Center for the Arts at The Ohio State University in Columbus, Ohio. Other works include *Necessary Beauty* (2008) and *Landing/Place* (2005). Miller is a professor emerita of dance at The Ohio State University. Her current projects include *Dance Fort*, a digital book on the creative process of the Bebe Miller Company.

Jennifer Monson, a choreographer, is the founder and artistic director of iLAND (interdisciplinary Laboratory for Art Nature and Dance) and professor of dance at the University of Illinois Urbana-Champaign. In 2000 she initiated the multiyear dance project *Bird Brain*, and in 2013 she created *Live Dancing Archive*, a project that combines improvisational dance with video installations and Web-based archives. Monson has collaborated with many artists, including Zeena Parkins, DD Dorvillier, Yvonne Meier, and David Zambrano.

Jayachandran Palazhy, a choreographer and teacher, is the artistic director of Attakkalari Centre for Movement Arts in Bangalore, India. He is also the director of the Attakkalari India Biennial and the FACETS International Choreography Residency. His collaborative productions include *AadhaaraChakra — A Dancelogue* (2012) and *For Pina . . .* (2010). A physics graduate from Kerala, Jayachandran trained in Indian classical and folk dance, Western dance idioms, and the martial art practice of *kalarippayattu*.

Juhani Pallasmaa is an architect, a designer, and professor emeritus of the Helsinki University of Technology. His many publications include *The Thinking Hand* (2009) and *The Eyes of the Skin* (2005). He has served as rector of the Institute of Industrial Design, professor and dean of the Faculty of Architecture, and director of the Museum of Finnish Architecture, Helsinki, and has held several visiting professorships in the United States.

Alain Platel, a director and choreographer, cofounded les ballets C de la B in 1984, which has become a significant platform for European performing artists. Recently he created *tauberbach* (2014) and *Coup Fatal* (2014) in partnership with longtime collaborator Fabrizio Cassol, a Brussels composer. He has also collaborated with opera director Gerard Mortier on *C(H)ŒURS* (2012), a large-scale project, and with British film director Sophie Fiennes. Platel was trained as a remedial educationalist.

Marcia B. Siegel is a writer, lecturer, and teacher. She is a contributing editor for the *Hudson Review*. *Mirrors and Scrims — The Life and Afterlife of Ballet* (2010) is her fourth collection of reviews and essays; her other books include studies of significant American choreographers and choreography. Siegel is a former faculty member of the Department of Performance Studies, Tisch School of the Arts, New York University.

Laurajane Smith is head of the Centre of Heritage and Museum Studies, School of Archaeology and Anthropology, at the Australian National University, Canberra. She is editor of the *International Journal of Heritage Studies* and general coeditor of Routledge's Key Issues in Cultural Heritage series. Previously based at the University of York, United Kingdom, she has conducted research in the United States, UK, and Australia on the theory and history of heritage, including how it is memorialized.

Catherine J. Stevens is professor in psychology and director of research and engagement, and leads the music cognition and action research program in the MARCS Institute for Brain, Behavior, and Development at the University of Western Sydney. Her publications include *Thinking in Four Dimensions: Creativity and Cognition in Contemporary Dance* (2005). She researches the cognitive psychological processes in creating, perceiving, and performing music and dance, as well as human-computer interaction. Stevens holds a doctorate from the University of Sydney.

Meg Stuart is an American choreographer and dancer who works in Brussels and Berlin. In *Hunter* (2014), her most recent work, Stuart explores her body as a living archive. In her book *Are we here yet?* (2010) she reflects on her practice in conversation with writer, dramaturg, curator, and performer Jeroen Peeters. Stuart and her company Damaged Goods have an ongoing collaboration with the Kaaitheater, Brussels, and the HAU Hebbel am Ufer, Berlin.

Ivo van Hove is the general director of Toneelgroep Amsterdam, the Netherlands. His recent productions include *Roman Tragedies* and *Scenes from a Marriage*. Van Hove's work appears in international festivals such as the Edinburgh Festival, the Wiener Festwochen, and Festival d'Avignon. Van Hove has directed theater at venues including the Schaubühne in Berlin, the New York Theatre Workshop, and the Young Vic, London, and opera at the Flemish Opera and La Monnaie, Brussels.

INDEX

Note: Page numbers in italics indicate illustrations; page numbers with "n" indicate endnotes.

AadhaaraChakra—a Dancelogue (Palazhy), 200, 202–3, 206–8

abjection, 271, 273, 274–77, 290

absence, 266–67

abstraction, 119, 244–45

Abulafia, Todros, 312–13

accuracy, 95–96, 98, 101

Acosta, Niv, 215

acting, 238

"action observation network" (AON), 89, 94

Adam, Adolphe, 148, 169, 172

Adams, Diana, 160, 178

adaptations, 25, 87, 206, 234, 239, 247

aesthetics: of architecture, 47, 51–52, 224; of classical dance, 206, 234; and cognitive psychology, 103; and dance studies, xiv, 8; and Diaghilev's Ballets Russes, 230–31; and dialogue, 123, 125; and experimental dance, 266; and flow, 297–301, 304; and heritage sites, 127; and historiography, 254; and in-between space, 212–13; intelligence, 49; physical, 7–8, 217, 271, 288; postmodern, 120, 122; of slow, 62; theory of, 220n6

Afrofuturism, 312

Agamben, Giorgio, 211–12, 220n11

agency: of angels, 302–3, 310, 313; and apparatus, 212; of the body, 2; cognitive, 20; cultural, 129; and location, 266; political, 139–40, 298–99; of presence, 204; social, 276; and technologies, 294

AHD (authorized heritage discourse), 127–29

Alexander, Christopher, 50

allegory, 188–89

Alonso, Alicia, 153, 175

Alpine, Alyssa, 185, 187, 188

Amaya, Carmen, 83, 86n5

Andersen, Ib, 165, 168, 179

Andrade, Oswald de, 188–89

angel of history, 308, 309–10, 312, 314–16

angelology, 297–317

Angelus Novus (Klee), 210, 309–10, 312, 318n27

animals, 59, 80, 113, 202, 264–67, 299, 304–7, 318n23

"Animate Dancing" (Forti), 80

antiflow (blocking), 298–300, 307

Antigone Sr./Paris Is Burning at Judson Church (L) (Harrell), 214, 221n24

antihistorical physics, 300–307

AON (action observation network), 89, 94

Apollo (Balanchine), 122, 146, 156–69, *161–63, 166–67*

Arabian Nights, 240–43

archaeology: performative, 9; of presence, 9

architecture, 46–52, 200, 202–3, 211, 224–25, 293–95

archival art, 6

archival impulse, 6–7, 10

archival turn, 2, 6

archive fever (*mal d'archive*), 5, 13n22

archive(s): body as, 1–10, 19–20, 28–30, 39, 183–89, 223, 227, 263–64, 268–91; choreographic, 209–19; creative use of, 14nn30–31; defined, xv, 4; and Derrida, 4–5, 13n18; digital, 264; embodied,

30, 40, 74, 80–81; and Foucault, 2–4, 115, 314; "gendered," 278; history of, 4, 15n33; as improvisational method, 263; and memory, 5–6, 63–64, 67–68; and notation, 36–40; and original performances, 118–25, 168–69; and painting, 144–45; and performance, 1–10; and politics, 4, 6; and retrieval, 5, 227–28

Are we here yet? (Peeters, Stuart), 55–57

Aristophanes, 121

Aristotle, 47

artificial grammar, 97–98

artist statements, 117–25

Ashwill, Mark, 219, 222n39

associated memory, 99–101

associative learning, 99–101

Asylmuratova, Altynai, 248, 259

Attakkalari Centre for Movement Arts, 200–208

audience: and archives, 9, 192; of Balanchine's ballets, 153–56, 161, 164; and cognitive psychology, 102–3; development, 96–99; experience, 263–66, 295; and memory, 200, 205, 251, 293; and modern ballets, 238–39; and *Para-Dice*, 184–85; participation, 206–8; reactions, 69, 85, 88, 94, 144, 275, 283–89; and revivals, 252–55; and staging, 214–16

Auinger, Sam, 205

aura, 11n3

auratic, 11n3, 210, 218

authenticity, 149, 151, 169, 234, 249–51

authorized heritage discourse (AHD), 127–29

awareness, 29–33, 36, 47–50, 58–60, 91–92, 96, 198, 223–24, 304

awareness, somatic, 73–81

Ayupova, Zhanna, 248, 259

Baddeley, Alan D., 99–100

Bakst, Léon, 234, 240, 247, 257

Balanchine, George, 149, 170, 187, 230, 245; *Apollo*, 122, 146, 156–69, 161–63, 166–67; *Ivesiana*, 84–85; *Night Shadow*, 83; *Prodigal Son*, 84; *Swan Lake*, 167–68, 180, 237–38, 257; *Union Jack*, 164, 179

Balanchine Foundation Video Archives program, 166

Baldina, Alexandra, 243

ballet: *Apollo*, 122, 146, 156–69, 161–63, 166–67; and architecture, 293; archival film, 168–69; classical, 237–39, 243; and cognitive psychology, 89; and David Gordon, 122; discovery of (Kent), 82–85; documentation, 252–54; and exoticism, 239–43; and Fokine, 229–55; *Giselle*, 146–58, 147, 152, 157, 168–76; Kirov corps, 241–42, 246, 248, 249–51, 253; and memory, 68; narrative, 146–69, 245–46; romantic, 153, 169, 176. *See also* body; dance; movement

ballet blanc, 158

Ballet Plastique (Crowner), 144

Ballet Russe de Monte Carlo, 243, 244, 260

Ballets Russes de Serge Diaghilev, 148, 158–59, 229–55, 260

Balzac, Honoré de, 148, 171–72

Banes, Sally, 20n1, 239

Barker, Francis, 217

Barnes, Edward, 118

Baronova, Irina, 249, 259, 262n40

Barr, Margaret, 99–100, 108n33

Baryshnikov, Mikhail, 117, 155, 164–65, 177, 246, 248, 258

basic neurocellular patterns (BNP), 59

de Basil Ballet Russe, 234–35, 243, 260

"bastard dance," choreographic exercise (Platel), 25

Baudelaire, Charles Pierre, 148, 171

Bausch, Pina, 23–24

Beaumont, Cyril W., 151, 155, 229, 233–34, 241, 255

Benjamin, Leanne, 238–39, 257

Benjamin, Walter, 2, 11n3, 209–10, 219n2, 299, 308–11, 318n27

Benois, Alexandre, *230*, 234, 257
Bergé, David, 216
Berger, John, *79*
Bergman, Ingmar, 69–70
Berne Convention, 235
Bessmertnova, Natalia, 154, 175
bharatanatyam (classical Indian dance), 203, 206–8
Bharucha, Jamshed J., 93
BIRD BRAIN Project (Monson), 263–66
The Birds (Aristophanes), 121
black performance art, 274–77, 308–17
black physics, 299–300, 315–17
blocking (antiflow), 298–300, 307
Blues (Hay), 198–99
Blues for the Jungle (Pomare), 275–76
Blum, René, 260
BNP (basic neurocellular patterns), 59
Boal, Peter, 165, 168, 179
body: agency of, 2; and architecture, 293; as archive, 1–10, 19–20, 28–30, 39, 183–89, 198–99, 223–25, 227, 263–64, 268–91; bodiedness, 1, 227; bodiliness, 217; and cognitive memory, 1, 87–103; developmental processes, 58–60; and environment, 265–66; and ephemerality, 312–13; as field site, 35; and flow, 303–4; and history, xv, 8; imprinted, 2–4; and kalarippayattu, 200–202; and knowledge, 1–3, 5, 31–40, 75, 183, 186, 279; and logisticality, 305–8; and memory, 46–50, 68, 72, 110–14, 193–97, 200, 279; and metaphor, 46–50, 303; and painting, 143–45; and performance art, 70–72; and pleasure, 61; and queer performance, 268–91; relational, 217, 302, 308; and return, 315; and the senses, 32; social, 25; and somatic awareness, 73–81; and technologies, 293–95; transmission, 33–34, 279; and tremulous histories, 209–19. *See also* dance; embodiment
Body-Mind Centering®, 60
body work, 56–57

Bolender, Todd, 84, 86n10
Bolm, Adolph, 158, 177–78, 235, 257, 261n22
Bonjour Madame (Platel), 24–25
Borodin, Alexander, 250–51
Bourgeois, Louise, 48
Bournonville, August, 168, 180, 256
Brockmeier, Jens, 10n1, 15n33
Brubach, Holly, 243
Bruhn, Erik, 148, 167–68, 180
Bruner, Jerome, 39
butoh (Japanese dance form), 211, 213

Campbell, Sue, 131
campus design, 33–34
capoeira, 89
The Caravan Project (Eiko and Koma), 213
Carnaval (Fokine), 232, 233–34
Carrington, Calvin, 43
Carter, Walter, 298, 299–300, 308–17
Casey, Edward S., 47
A Catalog of Steps (Dorvillier), 218–19
cellular consciousness, 58
Center for Creative Research (CCR), 123
Cerrito, Fanny, 154, 176
Chair, Alternative 1 Through 5 (Gordon), 118
The Chairs (Ionesco), 120
Chaliapin, Feodor, 250, 259
Chopin, Frederic, 244–45, 258
Chopiniana. See *Les Sylphides*
choreographer, defined, 27. See also *specific choreographers by name*
choreographic angelology, 297–317
choreographic inhabitation, 216–17
choreographic interpretations, 146–69, 233–51, 254
choreographic language, 198–99
choreographic space, 303
Choreographing History (Susan Leigh Foster), 74
choreography: angelical, 302–4, 307–8, 312; and architecture, 50–52, 293–95; as archive, 191, 209–19; and Balanchine's ballets, 83–85, 146–69; and

"bastard dance" exercise, 25; and cognition in dance, 90, 92–93, 95–103; and embodied memory, 200–208; experimental, 278–83; and flow, 297–304, 307; and Fokine's ballets, 229–55; and Lemon's black physics, 299–300, 308–17; and monster trucks, 41; and movement, 68, 303; and notation, 37, 233; and *Para-Dice*, 185–87; process of, 193–97, 264–66; research, 8, 64; as technology of transmission, 300; transmission of, 198–99; and "Use Me" exercise, 55–57
Choura (Brubach and Danilova), 243
Christensen, Lew, 159, 178
chronopolitical acts, 312, 315
chunking, 90–91, 96
CI (contact improvisation), 76–77, 271–73, 278, 281, 289–90, 291n1
city spaces, 204–5
classical ballet, 82, 162, 237–39, 243
Clerc, Florence, 253
Cochrane, Chris, 268–91, 270, 274, 286
cognition: and creativity, 89, 92, 103; and dance, 7–8, 87–103, 200; embodied, 1–2, 19–20, 20n2, 28–30, 34, 39–40, 88–89; and emotion, 49, 92
collaborations, 34, 102, 122, 202–5, 225, 268–86
collective identity, 126–27, 223–24
collective memory, 1, 87, 112, 129, 133–34, 202
collective performative acts, 130
commonsense narratives, 126, 138
competitions, 7–8
conceptual art, 224–25
conceptual dance structures, 7, 19, 214
Confronting Images (Didi-Huberman), 212–13
connective tissue, 81
consensus narratives, 138–39
contact improvisation (CI), 76–77, 271–73, 278, 281, 289–90, 291n1
contemporary dance, 76–77, 87–103,
143–45, 183–89, 194–97, 200–208, 223–25, 237–38, 250
context-dependent memories, 90, 99–100
continuity, 306–7
Convention for the Safeguarding of Intangible Cultural Heritage (UNESCO), 127
Coolidge, Elizabeth Sprague (née Penn), 158, 177
Cooper, Dennis, 268–91, 286
Cope, Jonathan, 238, 257
copyright, 235, 249–51
Coralli, Jean, 148, 173, 233, 256. See also *Giselle*
corporeality, 206–8, 217, 279. *See also* embodiment
"Corpus" (Nancy), 75
costumes, 124, 203–5, 214, 234, 244–45, 251–54
Craine, Debra, 249–50
creative expression, 29–30, 62
creative intuition, 48–49
Cries and Whispers (Van Hove), 69–70, 70
Crisp, Clement, 250
critical intimacy, 210, 220n5
Croce, Arlene, 122, 245
Crowner, Sarah, 144
Cruz, Felix, 275
cues, 90, 99–101
cultural amnesia, 13n28
cultural anthropophagy, 188–89
cultural difference, 183–89
cultural identity, 223–24
cultural knowledge, 28–30, 32–34, 37–39
cultural memory, 6, 13–14n28
Cunningham, Merce, 67, 184
"A Cyborg Manifesto" (Haraway), 294–95

Damaged Goods, 55–57
d'Amboise, Jacques, 146, 160–66, 161–62, 171
dance: and archives, 1–10; and cognitive memory, 7–8, 87–103, 200; competitions, 7–8; conceptual structures of, 7,

19; contemporary, 76–77, 87–103, 143–45, 183–89, 194–97, 200–208, 223–25, 237–38, 250; and cultural difference, 183–89; discovery of (Kent), 82–85; and flow, 297–304, 307; and gender, xvi n4, 4, 8, 89, 185, 217, 278–82; history, xiv, 233; interpretations, 234; kalarippayattu, 200–202; and Lemon's *How can you stay*, 308–15; and logisticality, 305–8; modern, xiv, 183–87; multimedia, 202–7; research, 263–67; theater, 23–27, 118–21, 183–89, 229–55, 268–91; and tremulous histories, 209–19; writers and scholars, xvi nn2–3, xvii n5, 15n35, 16n38, 16nn43–44, 20n1. *See also* ballet; body; movement

dancelogue, 202–5

Dancing Henry Five (Gordon), 120, 125

Daneman, Meredith, 238

Danilova, Alexandra, 234–35, 243, 245, 257

Danspace Project, 120, 218–19

Dawson, Robbie "Flying," 42

De Bruyckere, Berlinde, 71, 72

declarative (explicit) memory, 91–93

Delany, Samuel R., 209–10

Deleuze, Gilles, 211, 220n10, 298

de Man, Paul, 297–99, 307

Denham, Serge, 260

Derrida, Jacques, 2, 4–5, 12n18, 279, 298

design, 33, 42, 50–51, 241, 265, 293–95

devadasi traditions, 203, 206, 208n2

Diaghilev, Serge de, 148, 158–59, 173, 229–52, 260

dialectical image, 210, 213, 218

dialogue, 57, 69, 79, 118, 121–23, 125, 205, 215

Diary of an Image (Dorvillier), 218–19

Didi-Huberman, Georges, 212–13, 215–16, 315

digital archive, 264

digital performance, 293–95

disability, 23–27

disembodied heritage, 127

disorientation, 314–15, 316

dissemblance, 217–18

docufictional travelogue, 202–5

documentation, 230, 252–54, 263–65

Dorvillier, DD, 218–19

double consciousness, 183

Doubrovska, Felia, 84, 86n7

dramatis personae, 169–81, 255–59

Druet, Eugène, 75

Drummond, John, 252

Drury, Lindsay, 285

Du Bois, W. E. B., 183

duets, 56–57, 76–77

Duncan, Isadora, xvi n4, 77–80, 238, 241, 254–55

Dunham, Katherine, 275–76

Dupond, Patrick, 246, 259

The Dying Swan (Fokine), 249–51

Edinger, E. F., 52

(the efflorescence of) Walter (Lemon), 314

Eglevsky, André, 248, 259

1856 Cessna Road (Lemon), 316

Eiko, 213

Ek, Mats, 149, 174

Elssler, Fanny, 154, 176

embodiment: and angelology, 305–6; and archives, 30, 40, 74, 80–81, 263; and Body-Mind Centering®, 60; and cognition, 1–2, 19–20, 20n2, 28–30, 34, 40, 88–89; and cognitive psychology, 87–103; of consciousness, 28; defined, 31–32; and existence, 46–52; and heritage performance, 126–40; of history, 223–28; and identity, 186; and improvisation, 263, 271; and kinesthetic memory, 193–97; of knowledge, 1–3, 28–43; metaphor, 303; and painting, 144–45; of physics, 300–301

embryological development, 60

emotions, 49–52, 126, 130–39, 151, 168, 224, 237–38

empathy, 50–52, 131, 137, 204

enactive knowledge, 30, 35, 39–40

engagement, registers of, 131, 132–34, 137–38

English country dance, 297–98

enhancement, bodily, 294

Entranced Earth/Terra em Transe (Rocha), 190

entrance narratives, 131, 135

environmental dance projects, 263–67

ephemera, photographs, 67–68

ephemerality, 28–29, 31, 33, 35, 124, 204, 263–64, 293, 312–17

episodic memory, 91–92

Eritrean National Music and Dance Troupe (Sbrit), 194–97

existence, 46–52

Exit/Exist (Maqoma), 223–25

exoticism and ballet, 239–43

experience, 200–208

experiential time, 50

experimental method, 88, 93, 104n1

experimental performance, 204–8, 266–67, 268–91

experimental studies, 29, 32–33, 88–91, 93–101, 108n35

explicit (declarative) memory, 91–93

expressive movement, 29–30, 36–40, 79

eye focus, 206–8

eye movements, 94–96

Fabião, Eleonora, 314

failure trope, 273–74

Fairchild, Robert, 165–66, 179

familiarity, 96–99

fault lines (Stuart), 55

fear, 273–74

Feingold, Michael, 120

female representation, 8, 216–17

fieldwork, 9, 35, 36–40

Fighting over Fokine (TV special), 249–51

Figueroa, Graciela, 184

film: of *Apollo*, 160–61, 164–68; archival, 25–27, 168–69, 219n4; of Ballets Russes, 230, 235, 237, 241–43, 245–46, 249–51; and documentation, 252–54; of *Giselle*, 149, 155–56; in multimedia

productions, 190n6, 202–7; staging of, 69–72; of *Them*, 269–70, 273, 276–77, 280, 287–88, 292n12

Films medicaux (Van Gehuchten), 26, 27

Finlay, Chase, 165–67, 167, 180

The Firebird, 229, 234–39, 236

fixation, 94–96

Fleming, Donald, 270, 270–71, 282, 286–87

flow, 297–304, 307, 317

fluency, 97–99

Fokine, Isabelle, 249–51, 253

Fokine, Michel, 229–55, 232; *Carnaval*, 232, 233–34, 256; *Cléopâtre*, 258; *The Dying Swan*, 249–51, 259; *The Firebird*, 229, 234–39, 236, 256; *Le Dieu Bleu*, 258; *Le Festin* (Fokine et al.), 229, 234, 255; *Le Spectre de la Rose*, 243, 246–51, 258; *Les Sylphides*, 233, 243–46, 244, 252–53, 256; *Petrouchka*, 234, 239, 256; *Prince Igor*, 233–34, 250–51, 256; *Schéhérazade*, 234, 239–43, 240, 253, 256

Fokine, Vitale, 234, 249

Fokine Estate Archive, 235, 249–51, 262n40

folk traditions, 206

Fonteyn, Margot, 236, 237–39, 257

Fordeyn, Rob, 214

forgetting, 129, 209, 215–16, 218, 315–16

Forsythe, William (Billy), 102, 194

Forti, Simone, 80–81

Foster, Hal, 6

Foster, Susan Leigh, 74

Foucault, Michel, 2–4, 115, 212, 314

found sounds, 205

Fracci, Carla, 149–50, 174

Freud, Sigmund, 5, 12n18, 48

Fuller, Loïe, 75–77

Fullington, Doug, 169

The Future of the Image (Rancière), 217–18

Galván, Israel, 212

ganjifa cards, 207

Gardner, Howard, 49

Garis, Robert, 164
Gartner, Vallejo, 283
Gautier, Théophile, 146–55, 170, 181n2, 246, 259
gay performance art, 268–91
Geertz, Clifford, 44n3
Gehmacher, Philipp, 55
gender theory, 278–82
genealogical research, 3–4, 115
Gere, David, 80, 279
gesture, 10, 39–43, 44n6, 77–79, 204, 270–73, 279, 287–89
Gilberts, Laura, 188
Giselle (Coralli and Perrot), 146–58, 147, 152, 157, 168–76
Gish, Lillian, 246–47, 259
Glazunov, Alexander, 244, 258
Godard, Jean-Luc, 218, 221n36
Godden, Duncan R., 99–100
Goffman, Erving, 191
Goldman, Danielle, 281
Gordon, Ain, 118
Gordon, David: Chair, Alternative 1 Through 5, 118; Dancing Henry Five, 120, 125; Life Without Men, 118; Old Work as New Work, 124; One Act Play, 118; Punch & Judy Get Divorced, 117–18; Random Breakfast, 118; Shlemiel the First, 124; Trying Times, 122–24; Trying Times (remembered), 124
Gordon, Michael, 120
Gould, Peggy, 188
Graham, Martha, 83, 86n5
Grahn, Lucile, 154, 176
grammar, of dance, 87, 92–93, 97–98, 103
Gramsci, Antonio, 138
Greek mythology, 164, 177, 179. See also Apollo
Grigoriev, Serge, 229, 237, 241, 255
Grisi, Carlotta, 148, 153–54, 172
Grub Street, 148, 172

habit, 42, 270
Hagendoorn, Ivar, 93

Hahn, Tomie, 37–38
Halprin, Lawrence, 50
Haraway, Donna, 294–95
Harney, Stefano, 305
Harrell, Trajal, 211, 213–16, 219n4, 220n7
Harries, Karsten, 50
Hassabi, Maria, 216–18
Heebink, Marieke, 70–72, 71
Heine, Heinrich, 146, 153–54, 171
Hennessy, Keith, 283, 284
Henry V (Shakespeare), 120
heritage performance, 126–40
Hijikata, Tatsumi, 211, 213–14
Hiroshima, 214–15
historical consciousness, 307, 313
Historie(s) du cinema (Godard), 218, 221n36
historiography, 254–55
history: and angelology, 297–317; corporeal effects of, 76; and dance studies, 8, 10; defined, 11n2; embodied, 223–25; in images, 209–10; and the imprinted body, 2–4; and memory, 215
A History (Miller), 193
HIV, 272, 283–84, 287, 290
Houston-Jones, Ishmael, 268–90, 270, 274, 284, 286
How can you stay in the house all day and not go anywhere? (Lemon), 308–9, 311, 316
Hübbe, Nikolaj, 165, 166, 168, 179
Huyssen, Andreas, 6, 13n28, 15n33
hybrid dance theater, 183–89
hyperbolic dance, 7–8, 15n38

iconography, 217
ideal dancer, 301–3
identity, 126–27, 133–34, 137, 183–89, 223–24, 276, 280–82
image, 209–19
Images in Spite of All (Didi-Huberman), 215–16
imagination, 126, 130–31, 200–208, 215–16
iMAP/Ridgewood Reservoir Project (Monson), 263

Immersive Kinematics, 296n2
implicit learning, 97–98, 103, 107–8n29
implicit memory, 91–92
impressions, 205
imprinted body, 2–4
improvisation, 57, 68, 76–81, 90, 191, 203–5, 245, 263–64, 266, 268–91
in-between space, 203, 207, 266
"incalculable choreographies," 279
incoherence, 307
Indian traditional performance, 200–208
intangible heritage, 127–29
intelligence, 39, 49
Intelligence Reframed (Gardner), 49
intention, 36, 97, 102–3, 157–60, 165, 198–99, 201–2, 207, 253
interference, 307, 312, 313, 314
intergenerational communication, 133–34
interpassivity, 298
interpretations, choreographic, 146–69, 233–51, 254
intuition, 49, 224, 251
Invitation to the Dance (Weber), 246
Ionesco, Eugène, 121
Ives, Charles, 84–85, 86n9
Ivesiana (Balanchine), 84–85

Japanese dance, 30, 35–40
Jessen, Victor, 243
Jillana, 160, 161, 178
Joffrey, Robert, 252, 259
Johnson, Mark, 47, 49
Jones, Leroi, 275–76
Jones, Niall Noel, 287
Judson Church, 118, 122
Jung, Carl, 48
Justament, Henri, 169

kalarippayattu (Indian martial art form), 200–202
Kalela, Jorma, 129
Karalli, Vera, 229, 255
Karsavina, Tamara, 148, 173, 229, 231,

234–39, 236, 242–43, 245–46, 249, 253, 255
Kaye, Nora, 84, 86n8
Keightley, Emily, 130
Kent, Allegra, 161
Kessler, Gregory, 33
kinesiology, 293
kinesthesia, 73–81
kinesthesis, 91
kinesthetic memory, 68, 101, 193–97
kinetic-historical function of angels, 299
Kirov Ballet, 241–42, 246, 248, 249–51, 253
Kirshenblatt-Gimblett, Barbara, 129
Kirstein, Lincoln, 231, 256
Klee, Paul, 210, 309–10, 318n27
Kleist, Heinrich von, 299–301, 303–4, 306–7, 310–14
knowledge: archived, 191–92; and the body, 1–3, 5, 31–40, 75, 183, 186, 279; building of, 33–34, 40, 42, 63; and embodied cognition, 19–20, 28–30, 87–103; enactive, 30, 35, 39–40; environmental, 263–64; and heritage performance, 127–31
Kochno, Boris, 229, 255
Kolb, Igor, 248, 259
Koma, 213

Lac, Thibault, 214
L'Académie française (the French Academy), 148, 172
Lakoff, George, 47
Landing/Place (Miller), 195–96
Landsberg, Alison, 130–31, 137
landscapes, 263, 266–67
Langer, Suzanne K., xvii n5
language: and the body, 112, 279; choreographic, 198–99; and cognitive memory, 1, 87; and conceptual structures of dance, 7, 19; and gesture, 44, 78; and grammar, 92–93; and intention, 9; in kalarippayuttu, 202; and knowledge of

dance, 94; and learning, 39, 101–2; and metaphor, 47; and *Para-Dice*, 184–85; physical, 25, 27; and rechoreographing, 117

La Presse (journal), 150

Late Spring (Ozu), 308–9

Latin American art, 183–89

Lawrence, Robert, 241–42

learning, 39, 101–2, 131–32, 134

LeClercq, Tanaquil, 84, 86n8

Le Corbusier, 48

Le Festin (Michel Fokine, et al.), 234

Legris, Manuel, 249, 259

Leibniz, W. G., 301, 306

Lemon, Ralph, 220n7, 221n21, 299–300, 308–17; *1856 Cessna Road*, 316; *How can you stay in the house all day and not go anywhere?*, 308–9, 311, 316; *some sweet day*, 198; *(the efflorescence of) Walter*, 314

Le Pavillon d'Armide (Fokine), 229, 230–31, 239

Lery, Jean de, 187–88

les ballets C de la B, 23–27

Le Spectre de la Rose (Fokine), 243, 246–51

Les Sylphides (Fokine), 233, 243–46, 244, 252–53

Levinas, Emmanuel, 210

Levinson, André, 238, 243, 257

Lévi-Strauss, Claude, 187

librettos, 146–49, 154–58, 167–69

Lichine, David, 260

Liepa, Andris, 243

Lifar, Serge, 159, 178, 248–49, 259

Life Without Men (Gordon), 118

Lima, Lucas de, 285

Linyekula, Faustin, 211

lithographs, 153–54

live art production, 285

Live Dancing Archive (Monson), 263–66

live productions, 251–52

Llinás, Rodolfo, 36

location, 266

logisticality, 305–8

logomotion practice, 80

L'oiseau de feu. See *The Firebird*

London Coliseum, 250

long-term memory (LTM), 90–93, 95–96, 99–101

Lowenthal, David, 128, 130

Lutz, Martin, 205

Macaulay, Alastair, 153

Mackrell, Judith, 250

MacMillan, Kenneth, 153

Mad Brook Farm, 80–81

Mademoiselle de Maupin (Gautier), 148

Madison, James, 133, 135–37

Mahomet Aquifer Project (Monson), 263

Makarova, Natalia, 154, 175

Makhalina, Yulia, 259

Manifesto Antropófago (Andrade), 188

Manual for the Arrangement and Description of Archives (Muller, Feith, and Fruin), 12n17

manuals, 56, 169

Maqoma, Chief Jongusobomvu, 223–24

Maracci, Carmelita, 83

marionettes (puppets), 299, 303–4, 306–7

Markova, Alicia, 151, 155, 174–75

Martins, Peter, 163–65, 168, 178–79

masculinity, 268–91

Mason, Monica, 238–39, 258

Massine, Léonide, 230, 256, 260

material ephemerality, 312

material heritage, 127–29

mature dancers, 99–101

McBride, Patricia, 163

McNeill, David, 44n6

meaning, 126–40

media. See multimedia dance production

mediation, 205

Meents, Tom, 41

Memoirs (Fokine), 233

memory: antihistorical, 300–307; and archives, 1–10, 63–64, 67–68; and the body, 46–50, 68, 72, 110–14, 125, 193–97, 200, 279; and cognition in dance, 1, 87–103; and contemporary dance, 224–25; context-dependent, 90, 99–100; cultural, 6, 13–14n28; defined, 11n2; and Derrida, 4–5; experimental studies, 88–91, 93–101; and exposure, 93, 96–99; externalized, 50; and heritage performance, 126–40; impervious to history, 301–2; implicit, 91–92; and Lemon's How can you stay, 308–17; and logisticality, 305–8; and multisensory learning, 41–42; and notation, 36–40; somatic, 200–208; spatial, 200; theatre of, 140; tremulous histories, 209–19; types of, 90–92; of the viewer, 293; and witnessing, 215–16; and writing about dancing, 67

Merleau-Ponty, Maurice, 46

metaphor, 47–50, 253, 303–7

method, 198–99

Metropolitan Opera, 153, 246

Meyer, Leonard B., 93

Michelangelo, 47

migration, 263–67

mind-body split, 1, 7–8, 34, 43n2, 46, 68

Missing Foundation, 222n39

Mitchell, Arthur, 187

mnemonics, 102, 129–30

modern dance, xiv, 183–89

Modern Gestures: Abraham Walkowitz Draws Isadora Duncan Dancing (Albright), 77–80

modernism, 238, 255, 298

modifications, by dancers, 235–37

Moholy-Nagy, László, 293

Momiji no hashi (Japanese dance), 37

monster truck: Maximum Destruction, 41; Stone Cold 3:16, 43

Montpelier (Virginia), 135–36, 135–37

monumental heritage, 138–39

Monument to Balzac (Rodin), 210–11

mood, 49, 100

Morrison, Toni, 73

Moten, Fred, 299, 305

The Motion of Light in Water (Delany), 209

motor memory/control, 87–89, 92, 94, 101

movement: architecture of, 224–25; and archives, 9–10, 191–92; at Attakka-lari Centre, 200–208; and cognitive memory, 7–8, 87–103; and embodied knowledge, 28–43; and expression, 29–30, 36–40, 238; and flow, 297–304, 307, 317; and gender theory, 278–81; and gesture, 78, 238; and improvisa-tion, 271–72, 281; and Isadora Duncan, 77–79, 257; and location, 266; and monster trucks, 40–42; and notation, 36–40; and Simone Forti, 80–81; and tremulous histories, 210–19; vocabu-lary, 90–91, 200

multimedia dance production, 204–7

multimodality, of dance, 100–101, 106n16

multisensory orientations, 41–42

Muñoz, José Esteban, 273–74

muscle memory, 91

Museum of Modern Art, 198–99, 210–11, 213

museums, 126–40

music, 87–93, 99–101

NAGARIKA documentation project, 200–208

Nancy, Jean-Luc, 75

Napoli, or The Fisherman and His Bride (Bour-nonville), 168, 180–81

narrative ballet, 146–69, 245–46

National Museum of American History, 133, 137–38

navigation, 264–66

neuroscience, 6, 48

neutral media, 301

new kinaesthetics, 298–300

new physics, 301, 306

Newton, Isaac, 301

New York Daily News, 290–91

Nietveld, Chris, 69–70, 70

Nietzsche, Friedrich, 212

Night Shadow (Balanchine), 83
Nijinska, Bronislava, 82–83, 85n2, 229–30, 255
Nijinsky, Vaslav, 83, 148, 174, 229–30, 234–35, 241–43, 245–47, 251, 253, 255
Nishimura, Mina, 215
Noë, Alva, 48
Nora, Pierre, 13n28, 63
nostalgia, 6, 231, 239, 253–54, 281, 285
notation, 32, 36–40, 102, 169, 181, 233, 254, 293. *See also* scores
Nureyev, Rudolf, 167–68, 180

observation, 28–30, 32–40, 87–103
Old Work as New Work (Gordon), 124
One Act Play (Gordon), 118
On the Marionette Theater (Über der Marionettentheater), 1810 (Kleist), 299, 301, 303–4, 310
ontogenetic movement, 59–60
operas, 250
"Orta or One Dancing" (Stein), 77–79
Osborne, Elisa, 185–86, 187, 188, 188
Osipova, Natalia, 154, 175–76
Otzar Hakabad (Abulafia), 312–13
Ozu, Yazujirô, 308–9

painting, 143–45
Para-Dice (Hoffbauer), 183–89, 188, 190n6
Paris Is Burning at Judson Church (XS, S, M (Mimosa), L, XL, Jr., Made-to-Measure) (Harrell), 213–14
Parker, H. T., 241–42, 258
P.A.R.T.S., 218, 222n37
Paul Sacher Foundation's Archive and Research Center, 158
Pavlova, Anna, 83, 86n5, 229, 235, 243, 245, 253, 255
Paxton, Steve, 80, 291n1
Pehrsson, Anna, 143–44
Peracini, Giovanni, 256. *See also* Coralli, Jean
perceptions, 73–74, 88–89, 92, 95, 97–98, 101–3, 193

performance: of *Apollo* (Balanchine), 122, 146, 156–69, *163*, 166–67; and archives, 1–10, 118–25; at Attakkalari Centre, 200–208; and choreographic angelology, 311–17; and choreographic language, 198–99; and cultural difference, 183–89; of Diaghilev's Ballets Russes, 229–55; and environmental dance projects, 263–67; experimental, 268–91; and flow, 297, 302–4, 317; of *Giselle*, 146–58, *147, 152, 157*, 168–76; heritage as embodied, 126–40; and librettos, 146–69; and live bodies, 17n45; and memory, 87–103, 225; and new technologies, 293–95; and painting, 143–45
performative, 9, 57, 126–27, 201, 319n31
Perrot, Jules, 148, 173, 256. *See also Giselle*
Persona (Bergman), 70–72, *71*
Petipa, Marius, 148, 156, 167, 169, 172–73, 233, 256
Petrouchka (Fokine), 234, 239
Phaedrus (Plato), 63
Pheiffer, Jeremy, 275
Phelan, Peggy, 17n45
photographs, 67–68, 207, 214–16, 218–19, 234, 243, 252–53
physicality, 25, 27, 268–91
physical theater, 23–27
physics, 298–309, 312, 315–16
Pickering, Michael, 130
pitie! (Platel), 24
Plato, 63
pleasure, 61
politics, 1, 4–5, 183–89, 223–25, 268–91, 297–301
Polovtsian Dances (Fokine), 233–34, 250–51
Pomare, Eleo, 275–76
Pompidou Centre, 281, 284, 285
Pontbriand, Scott, 40–41
postmodern dance, 80, 183–89, 272
power, of archives, 1–5
Power Booth, 122–23

Preobrajenska, Olga, 245, 258
presence, 35, 208, 210, 219n4, 276, 280, 282, 287
primitive reflexes, righting reactions, and equilibrium responses (RRR), 59
Prince Igor (Fokine), 233–34, 250–51
procedural (implicit) memory, 91–92
Prodigal Son (Balanchine), 84
progressive nostalgia, 284
proportionality, 47
proprioception, 91–92
prosthetic memories, 130–31, 136–37
prosthetic memory, 13n25
Punch & Judy Get Divorced (Gordon), 117–18

quality, of movement, 200–208
queer: identity, 280; performance, 268–91; theory, 272–74; utopia, 273–74
Quinn, Anthony, 186

race, 183–89, 221n21, 271, 274–77, 287, 294, 306, 317
radical black dance theater, 275–76
Radio Canada Montreal, 160
Ralph, Philip, 247
Rancière, Jacques, 217–18
Random Breakfast (Gordon), 118
Ratmansky, Alexei, 257
Ravel, Mathieu Desseigne, 24
Rawe, Tom, 185, 186, 187
reactions, 59, 61, 72, 205, 231
recall, 90, 99–101, 193, 200
rechoreographing, 117, 167–68, 233
recognition, 127–29, 134–36
recollection, 124, 131, 200
recombinant poetics, 290
reconstruction of *Them*, 268–91
recording performance, 237–38, 247–51, 254–55
reinforcement, 133–39
relational body, 217, 302, 308
remembering, act of, 5, 6–7, 126, 128–31, 274–75, 315–16

repetition, 9, 29, 35, 39, 77–79, 90, 96–99, 101, 186, 264, 312–13
répétition generale, 229, 261n1
reproductive nostalgia, 285
research, 1–10
resonance, 80, 119, 200, 268
restaging, 229–55, 268–91; of exhibitions and installations, 14n30
revivals, 158, 231–32, 234, 251, 252–55, 268–91
rhythm, 193–94, 197
Richardson, Joanna, 148
Rilke, Rainer Maria, 48, 52
Rimsky-Korsakov, Nikolai, 240–42, 258
rituals, 201, 203–4, 224
Robert, Grace, 247
robotics, 294–95
Rodin, August, 210–11
romantic era, 148, 153–54, 156, 169, 176
Rorty, Richard, 49
RRR (primitive reflexes, righting reactions, and equilibrium responses), 59
Rubinstein, Ida, 234, 242, 253, 257
Rudner, Sara, 187, 189n4
Runa, Romeu, 24
rupture effect, 207
Russell, Francia, 160, 178
Ruzimatov, Faroukh, 241, 248, 250, 258

saccades, 94–95, 107n24
sadir (solo dance form), 206, 208n2
St. Denis, Ruth, 241, 258
Saint-Georges, Jules-Henri Vernoy de, 146–47, 171
Samuel, Raphael, 129, 140
Sanchez, George Emilio, 185–89, 187–88
Sandstrom, Philip, 122–23
Sarah Bernhardt Theater, 159
Sbrit (Eritrean National Music and Dance Troupe), 194–97
Schéhérazade (Fokine), 234, 239–43, 240, 253

schematic expectations, 93–96

Schiller, Friedrich, 297–99

Schlemmer, Oskar, 293–94

Schorer, Suki, 163

Schwartz, Hillel, 297–98, 300

scores, 50–51, 68, 84, 148, 169, 191, 199, 205, 207, 216, 241, 253–54, 266, 278, 282, 304, 316. *See also* notation

Scully, Patrick, 283, 284

Seaman, Bill, 290

semantic memory, 91–92

Sensational Knowledge: Embodying Culture through Japanese Dance (Hahn), 37–38

A Sense of Sight (Berger), 79

senses: and architecture, 46–52; auditory-visual integration, 102; and environmental dance projects, 264–67; inputs, 36, 201–2; and kinesthetics, 73–81, 91; and memory, 90, 112–13; multisensory orientations, 41–42; perception, 58, 203–5; and pleasure, 61; transmission, 32–34

sentient archive, 2

sequencing, 90–91, 92, 97–99, 159

Serra, Richard, 218–19

Serres, Michel, 299–300, 302–3, 306, 317

Setterfield, Valda, 117–20, 122, 124

Seymour, Lynn, 152–53, 175

Shakespeare, William, 120

Shanks, Michael, 9

Shlemiel the First (Gordon), 124

SIP (Sustained Immersive Process)/Watershed (Monson), 263

"The Site of Memory" (Morrison), 73

Sketch for a Score for a Mechanized Eccentric (Moholy-Nagy), 293

skill acquisition, 90–91

Slave Ship (Jones), 275

slow, 62

Smith, Anna, 97, 107n27

Smith, Marian, 169

social body, 25

Solaris (Tarkovski), 308–9

SoloShow (Hassabi), 216–18, 221n29

somaesthetics, xvii

somatic awareness, 73–81

somatic memory, 200–208

Somes, Michael, 237–38, 257

some sweet day (Lemon), 198

sounds, 30, 41–42, 61, 205, 207, 216, 269–70, 278

Southland (Dunham), 275–76

spatial awareness, 73–81

spatial choreography, 50–52

spatial memory residues, 200–208

Spessivtseva, Olga, 149, 168, 174

Stallings, Carl, 117

Steedman, Carolyn, 12n15

Stein, Gertrude, 77–80

Steiner, Rudolf, 48–49

Stepanov, Vladimir, 169, 181, 254

stereotypes, 183–89

Stiefel, Ethan, 164, 179

Stokes, Adrian, 46

Stoler, Ann Laura, 11n5

Stravinsky, Igor, 122–23, 157–59, 161, 164–65, 177, 239, 258

structure, 93, 96–98, 101–3

Stuart, Meg, 55

Stuart, Muriel, 83, 86n6

subaltern, 185, 189n2

Sumner, Carol, 163

Suzuki Roshi, 68

Swan Lake (Balanchine), 167–68, 180, 237–38, 257

Sweigard, Lulu, 7

Taglioni, Marie, 154, 176

Takami, Asako, 309

Taken by Surprise (Albright and Gere), 80

Tallchief, Maria, 84, 86n8

Tanz im August festival, 281, 284

Tarkovski, Andreï, 308–9

Taruskin, Richard, 239

Taylor, Diana, 129–30

Tcherkassky, Marianna, 246, 248, 258

Tchernichova, Liubov, 237, 257
technologies, 4, 6–7, 293–95
temporality, 303, 312
textual archive, 12n17
textuality, 217
Tharp, Twyla, 184, 186–87
Théâtre du Châtelet, 229
theaters of memory, 115, 140
Them (Houston-Jones), 268–91, 270, 275, 289
Thesis on the Philosophy of History (Benjamin), 309
thevarattam (folk dance), 206, 208n1
Thomson, Stephen, 214
Titus, Antoine, 169
Todd, Mabel Elsworth, 7, 19
Tomalonis, Alexandra, 244
touch, 73–81
Toumanova, Tamara, 149, 174
Traces of Light: Absence and Presence in the Work of Loïe Fuller (Albright), 75
transferential spaces, 130–31
transmission: and angels, 302–3; of dance, 191; of dance through language, 198–99, 243; embodied, 29–43, 201; and heritage performance, 129–30; of knowledge, 32–34, 130; and physics, 300
The Tremulous Private Body (Barker), 217
Triadic Ballet (Schlemmer), 293
Tristes Tropiques (Lévi-Strauss), 187
Trying Times (Gordon), 122–24
Trying Times (remembered) (Gordon), 124
Tudor, Antony, 153

Über der Marionettentheater (On the Marionette Theater), 1810 (Kleist), 299, 301, 303–4, 310
Ulanova, Galina, 149–52, 174
Ullman, Michael T., 92
unaccountable situations, 199
unauthorized performances, 129–30
The Undead (Houston-Jones), 283
understanding, 126, 128–31, 139–40, 225

UNESCO World Heritage List, 127
Union Jack (Balanchine), 164, 179
Unsafe/Unsuited (A High Risk Meditation) (Houston-Jones), 283, 284
Untitled (Serra), 218–19
Used, Abused, and Hung Out to Dry (Harrell), 211, 213–15
"Use me" choreographic exercise (Stuart), 56–57

Van Gehuchten, Arthur, 25–27
vaythari (verbal commands), 202
Verdy, Violette, 146, 147, 149–52, 152, 154–56, 157, 170–71
veridical expectations, 93, 95
video, 263–64. See also film
Vidich, Arturo, 288, 289
Vidlar, Ondrej, 214
Vienne, Gisele, 284
viewers. See audience
Villella, Edward, 149, 152, 157, 163, 163, 165, 179
violence, 305–6, 311, 313
virtuosity, 7–8, 16n38, 62, 237, 247, 251
Vishneva, Diana, 154, 175
visitor interviews, 133
visual attention, 93–97
vocabulary, of dance, 90–93, 94, 223
Volochkova, Anastasia, 250, 259
A Voyage to the Land of Brazil (Lery), 187
vsprs (Platel), 25–27
Vulpian, Claude de, 249, 259

Walker, Jonathan, 270, 274, 282
Walkowitz, Abraham, 77–80
Wang Shu, 51
We Are All Flesh (De Bruyckere), 71, 72
Weber, Carl-Maria von, 246–47, 258
Weinstein, Arnold, 118
Werkbund movement, 293
Wertsch, James, 128–29
What is Black Music Anyways . . ./Self-Portraits (Linyekula), 211
White, David, 122–23

Wilde, Patricia, 161
witnessing, 210–19
Wittgenstein, Ludwig, 52
WM (working memory), 90–91
Wölfflin, Heinrich, 46
Wolf Trap, 248
women, xiv, 216–17, 282
working memory (WM), 90–91
"Writing the Moving Body" (Albright), 77

Xhosa (South African cultural group and language), 223–25

YouTube, 244, 246, 247–48

Zakharova, Svetlana, 258
Zalinsky, Konstantin, 258
Zorba the Greek (film), 186